Ground Down by

Anthropology, Culture and Society

Series Editors:
Jamie Cross, University of Edinburgh,
Christina Garsten, Stockholm University
and
Joshua O. Reno, Binghamton University

Recent titles:

The Limits to Citizen Power:
Participatory Democracy and
the Entanglements of the State
VICTOR ALBERT

Becoming Arab in London:
Performativity and the
Undoing of Identity
RAMY M. K. ALY

Anthropologies of Value
EDITED BY LUIS FERNANDO
ANGOSTO-FERRANDEZ
AND GEIR HENNING
PRESTERUDSTUEN

Dream Zones:
Anticipating Capitalism and
Development in India
JAMIE CROSS

Ethnicity and Nationalism:
Anthropological Perspectives
Third Edition
THOMAS HYLLAND ERIKSEN

Fredrik Barth:
An Intellectual Biography
THOMAS HYLLAND ERIKSEN

Small Places, Large Issues:
An Introduction to Social and
Cultural Anthropology
Fourth Edition
THOMAS HYLLAND ERIKSEN

What is Anthropology?
Second Edition
THOMAS HYLLAND ERIKSEN

At the Heart of the State:
The Moral World of Institutions
DIDIER FASSIN ET AL.

Anthropology and Development:
Challenges for the Twenty-first
Century
KATY GARDNER
AND DAVID LEWIS

Organisational Anthropology:
Doing Ethnography In and
Among Complex Organisations
EDITED BY
CHRISTINA GARSTEN
AND ANETTE NYQVIST

Children of the Welfare State:
Civilising Practices in Schools,
Childcare and Families
LAURA GILLIAM
AND EVA GULLØV

Anthropology's World:
Life in a Twenty-first Century
Discipline
ULF HANNERZ

Flip-Flop:
A Journey through
Globalisation's Backroads
CAROLINE KNOWLES

Faith and Charity:
Religion and Humanitarian
Assistance in West Africa
EDITED BY MARIE NATHALIE
LEBLANC AND LOUIS AUDET
GOSSELIN

The Anthropology of Security:
Perspectives from the Frontline
of Policing, Counter-terrorism
and Border Control
EDITED BY MARK MAGUIRE,
CATARINA FROIS
AND NILS ZURAWSKI

Private Oceans:
The Enclosure and
Marketisation of the Seas
FIONA MCCORMACK

Contesting Publics
Feminism, Activism,
Ethnography
LYNNE PHILLIPS
AND SALLY COLE

Food for Change
The Politics and Values of Social
Movements
JEFF PRATT AND
PETER LUETCHFORD

Base Encounters:
The US Armed Forces
in South Korea
ELISABETH SCHOBER

Checkpoint, Temple, Church
and Mosque:
A Collaborative Ethnography
of War and Peace
JONATHAN SPENCER, JONATHAN
GOODHAND, SHAHUL
HASBULLAH, BART KLEM,
BENEDIKT KORF AND
KALINGA TUDOR SILVA

Race and Ethnicity
in Latin America
Second Edition
PETER WADE

The Making of an African
Working Class:
Politics, Law and Cultural
Protest in the Manual Workers'
Union of Botswana
Pnina Werbner

Ground Down by Growth

Tribe, Caste, Class and Inequality in Twenty-first-century India

Alpa Shah, Jens Lerche, Richard Axelby,
Dalel Benbabaali, Brendan Donegan,
Jayaseelan Raj and Vikramaditya Thakur

PLUTO PRESS

First published 2018 by Pluto Press
345 Archway Road, London N6 5AA

www.plutobooks.com

British Library Cataloguing in Publication Data
A catalogue record for this book is available from the British Library

ISBN   978 0 7453 3769 2   Hardback
ISBN   978 0 7453 3768 5   Paperback
ISBN   978 1 7868 0204 0   PDF eBook
ISBN   978 1 7868 0206 4   Kindle eBook
ISBN   978 1 7868 0205 7   EPUB eBook

This book is printed on paper suitable for recycling and made from fully managed
and sustained forest sources. Logging, pulping and manufacturing processes are
expected to conform to the environmental standards of the country of origin.

Typeset by Stanford DTP Services, Northampton, England

Simultaneously printed in the United Kingdom and United States of America

Contents

List of Illustrations

MAP

TABLES

Series Preface

As people around the world confront the inequality and injustice of new forms of oppression, as well as the impacts of human life on planetary ecosystems, this book series asks what anthropology can contribute to the crises and challenges of the twenty-first century. Our goal is to establish a distinctive anthropological contribution to debates and discussions that are often dominated by politics and economics. What is sorely lacking, and what anthropological methods can provide, is an appreciation of the human condition.

We publish works that draw inspiration from traditions of ethnographic research and anthropological analysis to address power and social change while keeping the struggles and stories of human beings' centre stage. We welcome books that set out to make anthropology matter, bringing classic anthropological concerns with exchange, difference, belief, kinship and the material world into engagement with contemporary environmental change, the capitalist economy and forms of inequality. We publish work from all traditions of anthropology, combining theoretical debate with empirical evidence to demonstrate the unique contribution anthropology can make to understanding the contemporary world.

Jamie Cross, Christina Garsten and Joshua O. Reno

Preface

Alpa Shah and Jens Lerche

Growing inequality is undoubtedly one of the most significant political challenges of our time. Income inequality, the gap between the rich and everyone else, has dramatically escalated in the last 30 years in many parts of the world, not least the US and the UK. Oxfam (2016) recently reported that the richest 1 per cent now have more wealth than the rest of the world combined.

India, once to some extent shielded from the market forces of global expansion, is now no longer an exception. Right behind the US, China and Germany, and ahead of the UK, India ranks fourth on the list of dollar billionaires.[1] The Indian wealthy now increasingly mark the country's landscape with their air-conditioned malls, gated communities and high-rise apartments with swimming pools. But there is also an India of dislocation and despair. The 'trickle down' of India's spectacular growth rate is a very slow drip. Armies of migrants from the countryside live under tarpaulin tents, with almost no citizenship rights, while building the infrastructure that is to sustain the Indian boom. Indebted farmers are committing suicide. Protests are increasing against displacement for mining and industrial development. Marking poverty in a land of plenty, around 800 million Indians survive on less than $2 a day (Kannan 2012: 36). Indeed, it is now no longer news that 8 Indian states have more poor people than 26 of Africa's poorest countries put together (Alkire and Santos 2010).

What is less well known is that social discrimination marks the contours of poverty in India; that certain social groups – India's low castes and tribes – are overwhelmingly represented among the poor. *Ground Down by Growth* asks how and why, despite India's celebrated economic growth, the marginalisation of low castes and tribes persists in the country. It explores the inextricability of identity-based oppression – of caste and tribe in particular, but also region and gender – and class relations in the belly of the Indian boom. In this Preface, we provide the backdrop to the questions we ask in this book and how we seek to address them.

ECONOMIC GROWTH, INEQUALITY AND POVERTY

Alongside China, India is the world's fastest growing major economy and the two are predicted to become the world's largest and most dynamic economies of the future. Marking a stark contrast to a European climate of sluggish growth and economies falling in and out of recession, the story of Indian growth has been celebrated since the 1990s when the country liberalised and opened up its economy, and Coca Cola, McDonald's and the global IT sector came marching in. India's Prime Minister, Narendra Modi, riding the wave of GDP figures, marked his first anniversary in power in 2015 with further promises of dazzling growth, strengthening his central policies to attract foreign investment and ensure ease of conducting and expanding business in the country.

The forces of neoliberalism, underpinned by a liberal political commitment to maximum individual autonomy entwined with a laissez-faire economic ideology, have been sweeping the world since the 1980s.[2] This absolute commitment to the free market and state-sponsored privatisation started to take root in India in the same period and spread from the 1990s on, when the country officially liberalised its economy. International trade burgeoned, multinational companies lined up to enter India's mineral-rich resource areas and outsourced to the country to make use of its cheap labour for the global market, while state controlled industries and sectors were privatised.

Proponents of high growth rates claim that economic liberalisation is also good for the poor;[3] that eventually its benefits will trickle down even to those who are right at the bottom of the economic pile. The idea that growth inevitably leads to reduction of poverty has a long history, despite those who have powerfully argued that development and underdevelopment constitute two sides of the same coin.[4] The 'inclusive growth' that is promoted by the World Bank (2002) and others is the latest incarnation of these neoliberal policies. For these policies, there is no bar to growth, and poverty reduction replaces equity[5] as the central moral concern. In India, 'inclusive growth', placing economic growth and deregulated markets at the centre of poverty reduction, have been backed by eminent economists. Jagdish Bhagwati, Professor of Economics and Law at Columbia University, claimed to be the intellectual inspiration behind the economic reforms of 1991 which liberalised the Indian economy (Bhagwati 1993). With his co-author, Arvind Panagariya, in *Why Growth Matters*, Bhagwati has reinforced his case for privatisation and liberalisation with less protection for labour (Bhagwati and Panagariya 2013).

Critiques of inclusive growth argue that inclusion in these models is thought of in the very narrow sense of enabling everyone to take part in markets; there is little consideration of whether this growth increases inequalities (Saad Filho 2011) and yet evidence from across the world indicates that inequality is rising (Piketty 2013). A new paradigm challenging inclusive growth is emerging. In 2017 Oxfam followed up the previous year's report on the 'economy for the 1%' with one on the 'economy of the 99%', now showing that just eight men owned the same amount of wealth as the poorest half of the world (Oxfam 2016, 2017). It also argued that the incomes of the poorest 10 per cent of people increased by less that \$3 a year between 1988 and 2011, while the incomes of the richest 1 per cent increased 182 times as much.[6]

Indeed, economists commenting on India – not least Jean Drèze and Amartya Sen (2013) – have challenged India's so-called inclusive growth policies of alleged trickle down, dubbing it an 'uncertain glory'. The Cornell economist, Kaushik Basu (2008), has warned that most of India's aggregate growth has led to a rise in incomes at the upper end of the income ladder. In 2010, India's 100 wealthiest people had increased their combined worth to \$300 billion, a quarter of the country's GDP, while income inequality, as measured by the Gini index, had also grown (Kannan 2012: 44; Anand et al. 2014: 4). The fruits of economic growth barely reached the poor. Throughout more than 20 years of neoliberal reforms, the rate of poverty reduction has been much less than the rate of economic growth.[7]

Notably, in 2004, the Indian government set up a National Commission for Enterprises in the Unorganised Sector headed by some of its best applied economists – (the late) Arjun Sengupta, K.P. Kannan, Ravi Srivastava and the civil servant V.K. Malhotra. The commission published a series of important and controversial reports that challenged India's 'inclusive growth' policies. K.P. Kannan (2014) has recently brought out some of its conclusions in his book *Interrogating Inclusive Growth* and the key arguments are also presented in this book. The commission's economists showed that by 2004–05, despite decades of economic growth, 77 per cent of Indians were poor and vulnerable, living on less than Rs.20 (30 cents US)[8] a day; that less than a quarter of Indians enjoyed the fruits of India's economic growth, and that the most vulnerable of Indians were bypassed (NCEUS 2009).[9]

These conclusions were reached even though India has many pro-poor schemes, which include the distribution of food staples at subsidised prices through the 'fair price' or 'ration shops' of the public distribution system. There is also a rights-based public employment guarantee scheme, the National Rural Employment Guarantee Act which, since 2005, has provided up to 100 days of paid employment per year for members of rural households.[10] A social health insurance scheme was introduced in 2008 to cover segments of informal/unorganised workers and poor households, but has had limited impact.[11]

The reports of the commission were, unsurprisingly, not appreciated by the government of the time; the commission's work was cold-shouldered and its website was closed as soon as it had finished its work in 2009, making its reports harder to obtain.[12] Nevertheless, the messages are out there and they are remarkably clear. By 2010 a little more than two-thirds of the population was still poor and vulnerable (Kannan 2012). Some advances have been made in reduction of absolute levels of poverty. But – although people are slightly better off – they are less equal than before. Income and wealth inequality is increasing in the India that is being celebrated for its growth rates.

THE ECONOMIC DATA ON SOCIAL DISCRIMINATION
IN THE BELLY OF INDIA

Significantly, as K.P. Kannan argues in this book, the economists of the National Commission for Enterprises in the Unorganised Sector showed that Indian poverty was marked by certain social characteristics based on caste and religion (more than others which also mattered, like gender or region).[13] Throughout the country Dalits (or Scheduled Castes; those who were previously called Untouchables), Adivasis (Scheduled Tribes) and Muslims were worse off than all other groups. Social discrimination, that is, discrimination based on identity, marks the contours of poverty.

The persistence of discrimination based on identity in twenty-first-century India is particularly disappointing because at the time of Independence, the founders of the modern Indian made a range of radical efforts to eliminate it. In 1949/50 'reservations' (a form of affirmative action that relies on quotas), first introduced as colonial policy at the turn of the twentieth century, became a comprehensive nationwide system through the post-Independence Constitution of India, written by the Dalit leader B.R. Ambedkar; 15 and 7.5 per cent of government sector jobs and higher education seats were reserved for the Scheduled Caste and Scheduled Tribe communities respectively; together they were called 'Backward Classes'.[14] Seats were also reserved for Scheduled Castes and Scheduled Tribes in the national Lower House of Parliament (Lok Sabha) and in the state legislative assemblies, based on the percentage of their population in each state. These policies were intended to be temporary, but, following the recommendations of the 1980 Mandal Commission report, which evaluated the system, in the 1990s the quotas were extended; 49.5 per cent of all jobs in central government services and public undertakings were now reserved for Scheduled Castes, Scheduled Tribes and a poorly defined category of 'Other Backward Classes' (OBCs). There were other protective policies also targeted at Dalits and/or Adivasis, such as the Scheduled Castes and Scheduled Tribe Prevention of Atrocities Act 1989, various policies to protect Adivasi land rights in the Fifth and Sixth Schedule of the Constitution, and budgetary allocations though the Tribal and Scheduled Caste Sub-Plans.

However, despite all these measures to address the discrimination caused by caste and tribe, 60 years after Independence, the 2011 Census, for the first time since 1931, collected data on caste, in the recognition that caste remains a significant maker of disparity. Some activists and scholars have gone as far as to argue that there is a hidden apartheid in India.[15] Inequalities based on caste and tribe continue to be deeply implicated in the contours of poverty in India[16] and especially affect the position of Adivasis and Dalits.[17] The rate of poverty decline among Adivasis and Dalits between 1999 and 2009 was just over half the rate for all other communities[18] and in 2009–10, 82 per cent of Adivasis and Dalits were still below the international poverty line of PPP$2 a day (purchasing power parity). While incidence of poverty varies across the regions of India, Dalits and Adivasis are even worse off than Muslims almost everywhere (Kannan's chapter, this book). In 2004–05, 15 of India's 21 major states had 85 per cent or more of their Adivasis and Dalits living in poverty, and everywhere at least two-thirds of Adivasis and Dalits were poor (below the PPP$2 poverty line) (Kannan 2011; see also Kannan's chapter in this book). Being born Adivasi or Dalit appears to determine poverty more than where one comes from.

A rich heritage of scholarship within and on India means that poverty analyses of the country are some of the most sophisticated in the world. Senior planners, policymakers and economists, both in and outside government, pay great attention to counting the poor.[19] But as Sukhdeo Thorat (2017) laments, social discrimination in the Indian labour market – which has a vast impact on income distribution and poverty – has not received much attention in mainstream discourse in the social sciences in India (except in relation to gender discrimination).[20] Some recent studies have been increasingly interested in mapping the concentration of poverty among Adivasis and Dalits,[21] exploring discrimination against Adivasis and Dalits through macro-economic data and large-scale household surveys. Some have also paid attention to mapping discrimination in relation to work and employment.[22] They use the National Sample Survey Office consumer expenditure surveys to analyse the standard of living of Adivasis and Dalits in relation to other groups, or to map inequality and poverty for the two groups.[23] Others have used National Family and Health Surveys to construct 'caste development indices' for exploring regional disparities between Adivasis and Dalits and other groups. Still others have used the Economic Census to show that across all states Adivasis and Dalits are significantly under-represented in self-employment, the ownership of enterprises and the share of the workforce employed by them.[24] The more ambitious have tried to separate the particular spheres in which Dalits and Adivasis experience discrimination over and above households with the same profile, for example in education or housing.[25]

These 'disparity studies' – largely by economists – have been extremely important in highlighting the social characteristics of poverty in India. However, most have some limitations. They are, of course, inhibited by the nature and quality of the data collected. One small example is that one of the most comprehensive studies on Dalit and Adivasi inequality (Kijima 2006) concludes that education enables upwardly mobile migration but relies on data on permanent migrants and therefore cannot capture the massive importance of seasonal, casual labour migration of illiterate Dalits and Adivasis, which goes unrecorded. In addition, studies which depend on official poverty line figures in India are compromised because these figures have been based on the outdated cost of a basket of food necessary for the minimum calorie intake a person needs a day that was set in the 1970s.[26] More significantly, most of the studies are limited to descriptive analysis; for instance, whether a particular development input (such as landownership or access to education) decreases the welfare disparities between Adivasis and Dalits and the rest. They can only speculate about causal mechanisms.

Comparative developments in the study of race, class and inequality in the US have recently highlighted the limitations of disparity studies. Political scientist Adolph Reed Jr and Merlin Chowkwanyun, a historian of racial inequality, write:

Research precisely specifying racial disparities in the distribution of advantages and disadvantages, well-being and suffering has become common enough to have generated a distinctive, *pro forma* narrative structure. Quantitative data, usually culled from large aggregate data sets, is parsed to generate accounts of the many facets of apparent disparity along racial lines with respect to ... wealth, income and economic security, incarceration, employment, access to medical care, and health and educational outcomes ... [These accounts] tend not to add up to much beyond fleshing out the contours of the disproportionate relations, which are predictable by common sense understanding. Explanations of the sources of disparities tend to dribble into vague and often sanctimonious calls to recognize the role of race, and on the left, the flailing around of phrases like 'institutional racism' that on closer examination add up to little more than signifying one's radical credentials on race issues. (Reed and Chowkwanyun 2012: 150)

These quantitative studies tracing racial disparity across different metrics thus only serve to flesh out a picture we already see but, ultimately, political-economic relations and power are too easily reduced to statistical distributions and decontextualised indices of economic attainment. Reed and Chowkwanyun (2012) thus identify an impasse in the literature on race in the US stemming from its sidestepping of the potentially thorny causal questions about how such disparities are produced and reproduced in particular historical configurations through the changing forces of American capitalist social relations.

The problem of the inadequacy of analysing causes, processes and relations when faced with macro-economic data obtained through large surveys was well recognised by Pranab Bardhan (1989), who sought to encourage *Conversations between Economists and Anthropologists*. Bardhan and his collaborators proposed that anthropologists, with their in-depth studies, were better placed to capture the dynamics, processes and relations that it was not possible to reveal through the surveys. Fine-grained, detailed studies explaining rather than describing durable poverty are often called for by the research community but are rarely found in the established literature.[27] John Harriss (2007), some time ago, pointed out that poverty is more often than not thought of almost as a condition that one falls into, or is trapped into, or that one escapes from. Poverty research tended to focus on the characteristics of the poor, equating the study of poverty with studying poor people; looking at the outcome but not the means through which poverty persists, as David Mosse (2010) put it.

To explore how and why India's Adivasis and Dalits are at the bottom of the Indian social and economic hierarchy this book shows that we need to move beyond the measurement focus of much of the poverty research (whether it addresses absolute or relative poverty or takes on multidimensional indicators of poverty). Economic data needs to be complemented by an understanding of the lived reality of the poor, in particular a more grassroots approach to processes of inequality and how particular groups experience them. In doing so, this book embraces Bardhan's (1989) call for a conversation between economists and anthropologists, and explores the trends that economists have presented to us by undertaking country-wide detailed ethnographic studies. It takes as its starting point the proposition by Henry Bernstein (1992), John Harriss (2007) and, more recently, David Mosse (2010) that poverty must be understood through social relations, relationally. That is, it puts the historically developed social relations between Adivasis/Dalits and other groups at the centre of the analysis. These relations are, as most recently argued by Jonathan Parry (2014), more often than not unequal power relations and it is through them that poverty is produced and persists. This is something which cannot be captured through quantitative measurements alone. In short, we need to move to a qualitative, historically situated analysis of the relationship between inequality and poverty and social discrimination.

OUR PROGRAMME OF RESEARCH

To explore the processes of inequality, we – Alpa Shah and Jens Lerche – conceived, led and executed a Programme of Research on Inequality and Poverty from the Department of Anthropology at LSE.[28] The Programme of Research was based on long-term in-depth ethnographic research, living with Adivasis and Dalits, placing their perspectives and experiences at its centre, and understanding their situation in relation to that of other local groups and in relation to the wider political economy of the region, with the aim of comparing across sites in the country. Our focus – across the sites – was to understand and compare the changing situation of Adivasis and Dalits in the context of oppression, exploitation and discrimination; livelihood patterns and related land and labour and migration patterns; intra-caste/tribe and gender relations; and also in relation to their own social struggles.

We should note at the outset that we have not worked with Adivasis in the north-east states of India who, at a national level (as shown in Kannan's chapter), fare much better than the Adivasis of peninsular India. We should also note that Adivasis and Dalits are not the only groups that suffer disproportionally high levels of poverty. Low-status Muslim groups, in particular, are also at the receiving end of economic and social discrimination (as Kannan also shows). The groups called 'Denotified Tribes' (previously classified by the British as 'Criminal Tribes') also live in deplorable conditions and are stigmatised, but are not discussed in this book. In this book we limit ourselves to the study of relations of class and ethnicity/identity in the context of Adivasis and Dalits in peninsular India, while acknowledging, where possible, wider trends involving other social groups.

We recruited a team with previous ethnographic field research experience of either having worked with Adivasis or Dalits or on issues of inequality and poverty through serious long-term field research.[29] The choice of our sites of field research (Himachal, Kerala, Maharashtra, Tamil Nadu and Telangana) drew on the strengths of the previous experiences of this team (Richard Axelby, Jayaseelan Raj, Vikramaditya Thakur, Brendan Donegan and Dalel Benbabaali), and we of course brought our comparative experience from Jharkhand and Bihar (Alpa Shah) and Uttar Pradesh (Jens Lerche) to the mix.

We developed a programme of research that would allow each researcher to follow their interests, develop and write articles and books of their own in the more classical approach of anthropological field research, which relies on the 'lone anthropologist', but we also designed a programme of research training, research questions, research methods and writing to generate research that was explicitly comparative. Our first six months were based in London, from January 2014, when we ran workshops and a series of intensive fortnightly, sometimes weekly, seminars to develop our collective research questions, themes and methods, discussing the work of economists, sociologists, development studies specialists, geographers and anthropologists who have deliberated on questions of inequality, poverty, labour, tribe, caste and class with them to develop our own collective programme of work. In this period, we established a set of methods to be used across each site – a collectively designed household survey, genealogical and generational histories, archival research, key interviews – to explore an agreed set of issues, themes and dimensions of social transformation. Alongside these collectively designed methods, most importantly, all the ethnographers were to live as participant observers amid the Adivasi and Dalit families they write about.

The following year, the ethnographers of the chapters of this book immersed themselves in their field sites, conducting in-depth field research. While these were all situated studies, most often in a village context, they were by no means bounded village ethnographies.[30] As this book will show, all of our studies began with the premise that a deep understanding of a particular locality in relation to its wider context was necessary to understand the changes taking place across the country. Every study both contextualised and used the in-depth understanding of particular localities in relation to the processes of a much wider regional political economy. All the ethnographers moved in and out of the localities where they were based, to understand the movement of people and processes across the country – whether it was following Adivasi migrant labour found in the tea plantations of Kerala back to their homelands in the Santhal Parganas in Jharkhand, or whether it was to follow Gujjar herders who had moved from the High Himalayas to the plains of Punjab.

We met throughout the course of fieldwork to discuss, share, compare and develop analyses. As a team, we met three months into fieldwork to assess and reshape a piloted household survey and then again six months into field research to compare findings, discuss emerging analysis and themes. We also shared and discussed regular field reports from each site. The postdoctoral researchers visited one other ethnographer from the group and had a different ethnographer visit their site. To nurture better questions and comparative analysis we, Alpa Shah and Jens Lerche, visited each of the five field sites and worked closely with all the ethnographers over the course of the research. In all cases we were actively involved in the choice and delineation of field sites, working on the focus of the specific areas of research in each site, and, as the research evolved, encouraging the exploration of particular research questions as they became evident from the sites and following specific directions, such as moving with migrant labour to their home or to distant labouring sites.

Finally, on return from fieldwork, we embarked on a 15-month programme of writing together, holding three formal book writing workshops, developing the emerging comparative analysis through every draft of the book, presenting together at one conference. Throughout the two years of writing that have gone into this book, we were actively involved in developing and rewriting each chapter in light of the overall analysis that was emerging and in relation to the other chapters. From this has grown the overall analysis of *Ground Down by Growth* presented in the chapter that follows. Our Programme of Research on Inequality and Poverty is therefore one of the first concerted efforts by a team of anthropologists to work closely together across different sites to comparatively address a collective research question and to write together about it. To reflect the collective nature of our research and writing, we therefore present our book not as an edited but as a multi-authored one.[31]

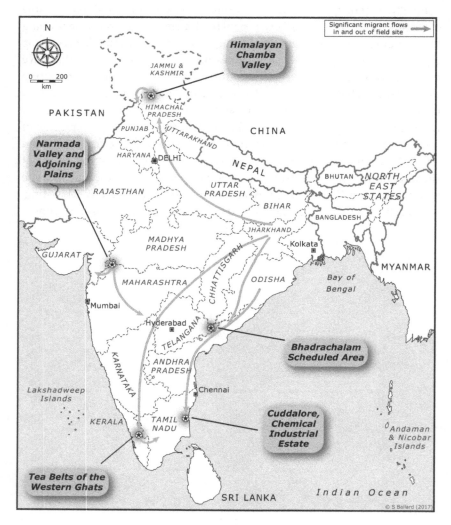

India, showing our field sites and main migration patterns

1

Tribe, Caste and Class – New Mechanisms of Exploitation and Oppression

Alpa Shah and Jens Lerche

Capitalist modernity across the world was expected to diminish the salience of older forms of identity-based relations. In India, differences based on caste and tribe were to disappear. But, despite economic growth, the conditions of India's Adivasis and Dalits have flouted these rosy expectations. *Ground Down by Growth* travels the length and breadth of the country to explore how and why Adivasis and Dalits (also known as Scheduled Tribes and Scheduled Castes),[1] remain at the bottom of Indian society.

One of the first collective efforts by a team of anthropologists working on the same questions across different sites, *Ground Down by Growth* brings to light the real-life stories of the struggles of India's low castes and tribes across the country. The fate of India's Adivasis and Dalits is globally important for many reasons, not least that together they make up 1 in 25 people in the world. Most importantly, as we argue here, their stories show us the ways in which economic globalisation has re-entrenched identity-based social oppression (by which we mean here, tribe, caste, gender and region, but which could include race, ethnicity, sexuality), making it inseparable from class relations, a process we conceptualise as 'conjugated oppression'. This book's potential significance, then, derives not simply from the number of people its analyses address directly, but also from the more general theoretical argument it makes about how the spread of capitalism today is enlisting and intensifying previously existing relations of domination based on inherited and indelible social identities. In exploring the relation between inherited social identities and the often-observed divergence between haves and have-nots, the book adds weight to the argument that the failure of 'trickle-down' models of growth and the persistence of social disparities under contemporary capitalism are two sides of the same coin.

Ground Down by Growth explores the changing historical processes through which Adivasis and Dalits across the country remain worse off than all other groups. It poses a challenge to proponents of India's economic growth as it shows that neoliberal capitalism, far from enabling the benefits of its growth rates to trickle down to all groups, has further entrenched inequalities based on pre-existing unequal social divisions. *Ground Down by Growth* shows the ways in which inequalities of caste and tribe (and region and gender) take shape through class relations across the country, morphing older forms of identity-based discrimination and marginalisation into new mechanisms of exploitation, oppression and subjugation. Specifically, we propose that the entrenchment of social difference in the expansion of capitalism takes place through at least three interrelated processes: *inherited inequalities of power*; *super-exploitation based on casual migrant labour*; and *conjugated oppression* (that is the intertwined multiple oppressions based on caste, tribe, class, gender and region). The book also explores the struggles Adivasis and Dalits wage to cope with the situation they find themselves in.

OUR FIELD SITES

The long history of marginalisation of India's Adivasis and Dalits is reflected across our sites. In the past, the Indian caste system kept the Dalits as 'Untouchables', firmly below and outside a hierarchy of endogamous kinship groups. There, they constituted a class of unfree agricultural labourers[2] and other manual occupational groups working for the dominant classes who were higher than them in the caste hierarchy. The dominant classes controlled the land and appropriated the surplus value of the Dalits, preventing them from cultivating land on their own. Compelled to act at the behest of the landlord,[3] they constituted what scholars have called, 'agrestic slaves' (Kumar 1965, Vishwanath 2014). An oppressive discourse of purity–pollution,[4] permeating religious, cultural, social and economic interactions, was part of the means of their domination and subordination.[5]

There were of course regional variations. Bondage and oppression was harshest in the intensively cultivated, irrigated river plains and delta regions, from the Gangetic Plains to parts of coastal Kerala and Tamil Nadu. In the dryer regions, where labour was at a premium but land less so, they might even have had some plots of land.[6] There were also differences between Dalit castes; village servants, for example, were more likely to have access to a small plot of land.[7]

The Adivasi or tribal groups of the hills and forests of India, in comparison, lived in relatively independent communities, with much more direct access to the means of their social reproduction because many were able to cultivate land and access forest resources without interference in, or domination or mediation of this access by caste groups.[8] Often they sought to keep away from outsiders,[9] and were stereotyped as wild and savage,[10] but Adivasis' autonomy regarding land and forests enabled them to be somewhat independent of the Hindu caste system. As Frederick Bailey (1961) argued, there was a tribe–caste continuum, with some groups more autonomous than others. The closer the interaction of Adivasi groups with Hindu societies of the plains, the more likely it was that their domination and exploitation became more like that of the 'Untouchables', so that some scholars have even called them 'tribal castes'.[11] Indeed, some scholars have argued that sections of Dalits came from tribal backgrounds, sometimes as subjugated hunters and gatherers of the lands conquered by warrior peasant groups.[12]

The colonial powers officially abolished slavery in India in 1843, but this simply led to its transformation into bondage through relations of debt; what has been called debt bondage by scholars.[13] Colonialism also reinforced the stigmas of caste and tribe. There is a well-known history of high caste collusion with the colonial administrators which reinforced the caste system and kept Dalits at the bottom of the social hierarchy. There is also a less well-known history of the appropriation of Adivasi forest and land resources that led both to their persistent dispossession but also to their fight back through rebellions, resulting in some protective legislation of their territories,[14] and their migration into ever more remote sites, seeking to keep the state at arm's length. Dalit resistance also began to take shape, led by a whole set of both high-profile and less well-known movements and people.[15]

The Dalit leader B.R. Ambedkar outlined the conditions and stigmatisation of Dalits by way of a stylised 20-point code that 'Touchables' in all villages would set for 'Untouchables'. These included segregated living quarters in the village with Untouchables relegated to the outskirts, marking a more general principle that Untouchables should stay clear of Touchables so that the Touchables could avoid their 'distance pollution' and their 'shadow pollution'. The code also prohibited wealth acquisition for Untouchables. There was also the requirement that 'he must wear the marks of his inferiority for the public to know and identify him such as: having a contemptible name; not wearing clean clothes', nor shoes, silver and gold ornaments. The code also listed duties of the Untouchables which included, among other ritual and practical duties, that 'on certain festivities, the Untouchables must submit their women to members of the village community to be made the subject of indecent fun' (Ambedkar 1989). Combined with the knowledge that these principles would be enforced through abuse, boycotts, beatings, and killings if necessary, Ambedkar's outline of the situation faced by Dalits provides a fitting description of untouchability in practice during the late colonial period.

With Independence, economic growth, development and modernisation were supposed to eliminate caste and tribe,[16] as well as poverty in India. Indeed, as outlined in the Preface, an ambitious programme of affirmative action for Dalits and Adivasis was introduced, and in the decades following Independence extreme oppressive historical forms of exploitation, such as hereditary life-long debt slavery, have been pushed to the margins, as have the most virulent forms of oppressive social practices based on purity–pollution. But scholars have argued that though the boundaries between Hindu (non-Dalit) castes may now be more permeable than in the past,[17] segregation between the Hindu castes and Dalits/Adivasis persists.[18]

Our book shows that despite substantial changes and some improvements, Adivasis and Dalits are still worse off than all other groups across all our sites, and still suffer from severe disadvantage and entrenched discrimination. Importantly, the sites of exploitation, marginalisation and oppression, and the ways in which Adivasis and Dalits are overwhelmingly trapped at the bottom of the Indian social and economic hierarchy, are both continuous with and also different to those of the past. Although the ideology of caste based on purity and pollution may be diluted, as a social relation of oppression, caste and tribe continue to be pervasive in contemporary India.

Our stories begin in the run-down tea plantations of the Peermade belt in Kerala where, from the 1860s onwards, Dalits from the villages of Tamil Nadu were brought to work as indentured labourers in the tea plantations developed by the colonial planters. This is the site of Jayaseelan Raj's research. Though Kerala is known the world over for its high levels of education and its unparalleled success within India in relation to human development, our book reveals a story of centuries of exploitation hidden in the midst of the beautiful rolling landscape of tea estates, the site of many a tourist visit to India.

Here, the processes of cutbacks in the terms and conditions of labour that accompanied economic liberalisation were sharpened by a global collapse of the tea economy in the 1990s. While some plantations started to close down, others were taken over by Indian multinational companies which used the moment to put much more precarious working conditions for labour into place.

Dalit men overwhelmingly lost their permanent work in the estate tea factories and Dalit women saw their permanent tea plucking jobs being cut back too. Though the jobs were very low paid, at least they had come with security of employment and also some welfare benefits (such as free healthcare, housing and the promise of pensions), but these benefits were cut back too. It was predominantly older Dalit women who continued to hold permanent tea plucker jobs in the tea plantations, thus at least providing the family some security of housing.

The Dalit youth – now more educated than their parents – tried to find better jobs in the cities back in Tamil Nadu. The best that most of them could get, though, was semi-skilled work: dyeing textiles and stitching and making garments or operating machinery. Away from the confines of the tea plantations many of these Dalits chose to hide or change their surnames in the face of overt caste discrimination in Tamil Nadu. Caste in India is often indelible in one's surname, and this made it difficult for these tea plantation Tamil Dalits to get a house or a job and much else when people knew their surname.

Jayaseelan Raj details how the local trade unions have been co-opted by the management of the tea plantations. However, in August 2015, 12,000 Dalit women tea pluckers in the Munnar tea belt, mobilising in a month-long strike, showed exceptional courage in fighting against the deteriorating terms and conditions of work that they increasingly face. Though they were not as successful as they had hoped, remarkably they bypassed the unions' formal leadership, charging them with nepotism and corruption, and mobilised autonomously to fight for higher wages.

The bargaining power of this local labour force – and their access to this kind of work – is, however, increasingly being undercut by the plantation owners bringing in seasonal migrant labourers who are even poorer than the local Dalits. In the Peermade this is Adivasi migrant labour from Jharkhand (Santhals), whom Jayaseelan Raj followed back to their homes in eastern India. They are brought in to do the tea plucking work that Dalits are compelled to move out of. For the tea plantation owners, the Adivasis are a cheaper, more docile workforce that can be hired on a casual piece rate basis without any of the rights the permanent Dalit workers had to housing, pensions and healthcare. Usually brought in just for eight to ten months a year, displaced from their kinship support networks, and not speaking the local language, they are not in a position to mobilise – as the Dalit women have done – against the plantation management.

From Kerala, the book moves east to the coastal belt of Cuddalore district in Tamil Nadu where Brendan Donegan worked. This region, an erstwhile landlord-dominated agricultural belt, has, again with economic liberalisation, been targeted by the State Industries Promotion Corporation for Tamil Nadu for the development of highly toxic chemical and pharmaceutical industries now lining the Bay of Bengal. The one that has an immediate impact on Donegan's site is a newly established gelatine factory whose entire production is for export. It is run with a business partner in Japan, has joint ventures in China and Taiwan, and makes gelatine from cattle bones for gelling agents in food, pharmaceuticals, photography and cosmetics, and hence locally is called 'the bone factory'.

The shift from agriculture to industry has meant that Dalit and Irula Adivasi labour is no longer bonded in agricultural servitude to high caste landlords. However, while Dalit women still primarily work in the village, Dalit men are now incorporated into the lowest rungs of the chemical industry – in Donegan's village most are working in daily contract wage work, cleaning bones with toxic chemicals. The jobs are controlled by the erstwhile landlords whose relatives own the factories, get the permanent jobs, and who themselves now dominate the supply of labour and material to the factories, apart from having moved out into other lucrative and powerful positions like operating a tollgate on the highway, becoming a Member of Legislative Assembly of Tamil Nadu, a film director or owning a five-star hotel.

The overall transition in the village is the classic one from field to factory, but one that is underwritten by a stark caste divide in which the low castes occupy the most precarious of jobs in the informal economy, in this case the dirtiest tasks of cleaning animal bones. Meanwhile the Irulas, who have not been given Scheduled Tribe status by the government, stick to agricultural labour and fishing: none do factory work. A few Irulas add long commutes to already lengthy working days to work in Pondicherry on construction sites, or migrate seasonally.

Though there is no upward mobility for the Adivasis, for some Dalits affirmative action, together with a long history of missionary work and related Dalit mobilisation,[19] have enabled them to occupy state sector jobs, albeit in the lower echelons (mainly in the police). However, as the Dalits in the factories try to rise against their exploitation, their bargaining power is being increasingly cut by seasonal migrant Adivasi and Dalit labour, again brought in from eastern India (Odisha, Jharkhand, Bihar), repeating a process that we also saw in the tea plantations of Kerala. Super-exploited, these migrants live in squalid conditions. There are often 40 to 70 people in one room operating as a dormitory, where they have to share the spot in which they sleep in shifts. And they work longer hours for less pay than any of the local low caste labour.

From Tamil Nadu, we move to the heart of the country to the banks of the Godavari in Bhadrachalam, Telangana where Dalel Benbabaali was based. Typical of the Adivasi-dominated areas of central and eastern India (in the states of Jharkhand, Chhattisgarh and Odisha), this is a place where Adivasi land rights have been constitutionally protected but which also contains a wealth of India's natural resources (coal, iron ore, bauxite and timber). Despite a long history of social movements, which most recently includes the Naxalite revolutionary struggle and the formation of the new state of Telangana from the erstwhile Andhra Pradesh, Adivasi land and forest rights in these areas have been successively eroded.

Benbabaali's research focused on the processes through which Adivasis (mainly Koyas), who were once rich in land and forest resources, were made increasingly poor. First, Kamma and Reddy landlords who came to the area from Coastal Andhra Pradesh in the 1800s in search of land for agriculture, took over the land of the Adivasis and controlled their labour, and that of the Dalits (Malas and Madigas), through relations of servitude. Subsequently, and under the control of these new dominant caste landlords, Adivasis were further dispossessed of their land for industrialisation and economic growth. A paper factory of the Indian Tobacco Company Paperboards and Speciality Division, which prides itself on being the largest manufacturer of packaging and graphics boards in South Asia, was set up and local Dalits became increasingly dependent on the low-paid casual labour in this paper factory while Adivasis became ever more dependent on the landlords for work as agricultural labour.

Since India's economic liberalisation, these areas have been the targets of large multinational corporations seeking to harvest the natural resources which lie underground. The Indian Tobacco Company has not only taken over land for its operations but is also increasingly destroying the surrounding forested areas, which is a crucial livelihood resource for the Adivasis, by replacing the diversity of the local forests with eucalyptus plantations which kill most local flora and fauna. The increase in the production of the factory that has accompanied liberalisation has also meant an increase in its need for natural resources, in this case wood. Wood imported from Southeast Asia is being replaced by new local plantations of eucalyptus. As is typical with this form of development that has come with economic liberalisation, many of these plantations are on land that has been illegally encroached on. The industries are so powerful and have such influential relationships with the state that even well-meaning, locally posted state officials who want to challenge this encroachment cannot do much.

Benbabaali shows that the main local beneficiaries of this industrial development have been the Kamma and Reddy landlords whose sons and daughters now aspire to move not only out of the area but also out of India to live in the USA. The son of one particular Kamma landlord, a well-heeled doctor, in fact now owns six different private hospitals in the US and has his own private jet plane to get from one hospital to the next. Meanwhile, the mainly landless Dalits work under casual contracts in the factories and in the cotton fields of the Kammas, their access to work controlled by the Kamma lords and at their beck and call. The Adivasis have more land to fall back on, enabling them to keep some autonomy from factory work, which they do not like. However, it is questionable how long they will be able to maintain this autonomy and some of them are already in the same situation as the Dalits. Moreover, none of these Dalits and Adivasis are likely to get the permanent factory jobs that are monopolised by people from non-Dalit/Adivasi communities. With their displacement by development and increasing housing and land rental prices, many have found it so expensive to live in the area that they have been reduced to living in plastic tents on occupied land, fetching water from a leak in a pipe, as a way to fight for a home.

From these Adivasi heartlands, *Ground Down by Growth* travels to the high mountains of Chamba in Himachal Pradesh where Richard Axelby worked. Here, Muslim Gujjar Scheduled Tribes and Hindu Gaddi Adivasis have survived with their buffaloes, sheep and goats for centuries in the extreme climate of the Saal valley and beyond, into the high Himalayas, as nomadic agro-pastoralists. In what is perhaps one of the first comparisons of Muslim and Hindu Adivasis, this chapter explores how population pressure, coupled with the limited number of grazing permits, means that both these groups have had to diversify out of nomadic agro-pastoralism, but have done so in different ways.

As a minority religious and ethnic group in Himachal, the Gujjars have seen little benefit from the forms of state assistance supposedly afforded them by their Scheduled Tribe status. On the other hand, while a few Gaddis have gained from affirmative action measures, the majority struggle to survive by combining small-scale agriculture and insecure precarious forms of wage labour. While Gaddis deal with uncertainty by 'turning inwards' to draw on the mutual support of the village community, Gujjars have reached out to external actors though the benefits of doing so are neither widely nor evenly distributed.

Unlike the banks of the Godavari River or the coastal belt of Tamil Nadu, there is no immediate oppressor impacting on the Adivasis in this Himalayan region. They are nevertheless marooned at the bottom of the social hierarchy compared with the upper castes and even the Dalits in the same hills and valleys. The higher castes have continued to own the best agricultural land, get the best education, and significantly more and better government jobs as well as better private sector jobs. Axelby argues that the historically close ties of the upper castes to the old royal court and businessmen in the nearby Chamba town enabled them to access profitable new positions as they emerged, post-Independence, and as the urban economy developed. However, for Gaddis and Gujjars there was no easy way to move away from an existence as herdsmen, petty farmers and labourers. Since the unskilled road project work in the Saal valley is given to incoming seasonal migrant labour from Bihar, Jharkhand and elsewhere, the Gujjars and Gaddis have to migrate for short-term, seasonal, informalised roadworks throughout the high mountains of Himachal Pradesh.

From the mountainous Himalayas of the old princely state, the final port of call is the Narmada River in Maharashtra where Vikramaditya Thakur lived with the Bhil Adivasi people. This is a site that attracted much international attention when a large dam – the Sardar Sarovar dam – was built in the name of development in the Satpura hills. Despite a huge international protest in the 1980s against the building of the dam, its reservoir flooded the surrounding villages displacing more than 30,000 people.

Vikramaditya Thakur's chapter compares the Bhil Adivasis who are still in the hills, with those who were moved to resettlement colonies in the agricultural plains, and with those who have a long history of living in the caste-dominated villages in those very plains. In the deforested hills, the Adivasis still rely on tilling whatever land they can access and migrating as seasonal agricultural labour to the sugar cane plantations of Maharashtra. Displaced by the dam, their counterparts who have moved to the resettlement colonies and been given unalienable land have inserted themselves into the insecurities of the cash crop economy – farming genetically modified Bt cotton, and papaya and bananas – in the plains. We see here a slow class differentiation taking place among the Adivasis and it is interesting to note that those who were resettled in the plains were led by the better educated Adivasis who were once the local activists of the movement against the Narmada dam. They have learnt about cash crops from the nearby dominant Gujar farmers who sold them the land for resettlement and whose sons and daughters are themselves moving out of agriculture.[20] In the nearby Gujar-dominated villages, we find a different group of Bhil Adivasis who have historically been the agricultural serfs of the Gujar landlords but, in more recent times, have been able to 'free' themselves to work as manual labour in the brick factories.

Though the resettled Adivasis have embarked on the kind of farming which was once the domain of the Gujars, and there are some signs of class differentiation among the Adivasis, Thakur is not optimistic regarding any trajectory of significant upward mobility. Without the cooperative agro-industrial moorings of Gujar farmers and with no social networks to access government and business circles, the Adivasi farmers are at the mercy not only of the vagaries of the weather but also of moneylenders and shrewd traders. Meanwhile, the stakes have changed and the sons and daughters of the Gujar landlords now seek well-paid government or private jobs outside the village and in the USA. Moreover, Thakur predicts that though the Adivasi youth aspire to better, English-medium education and better state sector or private sector jobs, the resettled Adivasis in fact face the same fate as their counterparts in the caste-dominated nearby village and as those in the hills. That is, cycles of back-breaking work as migrant agricultural labour in the farms of Gujarat and in the brick kilns of nearby states.

SURPLUS POPULATIONS?

What emerges across our sites is that the processes which keep Adivasis and Dalits at the bottom of the Indian social and economic hierarchy are dependent both on the continuities of inherited inequalities of power they are subject to and directly linked to the changing ways in which capitalism is expanding across the country. Whereas the village was once the primary site of the subordination and exploitation of India's Dalits, as agriculture has lost its central role in accumulation for the dominant castes the sites of exploitation and oppression for India's low castes have also shifted to the non-farm economies. And where some of India's tribes could continue to live off shifting cultivation, tilling their lands and foraging, or nomadic pastoralism, population pressure combined with their increased dispossession in the name of what has been called development means that they also face new sites of exploitation and oppression.

Though there are differences between Adivasis and Dalits (to which we return later), between individual Adivasi and Dalit communities, and within Adivasi and Dalit communities (in relation to gender and internal stratification), across the country both groups now practise multiple livelihood strategies which mix farm work (on their own land if they have any) with hard manual labour in the most uncertain, precarious and exploitative work conditions, within an India-wide informal economy that serves the interests of capital. This is so whether they end up working in construction in Chennai, in the chemical factories of Cuddalore or the garment factories of Tiruppur, in the tea plantations of Kerala, the paper factory in Telangana or the brick factories of Maharashtra and Gujarat.[21]

The purchase of the idea that the generation of wealth and poverty are different sides of the same coin, an integral part of the way in which capitalist growth works[22] is gaining new currency to explain recent trends in inequality across the globe. The recent Oxfam reports *An Economy for the 1%* and *An Economy for the 99%* (2016, 2017) are part of a wider literature which connects capital and labour, arguing that the huge concentrations of wealth and income are exacerbating inequality because of the increasing return to capital versus labour.

> In almost all rich countries and in most developing countries, the share of national income going to workers has been falling, meaning workers are capturing less and less of the gains from growth. In contrast, the owners of capital have seen their capital consistently grow (through interest payments, dividends, or retained profits) faster than the rate the economy has been growing. (Oxfam 2016: 4)

Capitalism produces more and more wealth for some but at the same time it also creates processes that displace people, that dispossess people and that turn them into paupers.[23] Generally, modern-day capitalism is so capital intensive that it creates fewer jobs. Some scholars have argued that as fewer people are involved in the production of wealth, more and more people are made superfluous and threatened with poverty or pauperised.[24] Tania Li (2010) and Jan Breman (2016) have called those who face this fate, 'surplus populations'.

However, when such arguments turn from a diagnostics of the precarious and informalised nature of work into a claim of widespread unemployment and pauperisation,[25] they run counter to the evidence of our research. The condition of most people across our sites is not cyclical unemployment, or partial integration into capitalist production, or pauperisation resulting in 'surplus population'. People are working and they are working hard; the problem is that most of them have been incorporated into the economy on very adverse terms from which they gain little benefit while they lose much. This is because capitalist growth in India, as elsewhere, has not led to a growth in secure employment that may improve the conditions of the poor,[26] only informal insecure work creating a highly exploitable labour force.

Indeed, decent jobs are so few and far between in today's India that Jonathan Parry (2013) has asserted that the biggest divide within the labouring classes is between the 8 per cent of the workforce in formal sector regular jobs (those that have *naukri* or secure employment) and the rest (those that have *kam* or insecure wage labour). This divide marks a significant difference in job security, pay, type and conditions of work, housing, health insurance, pensions, and so on, and ability to unionise. The majority of Indian workers – 92 per cent – are engaged in precarious work (what Parry calls *kam*), either in the small-scale informal sector or in informalised employment for formal sector enterprises.[27] They have no security of employment and no welfare benefits – no medical benefits, no insurance, no pensions. These are workers trapped in low wages or vulnerable self-employment and miserable work conditions, hired on a contract and fireable at a moment's notice. The precarity of work has become so widespread a reality that economists of the National Commission for Enterprises in the Unorganised Sector have aptly dubbed informalised workers as 'the Common People', the *Aam Aadmi* (see also Kannan's chapter).

Unprotected, informal labour in India is pervasive, in spite of a wide set of labour laws.[28] But, as pointed out by the National Commission for Enterprises in the Unorganised Sector (NCEUS 2007), labour laws are simply not implemented or enforced for informal labour. Moreover, in 2017 the government was even pushing through a major labour law reform which might well get rid of the little protection that is, at least in theory, offered by these laws.

The increase in unprotected, informal workers outside of agriculture is part of a wider trend that has taken place since the 1980s as governments have liberalised and privatised their economies and integrated them into a global market. Businesses in both rich and poor countries deepened and extended their reach to new areas and sectors, surviving increased global competition by relying on a flexible, informalised, cheaper and more docile workforce. In most parts of the world, we have therefore not seen what was expected to be the standard development trajectory, based on European industrialisation, which teleologically predicted a move from agriculture to industry and the formation of a 'proletarian' condition, with workers solely reproducing through labour relations with the potential to self-identify as proletarians.

While full-time work in agriculture has declined rapidly across the global South, there is no overall move towards a doubly 'free' class of a mainly industrial labour force – 'freed' (that is, dispossessed) from access to the means of production such as landownership, and 'free' (that is, forced by economic compulsion) to sell their labour power. Instead, groups of 'more-or-less' free labourers (Banaji 2003) have been constituted, often with at least one foot in agriculture and the other in informal and insecure work and precarious petty commodity production outside of agriculture.[29] This non-proletarian condition, which Henry Bernstein (2007) calls 'classes of labour', can be viewed as a new permanent reserve army of labour,[30] facing 'terminal marginality within global capitalism.'[31] It is the fate of most of the working population of Latin America, Africa and Asia, and, according to some, even of China.[32] Such 'classes of labour', are, as we show in this book, however, only part of the picture.

RETHINKING CAPITALISM AND CLASS, RACE AND CASTE-TRIBE

'Class relations', as used in this book, refers to people's relations to each other as they are shaped by their relationship to the means of production and the appropriation of surplus from labour, and by their social reproduction.[33] What our book highlights is that class relations are inseparable from other axes of social oppression such as race or ethnicity; in our case, caste, tribe, gender and region. This is central to an understanding of contemporary agrarian change and the spread of capitalism, and, as we argue in the final chapter of this book, has deep-seated consequences for how we think about political struggles.

When compared with the neighbouring upper caste households – whether it is the upper caste Hindus of the Himalayas or the Gujars of the Maharashtra plains, the Nadars of Cuddalore, or the Kamma and Reddies of Telangana – everywhere it is Adivasis and Dalits who occupy the most precarious rungs of the occupational ladder.[34] Industrialisation has not led to a generalised proletarian condition for them, not even in the village swallowed up by the industrial belt in Cuddalore, Tamil Nadu or in the Bhadrachalam village in Telangana dominated by the Indian Tobacco Company paper factory. Formal sector regular employment is dominated by the higher castes. All other main caste, ethnic and religious groups are under-represented in formal sector regular employment but, in the last decade, the large group of castes belonging to 'Other Backward Classes' (OBCs) have significantly improved their access to this kind of work, and a divide is now also opening up between Adivasis, Dalits, Muslims and all other social groups in accessing regular formal work. Self-employment outside of agriculture is also not a rewarding survival strategy for Adivasis and Dalits. Not only are they under-represented among the self-employed, but self-employed Adivasis and Dalits are significantly poorer than all other social groups of the self-employed. This is clear from National Sample Survey data.[35] It is not just, as Parry (2013) asserts, that the biggest divide within the labouring classes is between those who have *naukri* and those who have *kam*. What is crucially at stake is the fact that, in comparison to the dominant castes, Adivasis and Dalits overwhelmingly have just *kam*.

The stories presented here suggest that Adivasis and Dalits have no choice but to enter work lives shaped by global patterns of capitalist accumulation which appropriate (rather than negate) social differences and entrench them. They suggest that it is impossible to consider a class analysis without at the same time considering other axes of social oppression (here, caste, tribe, region and gender) in the processes of capitalism.

In recent years, theories of intersectionality have gained a lot of purchase in attempts to draw attention to how injustice and social inequality occur on a multidimensional level involving several social identities that 'interact with each other' (such as gender, race, social class, ethnicity).[36] While important in placing multiple identities on the agenda, we find these theories inadequate to explain the inextricability of the ways class relations and identity shape each other. This is because in most analyses of 'intersectionality', different categories are nearly always treated as independent 'variables' that may or may not 'interact' or 'intersect' or 'correlate' in a particular circumstance. Moreover, class is treated as a social category rather than as constituting people's social relations as they are shaped by their relationship to the means of production and reproduction. In contrast, we draw attention to the fact that identity-based social oppression is constitutive of and shapes people's relationship to the means of their production and reproduction, placing centre stage the analysis of the political economy under which class relations, caste, tribe, gender and region are inextricably linked.[37] In doing so we draw inspiration from a tradition attempting to understand the relationship between race and political economy that goes back to Marx,[38] has been developed in the North American and European context, and which has been revived and taken further in recent years.[39]

In the late 1940s, Oliver Cox in his *Caste, Class and Race* (1970 [1948]), tracing European colonialism in the Americas after 1492, proposed that race prejudice was a ruling-class instrument justifying the exploitation of a group or its resources. Though there were debates about the extent to which hierarchical racial differences were essential or cultural or material, Cox's insights were developed in different ways and to different degrees by various authors to show that race and class were not fundamentally distinguishable, not dichotomous, but overlapping in a singular system of social power and stratification rooted in political economy.[40]

In Europe in recent years, Stuart Hall (1986), drawing inspiration from Gramsci's non-reductive approach to questions of class, similarly deliberated on the interrelationship between class and race in the expansion of capitalism. He urged us to see the ways in which capitalist development preserves, adapts, harnesses and exploits the culturally specific character of labour power rather than systematically eroding these distinctions as an inevitable part of progress in world history. He said that:

> The ethnic and racial structuration of the labour force, like its gendered composition, may provide an inhibition to the rationalistically-conceived 'global' tendencies of capitalist development. And yet, these distinctions have been maintained, and indeed *developed and refined*, in the global expansion of the capitalist mode. They have provided the means for differentiated forms of exploitation of the different sectors of a fractured labour force. (Hall 1986: 24)

Arguing that racism is best understood as a social relation of oppression rather than as solely or primarily an ideology, David Camfield (2016) has recently argued that racism remains a very real feature of the contemporary world because of two dimensions of capitalism. The first is imperialism and the profitability of racism, and the second the efforts of dominant groups to preserve their advantages relative to the racially oppressed (Camfield 2016). A recent special volume of the *Journal of World Systems Research*,[41] set in critical dialogue with Cox's early study, further proposes that the racialised subordination and creation of 'redundant' populations,[42] including along lines of ethnicity, is an essential part of global capitalism. Indeed, Anna Tsing (2009: 148), reflecting on 'Supply chains and the human condition', has argued that diversity in the form of gender, race, national status and other forms is structurally central to global capitalism, and not 'decoration on a common core'.

In India, the inseparability of identity and class in the processes of capitalism is a point increasingly voiced by Dalit scholars (Guru and Chakravarty 2005; Teltumbde 2010). It has also been expressed in the critiques and self-critiques of radical Marxist movements (see Ghandy 2011, Ismail and Shah 2015 and Srinivasulu 2017 on the Marxist Leninists/Maoists; and Lerche 1999 on the Communist Party of India [Marxist]). These political critiques are supplemented by historical analyses[43] and the rare agrarian class analysis, such as that of the late Arvind Das (1984). Some have more recently shown how capital segments and fragments labour through the manipulation of caste, gender and other non-class social identities (Harriss-White and Gooptu 2000) and others have explored how contemporary processes of primitive accumulation under financialisation accentuate local dynamics of race/ethnicity, gender and class (Whitehead 2016).[44]

These are important contributions but they are exceptions to a general unease, especially within the left, about exploring the mutual constitution of class relations and social difference, and a general preference for viewing class and social difference as opposing binaries. Raj Chandavakar, in his critique of labour historiography, aptly points out that part of the reason for this omission is perhaps an incipient fear that, 'To recognise that the working classes were fragmented by the very processes which constituted them has appeared to some as nothing less than the rejection of the concept [of class] itself or the denial of the possibility of class consciousness' (Chandavakar 1999: 208).

But the centrality of the social fragmentation (or, in Hall's terminology, cultural fragmentation) of the workforce under capitalism has a long history. Kevin Anderson (2010) has recently highlighted how even Marx, in the last decades of his life, started seriously thinking about the significance of ethnic divisions within the workforce and how ethnic groups were used against each other in capitalist growth – whether it was in the context of Irish workers in England or Polish workers in Russia.

The racial fragmentation of workers is, perhaps, nowhere better developed than by Etienne Balibar (1991a, 1991b). Focusing first on colonial Spain, Balibar shows how the ruling classes constructed themselves as a pure race, thus enabling their mastery over the labour of those they construed as races different from and inferior to themselves. He argues that the primitive accumulation of capital in the colonies was based on conferring on the Spanish race 'a fictive nobility to make it a "people of masters"' exactly when Spain, as the largest of the colonial empires, was conquering and dominating by terror, genocide, slavery and enforced Christianisation' (Balibar 1991a: 208). Then, Balibar argues, the Industrial Revolution and the expansion of capitalism accentuated these processes of stigmatisation and gave rise to 'the new racism of the bourgeois era which has as its target the *proletariat* in its dual status as the exploited [...] and politically threatening population' (Balibar 1991a: 209). Drawing on Louis Chevalier (1981 [1973]), Balibar proposes that the processes of stigmatisation discursively created the 'labouring classes' as the 'dangerous classes', a category used to stigmatise the bottom of society in nineteenth-century France as a 'breeding ground' for thieves, prostitutes, beggars and 'evildoers of all sorts' who are 'an object of fear to society' and therefore 'dangerous' (Balibar 1991a, 1991b).

Balibar argues that after the Industrial Revolution, not only were the labouring classes discursively created as a degenerate and dangerous race, they were divided into two: those who were made to be no longer dangerous and those upon whom 'dangerous' characteristics were displaced, that is, primarily foreigners, immigrants and colonial subjects. The privileges of the first group might include citizenship, voting rights and so on, while the latter were excluded from such positions and markers (Balibar 1991a: 208–11). Balibar argues that in the global North (he focuses on France) the divide runs between immigrant workers and those considered proper national workers, and this relates closely to hierarchies of work. The relative privileges – real or perceived – of the national workers can only be maintained if they are exclusive and restricted. Working-class racism, that is, racism between those groups who perceive themselves linked to the dominant classes, and the 'dangerous' parts of the labouring classes, plays a major role in the workings of class racism in capitalist accumulation (Balibar 1991b: 224–26).

Balibar has called this process of stigmatisation of the working classes by the ruling elites, and their internal conflicts, 'class racism'. We argue that in India a similar stigmatisation of certain sections of the labouring classes is also central to the workings of capitalism and especially affects the position of Adivasis and Dalits. But racism is only one aspect of the oppression they face. In India, tribe, caste, ethnicity, gender and region are crucial elements shaping the specific ways in which, under capitalism, the dominant classes and castes ally with some segments of the working population to maintain and reinforce difference and defend the (for many, quite meagre) privileges and resources that they have from those below them in the social hierarchy through the social stigma they attach to them.[45]

Specifically, our research leads us to propose that the entrenchment of social difference in the expansion of capitalism takes place through at least three interrelated processes. The first is through historical *inherited inequalities of power*, in which powerful outsiders, the state, and locally dominant groups continue to mediate and control the adverse incorporation and marginalisation of Adivasis and Dalits in the new economies. The second is through the *super-exploitation of casual migrant labour*, in which local labour power is undercut by a more vulnerable workforce brought in from a different region (and of a different ethnicity) on worse terms and conditions, enabling capitalists to fragment the overall labour force and therefore better control and cheapen it. Third, *conjugated oppression* – the inextricability of multiple oppressions based on caste, tribe, class, gender and region with class relations – is a constitutive part of all the other processes and should be seen in relation both to all India stigmatisation and to further division of the working classes, specifically inter-group and gender differences, between and within Adivasis and Dalits, men and women.

Inherited inequalities of power

The ways in which global processes of the expansion of capitalism actually work through locally dominant caste groups and the ways in which this impacts on Adivasis and Dalits is striking across our sites. Many of the upper caste Hindus, Gujars, Nadars, Kamma and Reddies who used to command hegemonic power at village level through caste-based hierarchical land, labour, social and political relations, have transformed themselves into major or auxiliary players in the new economy. Though their access to livelihoods in the informal economy for Dalits and Adivasis occurs beyond the old bounds of the patronage of village hierarchies, it is thus nevertheless shaped by processes of inequality involving their inherited powerlessness in relation to the power of dominant social groups and institutions.

The implications are that the poverty of the Adivasis of central and eastern India cannot be understood without accounting for the continuing long-term impact of the higher caste outsiders who have come to take away their lands and resources. This is the case whether it is the banks of the rivers they lived off which have been flooded by the building of dams made to serve rich farmers, or whether it is land taken away first for agriculture for the dominant castes and then for industrial development projects, a paper factory or a mine belonging to large multinational companies whose owners live in palaces in Mumbai or Kensington. Similarly, the poverty of the Dalits of Kerala cannot be understood without taking into account the history of how they were brought in as indentured labour by the British tea planters to pluck tea and how, with the tea crisis, the multinational and Indian companies that own these plantations have taken from them even the modicum of security that these jobs offered, thrusting them into the garment sector in which they make clothes for national and international outlets such as Gap.

For many of our sites, the forces shaping such developments are very visible and violent. For instance, for the Adivasis and Dalits of the Telangana village, the processes reinforcing existing inequalities have a very real local presence in the shape of the old local Kamma landlord, who not only controls access to informalised jobs and patronage in the nearby paper factory but who also tries to determine to what level Adivasis and Dalits can be educated. Indeed, a local teacher reported that the Kamma landlord filed a case against him when he tried to convince the government to extend classes in the village school to 10th grade (the equivalent of GCSEs); the landlord did not want the Dalits and Adivasis to become more educated than he was.

Similarly, we cannot understand the plight of the Dalits of Tamil Nadu unless we understand that the dominant caste landlords under whose patronage they worked as bonded labour now control their access to industrial work, in close collaboration with their powerful caste brethren who are in charge of the 'bone factory' producing gelatine for the global market. The dominant castes colonise the best jobs and ensure that Dalits only have access to the worst jobs in the most polluted circumstances. Meanwhile, for the Dalit tea plantation workers in Kerala, their conditions are explicitly shaped by the class of higher caste plantation administrators and officials who cut their wages, undermine the security of their permanent work status, and cut their gratuity benefits under the pretext of a crisis in the tea economy.

Even where the power of the local landlords to control the fate of Adivasis and Dalits has declined, or where the immediate powers shaping local conditions may seem distant and abstract – such as for the Adivasis in the Saal valley in the Himalayas – for all the Dalit and Adivasi groups we have worked with, their ongoing adverse inclusion into the economy is based on historical disadvantage and institutionalised discrimination.

This history legitimises the fact that, today, Adivasis and Dalits have less land, capital, education and political clout than others and therefore are consigned to low-end work. So even where Dalits and Adivasis do not face overt discrimination by higher castes, they are still disadvantaged in relation to other social groups. In some of our cases the historical disadvantage and powerlessness is extreme, such as for Irulas in Tamil Nadu, who have little recourse when faced with government officials who deny them their tribal certificates. Or, for instance, in the case of the Bhil Adivasi farmers who are forced to watch their papaya crop rot in the fields as traders, unpunished, renege on deals to pick it up. (The only get relief they get is when Gujar farmers use the strength that only they have, to force government to provide a minimum of support to all papaya growers.) In Telangana, where there is overt discrimination in certain contexts, it is notable that in the vicinity of the paper factory only the Kamma street (and not the Adivasi or Dalit ones) has a tap for almost every house and a concrete road built by the factory. Elsewhere the disadvantage is more mundane. The Adivasis in the Himalayas, for instance, found that their historical position at the social and physical extremes of society left them without entry points or means to access decent work in government or the private sector. They were only able to add road construction work, local petty business or migration to rear cattle in Punjab to their livelihood strategies.

Moreover, across all our sites, Adivasis and Dalits were less educated than all other groups. Where we have evidence that maps education onto occupation, the pattern is that precisely the same levels of education yield better jobs for general castes than they do for Adivasis and Dalits. This is also the case for the Bhils who, within the last generation, finally obtained access to education only to find that the Gujar farmers had monopolised the good private sector jobs of the region. This confirms a more general

pattern, highlighted by K.P. Kannan in his chapter, that for the socially disadvantaged groups the level of education required to cross the threshold
of poverty and vulnerability is much higher than for those in a socially
advantaged position, and the speed at which it happens slower.[46]

These inherited inequalities of power, underwritten by caste relations,
mark the ways in which capitalism in India has spread and has thus
reproduced the poverty of the country's low castes in new contexts and
new ways. Poverty is thus not only the result of processes based on the
relationship between structurally unequal people, but also an effect of the
inherited structural ability of certain social groups to continue to assert
power and shape social and economic relations accordingly.

The liberalisation which is driving the ways in which capitalism is
expanding across the country is, of course, a state-driven process. And
though these processes are not unilinear, and can vary between regions and
across political parties,[47] the Indian state is nevertheless part and parcel of
these persisting inherited inequalities of power. The dam on the Narmada
River which flooded the Bhil Adivasi villages was a government project. The
breach of the Fifth Schedule of the Constitution allowing the establishment
of the paper factory in Bhadrachalam was so blatant that its illegality was
acknowledged by official government documents, as was the fact that it
happened at the cost of the rights of local Adivasis. An implicit ingredient
of the industrial policies in Tamil Nadu and elsewhere (including in the
Peermade tea plantations) is that labour laws such as those limiting the use of
contract labour are not enforced. And in the Saal valley, as everywhere else,
the outsourcing of government work to private contractors has diminished
the efficacy of reserving government jobs for Adivasis and Dalits.

The super-exploitation of migrant workers

Economic growth crucially uses the low status and social difference of
migrant labour, their region and language-based alien-ness, to undercut
local low caste workers and resolutely make the overall labour force insecure
and super-exploitable. Of course, the use of racial difference of migrant
labour in the organisation of capitalist production has a long history that
dates back to African slavery and Asian indenture systems. Today, many
countries of the global North are dependent on migrants from less developed
countries who are highly precarious, whether it is Latinos in the USA or
North Africans in France. In India, the oppression of migrant labour is not a
product of external immigration (as in the French/European and US cases)
but 'internal alien-ness'[48] based on low caste, tribe and region status. This
internal labour circulation is central to cheapening and controlling labour
inside and outside the labour process.

The Inter-State Migrant Workmen (Regulation of Employment and Conditions of Service) Act, 1979 makes it illegal to treat migrant labour worse than local labour. But every year people find themselves in circumstances where they are migrating to a new place where they most often do not speak the local language, doing manual labour under living conditions and with wages that few locals would agree to, getting work for only a part of the year. They hold on to what little assets they might have back at home.

India's development trajectory, rather than resulting in the formation of an urban proletariat, has led to people who keep whatever little land they may have in rural areas while at the same time migrating to work seasonally in more urban sectors. Marginal and small farmers are increasingly turning to seasonal labour migration. These are the scores of circular migrant labourers, those whom Jan Breman has devoted his life to analysing and whom he has called 'wage hunters and gatherers' (Breman 1996), transcending and working across both the agricultural–industrial and the rural–urban divides.

The numbers are very difficult to establish for there is no survey that captures seasonal labour migrants. The official Economic Survey 2016–17 now estimates internal seasonal labour migration in India to be about 140 million, upping the stakes on an earlier estimate of 80–100 million.[49] On the basis of how this migration works within households we suggest that these are still very modest estimates, as they do not include all the people per household *affected* by seasonal casual labour migration (even if at any one moment in time all are not engaged in the migration). For the very point of such migration is that a household needs multiple means of livelihood to survive and the migrant should not be considered separate from the other members of the household (for example, people often take turns to migrate within households). Seen this way, several hundred million people – 560 million if we assume that for each migrant there are three other members of the household – are fundamentally *affected by* seasonal casual labour migration.

The anthropologist Claude Meillassoux, some time ago, in the context of Southern Africa, pointed out how such labour migration involves a distinctive mode of exploitation, as it relies on dividing local workers reproducing themselves entirely within the capitalist industries and the rotation of a rural labour force which only partly reproduces itself in the same way (Meillassoux 1981 [1975]: 120–25). We use the term 'super-exploitation' to describe the condition under which capital cheapens labour from the countryside far below the standard cost of a local worker by not only giving them lower pay and worse terms and conditions of work, but also by omitting the cost of their reproduction back at home.

Importantly, this double local and rural rotational migrant labour market is dependent on various forms of discrimination. Meillassoux (1981 [1975]: 120) highlighted that the processes which enable this double labour market to function are reinforced by a racist ideology that classifies the migrant workers as a priori unskilled and therefore relegated to low pay and unstable employment. Racism creates a hostile social environment around these workers, making it difficult for them to put forward their demands, demonstrate publicly or ally with local workers. Crucially what we find is that this oppression of seasonal labour migrants has both a caste/tribe dynamic and a regional dimension; they face conjugated oppression, a concept developed in the next section.

To take the caste/tribe dynamic of the oppression of seasonal casual labour migrants first – Adivasis and Dalits are overwhelmingly represented among this group.[50] A recent government report on migration shows that Adivasis and Dalits form a disproportionately large percentage of migrant workers – much higher than their share of the overall population – across nearly all sectors and they dominate numerically among migrant workers in the low skill, back-breaking brick kiln and construction sectors.[51]

The main migration patterns are shown in our map at the front of the book. The Adivasi households of Maharashtra make a living in this manner, as do the young Dalit plantation workers from Kerala and some of the Irula Adivasi households in Tamil Nadu. The Adivasis from central and eastern India survive the year by migrating to work as the most exploited of the informalised workforce in the industries and tea estates studied in South India. The isolation of the Adivasis on the tea plantations and of the Odisha migrants in the bone factory is intense, as they do not speak the local language. Others, such as Adivasis in the Himalayas, find work through shorter-term, migratory labour contracts closer to their homes, although they also have to go further and further afield to find work as other seasonal in-migrants from Jharkhand, Bihar and elsewhere are considered more malleable by local labour contractors.

Although for some – such as the Bhil Adivasis of the Gujar-dominated village of Mankheda in Maharashtra – seasonal migration may be a way out of even more oppressive relations in the village,[52] the new labour relations of migration inevitably involve new forms of oppression and exploitation. Chains of labour contractors organise long-distance seasonal migration and, for many at the bottom end of the labour hierarchy such as the Bhils, lump sums paid in advance tie them to a specific contractor. In Tamil Nadu, the contractor who brings the Odiya workers in to the bone factory pockets a significant proportion of their wages, allegedly to pay for their overcrowded dorm where there is only space for them to sleep in shifts. Everywhere the migrant workers live in squalid conditions. The Adivasis of the Saal valley working on road construction sleep in tents and huts, often under freezing conditions in the high passes of the Himalayas. In the Kerala tea plantations, the workers from Jharkhand are given the worst accommodation on the estates, with several families having to share one small tenement house. Meanwhile the Bhil Adivasis live in straw- and plastic-tented camps at the brick kilns or in the sugar cane fields.

Region also overlaps with caste/tribe to divide the workforce and ensure that the labour power of local low caste labour is undercut by migrant low caste labour brought in from other parts of the country. Seasonal labour migration is of course a huge part of the everyday life of poor Adivasis and Dalits, as well as of other low castes and Muslims across India. This is especially the case in the poorest regions of India, in particular central and eastern India. Typically, the most exploited of seasonal migrant labour comes from central and eastern India (Jharkhand, parts of Bihar, Chhattisgarh, Odisha, parts of Madhya Pradesh, and parts of Andhra/Telangana). These are regions which historically have been less developed, and where households are otherwise dependent on agriculture. Unless year-round work opportunities are at their doorstep, both Adivasis and Dalits in these regions will have at least one or more members of the household migrating away to work in brick factories, agricultural fields, garment work or as construction labour – overwhelmingly jobs that are classified as low skilled and remunerated accordingly. We have found Adivasis (and Dalits) from Jharkhand doing the most physically demanding jobs with the worst remuneration in brick factories in Calcutta (Shah 2006), in the chemical factories in Tamil Nadu (Donegan's chapter here), in the tea plantations of Kerala (Raj's chapter), in construction sites in Delhi (Lerche et al. 2017), and in agricultural work in Gujarat (Thakur's chapter).

This labour circulation is central to cheapening and controlling labour inside and outside the labour process in contemporary India, to keep the 'social cost of production' (as Raj calls it here) as low as possible. The oppression of this migrant labour workforce in relation to the local low caste workforce happens in at least two ways – both inside and outside of the production process. To take the labour process first, migrant labour from these central and eastern Indian regions is usually the lowest paid in the regions to which they are migrating and the terms and conditions of their work are, crucially, even worse than those of local Dalit or Adivasi labour. While local Tamil Dalit contract workers in the bone factory usually do one eight-hour shift, six days a week, the eastern Indian migrants regularly work between one and four shifts in a row, seven days a week. They achieve this seemingly impossible feat by means of an informal understanding with other workers and supervisors, in which workers take turns to sleep in a corner of the factory. In Kerala, the Adivasi workers from Jharkhand are employed as casual workers. They will not even be considered for promotion to temporary worker status, let alone permanent worker status, while most of the Tamil Dalit workers have permanent status or, at the very least, temporary status. This denial of temporary/permanent work status means that the Adivasis do not have a provident fund, annual leave, medical leave and other benefits that are provided to the permanent and temporary workforce. They are paid less than half the minimum wage in all other sectors in Kerala.

Outside the production process the low caste seasonal migrant workers are also more prone to oppression and exploitation than the local low castes. Their living conditions are usually far worse than those of local labour. In Kerala, for instance, several Adivasi families from Jharkhand are forced to live in each small tenement that would normally be for one local Dalit family only. Moreover, they do not speak the local language so are unable to negotiate and bargain for themselves, most often having to rely on their contractor.

As pointed out by Raj, since the migrant workers from Jharkhand are not recognised as proper workers on the tea estates, they are also not eligible for welfare measures outside the plantations; officially, for the Keralan authorities, they simply do not exist. They do not have access to the Public Distribution System under which subsidised rations of rice, dal and kerosene are available to the poor and that other workers benefit from.[53] They are treated along the same lines as immigrants in many other countries. For instance, in China circular migrants working in the big cities do not have the same rights as those with urban *hokou*. Seasonal migrant workers in India are, in effect, not seen as citizens of the state when migrating as they do not even have access to amenities for the local poor in the places they migrate to.

The seasonal migrant workers are dependent on their own reproduction in their domestic economies to supplement their migrant labour power and this social cost of reproduction back at home is never taken into account in their remuneration in the places to which they migrate. Indeed, it constitutes the very basis upon which the overall workforce is cheapened. Wherever they end up staying in their places of migration they usually become the most marginalised of local communities; landless, uneducated and with not even a caste certificate to their name – as in the case of the Odiya camp dwellers in Bhadrachalam, who are mostly a Dalit group called Doms that originally came from Malkangiri in Orissa to build the Sileru dam and then the paper factory.

What we see is that economic growth in India has crucially used the low status and social difference of migrant labour, their region and language-based alien-ness, to undercut local low caste workers and make the overall labour force completely insecure and super-exploitable. Workers divided by caste and region are less able to resist managerial control – they can be better 'tamed' to put it in Jan Breman's words – meaning more is extracted from the workers. Workers from outside the region are working for lower wages and under worse conditions, often doing jobs that local workers will not do for the same terms and conditions, and therefore the workforce is cheapened for the employers. In today's India this seasonal casual labour migration is a crucial part of the conjugated oppression – discussed in the next section – at the heart of capitalist accumulation that fragments the labourers, keeping Adivasis and Dalits at the bottom of the Indian economic and social hierarchy.

Conjugated oppression

To explore the multiple forms of oppression simultaneously at work in India, we take inspiration from Philippe Bourgois's (1988, 1989, 1995) conceptualisation of 'conjugated oppression'. For Bourgois, 'conjugated oppression' is useful to capture how 'an ideological dynamic of ethnic discrimination … interacts explosively with an economic dynamic of class exploitation to produce an overwhelming experience of oppression that is more than the sum of the parts' (Bourgois 1995: 72). Bourgois used the concept first in relation to two ethnic groups of workers on banana plantations spanning the borders of Costa Rica and Panama and the different kinds of oppression they faced (Bourgois 1988, 1989), but then also transported the concept to express the many forms of oppression faced by Puerto Ricans in New York for whom a drug like crack had an explosive appeal (Bourgois 1995). We expand Bourgois's 'conjugated oppression' to express how multiple axes of oppression – such as caste, tribe, gender and region (but which could include race, ethnicity or sexuality in other contexts) – are constitutive of and shape class relations, inseparable from each other in capitalist accumulation.

Although we focus here on the spread of capitalism, we do not see conjugated oppression as limited to capitalist relations – it can be an aspect of any society with exploitative relations. In India, as shown, conjugated oppression of class, caste and tribe started long before the spread of capitalism. Stigmatisation takes place in different ways for the different communities. Caste-based oppression, especially of 'Untouchable' castes, was part and parcel of the creation and maintenance of a large rural proletariat of agrestic slaves in pre-colonial times. Despite the banning of untouchability by the Indian Constitution in 1950, stereotypes often ascribe impurity and filth to Dalits. For the Indian tribes the issues were different, as their forest autonomy enabled them to be somewhat outside the Hindu caste system – except, of course, when their areas were conquered or encroached upon by outsiders. But they are still discursively constructed as part of the 'dangerous classes', as wild, savage and barbaric.

In some of our cases the stigma experienced is so explicit that it excludes Dalits and Adivasis from certain jobs. Raj, for instance, documents some of the most clear-cut cases of overt work-related discrimination. The textiles and garment sector factories in Tamil Nadu were unwilling to employ semi-skilled Dalits and there were cases of entire communities of Dalits hiding their name and caste background for years in order to get work.[54] For others, for example a Dalit plumber in a Kerala town, it was the everyday discriminatory behaviour of work colleagues and bosses that made it impossible for him to stay in the job – had he stayed on, it would have been at the cost of his sanity and self-respect.[55] Going back to their villages in Tamil Nadu was not seen as a viable escape from these processes of oppression as the stigma of pollution attached to being Dalit were still prevalent there. For instance, upper caste tea shop owners were reported to discourage Dalits from entering their shops by providing tea in dirty cups and demanding the exact sum of money for the tea even if they had change to give back. Back in the tea plantations, the Dalits are stigmatised not only as Dalits but also, as Raj argues, because of their history of once having been enslaved bonded labour, because they were Tamil speakers in Malayali Kerala, and because they were from the 'wild' highlands rather than from the settled and 'civilised' lowland valley. These varied processes of conjugated oppression lead Raj to argue that economic mobility does not come with social mobility for the tea plantation Dalits.

Meanwhile, at the bone factory in Tamil Nadu, local Dalits and Adivasis, as well as migrant workers who are also mainly Dalits and Adivasis, do the dirtiest jobs, dealing with animal bones in the smelly, unhygienic heart of the factory. In Telangana, Benbabaali reports not only the presence of these stigmas but also how they are used to divide and rule workers – so Koyas are constructed as 'rebellious' by the Kamma landlord and Lambadas as 'obedient', thus enhancing the preferential employment of the latter in his fields or as informalised labour in the paper factory. At another field site, in the plains of Nandurbar, Thakur informs us, the Gujar farmers hurl abuse and taunts at their Adivasi Bhil labourers. And in Himalayan Chamba, Axelby reports how a government official described his fellow caste Hindus as 'hardworking' and 'progressive' in contrast to the 'ignorant and lazy' Gaddis and 'dishonest' Gujjars, while wealthy upper castes and the upper Muslim groups of Chamba town stigmatised the rural Gujjars as dirty, ill-educated and dishonest.

While Adivasis and Dalits (as well as Muslims) are overwhelmingly informalised, so are major sections of other relatively low-ranking castes. The process of conjugated oppression often also maintains and strengthens the divides between these groups as the non-Dalit/Adivasi low-ranking castes may kick downwards, as highlighted by Raj in relation to urban informalised workers' discrimination against Dalits, and as reported by Donegan from Tamil Nadu where the Adivasi Irulas suspect that culprits from the Nattar fishing caste (who are higher up in the caste hierarchy and officially registered as OBCs) were behind stealing the engines and destroying the nets of their new fishing dinghies, expecting to – and succeeding in – getting away scot free. The Vanniyar caste (also OBCs), with the tacit understanding of the Nadar factory management, has monopolised the semi-skilled contract work at the bone factory, keeping the Dalit Paraiyars confined to the more hazardous and poorly paid work on the factory floor. Underwritten by a broad acceptance from those classes and castes which are not at the bottom of the hierarchy, this conjugated oppression is essential to the social relations of inequality on the ground.

The Indian poor are also marked by conjugated oppression in ways that go well beyond the specificities of the workplace and its locality. Adivasis and Dalits in particular are not only 'othered'; in many instances they are the non-humans of India, the ones who can be discriminated against, the ones with no rights and the ones against whom atrocities can be committed with near impunity. Some of the most degrading stigmatising is most clearly exposed in the ways Adivasis have been treated in central and eastern India, as the 'dangerous classes' joining the Naxalite revolutionary struggle, but we have also seen this negative stereotyping in the ways in which Dalits across the country have been targeted as 'anti-national' in recent years (take for example the struggles around the suicide of the Hyderabad University Dalit student Rohith Vemula in 2016). The dominant classes in society still view the lives, lifestyles and customs of Adivasis and Dalits (and Muslims) as dirty or uncivilised, decry emancipatory politics from their midst as anti-national (that is, disloyal to the nation), and consider them in need of civilisatory education before they can join the 'nation'. What we have as a result of the construction of Adivasis and Dalits as 'dangerous classes', based on their conjugated oppression, is a super-exploitable workforce controlled, enforced and over whom is supported by an oppressive 'civilising' mission which is increasingly being meted out by the police and other state forces in collusion with corporate capital.

As is evident, crucial to the process of conjugated oppression are the differences within and the fracturing of the labour force, leading to different kinds of oppression experienced by the different groups at the bottom of the social and economic hierarchy.

A significant aspect which emerges through our collective work is that although the dominant economic analysis groups together Adivasis and Dalits (as Scheduled Castes/Scheduled Tribes), there are in fact vast differences in their experiences of inequality, poverty and stigmatisation which are important to consider. Those who have tried to differentiate the two have told us that Adivasis are worse off than Dalits. Poverty figures show that while poverty continues to be falling more slowly for both Dalits and Adivasis than for other groups, this decrease in poverty is particularly slow for Adivasis.[56] The data shows that Adivasis tend to have less schooling than Dalits[57] and that they are less likely to benefit from reservations.[58] The data also show that Adivasis are hardly represented among private sector regular formal workers, when compared to Dalits (who are themselves also under-represented compared to other groups).[59]

Although some of our material shows these differences between Adivasis and Dalits, other aspects of our work also challenge the perspective that Adivasis are worse off than Dalits. For instance, it is true that the Irulas of Cuddalore are much worse off on every front than the Dalits who live next door. The Dalits of Chamba are also much less isolated and much more integrated, and therefore have benefited from better jobs than the Adivasi Gaddis or Gujjars of Chamba. It is also the case that across all our sites, Adivasis have less schooling than Dalits. However, our work also raises serious questions about the universality of these trends and about how to think about poverty.

Landlessness is less common among Adivasis compared to the rest of the population, while it is more common among Dalits than among other groups. This is the case nationally as well as in most central and eastern states.[60] We suggest that whether Adivasis are worse off than Dalits depends largely on whether Adivasis have historically had access to land in their home areas and therefore this has a strong regional configuration. In the central and eastern Indian belt – as we find in Benbabaali's case of northern Telangana – local Adivasis are often in a better position than local Dalits for they have some access to land and forest resources that Dalits most often do not.[61] This gives the Adivasis some autonomy from dependence on landlords or factories and it may be one explanation why there is less class differentiation among Adivasis as well as, perhaps, more egalitarian gender relations than among Dalits (Shah forthcoming). It should also be noted that Adivasis reproduce themselves under generally more egalitarian conditions, as their homes continue to be in villages which are not as penetrated by the caste hierarchies that Dalits experience daily in the villages of the Indian plains.

The super-exploitation of migrant labour takes place differently for Adivasis and Dalits. Adivasis who have land (for instance in central and eastern India) may be better off in some ways than Dalits from the same region. Nevertheless, their seasonal migration is often driven by the inability to solely live off the lands in their home villages, as it is for the seasonal migrant workers from Jharkhand in the Kerala Peermade tea plantations (see chapter 3). In central and eastern India, land alienation is driven by population growth and the ongoing encroachment on their lands by dams (as in the case of the Narmada dam, see Thakur's chapter), factories (such as the paper factory in Bhadrachalam, see Benbabaali's chapter) and, not least, large-scale coal and mineral mining by major Indian and transnational mining conglomerates. 'Land grabs' may speed up further as the legal protection of Adivasi land is undermined. For instance, the attempts made in 2016 to amend the Chotanagpur Tenancy Acts and Santhal Parganas Acts in Jharkhand, to enable the use of agricultural land for industry, though unsuccessful, are the most recent manifestations of undermining the modicum of land and forest protection that Adivasis have had. The relative autonomy of the Adivasis in these regions from wider Indian capitalist processes is diminishing. Moreover, when the same Adivasi groups go to other parts of India as seasonal migrant labour, they are stigmatised as simple, uncivilised people who can be treated even worse than the local Dalits where they take up work.[62]

As important to consider as the difference in experience of inequality and poverty between Adivasis and Dalits is the intra-household difference between men and women within these groups, the differences in social relations of oppression entrenched in processes of accumulation. Across our sites, women do not get the most remunerative of work and are usually paid less than men for the same work. Across all our sites, women bear the greater burden of the social reproduction of the household in comparison to men, which is what ultimately enables the men from their house to work for their employers. This domestic work of reproducing the household, which enables employers to have workers, is of course never considered as 'work' nor is it ever remunerated.

It is also the case that, in comparison to women of higher caste households, where women are withdrawn into household work, at the bottom of the social and economic hierarchy both men and women do paid work outside the house. The Adivasi Koya women and the Dalit Madiga women in Telangana tend to do paid work in the fields (more than the Kamma women who stay in the household), the Dalit women in the tea plantations work, the Dalit women in Tamil Nadu work in the factories, the Adivasi Bhil women work outside the household alongside their men in brick kilns, in their own fields as well as those of others in the sugar cane and cotton fields. Although there are exceptions (for instance Irula women do not appear to do much paid work), we do not find evidence for the trend reported by some recent economic data that Dalit and Adivasi women are being withdrawn from the workforce.[63]

That Adivasi and Dalit women continue to do paid work outside the household has implications for the rise of patriarchy within households. The fine work spearheaded by Sylvia Federici (2004) and others has argued that pivotal in the spread of capitalism was a war against women and the rise of the 'patriarchy of the wage' (2004: 97–100), which turned women into housewives and violently repressed those who did not conform as witches. In India, scholars have reported that where there is upward mobility among Dalit and Adivasi families, it can indeed come at some intra-household cost, as women are then increasingly taken out of paid outside work and restricted to domestic work in the household, resulting in less equal gender relations (see Kapadia 1995 and Still 2014 for Dalits, and Higham and Shah 2013a for Adivasis).

Although we do see such patterns in our sites in certain households, there is no great move towards upward social mobility in any of our sites and no overall trend with regard to women being withdrawn from the paid workforce. In fact, in some of our sites, such as the Kerala tea plantations, neoliberal cutbacks have meant a feminisation of the workforce, so that it is the women who are left doing the paid work in the tea plantations and thereby keeping their homes secure, ensuring that the Dalit men who may move away to work at least have a house to return to. It is also the women here who have led the struggles against their exploitation, something to which we return in both Raj's chapter and the concluding chapter, 'The Struggles Ahead'.

Though patriarchy may be more muted within Adivasi and Dalit households than it is in those households further up the social hierarchy who remove their women from paid work, working outside the household is also more likely to expose Dalit and Adivasi women to the conjugated oppression of higher caste employers and contractors. And inter-household stigmatisation is likely to be experienced differently for different people. For instance, in Thakur's site women report sexual exploitation in particular when migrating out to work.

Capitalist accumulation is then dependent on the differentiated fragmentation of the labour force, in which caste, tribe, region and gender-based oppression are constitutive of class relations and significantly affect the position of Adivasis and Dalits in India.

MOVING FORWARD?

In the chapters which follow – on Kerala (by Raj), Tamil Nadu (by Donegan), Telangana (by Benbabaali), Himachal Pradesh (by Axelby) and Maharashtra (by Thakur) – this book presents the ethnographic research from which emerge the theoretical analyses we have presented in this chapter. Before we embark on these journeys, the economist K.P. Kannan presents, in the next chapter, the macro-economic data showing the country-wide patterns of the marginalisation of Adivasis and Dalits, the processes of which are explored in the ethnographies of the chapters that follow.

Our book shows the ways in which conjugated oppression – the multiple oppressions based on caste, tribe region and gender which are constitutive of class relations – persists in India and has transformed within the new economy of capital–labour relations through inherited inequalities of power and the super-exploitation of migrant labour, and the fragmenting and cheapening of the labour force. These relations do not always explicitly require the extreme purity–pollution rules of the caste hierarchy that once manifested themselves in India, and which have been diluted in Independent India through a set of interrelated economic, social and political processes. Instead they entail that Dalits and Adivasis, while now formally treated as full and equal citizens with the same freedoms as everyone else, are still stereotyped as dirty, childlike, ignorant, lazy people. They are still discursively constructed as uncivilised and potentially anti-national people. They are still a 'dangerous class' that can legitimately be treated worse than others, and have their rights violated, sometimes in very brutal and violent ways, in which other labourers may also be complicit. Moreover, purity–pollution norms have not disappeared and can always be reactivated as a means of enforcing power relations.[64]

There is ample evidence that, while India is more likely to see an increase in the recording of caste-based violence (through the Prevention of Atrocities Act for example), many Dalits have also experienced the changes in caste relations since Independence as a loosening of oppressive relations. What we show is that this is also a transition to a new form of conjugated oppression which maintains Dalits at the bottom of the social hierarchy. Some Adivasi groups have maintained degrees of autonomy in their social reproduction that are almost unheard of among Dalits, whose reproduction is dependent on other groups. For Adivasis, there are variations in how conjugated oppression works, depending not the least on whether they have maintained their autonomy and access to land and forests. However, even the Adivasis of central and eastern India are being more and more integrated into the capitalist economy as seasonal migrant labour, and when migrating they are experiencing greater conjugated oppression than the Dalits. Experiences of oppression are also likely to be gendered and differentially experienced by men and women from these communities.

In the midst of this bleak situation of India's low castes and tribes, it is of course true that the country has for many years also produced high-profile, well-to-do Dalits and Adivasis, from chief ministers to state officials and activists. There is evidence of some class differentiation within Dalits and Adivasis in our sites. The main process that cuts across conjugated oppression is the combination of education and affirmative action that has enabled some degree of upward mobility for a minority of Dalits and some Adivasis, and this has nurtured some degree of class differentiation within Adivasi and Dalit communities (though notably more for Dalits than Adivasis). In our cases, where reserved jobs have been acquired they have been on the lowest rungs of the state sector (as home guards, policemen and railway clerks for instance). Whether this will translate into generational mobility for these households remains to be seen. In most other cases where some degree of upward mobility appears to have been reached beyond that provided by affirmative action, as in the case of Dalit youth of the Kerala tea plantations, it is to work in semi-skilled jobs which are just as – perhaps even more – precarious than the permanent tea worker jobs their parents had.

The indications from our sites are indeed that for now most Adivasis and Dalits will not succeed in becoming significantly upwardly mobile in comparison to their higher caste counterparts. The only exception is a few Gujjar households of the Saal valley in Chamba who, over a forty-year period, have moved from setting up small roadside shops to becoming contractors and businessmen in their own right, in a league of their own in relation to their Gujjar brethren. The neoliberal cutback and informalisation trends of the last twenty-five years have shrunk the government sector and frozen private sector formal blue-collar jobs and have curtailed the possibilities of existing class mobility routes. The overwhelming majority of Adivasis and Dalits will negotiate the opportunities available to them in the best possible way, within the structural limits set by an absence of sufficient assets and capital, limited levels of education, absence of political connections and the very real constraints placed on them by their class relations and caste and tribe discriminatory practices – in short, by conjugated oppression.

However, as the very last chapter – 'The struggles ahead' – says, what we also hope to have done in this book is to place Dalit and Adivasi life-worlds centre stage; to show the ways in which Dalits and Adivasis try to create and transform ideas and practices of the 'good life' in response to the situations they find themselves in;[65] and how these life-worlds, in turn, may provide possible counteractions to these situations. Whether it is by forming caste associations, converting to religious movements, creating Dalit or Adivasi identity-based social movements or supporting Maoist guerrillas, in many places Dalits and Adivasis are struggling to challenge the structures of inequality that squash them. To return to Stuart Hall, capitalism works through the cultural specifics of labour power; and, in line with E.P. Thompson, it is from the specific life-worlds of different Adivasi and Dalit groups that specific class consciousness and class action against their circumstances takes shape. But, as we show, the precise form, direction or reach of such action is not predestined and cannot be taken for granted.

2

Macro-Economic Aspects of Inequality and Poverty in India

K.P. Kannan

This chapter analyses some of the all-India countrywide macro-economic data that show the position of Adivasis and Dalits vis-à-vis other caste and religion-based groups. Its focus on the patterns revealed by the macro data sets it apart from the chapters which follow which analyse the processes behind these patterns through in-depth ethnographic fieldwork.

This chapter shows that while there is a clear relationship between the work people do and degrees of poverty, there are also interrelated inequalities along the lines of caste, tribe and religion which overwhelm all other forms of inequality in India (such as region and gender). This is not to say that region and gender do not matter; a powerful combination of social (that is, caste/tribe/religion) group status, region and gender could produce either a highly favourable situation or an extremely debilitating one in terms of overcoming basic deprivation. But it is to highlight that caste, tribe and religion are the most salient markers of inequalities in degrees of poverty across the country. While such social dimensions of poverty have received some attention from scholars, most of the literature and analyses drawn on by policymakers have focused on regional and sectoral dimensions of poverty and only occasionally on the most disadvantaged social groups.

A national picture – across Indian states – is presented, mainly in relation to income/expenditure poverty but also incorporating basic indicators of education and malnutrition. The chapter will also examine the evidence on multidimensional poverty reported in the *Human Development Report 2010* (UNDP 2010) and its strong association with India's broadly defined social groups.

THE SOCIAL FACE OF HIGH POVERTY AMIDST HIGH GROWTH: A MACRO PROFILE

Since the 1980s, India's aggregate economic growth has been impressive, not only by historical standards but also contemporary Asian standards. With an average annual growth rate of around 6 per cent for two decades following the mid-1980s, and around 8 per cent in the decade after that, India has emerged as the one of the fastest growing economies in the world today.[1]

As highlighted in the Preface to this book, despite such an impressive growth performance and consequent euphoria among a good section of the elites in the country, there is an intense and ongoing debate about how far such a growth performance has benefited the majority of the ordinary people, known as the *Aam Aadmi* or 'the Common People'. Serious doubts and questions have been raised about the mantra of the market and the process of growth trickling down to the poor.

Several studies have questioned the wisdom of following policies of economic liberalisation and globalisation rooted in a narrow foundation of neoclassical economics that has been actively promoted (and often imposed) by the Bretton Woods institutions (Stiglitz 2002). In the context of countries like India such questioning has been based largely on the need for an inclusive development that should ensure the livelihood security as well as the development of capabilities of the vast majority of the poor in the country (Mehrotra and Delamonica 2007).

However, questions must be raised not just based on the need to ensure livelihoods or employment per se but also concerning the quality of work, whether work is 'formal' or 'informal'. As outlined in the opening chapter, overall, 92 per cent of the workers in India are informal workers (for a detailed analysis, see NCEUS 2007), a number that has remained stable for the last two decades. This is not only due to the dominance of small-farmer-led agriculture, where almost all workers can be classified as informal, but also because in the non-farm economy informal workers constitute about 75 per cent.

Does informal work, though, correlate to the incidence of poverty?[2] The National Commission for Enterprises in the Unorganised Sector, of which I was a member, was constituted in 2004 by the Government of India to examine the problems faced by the unorganised sector and unorganised workers – as the informal sector and informal workers are known in India. The defining features of the poverty line in India, as noted in the preceding chapter, have been subject to huge controversy.[3] The National Commission for Enterprises in the Unorganised Sector thus produced estimates of poverty in India based on different threshold levels, taking the then official poverty line as a benchmark. If the official poverty line was to be increased by 25 per cent, it would correspond to the international definition of 'extreme poverty' of PPP$1.25 (purchasing power parity) per capita per day, and if it was doubled it would correspond to the international definition of poverty of PPP$2 per capita per day. The National Commission for Enterprises in the Unorganised Sector called the former

'Poor and Marginally Poor' and the latter 'Poor and Vulnerable' – terms that we shall also use in this chapter.

The National Commission for Enterprises in the Unorganised Sector estimates, based on consumer expenditure data as well as the employment data from the National Sample Surveys, found that the group Poor and Vulnerable in India was closely associated with informal work status. It was found that in 2004–05 a little more than 76 per cent of the Indian population spent, on average, less than PPP$2 a day per person. It was also found that a similar percentage, 79 per cent, of informal workers were Poor and Vulnerable. In this sense, there was a close linkage between work status and poverty status.

Detailed subsequent work (see NCEUS 2007 and Sengupta et al. 2008) revealed that there is a clear and unambiguous 'social face' to the incidence of poverty and vulnerability in India and informal work status. It was found that the application of a single poverty line concealed more than it revealed about the state of poverty of different segments of the population. What was striking was that the population belonged to different poverty bands or poverty groups that represented a social hierarchy of poor.

Six categories of poverty and higher income were identified. The first, called 'Extremely Poor', consisted of those whose consumption expenditure did not exceed 0.75 of the official poverty line. The second, 'Poor', denoted those between the 'Extremely Poor' and official poverty line expenditure. The third, 'Marginally Poor', referred to those who did not have expenditure of more than 1.25 times that of the second category. The fourth group was the 'Vulnerable' and referred to those whose expenditure varied between 1.25 and 2 times that of the 'Poor'. The fifth group was called 'Middle Income' and its expenditure varied between 2 and 4 times that of the 'Poor'. The sixth and last category was referred to as 'High Income', whose expenditure exceeded by 4 times that of the 'Poor' group.

This may be summarised in terms of three groups viz. (a) the Poor and Marginally Poor, comparable to the international definition of 'extremely poor' with not more than PPP$1.25 per capita per day; (b) the Poor and Vulnerable comparable to the international poverty line of PPP$2 per capita per day and (c) those who are not poor and classified as Middle and High Income.

Table 2.1 presents the incidence of poverty in terms of these three groups and how it relates to social and religious groups: Adivasis/Dalits, Muslims, Other Backward Classes (OBCs) and Others.[4] The important point that emerges is the hierarchical association of the categories of the poor with the broad social groups of the Indian population, Adivasis and Dalits in particular, but also Muslims.

Table 2.1   Percentage distribution of population by poverty status and social groups, 2004–05 and 2009–10

		Population			
	Total	Adivasi/ Dalit	Muslim	OBC	Others
Poverty status 2004–05					
1. Poor and Marginally Poor	40.8	54.8	49.7	40.6	19.6
2. Poor and Vulnerable (incl. 1)	76.7	87.8	84.5	79.9	54.8
3. Middle and High Income	23.3	12.2	15.5	20.2	45.2
4. All	100.0	100.0	100.0	100.0	100.0
Poverty status 2009–10					
1. Poor and Marginally Poor	32.1	45.2	39.6	30.8	13.8
2. Poor and Vulnerable (incl. 1)	69.0	81.9	78.9	70.8	44.5
3. Middle and High Income	31.0	18.1	20.1	29.2	55.5
4. All	100.0	100.0	100.0	100.0	100.0

Source: NCEUS (2007) for 2004–05; Computed from unit level data from National Sample Survey 61st Round for 2009–10.

Thus, in every poverty group, the highest incidence of poverty is among the Dalit/Adivasi groups, followed by Muslims, OBCs and then the 'Others'.[5] The social face of poverty comes out most sharply when we focus only on the Poor and Marginally Poor and the Poor and Vulnerable (see Figure 2.1). It is clear that the burden of poverty is concentrated among the socially disadvantaged groups –Dalits/Adivasis and Muslims – to a very significant degree.

HOW EFFECTIVE IS THE 'TRICKLE-DOWN' PROCESS?

As the Preface to this book has outlined, neoliberal economic policies claim that aggregate economic growth, when pursued as an objective in itself, will trickle down to the poor and thereby help them come out of the poverty trap and provide more opportunities for them to share the fruits of further economic growth. While such a simple and simplistic notion has been challenged many a time, and while the history of economic growth provides valuable lessons of concerted action often designed and/or led by the state, it nevertheless remains a core principle and is usually used to justify policies to strengthen the working of the market mechanism. But to what extent has the 'trickle-down' process worked in the Indian context of a historically unprecedented acceleration in aggregate economic growth? Most significantly, how effective is any such trickle-down process for the groups which are acknowledged by official policy to be socially disadvantaged?

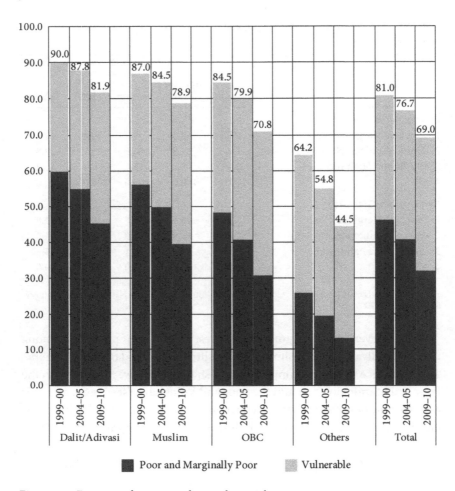

Figure 2.1   Poverty and poverty reduction by social group

To answer these two questions, we have worked out the percentage reduction in poverty in the two broad poverty groups with respect to aggregate economic growth in India for the last ten years, in Table 2.2. The results are revealing. During the first period 1999–2000 to 2004–05 the Indian economy achieved a growth rate of 5.7 per cent per annum while the incidence of Poor and Marginally Poor declined by just a little over one percentage point per year (or 5.1 percentage points in five years). When we examine the incidence of Poor and Vulnerable, the incidence declined by just 0.8 per cent per year (or four percentage points in five years).

Most important is the issue of the decline in poverty levels among the different broad social groups. During the first five years, the rate of reduction was lowest among the bottom social groups of Dalits/Adivasis and Muslims.

Table 2.2   A 'trickle-down' process? The pace of poverty reduction in relation to economic growth 1999–2000 to 2009–10

Period	Percentage point decline per annum in Poor and Marginally Poor					Growth*
	Adivasis and Dalits	Muslims	OBCs	Others	Total	
1999–2000 to 2004–05	0.98	1.00	1.50	1.26	1.02	5.74
2004–05 to 2009–10	1.92	2.02	1.96	1.26	1.74	8.16
	Percentage point decline per annum in Poor and Vulnerable					
1990–2000 to 2004–05	0.44	0.50	0.92	1.88	0.80	5.74
2004–05 to 2009–10	1.18	1.1	1.82	2.06	1.54	8.16

Note: * Aggregate economic growth rate per annum.

During the second five-year period, the rate of decline among these groups exceeded that of the top two social groups, but this small catch-up still leaves a large gap between the bottom groups and the rest, especially for those belonging to the Dalit/Adivasi groups. This differential rate of decline should therefore be viewed in relation to the backlog of poverty for these groups. It should also be viewed in relation to the population increase. When looking at absolute numbers, for these bottom groups the movement is largely from being more poor to less poor: the total number of 'Poor and Vulnerable' for these groups had increased in 2010. The largest increase is for the Adivasi/Dalit groups – 14 million (from 265 to 279 million) – whereas for Muslims the number increased by just 2 million (from 116.7 to 118.5 million). For the two groups of OBCs and Others at the upper end there has been a net decline of 1.6 million and 20.4 million respectively. The biggest gain has been to the socially advantaged group of 'Others'.

Table 2.2 also shows the overall poverty reduction for the four broad social groups, sharply bringing into focus that the burden is concentrated among the socially disadvantaged groups. Clearly, if there is a trickle down, it is not very effective; and especially not effective for Adivasis/Dalits and Muslims.

We must also ask whether the modest reductions in the proportions of poor and vulnerable are due to the growth process. The higher growth during 2004–05 to 2009–10 may have had some impact on the rate of decline, but it is also important to remember the number of poverty reduction schemes and programmes that are in place, as mentioned in the opening chapter.[6] Not least, the greater pace of poverty reduction in the second period has to factor in the impact of the National Rural Employment Guarantee. An evaluation of the Employment Guarantee for the first five years revealed that the additional wage earning of participating households was equivalent to 10 per cent of the consumption expenditure required to cross the official poverty line.[7] Measuring the impact of all these state-sponsored interventions on poverty would be a complex exercise but it can safely be said that they did make an impact on the poverty levels and that a trickle-down effect cannot lay claim to all of the (socially skewed) poverty reduction that actually occurred.

Poverty, though, should not be considered without its twin, inequality. As the Preface and opening chapter to this book argue, today, understanding inequality forms an integral part of understanding poverty. People also judge their position in relation to what others have or do not have, even in a situation of normatively anchored absolute poverty. Studies carried out on the different dimensions as well as the pace of economic inequality in India clearly show an increasing trend of inequality, especially since the early 1990s when the Government of India started its neoliberal economic reforms. Since government policy has a direct bearing on the distributional dimension of economic benefits, let us look at the official poverty line in relation to the economic growth performance of the economy. The official poverty line adopted by the government in India was based on a consumption basket that was adopted in 1973–74 (although its lineage goes back to the early 1960s). We therefore compare the poverty line per person per month expressed in Indian Rupees (Rs.) as a percentage of the per capita income per month, based on the estimation of gross domestic product (GDP). In 1973–74, the official poverty line was close to 58 per cent of the per capita income (Rs.51.10 as against a per capita monthly GDP income of Rs.88.14). This share has declined consistently and it stood at close to 12 per cent in 2009–10 (Rs.526 as against a per capita income of Rs.4402). Had the poverty line not been revised upwards in 2010, the share would have remained at around 10 per cent. As per the new official poverty line that is only equivalent to 12 per cent of the per capita GDP, while the incidence of poverty in India in 2004–05 was as high as 37 per cent! No further comment is required to show at what speed the economic growth in India has trickled down to the poor. It is in this context that our estimation of poverty at different threshold levels becomes important.

THE MULTIDIMENSIONALITY OF POVERTY

The measure of poverty and vulnerability that we have discussed so far relates to consumption expenditure (inability to spend the normatively specified level of money). This is a common way of measuring poverty in India. However, it is increasingly recognised that other dimensions of poverty that show basic deprivations are equally important. A first attempt to measure such dimensions has been to develop a combined index of multidimensional poverty. This multidimensional measure consists of (a) *standard of living* composed of access to/ownership of electricity, drinking water, sanitation, quality of housing, cooking fuel and certain assets, (b) *education* measured in terms of (i) average years of schooling and (ii) child school enrolment and (c) a measure of *health outcome* in terms of (i) child mortality and (ii) nutrition (for details, see Alkire and Santos 2010). The relevant data are available for a period quite close to our period of analysis (2000–08).

A detailed exercise for Indian states as well as social groups within the Hindu community (representing 83 per cent of the Indian population) has been carried out and published as part of the background papers for the *Human Development Report 2010* (UNDP 2010). The Multidimensional Poverty Index values for groups/states have been calculated along with the proportion of population who are considered multidimensionally poor by this definition. These are presented in Table 2.3. It first presents the situation of Hindu social groups by comparing them with other developing countries as well as Indian states. This is followed by the status of Indian states comparing them with other developing countries sharing a similar status.

The Multidimensional Poverty Index findings (based on data for 2005) have a remarkable resemblance to the hierarchical social order that we found in the case of income/consumption poverty. The proportion of poor (55 per cent for all India) in terms of the Multidimensional Poverty Index falls between the proportion of Poor and Marginally Poor (32 per cent) and Poor and Vulnerable (69 per cent) for 2009–10 as shown in Table 2.2 earlier.

The most multidimensionally deprived are Adivasis with 81 per cent of Adivasis being deprived. The situation of the Adivasis is closer to that of Rwanda, a country that ranked as the 13th most multidimensionally deprived out of the 104 developing countries included in the study. Within India, the situation of Adivasis resembles the average situation in the State of Bihar which ranked lowest, that is, as the poorest, of the Indian states. Dalits have the next highest incidence of multidimensional poverty of 66 per cent. Their situation is closer to the average situation in Nepal that ranked as the 23rd most deprived country or the average situation of the Indian State of Rajasthan. The situation of upper caste Hindus is the best among the four social groups within the Hindu population, but their situation resembles the average of Honduras that ranked 58th out of the 104 developing countries, and within India their average situation is closest to that of the State of Tamil Nadu.

Although strict comparison of the Multidimensional Poverty Index of one country or province with another is not advised due to differing periods of data, we may note that it is not too off the mark to bring in an international comparative perspective to convey a sense of relative position in a wider perspective. It could also help the country in question to reflect on its own relative position and the regional dimension that plays a big role in determining its national position.

Table 2.3   Multidimensional poverty among India's social groups and states in a comparative perspective

Category	Multidimensional poverty		Country	Multidimensional poverty	
	Index value	% of poor		Index value	% of poor
Comparing Indian social groups* with other countries/Indian states					
Hindu upper castes	0.157	33.30	Honduras	0.160	32.60
Dalits	0.361	65.80	Nepal	0.350	64.70
Adivasis	0.482	81.40	Rwanda	0.443	81.40
Comparing Indian states with other countries					
Delhi	0.062	14.20	China	0.056	12.50
Kerala	0.065	15.90	Philippines	0.067	12.60
Goa	0.094	21.70	Indonesia	0.095	20.80
Punjab	0.120	26.20	Guatemala	0.127	25.90
Himachal Pradesh	0.131	31.00	Morocco	0.139	28.50
Tamil Nadu	0.141	32.40	Djibouti	0.139	29.30
Uttaranchal	0.189	40.30	Namibia	0.187	39.60
Maharashtra	0.193	40.10	Swaziland	0.183	41.10
Haryana	0.199	41.60			
Gujarat	0.205	41.50	Nicaragua	0.211	40.70
Jammu and Kashmir	0.209	43.80			
Andhra Pradesh	0.211	44.70	Lesotho	0.220	48.10
Karnataka	0.223	46.10			
India	**0.296**	**55.40**	Cameroon	0.299	54.60
NE states	0.303	57.60	Bangladesh	0.291	57.80
West Bengal	0.317	58.30	Côte d'Ivoire	0.320	52.20
Odisha	0.345	64.00	Zambia	0.325	63.70
Rajasthan	0.351	64.20	Nepal	0.350	64.70
Uttar Pradesh	0.386	69.90	Senegal	0.384	66.90
Chhattisgarh	0.387	71.90	Malawi	0.384	72.30
Madhya Pradesh	0.389	69.50			
Jharkhand	0.463	77.00	Angola	0.452	77.40
Bihar	0.499	81.40	Rwanda	0.443	81.40

Note: *Accounting for 83 per cent of the Indian population.

Viewed from this perspective, there are only two Indian states that are close to the average of China; they are Delhi and Kerala. In fact, both are somewhat below China (ranked at 44th) and closer to the Philippines (ranked at 48th). But most Indian states do not match the record of the countries in Asia, especially those in Southeast Asia (except Laos and Cambodia). Their rankings are closer to the poor countries in Africa.

EDUCATION AS A LEVELLER, BUT INITIAL CONDITIONS MATTER

As outlined above, education (and absence of education) is one dimension of multidimensional poverty. In a long-term perspective, education is widely perceived to be a leveller in terms of overcoming situations of poverty and vulnerability. However, in the Indian context at least, its effectiveness varies across social groups. Table 2.4 presents the poverty status of social groups according to their educational attainments, and shows a clear relationship between the degrees of poverty and degrees of education. This is perhaps not surprising. What this table further reveals is that, for the socially disadvantaged groups, the level of education related to crossing the threshold of poverty and vulnerability is much higher than for those in a socially advantaged position.

Table 2.4 Percentage distribution of population in specific educational categories by poverty status and social group, 2004–05

Social category	Poverty status	Illiterate	Up to primary	Middle	Secondary and above but below graduate	Graduate and above	Total
Adivasis /Dalits	Poor and Vulnerable	91.2	89.7	80.7	65.4	47.8	85.0
	Middle and HIG	8.8	10.3	19.3	34.7	52.2	15.0
	All SC/ST	100.0	100.0	100.0	100.0	100.0	100.0
Others	Poor and Vulnerable	70.6	66.9	57.7	39.5	21.6	50.9
	Middle and HIG	29.4	33.1	42.3	60.5	78.4	49.1
	All Others	100.0	100.0	100.0	100.0	100.0	100.0
All	Poor and Vulnerable	86.1	83.3	71.2	52.4	29.7	72.6
	Middle and HIG	13.9	16.7	28.8	47.6	70.3	27.4
	All Population	100.0	100.0	100.0	100.0	100.0	100.0

Note: HIG: High Income Group; SC: Scheduled Caste; ST: Scheduled Tribe.

For example, nearly half of all Dalit/Adivasi graduates are Poor and Vulnerable but less than a quarter of the upper caste Hindu, Christian and Sikh graduates belong to this, the poorest group (48 per cent against 22 per cent). Likewise, a much smaller proportion of upper caste Hindus, Christians and Sikhs with only primary education are Poor and Vulnerable, compared to those Adivasis/Dalits who also only have primary education (67 per cent against 90 per cent). It is not only the Adivasis/Dalits for whom a higher proportion of better educated people are Poor and Vulnerable; Muslims and OBCs are also in a similar position. The Adivasis/Dalits, are, however, in the worst position when considering whether education translates to a better place on the poverty scales, followed by the two other groups in tapered order.[8]

It is clear, then, that social disadvantage strongly influences the degree to which higher levels of education and the reduction of poverty go together. Moreover, social disadvantage is also likely to be a summation of adverse initial conditions, especially for those at the bottom such as the Dalit/Adivasi groups. To summarise, education matters but when it comes to the most socially disadvantaged groups, underlying social and economic conditions seem to matter more.

REGIONAL DIMENSION OF SOCIAL INEQUALITY

In this section, we explore the regional-cum-social dimension of poverty and vulnerability. Differences in degrees of inequality between the Indian states matter. However, what the analysis below shows is that differences of inequality between different social groups are so overwhelming across the country that it relegates regional and even gender inequality to a secondary position. I report the findings of my earlier study on regional dimensions of poverty, and then examine the social dimensions of poverty within the regions, that is, the Indian states. Since social group-wise incidence of the Multidimensional Poverty Index at state level is not available, we shall proceed on the basis of consumption poverty data (see Table 2.5). Here we have classified the states by levels of performance by taking the difference in percentage points between the best performing state and the worst performing state and dividing it by three. States that score within the top third constitute the top level. States with scores within the next one-third makes up the middle level. The rest are included in the low level.

Several important points emerge. First, just as at the national level, in a majority of states the hierarchy Dalits/Adivasis – Muslims – OBCs – Others is reflected in the incidence of poverty and vulnerability. This exact hierarchy is reproduced in 12 out of 21 major states,[9] accounting for 75 per cent of India's population. Only in seven states are the Dalits/Adivasis only second worst off and in all these states it is Muslims who are at the bottom. In two other states OBCs and Muslims have swapped places. As shown in more detail below, this means that if one happens to be a Muslim or a Dalit/Adivasi there is an overwhelming chance that one will be in the bottom level, irrespective of one's regional location.

Table 2.5　State-wise incidence of poverty and vulnerability by social group

Total population	Dalit/Adivasi	Muslims	OBCs	Others
Top level				
PJ [47.5]			PJ [50.7]	TN [23.3]
HR [60.1]			JK [54.9]	PJ [26.5]
KE [61.0]			HP [58.0]	GJ [37.8]
			KE [60.9]	AP [39.4]
				HR [40.5]
				KE [45.6]
				JK [51.8]
				HP [55.3]
				JH [57.3]
				KR [59.0]
				WB [59.7]
				CH [60.4]
				MH [62.2]
Middle level				
HP [62.7]	JK [67.4]	PJ [64.3]	HR [64.9]	UP [63.0]
AP [64.5]	NEA [68.9]	KE [68.8]	AP [68.4]	NEA [63.5]
GJ [67.4]	PJ [71.1]	CH [72.3]	TN [72.3]	MP [63.7]
NEA [71.7]	HP [75.4]	TN [74.5]	WB [75.1]	RJ [63.8]
JK [72.7]	AP [76.7]	AP [74.6]	KR [75.4]	AS [63.9]
TN [72.7]			AS [76.7]	BH [76.6]
KR [74.9]			GJ [76.7]	
MH 75.5]				
WB [76.6]				
Low level				
AS [80.3]	KE [78.8]	HP [78.1]	RJ [78.3]	OR [78.2]
RJ [81.0]	TN [84.5]	GJ [80.2]	MH [78.6]	UK [81.1]
UP [84.3]	GJ84.7]	JK [81.9]	NEA [82.4]	
CH [85.9]	AS [86.1]	OR [83.7]	UP [86.3]	
MP [86.0]	WB [86.4]	MH [84.2]	MP [86.8]	
UK [86.9]	MH [87.3]	KR [84.7]	CH [87.4]	
JH [87.5]	HR [87.4]	RJ [85.6]	OR [88.6]	
OR [89.7]	KR [87.7]	UP [87.9]	JH [89.2]	
BH [92.5]	CH [90.8]	AS [88.7]	UK [89.4]	
	RJ [92.3]	NEA [88.8]	BH [93.0]	
	UP [93.1]	WB [89.2]		
	JH [93.8]	HR [89.9]		
	UK [95.2]	MP [90.9]		
	MP [96.1]	UK [93.8]		
	OR [96.4]	JH [94.4]		
	BH [97.3]	BH [95.5]		
India [76.7]	[87.8]	[84.5]	[79.9]	[54.8]

Notes:
1. Figures in square brackets indicate the proportion of Poor and Vulnerable.
2. AP stands for Andhra Pradesh and Telangana, AS Assam, BH Bihar, CH Chhattisgarh, GJ Gujarat, HP Himachal Pradesh, HR Haryana, JK Jammu & Kashmir, JH Jharkhand, KE Kerala, KR Karnataka, MH Maharashtra, MP Madhya Pradesh, NEA north-eastern states except Assam (Arunachal Pradesh, Manipur, Meghalaya, Mizoram, Nagaland, Sikkim and Tripura), OR Odisha, PJ Punjab, RJ Rajasthan, TN Tamil Nadu, UK Uttarakhand, UP Uttar Pradesh, WB West Bengal.

Second, the poverty hierarchy from Dalits/Adivasis to other castes is even more pronounced than these figures seem to indicate, as in most of the exceptions from it the difference in poverty levels for Muslims and Dalits/Adivasis are either insignificant and/or relate to states where the Muslim population only constitute between 1.5 and 4 per cent of the population. The change in the Muslim–Dalit/Adivasi poverty order is only of some significance in the group of north-eastern states and the four states of Jammu and Kashmir, West Bengal, Assam and Jharkhand.[10]

The most interesting case where the standard hierarchy is not in place is in the seven north-eastern states of Arunachal Pradesh, Manipur, Meghalaya, Mizoram, Nagaland, Sikkim and Tripura, which are taken as a group since individual state-level data are not available. Taken together, these states have an Adivasi population share of nearly 70 per cent and that could explain the relatively high rank of Adivasis (second position) among the four broad social groups. In states such as Arunachal Pradesh, Manipur, Meghalaya and Mizoram they might even be in top position given their social and political dominance there. Importantly, in these north-eastern states the Adivasi population referred to here has historically enjoyed a certain degree of economic and political autonomy, which has also resulted in relatively higher achievements in school education, health, women's autonomy, wages and so on.

The findings in Table 2.5 convey prima facie that what are often seen as 'regional' factors have less to do with overall state-level poverty than 'social' factors. For example, when one looks at the top performers in terms of all the population in a state, there are only three – Punjab, Haryana and Kerala. But when one looks at the social category of 'Others' (upper caste Hindus, Jains, Christians and Sikhs) there are 13 states at the top level followed by six in the middle level and only two at the low level. The situation changes dramatically for the bottom two groups of Muslims and Dalit/Adivasi populations. There are none at the top level, five in the middle and the remaining 16 states are in the low level. What this conveys is that if one happens to be in the upper category of 'Others' there is a great probability of being less Poor and Vulnerable irrespective of one's regional location. Contrariwise, if one happens to be a Muslim or a Dalit/Adivasi there is an overwhelming chance that one will be in the bottom level irrespective of one's regional location. The OBCs – socially perceived as an intermediate category – are in the intermediate position with regard to poverty and vulnerability, even from a regional point of view.

Several questions and issues can be raised on the basis of this macro-level picture of regional-cum-social dimensions of poverty and vulnerability in India. Even for a state like Kerala, known for its social equity in human and social development, the top-level position is a result of the better performance of the upper social category along with OBCs and to some extent Muslims. The bottom-level position of Dalits/Adivasis, even in Kerala, points to the implicit/subtle social exclusion and discrimination outlined in the next chapter of this book. From this macro picture, the performance of Punjab is relatively good since it does not show any social category at the bottom level. However, as we have seen earlier, a more comprehensive measure of poverty (say, the Multidimensional Poverty Index), points to a different situation. Here Kerala has out-performed all other states in India except Delhi, the national capital region. The proportion of multidimensionally poor in Kerala at 15.9 per cent is followed by Punjab with 26.2 per cent. Moreover, the performance of West Bengal raises a whole set of politically uncomfortable questions. With a supposedly 'pro-poor' government for a continuous period spanning a whole generation (34 years to be exact), its record in reducing poverty and vulnerability is disappointing to say the least. Its performance in reducing the multidimensionality of poverty is equally disappointing.

The picture of a regional-cum-social dimension of poverty and vulnerability in India is clear. The findings of this section point to the dominance of inequality based on social groups over regional inequality in the incidence of poverty. They do not, however, in any way underplay the crucial role of regional development. When there is a generalised situation of chronic underdevelopment, especially in situations of inadequate or mal-governance, the outcome could be detrimental to all sections. The findings for Odisha and Bihar are a stark example here, as all the social groups in these states are at the bottom level. In fact, 70 per cent of the total multidimensionally poor in India (as of 2007) is concentrated in the eight states of West Bengal, Odisha, Rajasthan, Uttar Pradesh, Chhattisgarh, Madhya Pradesh, Jharkhand and Bihar. In absolute terms, the three states of Uttar Pradesh (135 million), Bihar (77.3 million) and West Bengal (52.2 million) account for an overwhelming share (around 60 per cent) of the multidimensionally poor in these eight high-poverty states in India (OPHDI 2010).

THE OVERWHELMING NATURE OF SOCIAL INEQUALITY

In an earlier paper I have argued, on the basis of empirical evidence, that social inequality seems to be overwhelming both regional and gender inequalities (included in Kannan 2014: chapter 5). What this means is that some social groups identified as the most disadvantaged (Adivasis/Dalits in relation to this book) experience a high incidence of poverty in which regional factors play only a secondary role, while others (categorised in many of the tables in this chapter as Others) seem to experience less poverty and where they live has only a marginal impact on their well-being. When we extend this argument to see the situation of women, the emerging picture is the same as above: that the hierarchy from Dalits/Adivasis to Others is also of most importance for differences in gender inequalities.

For purposes of illustration, let me take the state of long-term malnutrition represented by chronic energy deficiency among women in the four broad social groups across states in India. Chronic energy deficiency is a powerful indicator of the state of absolute material poverty that conveys a basic sense of gender-sensitive human well-being in any society. The findings are given in Table 2.6. The first thing to note is that women from nine states in the socially advantaged group – Others – are all in the top level experiencing an incidence of chronic energy deficiency ranging from 8.3 per cent in Tamil Nadu to 26.8 per cent in Uttarakhand, followed by those in nine states in the middle level ranging from 27.7 per cent in Madhya Pradesh to 34.5 per cent in Maharashtra. No one from the 'Other' social category belongs to the low level.

At the opposite end of the spectrum, women belonging to the Dalit/Adivasi group in just two states viz. Kerala (24.1 per cent) and Punjab (26.7 per cent) belong to the top level. In another two states – Assam (34.5 per cent) and Tamil Nadu (36.1 per cent) – women's chronic energy deficiency belongs to the middle level. Dalit/Adivasi women from the remaining 14 states were at the low level with an incidence of chronic energy deficiency ranging from 36.4 per cent in Haryana to 58.4 per cent in Bihar. The other two groups come in between this range but those in half the states were in the low level.

It is also significant to note that there are only two states with high levels of achievement in relation to chronic energy deficiency as well as low inequality across social groups. One is Kerala, where the difference between the best performer in Kerala (Muslim women) and the worst performer (Dalit/Adivasi women) is only 8.5 percentage points. The other is Punjab, where the difference between the best performer (Others, comprising predominantly upper caste Hindus and Sikhs) and the worst performer (Dalit/Adivasi women) is 12.3 percentage points. Only in these two states are all the social groups at the top level.

While gender and region matter, this incidence of malnutrition among Adivasi and Dalit women across the country is also a powerful indicator of the significance of inequality between social groups. These inequalities follow the same lines as the social hierarchy for income/expenditure poverty explored earlier, with Dalits/Adivasis firmly at the bottom. It is thus clear that even when we think about poverty in a truly multidimensional context, one of the most significant factors (across the different dimensions) is the inequality between social groups across the length and breadth of India.

Table 2.6 Social-cum-regional-cum-gender inequality in long-term poverty: incidence of malnutrition (chronic energy deficiency) among women, 2005–06

Total	Dalit/Adivasi	Muslim	OBC	Others
Top-level states				
Kerala (18.0)	Kerala (24.1)	Kerala (15.6)	Punjab (18.0)	TN (8.3)
Punjab (18.9)	Punjab (26.7)	Tamil Nadu (20.7)	Kerala (18.6)	Punjab (14.4)
		Punjab (22.5)	Tamil Nadu (26.8)	Kerala (18.0)
		Maharashtra (23.8)		AP (22.2)
		Karnataka (26.9)		Gujarat (22.9)
				Chhattisgarh 26.2)
				Jharkhand (26.5)
				Haryana (26.6)
				Uttarakhand (26.8)
Middle-level states				
TN (28.4)	Assam (34.5)	AP (27.6)	Uttarakhand (27.2)	MP (27.7)
Uttarakhand	Tamil Nadu (36.1)	Chhattisgarh (28.9)	Assam (30.4)	UP (28.3)
(30.0) Haryana		Uttarakhand (29.6)	Haryana (33.1)	Orissa (30.7)
(31.3)		Rajasthan (36.1)	Rajasthan (33.3)	Assam (31.4)
AP (33.5)			Karnataka (34.9)	Bihar (31.4)
Karnataka (35.5)			UP (35.4)	WB (31.5)
UP (36.4)			Maharashtra (36.1)	Karnataka (31.7)
				Rajasthan (32.3)
				Maharashtra (34.5)
Lower-level states				
Maharashtra	Haryana (36.4)	UP (36.4)	AP (37.0)	
(36.2)	AP (38.4)	Gujarat (37.0)	WB (39.2)	
Gujarat (36.3)	Uttarakhand (39.3)	MP (37.4)	Orissa (39.6)	
Assam (36.5)	Karnataka (41.8)	WB (42.7)	Gujarat (40.5)	
Rajasthan (36.7)	UP (43.6)	Assam (46.0)	MP (42.2)	
WB (39.1)	Maharashtra (43.6)	Jharkhand (47.3)	Bihar (43.3)	
Orissa (41.4)	Rajasthan (44.1)	Haryana (49.0)	Chhattisgarh (44.8)	
MP (41.7)	Jharkhand (44.6)	Bihar (49.6)	Jharkhand (45.3)	
Jharkhand (43.0)	WB (45.2)	Orissa (63.5)		
Chhattisgarh	Chhattisgarh (46.6)			
(43.4)	Gujarat (48.0)			
Bihar (45.1)	MP (48.7)			
	Orissa (50.6)			
	Bihar (58.4)			
India (35.6)	**India (42.7)**	**India (36.0)**	**India (35.1)**	**India (27.5)**

Notes:

1. Body Mass Index below 18.5 is usually referred to as chronic energy deficiency. Since undernutrition, especially chronic energy deficiency, is both a manifestation and outcome of poverty, such deficiency can be considered an indicator of long-term malnutrition. To avoid temporary fluctuations in body weight, women who were pregnant at the time of the survey and those who had given birth within two months preceding the survey are excluded from calculating the index. Source: Computed from National Family Health Survey-3 data. Data for Himachal Pradesh was not available.

2. For acronyms of states, see note 2 of Table 2.5.

SUMMARY

In the increasingly unequal, rapidly growing India, it is not only what you do but also who you are that matters. Practically everywhere the highest incidence of poverty is among the Dalit/Adivasi group, followed by Muslims, OBCs and then the 'Others'. As this chapter has shown, while gender and region matter too, social group inequality overwhelms both regional and gender inequalities. The data presented here, as well as the ground-level reality, point to the entrenched social inequality and the pervasive nature of poverty among the Dalits and Adivasis. With the Adivasis of India finding themselves on a par with Rwanda and the Dalits at the level of Nepal when it comes to multidimensional poverty, India is still far from shining.

The Indian Constitution gives special treatment to those at the bottom of the social hierarchy and official policy at the national level and in a number of states has further identified other socially disadvantaged groups. But it is telling that, as shown here, even the effect of education on poverty levels is unequal, to the detriment of those at the bottom of the hierarchy. This is in spite of the flagship government affirmative action policies that should lead to the opposite outcome.

This social character of the high incidence of poverty in India points to the as yet 'unresolved social question', as Jan Breman put it (2010a). The rest of the book focuses on the social processes that shape the social character of poverty across five field sites in Kerala, Tamil Nadu, Telangana, Maharashtra and Himachal Pradesh. In relation to the macro data of this chapter, we should note that all five states are in the more affluent half of the Indian states: their Net State Domestic Product per capita are all in the top half of states. Despite being in the more affluent half of the Indian states, across these five states the data show that poverty is significantly more widespread among Dalits/Adivasis than among upper caste Hindus, Christians and Sikhs. The social processes behind these inequalities, as revealed by long-term ethnographic research in each field site, are the focus of the following chapters.

3

Tea Belts of the Western Ghats, Kerala

Jayaseelan Raj

In this chapter, I explore the processes that lead to the continual margin-alisation and exploitation of Dalit and Adivasi labour in and out of the tea plantations of Kerala, a state that is conventionally celebrated for its development model and for having improved the material conditions of its people. I show the ways in which neoliberal restructuring of the Indian tea industry has led to new vulnerabilities, new forms of exploitation, and new sites of oppression for Dalit and Adivasi labour.

Dalit labour from what is now Tamil Nadu, the state which is the focus of the next chapter, was brought to Kerala in the 1860s under the colonial system of indentured labour to the newly developed coffee and tea plantations. Since then these Dalit families have formed the major labour force in the tea plantations, doing the back-breaking work of plucking and processing tea. Debt bondage declined over the years and though the labourers remained lowly paid and exploited many were, over time, able to gain a modicum of protection from social security measures afforded to permanent or temporary workers by the 1951 Plantations Labour Act. In this chapter, I show how these minor, hard-won gains unravelled with the crisis in the tea economy which has hit the country since the 1990s. Many tea plantations closed, cut down production and were taken over by new companies which transformed the labour regimes to super-exploit an illegal casualised precarious labour force of Tamil Dalit women workers and new seasonal casual migrants from poorer parts of India, mainly Adivasis from Jharkhand and Muslims from the north-east of India.

Under this restructuring the plantation labour force, who previously had some security as permanent workers, was now made temporary or casual. As Dalit households began to diversify their livelihoods, it was mainly the women who were left to work in the tea fields (historically the majority of tea pluckers were women and the men worked in the tea-processing units, most of which were shut down). Moreover, the new companies started to bring in more vulnerable seasonal migrant workers – mainly Adivasis from

Jharkhand – to reduce the power of the Dalit workers. The migrants from Jharkhand were a mobile labour force who did not speak the local languages and who were not given permanent or even temporary contracts and thus formed a super-exploitable casualised labour force. In comparatively exploring the Jharkhand Adivasi labour vis-à-vis the Tamil Dalit labour on the tea plantations in Kerala, I show how caste, ethnicity and region are used in the contemporary Indian economy to divide labourers and make them more vulnerable and exploitable.

After five generations of living on the tea plantations, in the aftermath of the tea industry crisis, Dalit labourers were forced to seek work in the informal economy outside the plantations. Although some Dalits had moved out of the plantations in previous generations too, it is only since the crisis that members of most Dalit families had to seek work outside. They went to work in the construction sector in lowland urbanised areas of Kerala, in the garment sector in Coimbatore and Tiruppur in Tamil Nadu, and some even went back to their ancestral villages in Tamil Nadu. While some of these jobs came with higher wages than those in the tea plantations, they also came with the new insecurities that accompany casualised labour. Moreover, outside the tea plantations where they had been relatively isolated from other communities, many Dalits faced overt caste discrimination for the first time. Hence, I argue for the need to differentiate social and economic mobility as, for these Dalits, economic mobility within the labouring classes is not accompanied by social mobility.

I show how these new patterns of mobility were highly gendered as Dalit women tried to stay behind and keep their houses and jobs on the tea plantations, as low paid as they were, while the men moved to work outside. Despite these new forms of precarity, Dalit labourers have not been lying low. In the final part of this chapter I show how these new precarious gendered and caste-divided labour regimes were fought against in a remarkable month-long strike demanding better terms and conditions of work and pay that was led by Dalit women.

I draw on long-term ethnographic research that I carried out in the tea belts of the Western Ghats, home to almost all the tea plantation districts in South India. The region consists of the Nilgiri plantations in Tamil Nadu; plantations near Wayanad and Nelliampathy in the Malabar region of Kerala; those by the Ponmudi Mountains in the southern part of the Western Ghats; the Kannan Devan plantations encircling the hill town of Munnar and the Peermade tea belt in Idukki district, also known as the 'teapot of Kerala'. The Peermade tea belt, comprising 36 tea estates and a total area of 10,000 hectares of tea bushes, is where most of my research for this chapter was carried out between July 2014 and September 2015, with shorter periods in the years that followed. I also draw on events in Munnar and earlier doctoral field research in Munnar between January 2011 and February 2012.

The Peermade tea belt is known outside Kerala for its proximity to the Periyar Wildlife Sanctuary (popularly called Thekkady/Periyar Tiger Reserve) and also to the Sabarimala pilgrimage centre. During the pre-Independence period, the ruler of the princely state of Travancore had his summer palace in the hill station of Peermade. Today the sanctuary with its wild and exotic image, together with the hill station known for its beautiful tea gardens, makes the Peermade a destination that draws both foreign and domestic tourists. But the imagery of the idyllic tea garden of course disguises the history of the plantation workers' abjection and poverty perpetuated by the exploitative plantation system.[1]

I carried out the majority of my fieldwork for this chapter in a plantation I call the Hill Valley estate owned by the True Life Company.[2] Here I carried out a household-level survey of the tea lines,[3] generational histories, key interviews and of course participant observation. I followed Dalit workers to their new sites of labour in Coimbatore, Tiruppur and to villages back in Tamil Nadu to better understand their situation there and conducted interviews with them. I also spent time with the Dalit women workers who organised the 2015 strike in the neighbouring Munnar tea belt to understand the dynamics of their mobilisation and how it spread and was

Photo 1   Hill Valley estate in the Western Ghats, Kerala
Photo by Jayseelan Raj.

curtailed. And, lastly, I draw on ethnographic research I conducted with the Adivasi labourers from Jharkhand who were based on a neighbouring plantation in the Peermade, about 20 km from the Hill Valley estate in what I call Top View estate owned by the Auburn Company, and a two-week visit back to some of their homes in the Santhal Parganas in Jharkhand to better understand their background.

First, let me turn to a broader history of the tea plantations as a context to understanding the situation of contemporary Dalit and Adivasi labour.

THE HISTORY OF TAMIL DALIT LABOUR
IN THE KERALA TEA BELT

Kerala is renowned for its inclusive development model whose human development achievements are comparable to those of developed countries. For example, according to the Census of India, Kerala achieved a significantly high male literacy rate (94 per cent in 2011), female literacy (93 per cent), sex ratio (1084F to 1000M), highest life expectancy (75 years) and lowest infant mortality (12 deaths per 1000 infants) of all Indian states.[4] It is perhaps an irony that in a state that is so often cited as a model of egalitarianism, development and education in India, one finds the kind of oppression and marginalisation that is faced by its Tamil Dalit communities in the tea plantations.[5] To understand their history of persistent discrimination and oppression, it is necessary to outline the history of the labour regimes under which the Dalits and a minority of non-Dalits backward castes were brought to Kerala.

By the 1860s the British had established plantations in the Caribbean, South and Southeast Asia, and Southern Africa. Although slavery was abolished between 1833 and 1848, it was replaced by a softer version known as the indenture system, by which workers were brought from distant places to newly developed plantations.[6] Being the largest component of Indian emigration during the colonial era,[7] Tamil indentured workers – who mostly belonged to outcaste communities – were sent to coffee, sugar and tea plantations around the Indian Ocean. They went to Ceylon (Sri Lanka), Malaya (Malaysia), Burma (Union of Myanmar) and the princely state of Travancore (the South Indian state of Kerala). A comparatively lower number of Tamil workers were also received by Fiji, Guyana and Mauritius, where most workers came from northern India.[8] Tamil labour, particularly that of 'Untouchable' castes, had developed a reputation of being manageable, hardworking, and able to survive heavily forested highlands.

In India, the new plantations were developed in the highlands of the south-western Ghats (mainly in Kerala and Tamil Nadu) and the north-eastern hills (mainly in Assam and West Bengal). While the majority of workers on the plantations in the north-east were originally brought from Adivasi communities in Jharkhand and Odisha, and Gurkhas from Nepal,[9] it was Tamil-speaking Dalits who constituted the majority of the labour force in Kerala. Under this colonial indenture system in the 1860s, Tamil Dalits migrated from the Tamil-speaking regions in South India to the newly developed colonial plantations in the erstwhile princely state of Travancore.[10]

The Peermade highlands, then called the 'hills of Central Travancore', were inhabited by tribes of Mala-Arayans and Mannans.[11] In 1863 British colonial officials of the Madras Presidency and British missionaries established coffee plantations there and the local tribes were driven away from their land. Tea became a prominent crop when a leaf disease resulted in the decline of coffee cultivation. As tea cultivation was labour intensive, more and more workers from outcaste communities in Tamil-speaking regions of South India were brought to the plantations. They initially came through the indentured labour system under which the workers signed a legal contract which bonded them to the plantation companies. The workers were recruited by professional agents of the plantation companies who later became Kanganis,[12] that is labour contractors cum supervisors who recruited workers from their own villages and supervised the workers in the plantations. Under the legal contract the workers were provided with an advance to pay off their debt back home as they entered into an agreement to work for specific plantation companies for a period (generally five years) stipulated under the contract. Once an agreement had been made with the company, it was virtually impossible for the workers to free themselves as they were forced to stay with the company even after their contract period expired. The workers under the indenture system thus effectively became bonded labourers.

The workers were presented with an alluring, colourful picture of plantation life and work but when they got to the plantations there were no decent housing or sanitation facilities. Many of the workers died of malaria, fever and dysentery while clearing the forest.[13] The labour process was arduous and exhausting. Work was extracted from the labourers with a machine-like precision and any fault detected was dealt with severely.[14] Many workers tried to run away due to the routine inhuman treatment and the severe work conditions. However, this was rendered virtually impossible by the debt bondage system that was integral to the recruitment of indentured labour, and the sanctions that could be exerted in the case of any attempt to withdraw labour.

The workers were divided into labour gangs under the Kanganis who had recruited them. The Kanganis were responsible for the maintenance of their labour gangs and paid them directly. Potential recruits would be offered an advance that was made against wages from future labour.[15] This advance might be used to pay off debts in the village or be given to landlords to release bonded labourers so they could be freed to travel to plantations; they could only escape their exploitation back in their village by entering into a new contract for a new place of work and therefore new indebtedness.[16] The debt of the workers was further increased as their Kangani charged them for transportation and food on their way to the plantations. In the plantations, they had to work under a strict class order and hierarchy.

In 1865 the Travancore Criminal Breach of Contract Act was passed under which it was a crime for workers to break their contract of employment with the plantation companies. A magistrate's court was established in Peermade by the Travancore state for the purpose of prosecuting workers under the terms of the act. The act effectively prevented employees leaving the plantations for alternative work. Moreover, the act advanced no protection against exploitation.[17] In addition, the Coffee Stealing Prevention Act of 1879 prohibited workers from having any right to the product of their labour. It not only symbolised the dehumanised situation of the labourers, the point of whose existence was solely to labour, but also presented the plantation workers as potential criminals: the coolie beast who needed to be tamed.[18]

International pressure to end the indenture system became stronger across the British colonies in the early 1900s, when the brutality of the system was widely documented and reported.[19] Indian nationalists, as well as anti-slavery and labour activists in the West called the indenture system a 'new form of slavery'.[20] The legal contract between worker and tea plantation was outlawed by the 1920s, but the Kangani system through which the workers had been recruited and controlled continued. The role of Kanganis did change somewhat after the abolition of the indenture system. They continued to recruit workers but without the control provided by the indenture system, which had given them impunity in punishing the workers; and the workers were more 'free' to shift from one plantation to another. By the late 1940s the Kanganis had ceased to be contractors and their role was limited to that of wage-earning supervisors of the workforce.

Although Europeans dominated the plantation economy from the early stages until the beginning of the 1970s, Indian capitalists from dominant caste groups, particularly Brahmins, Syrian Christians and a few from the Nadar caste, had gained access to plantation ownership by the mid-twentieth century. The native planters, as part of their own nationalist discourse, challenged the European monopoly. The Diwan of Travancore state wrote that 'preference will be given to the *subjects* of the Travancore state in the registration of land suitable for the cultivation of plantation crops'.[21] This was directed to benefit the Brahmin, Nair and Syrian Christian communities as they were considered legitimate *subjects*, whereas the Dalits were not socially or politically legitimised to own land.

Following the declaration of the Diwan, the planters from the high caste communities were successful in lobbying for huge areas of land for the plantations, involving more than 10,000 hectares. These lands were acquired at throwaway prices or even at no cost at all.[22] By contrast, the absence of land rights for the plantation workers was never discussed. This historically evolved pattern of landholding in the region, highly influenced by the interplay between land and caste,[23] ensured that the outcastes were alienated from landownership and continued to be a cheap source of labour for the privileged class of planters.

The formation of Kerala state in 1956 led to a major transition from foreign European control of the plantations to native owners. This, however, was threatened by the formation of the first communist government in Kerala (and in India) in 1957 as it pressed for land reforms and the redistribution of large landholdings to landless peasants and tenants. The new plantation owners feared the loss of their plantations and other institutional agencies in their control. They lobbied against the communist government, and supported the massive *vimochana samaram* political agitation that started in 1958 (Liberation Struggle a.k.a. Christian and Nayar-led Moral Rearmament Movement). A significant number of the plantation owners in the Peermade tea belt were Syrian Christians and many of their families were at the forefront of this movement. The outcome was that the plantations were exempted from the land reforms. Neoclassical economists supported this by arguing that the plantations were the most productive part of agricultural economy and the advantage of economies of scale would be lost in a land reform.[24] In other words, the abolition of the plantation system was described as *killing a goose that laid the golden eggs*.[25] Thus the Dalit plantation workers were largely excluded from the processes of land reform and redistribution, as were the Adivasi (indigenous/tribal) communities whose land it originally was. In this way, land reform legislation did not undermine the historical land-based social hierarchies, contradicting the egalitarian communist ideology that was the new state rhetoric in Kerala.

The only consolation for the plantation workforce was the Plantation Labour Act of 1951, which introduced welfare measures and social security benefits. According to the act, the workers should be provided with housing, water supply, healthcare, school education for their children, crèches, canteens, compensation for accidents and injuries at workplaces, and paid maternity leave and annual leave. Other benefits, such as compensation for accidents and water supply, were not provided until 1970s, when the workers organised protests through various trade unions. In many plantations, the hard-earned welfare provisions such as healthcare, crèche facilities and paid annual leave were suspended by the mid-1990s, with the plantations citing the economic crisis in the tea industry as the reason. So the Plantation Labour

Act did benefit the plantation workforce, but only for a period between 1970 and 1990 and that only as a result of the workers' struggle. While the companies often take credit for offering these services, the state and central governments provided significant financial assistance for them. For instance, many plantation companies lobbied state governments to provide school education for workers' children and the companies thus saved having to spend money on the schools. Even then, some of the facilities, such as latrines and electricity, were not provided to the workers until 2000, when the central government funded the construction of latrines and the state government provided electricity to the plantation workforce.

The trade unions emerged as a powerful force in the tea belt in late 1960s and were instrumental in improving the work conditions of the workers through popular struggle. They also represented workers in the plantation labour committee that determined work conditions and wages. However, the relation between the workers and the trade union leaders was quite hierarchical since most of the trade union leaders were not of plantation worker background. They were sent by various political parties to set up branches in the plantation belts. The planters did everything possible to drive away those trade union leaders who opposed them. Within the plantations, many trade union conveners who connected the workers with the trade union leadership were assigned to the hardest work. The planters also filed a number of criminal cases against trade union conveners in an attempt to demoralise and distract them from concentrating on the workers' issues.

The tea industry in India boomed in the first three decades of the postcolonial period. By the late 1980s India was second only to China, with nearly 25 per cent of global tea production and employing 1.26 million people on tea plantations and 2 million indirectly. But the collapse of the international price of tea in the early 1990s led to a major crisis in the Indian tea industry. Arguably, this was due to neoliberal structural adjustments of the international tea trade.[26] Trade agreements between countries conditioned the tea trade between 1950 and 1990 but this changed by the early 1990s as a few major corporate firms that controlled the industry began to intervene much more in determining the price for tea.[27] Furthermore, the collapse of the Soviet Union, India's main trading partner for tea, augmented the crisis. Iraq then became the major buyer for Indian tea but this new market was lost following the Gulf War of 1990–91. The rising cost of production, decreasing productivity of tea bushes and the heavy export duty in India are cited as other factors that precipitated the crisis in the Indian tea industry. In 2012 Indian tea earned only Rs.4000 million in foreign exchange, in comparison to Rs.5420 million at its height in 1977:[28] a drastic decline in real terms.

The plantation owners undertook major reforms in both land and labour regimes which dramatically affected the fate of the labour force. Planters had realised the tourist and real estate value of the plantation lands. For instance, superintendent and manager's bungalows were being rented out for movie shoots and to Western tourists who might enjoy their imperial feel and would combine a trip to the plantations with a safari in the nearby national parks such as Thekkady.[29] The planters thus used the crisis as an opportunity to diversify the economic activities on the plantations. The Plantation Act had previously made illegal the use of the land under plantation for purposes other than plantation. These legal restrictions had been enacted primarily to guarantee jobs for the permanent workers. (They of course also ensured that the plantations were exempt from land ceiling restrictions.) In the aftermath of the crisis, the planters lobbied for a significant amendment to the Kerala Land Reform Act of 1963 which enabled them to use 5 per cent of the land for non-plantation purposes such as tourism, renting to property developers for new tourist resorts, and cultivating other agricultural crops. Of course, the new amendments were silent on the issue of land for the plantation workers while at the same time welfare benefits were suspended in the name of the crisis, eroding the hard-won gains made in the preceding decades. It is against this backdrop of an increasingly neoliberal regime, strengthening the position of the planters while state control over plantations declined, that we must understand the fate of Dalit tea plantation labour.[30]

NEOLIBERAL REFORMS AND CHANGING LABOUR REGIMES IN THE PLANTATIONS

Most significantly for the labour, new, more exploitative, work regimes were put in place, especially in estates such as Hill Valley, which were taken over by new companies. In the 2010–11 period at least ten other estates were also taken over by new companies and this drastically transformed the way plantations were run. Vacancies were not filled and permanent positions were replaced by temporary ones and, increasingly, casual ones. The plantation companies increased the workload and intensified supervision of the work and punishments (such as suspension of workers) for any lapses. The plantation association in Kerala was successful in forcing the plantation labour committee (a panel comprising labour commissioner, trade union representatives and the plantation companies' representatives) to increase the plucking rate[31] from 14 kg to 21 kg in January 2011, and then to 25 kg in January 2016.

Permanent workers are those workers who are guaranteed work at at least the minimum wage throughout the year and are entitled to welfare, including housing, medical care and sick leave, an annual bonus, a provident fund and retirement benefits. Temporary workers are not guaranteed work throughout the year, but still live within the tea estate and get work during the peak tea-plucking season. They are not eligible for retirement benefits, bonuses, medical care or sick leave, but they can access the provident fund. They are given housing that permanent workers do not want, or are allowed to build small huts next to the permanent workers' settlement. The position of the casual workforce is the worst. The Plantation Labour Act allows the employment of casual workers only for occasional work outside the everyday process of production (for instance logging) but this rule is increasingly breached. Since the employment of casual labour for mundane tasks is illegal, and since they also do not exist in the official registry of the company, they are in a most precarious situation and often have to find work outside the plantation as well. Another significant difference between the temporary and casual workers is that the latter are not eligible for provident fund or any social security benefits (see Table 3.1 in the Appendix for details of these three contractual positions).

In the Hill Valley estate, according to a retired field officer, before the crisis in 1995 there were around 700 workers of whom 500 were permanent and 200 temporary. At that time, the casual workers were recruited only during peak seasons, usually around 50 workers. By the time I did fieldwork in 2014–15, two decades later, there were only 174 workers of whom 133 were permanent workers, 36 temporary and 5 casual. This decline in the workforce to less than a quarter shows the impact the crisis had on the plantation production. The percentage of the temporary workforce declined from 29 per cent to 21 per cent and, in addition, the number of days they were employed fell. This increasingly made the temporary workers reliant on income from outside the plantation. In other words, the crisis had made the temporary workers more precarious than before. The permanent workers were protected from being laid off, but the plantation companies had significantly worsened their terms and conditions.

Although production also declined, workers were doing more work as a result of the crisis. One field staff member told me that he was doing three times the amount of work he used to do before the crisis, since the new company withdrew the two assistants who had been working with him before the new plantation company took over. While the Hill Valley estate was not yet employing a significant casual labour force, in neighbouring estates where I also did fieldwork a large part of the labour force was being replaced by casual labour. These were not the local Tamil Dalits but more vulnerable seasonal migrant labour brought from poorer parts of the country (Adivasi labour from Jharkhand in Auburn and Top View estates where I did fieldwork), whose predicament I will return to towards the end of the chapter. The employment of more temporary workers living in the

Top View estate, and casual daily wage workers from outside the plantation, is intended to cut what the planters call 'the social cost of production', since these temporary and outside workers need not be given any welfare benefits, and to maintain the alienated status of labour in plantation production. Thus different companies have employed different strategies in dealing with the temporary and casual workforce given their production needs in the crisis context: Top View estate returned to full functioning after a short period of partial shutdown whereas the cutback in the temporary workforce at Hill Valley estate was because it continued to struggle despite a new company taking over.

The new companies can be referred to as 'new generation companies' and fall within the genre of larger corporations who prefer subcontracting systems to the wage-labour system. In the case of Tanzanian sugar plantations, Holt Norris and Worby (2012) have noted that liberalisation of the domestic economy has led to vulnerability in the face of price fluctuations in world markets and the entry of new generation companies arriving from Mauritius who 'exercise a sovereign capacity to shape the conditions of their employees' (2012: 356) and have laid off a significant section of the workforce. The new managements in Peermade tea belt intensified contract work, strengthened surveillance of the workforce, and increased workloads in the name of increasing the 'efficiency' of the workforce in ways strikingly similar to what happened in the Tanzanian plantations. The companies have also used the crisis as an 'excuse' to radically alter production relations to their advantage. For example, they have temporarily shut down production units in line with their immediate production needs regardless of the strict labour laws against this. In many cases this meant shutting down the tea-processing factories where the majority of the men were employed. Each plantation used to have a processing factory on site but, more often than not, this is no longer the case.

Wages were frequently not paid on time and workers claimed that the company made money by holding them back, often for three additional weeks. The result was that workers often ended up taking loans from moneylenders at extortionate interest rates. For instance, if the worker is supposed to receive Rs.3500 after various deductions, the money the workers would lose is around Rs.175 to Rs.200 (at a 5–7 per cent interest rate for 20 days). The payment of 'service payouts'[32] for the retirees was also delayed. Many of the retirees I met were very distressed by the delay. Mary, a 59-year-old Tamil Dalit retired worker, told me that she would protest by immolating herself in front of the company office unless she got her service payout within a month.

The new companies also confiscated the kitchen gardens and common yards by the workers' lines and fenced them off so that the workers could not use them. They planted tea in these kitchen gardens; a reminder that the production of tea is all that matters in the plantations and the workers should not imagine a life outside those production relations. The workers not only lost whatever little material gains they had made but also were socially attacked as the occupation of the kitchen gardens and yards by the company inculcated a sense of psychological alienation in which the workers control nothing in the plantations; they were reminded that they were alienated labour only. In short, the casualisation of the workforce, suspension of welfare measures and withdrawal of the workers' right to use the immediate surroundings of their settlements became part of a quotidian process of material and social dispossession of the workers.

Significantly, as a result of these processes, the Tamil Dalit labour force on the tea plantations was increasingly feminised: the actual tea plucking was mainly done by women and this was, by far, the main task left. Whereas previously the gender ratio was around 50 per cent, by 2014–15, 85 per cent of the workers left on the Hill Valley estate were women (out of the 174 workers, 148 were women – 110 permanent women workers and 33 temporary women workers; and all the five casual workers were women). For the workers, this was also a strategy of making the best of a bad situation: if the women were permanent workers they would be provided with a (tiny) home for the family in the tea estate labour lines; a secure base also for the

Photo 2   Dalit tea pluckers bringing their day's harvest in for weighing
Photo by Alpa Shah.

other members of the household now working in informalised insecure jobs outside the plantation.

At the Top View tea estate, the workforce was being replaced by migrant Adivasi male and female workers from Jharkhand who were all casual workers a process to which I will return.

The plantation work is arduous. Female workers are mainly engaged in tea plucking and work eight-hour days. To be eligible for the daily wage of Rs.232, they have to pluck a minimum of 21 kg of tea leaves during ordinary periods and 18 kg during the low season (in January, February and August). In January 2016, this was increased to 25 kg/21 kg respectively. If they pluck below the minimum weight their daily wage is reduced. If they pluck more, they are paid additional money. From 21–34 kg, the workers are paid 60 paise/kg; from 35–44 kg, they are paid 90 paise/kg; and for any extra kilo above 44, the workers are paid Rs.1.20/kg. On Sundays, the minimum wage norm is not applicable and the workers are paid Rs.4/kg (so if the workers are able to pluck 70 kg, they will be paid 70 × 4 = Rs.280). Tea pluckers frequently complained that the supervisors and field officers often miscalculate the weight of leaves plucked in favour of the management, by overcompensating for the weight of the baskets at the weigh-in.

The few men who are today employed on the plantations engage in field-based tasks, such as pruning and spraying fertiliser, and some are also employed in the remaining factories. Factory work is divided into shifts and is mostly done by men. The workers are paid for an eight-hour shift but have to work overtime during the high season plucking months. The work in the factory is understood to be more hazardous than the field due to the dust of the crushed tea leaves. The inhaled dust causes lung disease and can result in other internal bodily damage. Spraying fertilisers in the fields also causes health issues, although the workers tend to talk more about the issues in the factories than the fields. Neither masks nor any other protective measures are provided for work in the factories and fields.

The severe labour cuts, the arduous work, suspension of welfare measures, and increasingly casualised work in the tea plantations, have resulted not only in the greater feminisation of the workforce but also in the movement of young people out of the plantations. Some workers looked for work in the nearby cities while living in the plantations but there were also others – sometimes whole households – who left the plantations entirely.[33] While it was previously common for workers to leave the plantations either after retirement or when there were no children to take over their job in the plantation, the economic crisis since 1995 acted as a significant factor in propelling more workers to leave.

In 2014–15, I conducted a household survey of the 25 labour lines in the Hill Valley estate and covered all the 136 households and 814 people to understand how households were diversifying their livelihoods in view of the crisis.[34] In each household the members whose income forms part of the income of the household are counted, irrespective of whether they work inside or outside of the plantation.

Before the crisis, the occupations of both the male and female workforce of different caste groups were very similar as they were mostly all plantation workers. By 2015, more than three-quarters of all male workers had moved into other work, as had nearly two-thirds of women workers (see also Figures 3.1 and 3.2 in the Appendix). The figures reveal important aspects of the changes in the subsistence of the Dalit plantation Tamils. There are differences of occupational patterns between men and women, and between Dalit and non-Dalit castes but they are not particularly extreme. It is evident that the main move is to non-skilled manual work outside the plantations for both men and women. At the same time, there are now also more men (20 per cent) and women (15 per cent) working in semi-skilled work. There is also, among Dalits, a reliance on National Rural Employment Guarantee work within the plantations. It is the older women (and some older men and newly married women) who rely on this work as it is considered easier manual labour. As Donegan reports for Other Backward Caste (OBC) women in Tamil Nadu in the chapter that follows, National Rural Employment Guarantee Act work is less stigmatised than other forms of labour including plantation work, which is why newly married women also pursue it. Furthermore, there is less chance for older people and the newly married women to diversify their occupations within the plantation-dominated society. Only very few people on the plantations have diversified into petty business or salaried work.

Beyond this general pattern, there are some differences worth mentioning. As I have argued earlier, more women stay in the plantations than men. The non-Dalit castes have been able to keep a greater number of the plantation jobs (than Dalit men) and have not had to engage in manual labour or National Rural Employment Guarantee work as much as Dalits. Keeping plantation jobs in this context is, of course, very important as, despite all the cutbacks, it allows at least some securities such as a house to live in. The relatively better position of OBC and high castes over Dalits is also reflected in the fact that the former have more salaried jobs than Dalits. Equally there are differences within the Dalit groups, particularly between Pallars and Paraiyars. Pallars have in general managed to keep more plantation work but they have also diversified less into semi-skilled work and salaried jobs than Paraiyars.[35]

Overall, though, most Dalit men have had to seek manual labour outside the plantations in the construction industry. Others have worked as semi-skilled labour, as masons in construction and as heavy machine operators in the towns of central and southern Kerala. Seven Dalit youths worked as taxi drivers, jeep drivers and auto rickshaw drivers in the nodal town.

The production in the plantations incorporated the Dalit women in a very economically active manner, with fewer restrictions than we see in some of the other sites discussed in other chapters. As the survey data shows, every single woman in the plantation engaged in paid work. The particular gender relations that evolve out of these production relations enable the women to migrate for paid work outside the plantation as well. Their manual labour diversification outside the tea plantations includes work in other plantations where it is available, and work in cardamom, coffee and pepper plantations. Unmarried Dalit women have attained semi-skilled and sometimes salaried semi-skilled jobs as sales girls in shops, housemaids (known as 'home nurses'), and assistants in ayurvedic massage parlours. As mentioned before, inside the plantations they are now often the ones that have permanent positions and thus they are the ones that guarantee the family house at the plantation.

Kerala is acclaimed for its high educational attainment, with the rare record of 100 per cent literacy in primary education[36] and a better educational record for Dalits than in other Indian states: 48 per cent of Dalits have reached the secondary level pass (7th grade or above), and 65 per cent have educational attainment above lower level education (above 4th grade) (see the preceding chapter of this volume). However, the educational level among plantation Dalits is low: only 30–35 per cent of the male Dalit plantation workers had more than five years of schooling and women had even less. The OBC and high caste workers are better educated than the Dalits (see Figures 3.3 and 3.4).

The overall occupational patterns of the plantation workers bear some relation to educational levels. Nine to twelve years of education is crucial for workers to move from unskilled to semi-skilled work (see Table 3.2).[37] That said, in order to access those kinds of jobs they are up against discrimination, both within and outside the plantations; to which I will return below.

MOVING TO COIMBATORE, TIRUPPUR AND VILLAGES IN TAMIL NADU FOR WORK

What this household-level data does not show is the migration of people, sometimes entire families, out of the plantations in search of better work. As I described earlier, people left to return to Tamil Nadu after five generations on the plantations. About 100 families from the Peermade tea belt had migrated to the manufacturing and industrial heartland of the Tiruppur–Coimbatore region since 1995 where they were employed as mainly semi-skilled casual labour. Most other families that left the plantations moved back to their ancestral villages in Tamil Nadu. I spent some time in both types of locations and in Tiruppur I interviewed 34 families who were working mainly in the textile and garment industry to understand their circumstances.

Tiruppur is a major garment manufacturing township which is around 50 km from Coimbatore, a large industrial township known as the 'Manchester of South India'. The owners of the mills and the stitching units are mostly from Gounder (Kongu Vellalar) and Naicker (Kamma) caste communities.[38] While there were Kallar and Gounder workers, there is a significant Dalit population among the workforce from the Paraiyar and Arunthathiyar castes. The plantation Dalits make up a small group amidst those working in the textile industry. Among around 30,000 workers in the dyeing units,[39] they account for about 400.[40]

The majority of the Tamil Dalits from plantations that I met were engaged in skilled and semi-skilled work in garment-related industrial units.[41] There are three kinds of production units where the Tamil Dalits work: dyeing (semi-skilled), stitching (semi-skilled) and marketing in larger firms (semi-skilled). Out of 34 Tamil Dalit men interviewed, 3 were working in the dyeing units as machine operators, 26 were working as tailors in stitching units, and 5 were working in the marketing departments of Chennai Silks, a large firm that exports clothes to the Gulf, Europe and North America. Some of them were married. The wives of some were housewives, others worked as sales girls in shops, and still others worked as tailors alongside their husbands. While the majority of the plantation Dalits were working as labourers in dyeing units, the three machine operators were interviewed because they were from estates neighbouring Hill Valley and were accessible.

In February 2015 machine operators in dyeing units were paid a daily wage of Rs.600 a day. The marketing executives were paid a monthly wage that varied between Rs.8000 and Rs.14,000, depending on experience. Tailors were paid on a piece rate basis dependent on how many pieces they stitched,[42] and daily wages based on this work varied between Rs.275 and Rs.750. The possibility of working twelve-hour days (8 am to 8 pm) could bring in Rs.700 to Rs.750. This occurs when the small stitching units receive large numbers of contracts from major firms that have direct connections with buyers abroad. In times of less demand, the tailors earn from Rs.275 to Rs.400 by working around eight hours (9 am to 5 pm).

Despite better wages in Tiruppur, workers experience a new kind of exploitation here. Regular employment in small stitching units is based on workers consenting to stay and work overnight to meet the deadlines of the larger firms. Dalit workers in the knitwear units told me that they often have to work without sleep for nights on end, while allowed to take only short naps. It is perhaps no surprise that suicide rates among the migrant workers in Tiruppur are high.[43]

The dyeing units, where people worked ten-hour days (8 am to 6 pm), have various problems; they are notorious for pollution, and dyeing and bleaching units are known to cause serious health hazards for long-term workers. The dyeing units were shut down on grounds of pollution in 2011 after the intervention of Chennai High Court. Many large units managed to reopen while the small units remain closed. The closures have meant that many Tamils have moved either to stitching units in Tiruppur or machinery manufacturing industries in Coimbatore. As such, driven by one crisis (in the plantations), to enter into another crisis (in the dyeing industry), and driven again elsewhere (to the stitching units), the plantation Dalits become part of India's 'footloose' informal labour (Breman 1996) that oscillates between different occupations in different industrial townships attempting to find less precarious jobs.

I also found three young women aged 19, 23 and 26, who moved to Tiruppur from the Hill Valley estate, working under the illegal '*sumangali* scheme'. The girls receive food and lodging from the company, and their wages will be paid only at the end of a contract term that ranged from 18 months to four years, or else in frequent instalments to the girls' parents. The end of the contract is supposed to be before the marriage of the girls and the saved wages are meant for paying their dowry. Such marriage schemes are a form of (outlawed) bonded labour. Both under the contract and sumangali systems, wages for work done are withheld to control and discipline the workers.

Tiruppur's dependence on and maintenance of this precarious casual and/ or bonded labour force is not at all hidden from the popular and academic discourses, nor is it a new phenomenon.[44] While there is no scarcity of labour laws applicable to the Tiruppur textile and garment industries, they are hardly implemented. Many workers I interviewed had never heard of a 'labour officer'. A supervisor who had seen the labour inspector visiting his stitching unit told me, 'the laws are made not for the workers, but for the labour officers to extract money from the employers'.

Working outside the plantations in the garment units of Tiruppur enabled a certain degree of economic upward mobility for Tamil Dalits, who earned more money than those who stayed behind. However, there are many disadvantages of having to move out of the plantation economy. First, these new forms of work are not secure nor guaranteed in the way plantation work once was. Second, whereas the plantations had enabled some form of housing, families who moved outside the plantations had to pay rent and often had facilities poorer than those in the plantations; many were living in the slums and ghettoes of the cities they moved to.[45] Finally, people who work outside are also subject to caste discrimination in a manner in which they are not in the plantations. In the next section, I explore these dynamics in greater depth through household histories.

HOUSEHOLD STORIES OF LIVELIHOOD DIVERSIFICATION: ECONOMIC VERSUS SOCIAL MOBILITY

In order to understand the patterns of migration and diversification of livelihoods within households since the tea industry crisis, and the relative advantages and disadvantages of work outside the plantations, I undertook ten detailed household case histories of families who had been living next to each other in 1980 in the Hill Valley estate. The brief life histories (see Table 3.3) indicate the severe impact of the crisis on the ability of plantation workers to stay on in the plantations across generations. This is the case both for sons, many of whom were unable to become permanent workers in their 'home plantation', and daughters who would have married within the plantation sector although outside of the 'home plantation' but who now often move out of the plantation economy with their new households. In all of the seven households that retained the plantation connection,[46] it was elder siblings who stayed back because they were able to get employment on the plantations. The younger ones had to leave. In addition, although a daughter of one house (house 1 in Table 3.3) only moved to a neighbouring plantation when she married, her mother left the plantations altogether and moved to live with her son in Coimbatore. This may at least in part relate to the stigma attached to parents living with their daughters as opposed to their sons.

Out of the ten families, the three from which many family members left the plantations in the years of the crisis between 1995 and 1998 are considered in greater detail to understand their vulnerability and mobility. The first of the three families is that of Sundaram (house 4 in Table 3.3). Sundaram, who is now 46 years old, was a temporary worker in the Hill Valley estate when the crisis hit the tea industry. He moved out of the plantation in 1997 along with his wife Kokila, his youngest brothers Ramesh and Robin, and his parents, when he was 27 years old. He has four siblings – one elder brother, two younger brothers and one sister. The elder brother Karuppasamy is a carpenter in the Hill Valley estate, one younger brother works in Tiruppur's textile industry as a tailor, and another brother is a manual labourer in construction in his native village, Nagaram in Tamil Nadu. His sister is married to a permanent worker in a nearby tea estate. Sundaram dropped out of school when he was nine to take care of his younger siblings. He began working as a servant for a Syrian Christian family in a valley town when he was thirteen. The Syrian Christian family 'recruited' Sundaram through their friend who was then field officer in the Hill Valley estate. It was common to recruit plantation workers' children as servants for relatives of the managerial staff. After five years, Sundaram returned to the plantation to become a temporary worker in the tea factory for eight years. The company did not promote him to permanent worker, allegedly due to the economic crisis, so Sundaram moved to Nagaram, his native village in Tirunelveli district of southern Tamil Nadu. He said he moved because he realised that he didn't have a future in the plantation. Sundaram's story is common for many youths who were temporary workers at the time of the crisis.

Back in Tamil Nadu, he managed to obtain a ration card, and rented a hut for Rs.500 per month. Having been employed as a manual labourer in the plantation, Sundaram could not manage to become a semi-skilled worker such as a driver or a mechanic. He became an assistant to a mason in his native village, earning a daily wage of Rs.350. Sundaram also went to southern Kerala whenever he could not find work near his village. Sundaram said that although wages were higher in Kerala (Rs.500), so was the cost of living. But he saved money by sleeping at the construction sites, relying on rice soups which he used to cook on a kerosene stove he carried with him.

For a brief period, he worked in dyeing units of the textile factories of Tiruppur. This paid better. When I asked him about the health hazards of the dyeing units, Sundaram responded, 'At the end of the day, what I care about is how much I could save for my family. I don't care about my health.' He used to be paid Rs.650 for working 9–10 hours a day. Although daily manual labour should not be more than eight hours, he had to work a bit more to keep his job secure. He lost his job after the government temporarily shut down the dyeing units because of the pollution.

Sundaram was more vulnerable to debt since his income was central to the reproduction of his household; his wife did not do any paid labour. Sundaram told me that he wanted his wife to concentrate on taking care of the children's education and not to bother about bringing income to the family. His father could not work due to health issues. His mother found work under the National Rural Employment Guarantee Act. His mother's income was a major addition to the family, but most of her money was spent on the 'tonics and pills' for her husband.

Sundaram, however, managed to save more money than his brother Karuppasamy who stayed back in the plantation, as his wage was much higher than the plantation wages. However, as evident from the narrative above, Sundaram lived the precarious life of a migrant casual labourer relying on various odd jobs, in contrast to the secure job of his elder brother in the plantation. There was a price to be paid to 'see some money,' as Sundaram expressed it.

Another price was overt caste discrimination. Sundaram observed that the future lies in the towns for Dalits. He wanted to move his family to the city not only for economic reasons and the education of his children, but also because he faced severe caste discrimination back in the village. He told me that 'upper caste tea shops discourage Dalits to enter into their tea shops through creating "unnecessary troubles"' such as providing tea in dirty cups, and asking for exact change (exact cost of tea-snacks). That is, even if the tea shops have lots of coins and smaller denominations, they would demand that Dalits pay the exact amount. Sundaram was disappointed that he could not afford to move his family to a town.

Sundaram could not tolerate explicit discrimination. He had enjoyed relatively egalitarian relations in the plantations where caste identity is overshadowed by the class order of the plantation production relations. The unbearable discrimination led him to join Viduthalai Ciruthaigal Katchi aka VCK (the Liberation Panther Party). Through this party, he became a community leader for the Paraiyar Dalits, and he was entrusted with the responsibility of resolving family feuds/conflicts within the group. In one of our meetings he told me that he didn't know much about Ambedkar. There is indeed no statue of Ambedkar, nor any socio-political organisation in the Hill Valley estate dedicated to the cause of Dalits as there is in many other parts of the country. He came to realise 'Ambedkar's sacrifice', as he puts it, only after moving to Tamil Nadu. The experience of caste discrimination away from the plantation in turn also led to a greater consciousness of caste identity/the Dalit movement among the Tamil Dalit plantation workforce. Whenever someone like Sundaram visited the plantations, he preferred to talk about the role of caste in Tamil villages and how divisive caste is there, unlike in the plantation where, according to Sundaram, 'people from different castes live like siblings'. However, the Dalit consciousness in the plantation often resulted in group formation on the basis of sub-caste identity as in the case of Sundaram himself. Sundaram talked about the unity of Dalits but he was still part of the Liberation Panther Party which has been identified with Paraiyar community in Tamil Nadu.

While Sundaram wanted to move his family to a big city, Ilaiyaraja actually did move his family to Chennai. Ilaiyaraja, aged 40 (house 2 in the table), left the plantation along with his parents and younger sister, for Chennai in 1997. He chose Chennai mainly because his ancestors came from a village which is located around 40 km from this city. Ilaiyaraja used to be a temporary worker and the economic crisis led to a loss of guaranteed work in the plantation. Ilaiyaraja's elder brother, Selvam, remained at the estate as he was a permanent worker.

Ilaiyaraja had studied up to 10th grade and his high school education helped him to obtain a job as a marketing agent for a cement company in

Chennai. He was paid Rs.7000 a month. His father passed away in 2008, and his mother was not working. His wife, Jayalakshmi worked as a sales girl in a textile shop in Chennai and she earned Rs.6500 every month. So, the total income of Ilaiyaraja and Jayalakshmi was Rs.13,500 per month.

However, for Ilaiayaraja, this income was not enough to survive as a 'lower middle-class' family in a major city as he needed to pay rent of Rs.5800 and Rs.270 for electricity and water supply, a monthly school fee of Rs.700 each for two children, cover the medical expenses of his mother, and a loan amount of Rs.1200 for his motorcycle. The rest was spent on food. He saved a maximum of Rs.1000 every month.

Ilaiyaraja could have chosen to stay at the family house in his native village to save money but instead he rented in another place to mask his caste identity. He told me that he doesn't want his children to feel the inferiority of being identified with the 'SC [Scheduled Caste] colony', or what is popularly called 'parai cheri', a derogatory term used for the Dalit colonies in Tamil Nadu.

Another family that moved out of the plantation is that of John, a 46-year-old Dalit Christian of the Pallar caste (house 1 in the table). John had also been a temporary worker, and, like Sundaram and Ilaiyaraja, lost his job. John went to Coimbatore with his parents in 1997. He has two older sisters and one younger sister. All of them were married to workers' families in tea estates in the Peermade tea belt. In Coimbatore, John became an assistant to plumber Murugan who had moved out of plantations in the late 1980s. After one year of training, John became an independent plumber in 1998 and is now a popular plumber in the area. According to him, he was busy and he didn't need to beg for work. He made around Rs.15,000 per month and supported his entire family; his father died three years ago, his mother is too old to work and his wife cannot find 'suitable' (non-manual labour) work. He has a son and a daughter aged 14 and 12 respectively and both are studying in a Christian management school. Despite John's success he said he had to lie about his caste (or he had to pretend to be a person of higher caste) to become friends with the upper caste petty capitalists in the industrial town of Coimbatore. It is these petty capitalists who provide work for John.

As mentioned, Karuppasamy and Selvam, the elder brothers of Sundaram and Ilaiyaraja stayed on at the plantations. Karuppasamy inherited his father's status as a permanent manual worker. His wife, Maria, is also a permanent worker and she inherited the work from her mother. Both Selvam and his wife are also permanent workers. The flip side is that Karuppasamy and Selvam do not earn half as much as their younger siblings outside the plantations. Selvam told me that the lack of money is a major problem when it comes to 'major spendings' such as hospital expenses, education of children, weddings, and ritualised gift exchanges. Both of them said that they have considered leaving the plantations on many occasions, but did not want to go back to their native villages. The relative protection from caste discrimination is something that needs to be considered as a positive effect of being in the plantation, despite the lower income.

The three ex-temporary workers Sundaram, Ilaiyaraja and John have one thing in common in their otherwise different trajectories outside the plantations: they now all experience *overt* caste discrimination, whereas the caste discrimination they faced in the plantations was of a more structural, much less overt, kind.

CASTE DISCRIMINATION: INSULT TO INJURY

Tamil Dalit workers in the plantations have a long history of marginal-isation, discrimination and stigma though the ways in which it has been experienced has changed over time. They came to the Kerala plantations as indentured labourers, often escaping the extreme direct oppression of caste discrimination in their native villages in Tamil Nadu, but within the Kerala context their status was also inferior to that of most other groups. The fact that they were Dalits combined with other aspects of their identity.

The vulnerability of being located at the bottom of the caste hierarchy as well as at the bottom of the class structure is magnified by anti-Tamil prejudice in Kerala – something that also affects other Tamil groups in Kerala such as Iyers, Vellalas and Tamil Muslims,[47] but far less so as these groups are integrated into the generalised identity of *Keraliyar*. However, for the Dalit Tamils of the plantations the Tamil identity is strongly marked by their origin as indentured labourers (effectively slaves), which gives them a near-permanent status as migrants; by their outcaste identity; and by being from the 'wild' highlands rather than from the settled and 'civilised' lowland valleys. This combines to give them low, stigmatised, social/cultural worth. Thus, hostility towards the Tamil minority in Kerala, in the main, is directed towards the estate communities and other Tamils perceived to be migrants from Tamil Nadu.

For example, the Tamil community in the Peermade tea belt was a major victim of a dispute between Tamil Nadu and Kerala over the Mullaperiyar dam, located at the border between the two states. They were soft targets for abuse whenever they travelled into the Malayali-dominated valleys, especially at the peak of the protests in Kerala against Tamils in November–December 2011. Some were beaten in the towns where they worked. During the protests gangs of Malayali youths went searching for Tamils arriving on buses at the valley towns. One Tamil estate worker who narrowly escaped being beaten told me, 'We Tamils had better learn to speak good Malayalam for self-protection. If we speak in Malayalam fluently, we could escape in the disguise of Malayali identity. We should be careful to give our children Malayali sounding names.' He said this with sarcasm as he escaped an attack by speaking Malayalam relatively well. Those from the Tamil plantations working in the small cardamom and tea plantations in the Udumbancholai region were beaten and were chased over the border into the Tamil Nadu town of Cumbum. The Tamils who owned agricultural land in the nearby areas were also terrorised and told not to return. Migrant workers from Tamil Nadu who came to Kerala to work in the construction industry in the valley towns were also beaten.

Within the plantations, the low position of the plantation workers is cemented by their educational levels, which are well below Kerala standards. Even for the better-educated plantation workers, stigmatisation and discrimination create obstacles to socioeconomic mobility within the plantation system. For example, in the Hill Valley estate, only if the workers' families are much better educated than the managerial staff's family members may they be considered for clerical jobs. Educational parity (or even slightly more than that) is not enough for someone from the workers' community to move up into the managerial staff position in the plantation system.

Moreover, field officer/factory manager positions within the plantations are mostly the domain of the higher castes, despite their small numbers in the plantation workforce. A few Dalits do get promoted to supervisory level, though usually only in the last two or three years of their service, but there is only one Dalit who used to work at the managerial level as an assistant field officer, the lowest rank at the managerial level. He was transferred to another estate in the middle of my fieldwork. While the percentage of high caste households is only around 8 per cent, their share in the semi-skilled workforce is 40 per cent (see Table 3.4). While I have not done systematic fieldwork in other estates in the tea belt, I have a general impression that this statistic (8–10 per cent of workforce of non-Dalits occupying 40–50 per cent of semi-skilled positions) is similar for other estates as well.

The Dalit assistant field officer, when asked about the possibility of promotion, told me that he would become field officer within two or three years but that he would not be promoted to assistant manager or manager because of the strong Syrian Christian network at the higher ladder of the management. For example, more than 60 per cent of the managerial staff are Syrian Christians in the ABH Plantations, another tea company in the Peermade tea belt whose owner is a Syrian Christian. So, the aspiration of Dalits to climb the higher ladder of estate management is often thwarted by the network of high caste Hindus/Syrian Christians.

Outside the plantations, the Tamil Dalits were able to get semi-skilled work as drivers and mechanics, but they were not able to enter into positions such as being clerks. They were also not able to get local self-government (*panchayat*) nominated assignments, such as contract clerks, contract drivers for hospitals, and office peons and sweepers of the local panchayat.[48] Unlike other caste groups, they do not have the networks required, and they lack the functional literacy which is necessary to assert themselves in the labour market. More importantly maybe, their identity as Tamil Dalits is stigmatised within Kerala society. The popular belief in Kerala is that Tamil Dalits are better at hard manual labour than the local Malayalis but that the Malayalis are better with their brains, and such stereotypes affect the way Tamils are appropriated into the labour market. The Malayali Dalits are located in between the Tamil Dalits and upper caste Malayalis in the categorical relations, as many of the Malayali Dalits would identify the Tamil Dalits as below them in hierarchical relations of ethnicity.

There were instances of the Tamil Dalits leaving work because of discrimination and humiliation. Makenthiran, a 21-year-old who worked as concrete specialist for a construction contractor in the valley town of Erumeli, had borne the brunt of jibes from his Malayali co-workers that he shared a room with in Kanjirapally town. One evening after work everyone got drunk, and began to call Makenthiran a '*pandi*'. 'Pandi' is an ethnic slur that refers to Tamils in Kerala and portrays the Tamils as 'uncivilised'. The term can be applied to all the Tamils, but is specifically used to refer to Tamil Dalits.[49] Makenthiran was provoked by the continuous abuse and reacted by engaging in a nasty fight with one of the co-workers. While others intervened and stopped the fight, the Malayali workers began to maintain a 'safe distance' (as Makenthiran calls it) from him. This led to psychological distress for Makenthiran, and he decided to return to the plantations.

The case of plantation Tamil Dalits in Tiruppur is, as I have argued earlier, even more distressing. The fear of caste discrimination is so severe that most Tamil Dalits from the Kerala plantations in Tiruppur hide their caste identity; I didn't come across anyone who revealed his or her caste identity. Workers told me that revealing their Dalit identity would affect their possibilities of getting a skilled/semi-skilled job. A senior finance manager of a large firm told me that nepotism is a major operator when it comes to appointments and that Dalits would not be considered even for clerical positions.

I came across other Dalits from Tamil Nadu villages hiding their real caste identity in Coimbatore and Tiruppur. But it is more difficult for them. The plantation Tamils can take advantage of the fact the Tamil high castes have little knowledge of the caste hierarchy and practices in Kerala. The plantation Dalits claim to belong to higher castes from Kerala (for example, they claim to be Christian Nadars) and will hide details of their ancestral villages and their relatives in Tamil Nadu to limit the chance of getting caught. Those who hide their caste have a better chance of getting a job or a house for rent than those who cannot or will not hide it. I met six families who became successful in getting a house in streets dominated by upper caste people simply because they lied about their caste. I also met with 17 families who returned to their ancestral villages in Tirunelveli district of Tamil Nadu. They shared with me stories of 'culture shock' as there they were confronted with caste insults and violence of a kind they had not experienced back in the plantations. They also had to use the public water tap and purchase their groceries at the Public Distribution System ration shop at separate times from the higher caste villagers, and faced caste segregation in the use of separate temples and burial grounds from the higher castes.

ADIVASI SEASONAL MIGRANT CASUAL LABOUR: FROM EASTERN INDIA TO KERALA'S TEA PLANTATIONS

As the Tamil Dalits leave the Kerala tea plantations, the plantation owners deploy a strategy often used by capital – as also shown in the next chapter in this book – to cut the cost of production and undermine the power of labour: they bring in more vulnerable seasonal migrant workers from poorer regions. Adivasi migrant workers from Jharkhand and Muslim workers from Assam form the majority among this new workforce in the Peermade tea belt. There are also workers from Odisha who were brought in to work

Photo 3 Adivasi migrant labour returning to Jharkhand, waiting at a bus stop
Photo by Jayaseelan Raj.

for smaller estates that cultivate tea, cardamom and coffee. All the migrant workers are maintained, illegally, as casual labour.

My own field research related to the new seasonal migrant labourers of Auburn Tea's Top View estate where Santhali, Munda and Lohra migrants from Godda and Dumka districts of Jharkhand were based. Here they formed almost a quarter of the total plantation workforce. In April 2015, there were 30 families and 12 individual Adivasis from Jharkhand (nine male and three female) at the Top View estate. The Jharkhand workforce constituted 23 per cent of the total workforce (57 workers out of 232).

Many of these workers had relatives in other estates as well, and many of them had worked as migrant workers in other parts of India before coming to the Top View estate. They had worked in road building in Kashmir and Himachal Pradesh, in the construction industry in Delhi and Bangalore, in sharecropping in West Bengal, and in meat processing industries in Pune. Some were educated and I found one casual labourer with an undergraduate degree in physics. Around ten families, all from the Santhal and Munda tribes, owned land back in Jharkhand where the cultivation was done by their family members. The landowning families came to the plantations for many reasons, including to make enough money to pay the daily wages of hired workers in their fields back home. Most of the landless families among the Jharkhandi migrants belonged to the Lohras, classified as a Scheduled Caste in Jharkhand. They migrated to different places across India as the scope for their traditional occupation as blacksmiths had declined over the years.

In March–April 2016, I visited the Dumka and Godda districts in Jharkhand for two weeks.[50] These are among the most 'backward districts' in the country.[51] Most of the migrant workers were from two villages called Jheratti and Sakri in Dumka and Godda districts respectively. The field visit was a follow-up of the fieldwork and interviews I had already carried out among the Jharkhandi workforce in the plantation. It specifically focused on further understanding of the factors that facilitated the migration of this workforce.

Santhals and Lohras were the two communities in both villages, and there were also a few Munda families in Sakri village. Around 30 Muslim families lived on the outskirt of Jheratti who were not part of the migrant labour force. The Muslims owned land and also owned petty businesses in the region such as brick kilns. The Adivasi Santals and Mundas owned most of the land while the Lohras were landless. However, landownership did not generate significant class divisions because the paddy from land was only enough for the annual consumption of the families who shared the land. They were able to cultivate only one, rain-fed, crop, as irrigation facilities in Jharkhand are poor and there is also a low-lying and receding ground water table. The rice is planted in June–July and harvested in October. The rice cultivation therefore requires only two to three months of work and all village[52] households had to seek work outside during the rest of the year. The landowners did not produce surplus rice for cash transactions, and therefore had to migrate for work just like the landless families.

There was very little non-agricultural employment available in the villages and the wages were also low, less than Rs.120 for women and Rs.150 for men. The daily wage for manual labour in the nearby towns was slightly better (Rs.200), but such work was not considered viable by the villagers because travelling to the towns would cost them more than the difference in the pay. National Rural Employment Guarantee Act work was paid a daily wage of Rs.159, but was only sporadically available.

The migration to the plantation was a new addition to a long history of migration in the area. The villagers were brought to the plantation by a Syrian Christian contractor who happened to be a friend of a managerial staff of the Top View estate. The contractor charged a commission of Rs.20 from each worker per day. This is an extortionate reward for simply being the middle man between the workers and the employer – more than the Rs.5–10 that most labour contractors received in the Cuddalore village we studied (see the next chapter) and less than the 15–20 per cent of the daily earnings that the labour contractor charged from the Bhil seasonal migrants from Nandurbar in Maharashtra (see Thakur's chapter). At the Top View estate, this commission was brought to an end after one year as the plantation got rid of the contractor following a petition from the Jharkhandi workers.

There are three major reasons for the recruitment of the new workers. It is the case that, as Tamil Dalits are leaving the plantations in greater numbers, the planters often face labour shortages during the high season. Second, and perhaps more significantly, the 'social cost of production' of Adivasi migrant labour from Jharkhand is extremely low compared to the social cost of the production for the Dalit Tamils, as the Jharkhandi workers are kept as casual workers while most of the Tamil Dalit workers have permanent status. This denial of temporary or permanent work status for the migrant labour means that they do not have the provident fund, annual leave, medical leave and other benefits that are provided to the permanent and temporary workforce. In Top View estate, although the recruitment of Jharkhandi Adivasi workers began in 2011, by September 2015 not even one of them had been promoted to temporary worker status. While many Jharkhandi workers left after 8 or 10 months of work, there were a few who had stayed for more than two years which, formally, entitled them to become permanent workers while those who had stayed for shorter periods should have been temporary workers. While the Dalit Tamils are also exploited, their permanent/

temporary worker status shields them from the super-exploitation faced by the Jharkhandi workers.

The final reason why planters are recruiting this new seasonal migrant labour force is that the Adivasi workers can be better controlled (or 'tamed' to borrow a term from Jan Breman [1989]) compared to the Dalit Tamil workers, specifically as casual labourers. Their lack of recognition in the plantation production system leaves them totally vulnerable as it also denies them facilities and welfare measures outside work. Their living quarters were of poor quality and very cramped. The condition of workers' line houses is bad in general in the estate but the better ones were provided to the Tamil Dalits, while the Jharkhand workers received only the 'left-over' houses. In addition, two Jharkhandi families had to share each small tenement house: they were provided only a 'half house', not the 'full house'.

They also do not have access to the subsidised ration of rice, sugar and kerosene which is provided through the Public Distribution System ration shops for workers who are registered as residents locally. They often demanded that the estate provide them with a certificate of residence in order to apply for the transfer of their ration card but to no avail. Moreover, hospital facilities are available only in the nodal town since the company had reduced facilities in the local clinic citing the economic crisis. Although they have access to schools, only one child out of at least ten Adivasi children attended local school. The workers told me that they were not sending their children to school because the medium of language is Tamil and Malayalam. Many workers had therefore left their children to be educated back in Jharkhand.

The linguistic alienation also led to their alienation from trade unions and subsequent inability to negotiate facilities due to the plantation workforce. They did not have membership in any trade unions. The trade union conveners in the Top View estate told me that the Jharkhand workers were not part of the trade union because they were casual workers, and that since many of them do not stay longer than ten months they could not be considered as part of the organised workforce. During my fieldwork, I noted that the Jharkhand workers were not part of any protest meetings in the estate. In fact, a clash between the local trade union leaders and the Jharkhand workers escalated when the latter went to work while the trade union called for a strike in the estate. I was told by a local supervisor that the trade union leaders did not inform the Jharkhand workers about the strike, and therefore they went to work in the field. The supervisor added that the trade union leaders do not speak Hindi and therefore were unable to communicate with the Jharkhand workers.

While the Tamil Dalits had also lost welfare provisions and suffered in the crisis-ridden plantations, they were part of the trade unions and had been able to sustain certain important positions, such as their temporary or permanent work status. The Adivasis from Jharkhand, in contrast, were unable to negotiate with the management or trade unions and *de facto* had no social and legal protection. In sum, the new seasonal migrant workers from poorer parts of India have become a super-exploited labour force that occupies the lowest, most precarious and vulnerable rung in the informal casual occupational ladder of the plantation economy.

THE STRUGGLES FROM BELOW

I have argued in this chapter that a crisis in the global tea economy ushered in neoliberal reforms that led to a casualisation of the workforce in the tea plantations of Kerala. Tamil Dalit workers had been brought in as indentured labourers in the colonial period but, over the decades, they won a modicum of security and protection in their low-paid manual labour jobs in the tea industry. With the crisis, as the plantations came under new regimes of control, labour rights were slashed, vacancies were not filled, permanent workers were replaced by temporary ones and, on many plantations, an illegal casual seasonal migrant labour force from poorer parts of the country was brought in. These changes meant that Tamil Dalit youths increasingly sought work outside the tea plantations in the urban areas of Kerala or back in Tamil Nadu in the manufacturing and garment sectors in Coimbatore and Tiruppur, and even in their ancestral villages in Tamil Nadu. In these new sites of work, while they often earned more money than back in the plantations, they were also subject to new insecurities as they joined the masses who make up India's informal economy. Moreover, while their structural position in the plantations was based on their historical class and caste position, it was only when they left the plantations that they faced overt caste discrimination to the extent that, significantly, almost everyone who went to work in Tiruppur tried to hide their caste. Back in the plantations, the increasingly precarious workforce was feminised, as it was Tamil Dalit women who were left to pick tea. The power of the local plantation labour was further undermined as the planters brought in a super-exploitable seasonal casual migrant workforce who, in the areas where I conducted fieldwork, were Adivasis from Jharkhand.

One would have hoped that the trade unions and the labour departments of the state (inspector of plantations or labour officers) would have challenged or prevented the casualisation of the workforce. Legally (according to the Plantation Labour Act of 1951), casual labour may only be used in the plantations to fulfil tasks outside the daily routine of the plantations and not for the routine work or picking tea – which is what the migrant labour is used for. However, the plantation companies, backed by the trade unions and local officials of the labour department (inspector of plantations and deputy labour officer), deny this migrant workforce not only permanent but also temporary status.

Kerala has historically been hailed for its public action[53] and working-class movements/trade unions.[54] The plantation labour had won certain rights through the Plantation Labour Act and largely through the action of trade unions. Today there are four trade unions in the tea belt that are affiliated to different parties – the Communist Party of India (CPI), Communist Party of India (Marxist) (CPI(M)), Indian National Congress and Bharatiya Janata Party. The trade union leaders wield tremendous influence over plantation production and are the purveyors of politics in the plantation. It is the trade unions, rather than political parties, that link the workers' association with the electoral politics in Kerala. They are the ones who negotiate with the plantation management regarding the bonus rate, working conditions and any other disputes that arise in plantation production. It is also the trade union leaders who decide who should be promoted from temporary work status to permanent work status.

Plantation workers in Kerala have historically been relatively better served than workers in plantations elsewhere in India. However, the trade unions, I will argue here, have degenerated. There are several aspects to this. In the context of the crisis the trade unions became involved in the structuring of new patterns of control and work, rather than unifying the workers to radically resist the restructurings. Thus they became agents of the social and political fragmentation of the workers and added to their economic distress. Neilson and Pritchard (2009) note in their recent study that trade union leaders skimmed profits for their own individual and party-political purposes by charging dubious commissions as a new 'cooperative' set-up of tea plucking was introduced, controlled by them. In line with others I argue that these changes were part of a wider emergence of a trade union bourgeoisie in Kerala and its role as a labour contractor that can hire and fire workers.[55]

The collective solidarity of the workers was also drastically affected by trade union-led factionalism and divide-and-rule policies. Polarisation among the workers with different trade union affiliations grew when the tea fields were divided up and organised on the basis of trade union affiliation. For instance, in one of the estates, three major trade unions (Central Indian Trade Union – CITU, INTUC – Indian National Trade Union Council and AITUC – All India Trade Union Council) divided the tea fields into three areas on the basis of the number of workers affiliated to each trade union. The total workforce was divided into three union work groups and the workers' wages depended upon the collective quantity and quality of the tea leaves picked by that group. This solution, which was meant to 'save' the tea plantations, thus created new divisions and factionalism between the workers of different trade unions.

Underlying all this is the fact that the workers did not have their own representatives in the unions and consequently were relegated to marginal positions in plantation politics. Trade union leaders in Kerala were neither plantation workers nor Tamils. The trade union leadership is primarily made up of non-Dalit Malayalam-speaking individuals and they have used the caste hierarchy to keep the plantation workers under control. Most of the trade union leaders from the district belong to Ezhava and Syrian Christian groups, and they have employed their sociocultural capital and networks to retain dominance in the trade union leadership. This is contrary to, for instance, what happened in the Tamil Nadu plantations (particularly in the plantations located around Tirunelveli and Udagamandalam) where the workers' discontent with the major trade union wings of Indian National Congress and Communist parties[56] led to the growth of trade union wings of Dalit political parties.

For the Adivasi seasonal casual migrant workforce there was not even the possibility of trade union membership. Rather than taking the lead in challenging the casualisation of the workforce and the plight of the Adivasis, one trade union leader in Peermade told me that the casual nature of the migrant workforce generates obstacles for providing membership to them in the unions.

However, to end this chapter on a note of optimism, towards the end of 2016, 8000 Kerala Tamil Dalit women workers in the Munnar tea belt defied the trade unions, the labour departments and the plantation owners in a remarkable and brave month-long strike to demand better terms and conditions of work. Keeping the trade union leaders at bay and even shouting slogans against the corruption of the union leaders, they demanded an annual bonus rate of 20 per cent, an increase in daily wage from Rs.232 to Rs.500, and proper implementation of welfare provisions in the plantations. The *Pembillai Orumai* strike prompted workers in other tea as well as rubber plantations in Kerala to take strike action against low wage and bonus rates. The media referred to the strike in Munnar as the 'Munnar Model' that was imitated across Kerala's plantation belt.

The Dalit women workers' strike posed a challenge not only to the tea companies and corrupt trade unions, but also to the acclaimed Kerala model of development and the ethnic stereotyping they faced within that model. Kerala has achieved human development goals comparable to economically advanced countries despite being economically poor, and its model has been highlighted as an alternative to the neoliberal development ethos emphasising free market policies. However, the 'pro-poor' policies of Kerala state have in large part left out the plantation workers. They did not benefit from land reforms of the 1960s and 1970s and have remained largely poor, landless labourers working within the exploitative plantation system. Moreover, the women plantation workers face intense triple discrimination in Kerala because they are Tamil, because they are Dalit, and because they are women.

As I have discussed elsewhere,[57] the plantation workers were relatively invisible within the development discourse of Kerala state, and they were not even acknowledged within the official list of outlier communities. The strike was headline news on the Malayalam and Tamil channels in South India, and English news channels such as NDTV and BBC had features on it. From 6 September to 20 October 2016, more than 30 per cent of news-hour discussions were allocated for the Munnar strike. Popular Malayalam weeklies such as *Mathrubhumi* and *Madhyamam*, and English weekly magazines such as *Frontline* and *Economic & Political Weekly*, published special articles on the strike. Both state- and national-level leaders of various political parties rushed to the site of the strike to have their support and solidarity recorded, solidarity groups were formed outside the tea belt and various activist groups outside established political parties wrote regular columns on the progress of the strike. A popular film director announced that he would be making a movie based on the strike.

The *Pembillai Orumai* strike led the trade unions to rethink their relations with the plantation workers. On the one hand, the state-level leaders of trade unions/political parties had to go to Munnar and declare that they were still with the workers. INTUC dismissed and dispersed the plantation federation of Munnar, and CITU – Communist Party of India (Marxist) – issued a statement declaring that the local leaders should be more conscious of the workers' issues and should have intervened earlier. Kodiyeri Balakrishnan, the state secretary of Communist Party of India (Marxist) declared that the party is with the workers, not with TATA Company.[58] The popular scholarly journal *Economic & Political Weekly* published two articles arguing that the strike exposed the miseries of tea workers across India, and that the workers should have a stake not only in the tea production but also in the larger, booming tourism industry. The government initiated a new monitoring system by which the inspectors of plantations have to update the labour conditions in tea plantations, including providing photos of the labour lines through the WhatsApp messaging system. The government announced a relief fund of Rs.50 lakh for the immediate improvement of labour lines in tea plantations. It was a major achievement of the strike that it succeeded in making visible the marginality of Kerala's tea workers[59] in the academic/ bureaucratic discourse, as a marginalised community.

In the end, mainstream political parties attempted to co-opt the women leaders. However, the collective solidarity and mobilisation of the women tea workers against the increasingly insecure conditions that were being brought right into their households as a result of neoliberal economic reforms is a poignant and powerful reminder that India's workers can and are trying to fight back.

Photo 4   Dalit women tea worker's strike
Photo by Jayaseelan Raj.

4

Cuddalore, Chemical Industrial Estate, Tamil Nadu

Brendan Donegan

Indian manufacturing is increasingly moving into rural locations, with major implications for social relations.[1] This chapter examines how conditions of Adivasis and Dalits and their positions within relations of inequality are changing while also being reinforced, in the context of a village that has seen an industrial estate grow around it over the past 30 years. The village I refer to as Melpuram (a pseudonym) is in Cuddalore district in Tamil Nadu, a southern state with one of the highest rates of factory employment in the country.[2]

As discussed for India as a whole in the opening chapter by Shah and Lerche, the processes of agrarian transition in Tamil Nadu that Adivasis and Dalits are part of are also taking place in ways that do not conform to models of urbanisation and industrialisation based on Britain's Industrial Revolution. There is not a large-scale movement of Adivasis, Dalits and other labourers from rural agriculture to urban industry in a process of proletarianisation. Instead, rural labouring classes are diversifying their activities and have moved away from an exclusive reliance on local agricultural wage labour towards combinations of agricultural and non-agricultural employment and self-employment, including temporary migration for work.[3] In this chapter we see the city and industry 'moving into the village', bringing employment opportunities that discourage out-migration, encourage in-migration, and create particularly fertile conditions for the transition of dominant caste landlord families into non-agricultural accumulation and new modes of dominance over the low caste groups who worked for them in the past.[4] In these circumstances, agrarian social structures and hierarchies with Adivasis and Dalits at the bottom adapt and persist instead of disappearing.[5]

The chapter is based on 12 months of ethnographic fieldwork conducted in Melpuram between 2014 and 2016. This fieldwork included detailed household surveys within the local Paraiyar Dalit community and a group who claim to be Irula Scheduled Tribe (this claim is contested by the District Administration), short household surveys among other local communities

(Nadar, Vanniyar, Gounder, Nattar, all of which are classified as Other Backward Classes [OBCs] by the central government), short individual surveys among migrant workers from the eastern and central Indian states of Odisha, Bihar, Jharkhand and West Bengal, as well as participant observation and life histories, genealogies and key informant interviews.[6]

Policy debates about industrialisation in rural areas often focus on losses and gains associated with the transition 'from field to factory', with particular stress on loss of access to land, related resources and agricultural livelihoods, and the question of whether local people get the jobs in industry they are often promised.[7] But an emphasis on loss of land needs to be tempered by an account of the impact of industrialisation on those who were landless,[8] not least Adivasis and Dalits. The question, 'Do local people get factory jobs?' that is often used to evaluate the local significance of industrialisation on people's livelihoods is too vague and needs to be replaced with more specific questions. Which factory jobs are obtained by which categories of people, under what terms and conditions, and why? How does the arrival of factory-based industrialisation change the life chances of Adivasis and Dalits and other groups of people over several generations, and why? And how does the impact of factory-based industrialisation on a specific locality extend beyond those who work in the factories?

Answering these questions in the context of this chemical industrial belt in India requires an explanation of why things turn out the way they do for Adivasis and Dalits. As this book shows across the chapters, for that the focus must be on the social and economic relations that Adivasis and Dalits are part of and not solely on Adivasis and Dalits themselves. I argue that in the villages in and around the State Industries Promotion Corporation of Tamil Nadu (SIPCOT) Industrial Complex in Cuddalore district, accumulation and class relations are constituted through the interaction of diverse elements which are shaped by caste: pre-existing patterns of social relations within and between particular sites of production and social reproduction; the possibility of creating new connections between sites (for example, by tapping into the immense labour pool of migrant workers from 'northern' states [as the east and central Indian states from which the migrant workers come are called locally], whose presence has become significant in Cuddalore and other parts of Tamil Nadu over the past decade); and the existence and (non-)implementation of governmental policies and programmes (with aims including enabling and regulating markets, protecting labour and the environment, affirmative action and social welfare). Clearly certain actors are dominant in this locality, but I also hope to show that there is more to this than mere dominance.

To some observers who have made a quick visit to the industrial estate, SIPCOT Cuddalore (as it is known) supports a simplistic narrative of corporate rule: big landlords ruled this region in the past, the factories rule it now.[9] However, my findings suggest a more complex picture. In the past, the dominant actors locally were big landlords who belonged to particular caste groups and employed labour from other caste groups (especially Dalits, Adivasis and OBC Vanniyars) to work in their fields. Today the factories employ local Dalits and Vanniyars through local labour contractors, the most powerful of whom belong to the big landlord families. Thus, rather than a simple transfer of power from big landlords to companies, what has happened in Cuddalore is better understood as a shift from dominant caste landlord capital to industrial capital *mediated* by local actors who were dominant in the old agrarian order. As argued in the opening chapter, this is a pattern in other parts of the country too. There is a sense in which industrialisation can be seen as contributing to a *fragmentation* of dominance, insofar as power previously concentrated in the hands of the small number of families who controlled most of the agricultural land is now slightly more dispersed. At the same time, the ongoing centrality of these families in the organisation of the local labour market contributes to – and is enabled by – the continuing significance of caste as a core structuring aspect of labour relations both locally and in India more generally.

The factories plug this corner of India into global production networks. One of the most important connections between the village of Melpuram and the 'global level' is the complex of buildings the villagers refer to as 'the bone factory'. Located a short walk from Melpuram, its production processes are audible in the village, day and night, as a background hum. The bone factory has been central to Melpuram's economy since its construction in the early 1990s. The company acquires bones of cows, oxen, bullocks and camels from all over India and processes them to produce gelatine (used in the production of foods, photographic film, cosmetics, medicine capsules and explosives), as well as ossein and dicalcium phosphate (used in poultry feed). All outputs are packaged, driven to Chennai, then flown to Japan, the location of the next stage of production in this global value chain. The global gelatine market is characterised by high demand from food processing and pharmaceutical industries, and a recent report predicts strong growth in the market between now and 2020, with the fastest growth rates in the Asia Pacific.[10]

This chapter develops the arguments outlined above through an empirical account of Melpuram, and is organised as follows. Section two provides a historically and regionally contextualised account of Melpuram today, focusing on productive activities and their distribution by caste. Section three discusses Melpuram's past and the changes it has experienced since the arrival of the factories in the 1980s, beginning with a general discussion, turning to non-Dalits and non-Adivasis, and then to Dalits and

Adivasis. Section four provides a detailed analysis of caste and occupations, while section five discusses the relationship between the bone factory and Melpuram, covering immediate relations of production as well as wider relations of caste, class, discrimination and exploitation, and struggles. A final section concludes.

Photo 5   SIPCOT Industrial Estate, Cuddalore, Tamil Nadu
Photo by Alpa Shah.

MELPURAM AND TAMIL NADU: AN OVERVIEW

Tamil Nadu is often presented as a success story of a *humane* development model that contrasts with the so-called 'Gujarat model'. While both states have managed to secure strong economic growth rates, Tamil Nadu has done so alongside strong welfare policies that have reached even the most marginalised groups – so that, for example, 'Infant Mortality Rate for Dalits in Tamil Nadu was 37 per cent, while the corresponding figure for India stands at 66 per cent'.[11] Pandian and Kalaiyarasu suggest that it is the 'competitive populism' of the two Dravidian parties at the heart of Tamil Nadu's electoral politics (Dravida Munnetra Kazhagam or DMK, the Dravidian Progress Federation, and All India Anna Dravida Munnetra Kazhagam or AIADMK, the All India Anna Dravidian Progress Foundation) that led to the state government's attention to 'the needs of the common people',[12] while in contrast, a single party has been in power in Gujarat continuously since 1995 (the Bharatiya Janata Party). Pandian and Kalaiyarasu (2013) suggest that one of the tangible outcomes of the state's 'growth plus social justice' model is the state's literacy rate, which in 2011 was 80.33 per cent, positioning Tamil Nadu in third place among the major states, after Kerala and Maharashtra. At the same time Tamil Nadu is, nevertheless, a more unequal society than states such as Kerala and Himachal Pradesh.

The position of Dalits and Adivasis in Tamil Nadu today reflects the size of these population groups and the long shadow cast by the agrarian history of the state. Dalits currently comprise 19 per cent and Adivasis 1 per cent of Tamil Nadu's population,[13] their relative electoral significance reflected in the extent to which the Dalit vote is courted by the parties competing in the state, and the Adivasi vote is not. Tamil Nadu's successful 'humane development' means the state's Dalit and Adivasi populations score better than Dalits and Adivasis in most other states on income poverty and a range of socioeconomic indicators, and even score better than castes classified as OBCs and general castes in some states, such as Uttar Pradesh, Telangana and Jharkhand.[14]

Bugge's (1994) account of the Coromandel Coast south of Madras (now Chennai, capital of Tamil Nadu) during the pre-colonial and colonial periods emphasises two features relatively absent from other parts of South India. First, commerce, with the ports of Cuddalore and Porto Novo (located a few kilometres to the north and south of my study village, respectively) playing an important role in the international network of trade that covered the Indonesian Archipelago and South China Sea.[15] Second, relatively free and mobile labour, as the pre-colonial rule of the Mughal *nawab* of Arcot (as the region was then known) had contributed to the decline of agricultural bondage prevalent in many other parts of South India.[16] Labour migration during the last decades of the nineteenth century also contributed to the relatively positive position of agricultural labour. Large numbers of agricultural labourers from South Arcot (which split into Cuddalore district and Villupuram district in 1993) migrated to Ceylon or coffee plantations in Coorg and the Nilgiris. While it is possible that some of this labour – in particular low caste Dalit labour – may have stayed on as plantation labour as in the case of the Tamil Dalit plantation labour that is the subject of the preceding chapter of this book, others returned after a few years with sufficient money to buy land and settle as smallholders.[17]

Nevertheless, colonial reports indicate that labour in South Arcot was only *relatively* free: approximately one-third of agricultural labourers in that part of Tamil Nadu were slaves under the *padiyal* (farm servant) system of debt bondage in the second decade of the twentieth century.[18] Most of these agricultural labourers belonged to two caste communities: Paraiyar Dalits (now classified as Scheduled Caste) and Vanniyars (now classified as OBC). South Arcot had the highest concentration of Dalits of any district in Madras Presidency at the end of the nineteenth century,[19] and colonial reports suggest it is likely that most of the padiyals were Dalit.[20]

Over the last three decades, the predominantly agricultural, rural district of Cuddalore has experienced significant industrialisation and urban expansion. As recently as the 1980s this region was one of the biggest rice-producing regions of South India, and to this day agriculture remains a major part of the local economy, with the 2001 Census of India listing more than 80 per cent of workers in rural Cuddalore as cultivators (24 per cent) and agricultural labour (57 per cent). In the early 1980s, the state government began constructing an industrial estate south of Cuddalore town (population 173,676 in 2011): the SIPCOT Industrial Complex, consisting of 26–29 factories[21] manufacturing pesticides, pharmaceuticals, chemicals, plastics, dyes and textiles. Sandwiched between a major north–south highway (the East Coast Road) and the river Uppanar, this is one of the most highly polluted industrial clusters in the country. The future of this region appears to involve further industrialisation and urbanisation.[22]

The village of Melpuram discussed in this chapter straddles the East Coast Road a few kilometres south of Cuddalore town. Melpuram has factories to its north and south, a railway track and the Uppanar River as its western and eastern limits. The railway, highway and river all run north–south, parallel to the coast, which is barely 2 km east of the river. For the purposes of this chapter, the territory within these limits comprises three elements: east of the East Coast Road lies a multi-caste settlement comprising residential streets arranged around a large Draupati Amman temple, while to the west there are agricultural fields and a settlement called Swami Nagar where the Irula Adivasis live.

The multi-caste settlement comprises approximately 120 Paraiyar Dalit households,[23] 60 Nattar households, 4 Nadar, 30 Gounder and 90 Padyachi Vanniyars, 3–4 Chettiar, 2 Naidu and 1 Muslim. The Gounders and Vanniyars of Melpuram operate as a single caste community today (and are treated as such in the quantitative analysis later in this chapter): in recent years Vanniyars have become wealthier and consequently marriage restrictions between these two castes have been relaxed. Thus, the two numerically dominant communities of the multi-caste settlement are Paraiyar Dalits and Vanniyars/Gounders – mirroring the fact that Paraiyar Dalits and Vanniyars have been the two numerically dominant communities in Cuddalore district since colonial times. Almost all the Dalits have small, dilapidated and airless concrete boxes that are supposed to serve as houses, courtesy of a government housing scheme for the poor in the 1990s. But most Dalits prefer to sleep and cook in thatch outhouses. In contrast, almost all houses in the multi-caste settlement are brick and concrete, more ornate, larger, airier and sturdier constructions. Most roads in the village are concrete.[24]

Swami Nagar comprises 126 households inhabited by families who claim to be Irula Adivasis. Swami Nagar residents, and social activists who have attempted to organise the Irula community in Cuddalore, told me Swami Nagar is one of only six settlements of Irulas in the district. The District

Administration, however, claims there are no Irulas in Cuddalore, and refuses to grant Irula Scheduled Tribe certificates to Swami Nagar residents for that reason. Almost all the houses in Swami Nagar are identical concrete boxes that follow a design that is marginally superior to those found in the Dalit colony (larger, with a raised veranda and stairs leading to the roof). These houses were built using government funds for post-tsunami relief, secured by a Chennai-based social activist who was, at that time, funded by the UK-based charity ActionAid UK. Like the multi-caste settlement, Swami Nagar has concrete roads, electricity and many water taps, but these amenities are very recent, having arrived in the past five years.

The nearby 'bone factory' employs more than one-third (35 per cent) of Melpuram's working male Paraiyar Dalits and 22 per cent of Melpuram female Dalits. For the men, the work consists of three main roles: 'packers', 'loaders' and 'tank workers'. Packers fill sacks. Loaders carry heavy (70–80 kg) sacks of bones and chemicals from trucks to storage facilities and conveyor belts, and carry sacks of end products (the chemicals sent to the factory in Japan, as well as waste) from conveyor belts to storage facilities to trucks. Tank workers serve the large tanks where bones are washed in acid to remove meat, climbing down into the tanks after the liquid has been drained in order to pack the bones in sacks and clean the tank. Dalit women sweep and clean, and also work alongside some of the men, sorting the good bones from bad. One hundred Dalits, Adivasis and OBC people from Odisha and West Bengal reside in Melpuram and work in the bone factory, carrying out many of the same tasks as male Paraiyar Dalits but also heaving coal for the factory's boiler. Taking into account both livelihoods and assets, the majority of Tamil Dalits and Adivasis and migrant workers are poor, the majority of Vanniyars, Gounders, Nattars and Nadars are middle income, and members of the big Nadar landlord family are rich. The following sections discuss the processes contributing to this distribution of livelihoods and assets in Melpuram.

FROM FIELD TO FACTORY: A BRIEF SOCIAL HISTORY

All caste communities in Melpuram trace the history of the village back to the arrival of the first Nadar in the early twentieth century. The Nadar community are an example of a low caste (but not Untouchable) community that successfully challenged and shifted their position within the caste hierarchy.[25] The Nadar community made this shift after moving into profitable fields of business and in a manner not unlike the Marwaris in North India, 'exploited emerging possibilities for education, employment, and legal and political contestation'[26] and adopted the practices of higher castes while also confronting them with violence when necessary. The father of the first Nadar of the village produced toddy (palm liquor) in Tirunelveli district, 400 km south-west of Cuddalore. A drought pushed him northwards to Cuddalore where he bought a toddy shop in Melpuram through government auction, and started producing toddy in 1935. People say he became wealthy by selling toddy to local people who got addicted, became indebted and lost their land to him.

A more general account of the area was given by a Vanniyar man from a neighbouring village who claimed that the British acquired most of the land in this area from Brahmin landlords and gave it to Reddys, Nadars and Chettiars (all non-Brahmin communities closely connected with British rule in Madras Presidency). When the Reddys and Chettiars living in and around Melpuram moved into town, they sold their land to the Nadars. This narrative fits with the historical record, which describes the Nadar community as an important force in the Tamil non-Brahmin movement in the first half of the twentieth century, which 'tapped into British unease over the preponderance of Brahmins in office, and appealed to widespread resentment of Brahmin domination and arrogance'.[27]

The first Nadar's sons owned at least 170 acres between them, in and around Melpuram. Vanniyars and Dalits claim that some of this land was acquired from Vanniyars and Dalits pressured to sell at a low price set by the politically well-connected Nadars on whom they depended for work as agricultural labour. The police refused to intervene; the affairs of the village were managed by the Nadar big landlord family alone, who had total power because everyone else depended on this family for work and because of their wealth and political connections. Alongside their agricultural operations, the family operated a tollgate on the highway and owned the only rice mill in the area. One male descendant was an elected member of the Tamil Nadu Legislative Assembly for Cuddalore until 2001 and is high up in the Dravida Munnetra Kazhagam party, another is a famous Tamil film director and a third owns a five-star hotel in Chennai.

Almost all land in the village belonged to the Nadars, and most residents of the village worked as agricultural labour for the Nadars until the early 1980s, with the exception of the Nattar fishers, who caught fish in the river and sold them locally. Labour and housing was divided on caste lines: Paraiyars and Vanniyars lived in the multi-caste settlement east of the East Coast Road and worked as agricultural labour in Nadar-owned paddy fields, while the Irulas lived in isolated huts within Nadar coconut farms, working as bonded labour watchmen.

In the early 1980s, the Irulas collectively walked out of the coconut farms and set up home on a plot of land given to them by a competing powerful large landowner belonging to the Naidu caste. This happened in the aftermath of an incident in which an Irula accused of theft was tonsured, brutally whipped, painted black-and-red and paraded around local villages by his Nadar farm owner. The branch secretary of the All India Anna Dravida Munnetra Kazhagam in Melpuram's Dalit colony helped the Irulas approach a Naidu former village administrative officer whose family owned over 200 acres in and around Melpuram, and had been hereditary trustees of Melpuram's main temple for 300 years. The ex-administrative officer offered the Irulas work as free agricultural labour in his fields and a plot of land to build a settlement where they could live together. The Nadar coconut farm owners let them go because of the power of the ex-administrative officer's family.

Following a trend common to this part of Tamil Nadu, the past two decades have seen the Nadar landlord family selling off land to finance their move into non-agricultural accumulation; mostly the land has been bought by local Vanniyars. Today almost all Dalit and Irula households are still landless, many Vanniyar households own 1 or 2 acres, and a small number of Vanniyar households own 5 acres or more. They say that today it is difficult to make small-scale agriculture profitable, in part because of rising wages for agricultural labour. A number of factors explain the rise in agricultural wages, which is associated with improvements in the bargaining power of agricultural labour. Causes include the increasing availability of other work, state welfare programmes (including but not limited to the National Rural Employment Guarantee Act), and the work of new caste-based social movements and political parties defending the interests of the labouring castes, in particular the Vanniyar party, Pattali Makkal Katchi (PMK), and the Dalit party, the Viduthalai Ciruthaigal Katchi (Liberation Panther Party). Notably, there is no party actively working on behalf of the Irulas, but a number of non-governmental organisations and mass-membership organisations have taken up their cause in Cuddalore district.

Before the factories, limited transport and information about work elsewhere exacerbated the Nadar monopsony in the village labour market; at one time, the Nadar owned the only bullock cart in the village. The proximity of Melpuram to the highway meant that as bus services became more regular and affordable, possibilities for finding agricultural and non-agricultural wage employment outside the village improved, usually at better daily rates. While the Paraiyar Dalits took up low-skilled contract work in the factories adjacent to the village, the Irula Adivasis engaged in fishing, local construction work and migrating for manual work elsewhere, and the Vanniyars increasingly found employment in and around the factories as semi-skilled labour.

Agricultural practices changed in response. Many Vanniyars stopped employing agricultural labour, turning instead to family labour and reciprocal labour arrangements, and the Nadar big landlord family shifted from labour-intensive crops such as paddy and groundnut to cash crops that require less labour such as *savukku* (casuarina) and coconuts, and eventually mechanised parts of cultivation. Whereas before all male and female labourers in the village worked as agricultural labourers close to home throughout the year, they were now forced to find alternative sources of livelihood, which in turn led to a shift in labour availability. Instead of Paraiyars and Vanniyars waiting outside the Nadar's house each morning, landowners now needed to go looking for labour in the labourers' homes (the Nadars do not enter the Dalit colony themselves but find Dalits to make enquiries on their behalf).

Other factors also contributed to the decline in agricultural labour opportunities. First, large areas of land (particularly those located on the banks of the brackish and polluted waters of the estuary) are no longer under cultivation because the soil is contaminated as a result of the 2004 tsunami (which surged up the estuary dumping salt water on the land), excessive groundwater depletion and a decline in the water table due to the intensification of agricultural, industrial and urban usage, and pollution from the factories.[28] The related need for deep borewells to access useable water for cultivation was an added cost too far for many. Second, in recent decades agriculture has been getting less support from the state, in Tamil Nadu and in other parts of India.[29] Third, the National Rural Employment Guarantee Act improved the bargaining power of agricultural labour, particularly for Dalit female labour.[30]

At the time of my fieldwork in 2015, the factories operating in the SIPCOT Industrial Complex employed 2500 permanent staff (including 10–15 women working as receptionists or accountants), 1000 executives and engineers, and 4000 contract workers. Fifty to sixty registered labour contractors each send on average 50–60 contract workers to the factories. Of the 4000 contract workers, 750–1000 are from eastern India (locally referred to as 'North India').

Permanent staff are directly employed by the company, can join unions, and are hard to fire once they shift from a training contract to a regular contract. Low-skilled contract labourers work for registered contractors and cannot, in practice, join unions and can be replaced whenever the factory wishes. Permanent staff get a gratuity (Provident Fund), Employee's State Insurance (ESI), salary increments and are paid at least three times what low-skilled contract workers earn. Contract labourers sometimes get ESI; there are differing explanations for why some get it and others do not. In 2015 permanent staff earned upwards of Rs.750 per day, low-skilled contract workers earned Rs.170–270 per day, and semi-skilled contract workers (electricians, carpenters, painters, fitters) earned Rs.400–700 per day. This last category of workers is gradually growing relative to the permanent workers, as in recent years most companies in the industrial estate have been replacing permanent workers in these roles with contract workers, along similar lines to companies elsewhere in India.

The companies tend not to employ people from the villages in and around the industrial estate as permanent staff; the companies *do* employ local villagers as contract workers, but also began employing migrant workers from other states on a large scale five years ago (the companies sometimes explicitly ask a contractor to provide, for example, '20 North Indians'). This new development reflects the massive influx of migrant labourers from Assam, Bihar, Jharkhand, Odisha, Bengal, Uttar Pradesh and Nepal into Tamil Nadu over the past decade.[31] As highlighted in the opening chapter of this book, the factories aim to recruit labour that will not disrupt production: it is believed that local villagers may experience a conflict of interest between working for the factory and the pollution caused by the factory to their village, and it is believed that non-local workers are less likely to unite to defend their interests and more likely to accept longer hours for less money. The non-local workers tend to stay in the villages closest to the factories where they work.

The 'bone factory' operates along similar lines. It employs 75 permanent staff (including 25 office staff) and 400–450 contract workers, including 100 skilled manual 'technical' workers. It processes 70 metric tonnes of bones every single day, and it runs 24 hours a day and 365 days a year. It draws most of its contract workers from the villages in and around the industrial estate, but does not employ people from these villages in a direct employment relationship. Most of the directly employed, permanent staff (machine operators, supervisors, administrators) are Nadars from the Madurai region; villagers claim this is because its CEO is also a Madurai Nadar. Most of the semi-skilled contract workers (electricians, painters, fitters) are local Vanniyars. Seventy per cent of the low-skilled contract workers are Paraiyar Dalits, mostly from Melpuram and neighbouring villages. Very few Irula Adivasis work in the factory, something I will return to below. The large-scale employment of migrant contract labour began in 2008, following a strike of permanent employees and local contract workers, another point to which I will return.

Eleven of the twelve registered labour contractors who send workers to the bone factory are residents of Melpuram and neighbouring villages, and the last is from West Bengal. Four of these contractors are Paraiyar Dalit, four are Nadar, two are Gounder and one is Vanniyar.

By now it should be clear that the impact of the factories on the residents of Melpuram is more complex than either 'industrialisation is good because it brings jobs' or 'industrialisation is bad because local people do not get those jobs'. Instead, the benefits and costs associated with the industrial estate are distributed unevenly, along lines of caste, class and gender. In this way, industrialisation reproduces and sometimes exacerbates pre-existing inequalities and constraints on social mobility. At the same time, industrial-isation has substantially contributed to the reorganisation of social relations in a direction that is mostly satisfactory to many Melpuram residents, and perhaps most of all to the Paraiyar Dalits. A generation of Dalits have worked their whole lives as contract labour in the factories, doing work that is dangerous and poorly paid but that they nevertheless find preferable to the poverty and indignities their parents endured as agricultural labour in the fields of the Nadar landlord. However, improvements for the Dalits during this period were based on them being dependent on the factories for work because there was also in the same period a significant reduction in local opportunities for agricultural labour; if the factories were not there, the Dalits would either have to migrate for work or would really struggle to find sufficient work locally. This generational shift has contributed to weakening of the landlord family's authority and power, but – as the next three sections show – contemporary social relations in Melpuram remain intensely marked by historical patterns of inequality and dominance.

LIVELIHOODS IN MELPURAM TODAY: INEQUALITY AND DOMINATION

This section provides a breakdown of livelihoods and education by caste and gender, based on the surveys conducted (see Figures 4.1 to 4.4) and discusses the related relations of inequality, dominance and discrimination.[32]

Within Melpuram's Nadar community today, the big Nadar landlord family is still in a class of its own compared to all other villagers, holding most of the cards when it comes to wealth, power and connections. They still own significantly more land inside and outside Melpuram than any other family (most of it given over to coconuts). But accumulation today is on a wider scale and almost all the Nadars have moved out of the village into town, renting out parts of their sprawling houses to the bone factory, which uses these buildings to house migrant workers (Tamil permanent employees and contract labour from Odisha and West Bengal). Two male line descendants live in town but run lucrative coconut-related businesses based in Melpuram. After Cyclone Thane severely damaged their coconut farms in 2011, these brothers have been the principal beneficiaries of the Agriculture Department's decision to 'focus a lot on this village' (as one Nadar put it) in its post-Thane reconstruction efforts, which provided Melpuram's coconut farms with 'crib' (tubeline) irrigation, fertilisers, seeds and a plant nursery in 2014. In 2015 these brothers recruited men from Andhra Pradesh to husk coconuts in preference to employing local Paraiyar Dalits.

Photo 6   Dalit Woman by Dalit houses built through the government scheme
Photo by Brendan Donegan.

Two male line descendants of the first Nadar live in the village, and one man whose mother was part of the same family (this man is retired, and previously worked as a moneylender, lending money to all castes). All are well off but Siva's household stands out. Siva is a retired managerial level government employee and consultant and owns the village rice mill and 20 acres planted with coconut. He employs Dalits to tend his land, and his wife is a labour contractor sending 70 people, almost all Dalits, to the bone factory. She also manages a small canteen behind their house, which sends food to another factory, and rents out two buildings, one to the bone factory, which uses the building to house migrant workers from Odisha, and one to an Indian-owned multinational security company, which uses the building to house Bihari security guards who work in the factory where Siva's wife sends food. Siva and his wife have three children, none of whom live in the village. Their son is a safety engineer who has worked on projects across India. Their daughters are both also married to engineers; one is a software engineer in the USA where she lives, the other a college professor of engineering in Sivakasi, a town located in Nadar country in southern Tamil Nadu.

Members of the Vanniyar community are in a different position. In almost all households surveyed the husband is the main breadwinner and the wife either does National Rural Employment Guarantee Act work only or combines this with small petty business (flower or snack selling for a few hours a day); Vanniyar women claim they don't do other work because 'there is none available'. In most households the men do semi-skilled contract labour. This may be for the chemical factories – as electricians, carpenters, painters or welders – but is more likely to be an ancillary or unrelated business in town: car painting, car mechanics, construction, lorry supervisors (for factories but indirectly, through a contractor). However, they say they see the bone factory as particularly polluting and smelly, and prefer to work in other factories. A larger section of them work for two fish processing businesses located in Cuddalore town, owned by men who grew up in Melpuram. One is Gounder, the other is Nattar, and both employ dozens of people (many from Melpuram) and allegedly turn over tens of millions of rupees every fortnight. They 'export' fish within India; locally caught marine fish are packed in ice at their factories and then travel by lorry and train across the country. The contract workers operate the ice machines and unload and load fish and ice. The son of the Gounder fish processing businessman transports Vanniyar women to and from National Rural Employment Guarantee Act worksites in his father's Bolero jeep, and was recently gifted a Rs.900,000 custom Harley Davidson motorcycle by his father. In addition, the community say that other households who have been most successful in securing lucrative livelihoods have moved away to Cuddalore town. It might also be that some Vanniyar and other OBC households have moved away after getting government jobs and therefore that the occupational figures underestimate how successful these castes have been in getting such jobs.

The Nattar fishers used to be entirely autonomous from the Nadar-dominated agricultural economy that other communities in the village were tied into; they were able to catch and sell enough river fish to support themselves to a standard that was higher than the Vanniyars. They now say fish stocks are insufficient and it is likely that – as the Nattars claim – fish stocks are down because the companies discharge toxic effluents into the river. However, the changing fortunes of the fishers may also be a product of increased demands being made on the fish stocks because there are more Nattar fishers now than there were before. Many have moved into other types of work, mostly semi-skilled contract labour jobs in the factories. Two relatively well-off Nattars are the fish processing businessman (see above) and one of the two main priests in the main village temple (the other main priest is a Gounder). The priest is also secretary of the local Nattar caste association, and has three sons working as engineers in Chennai and abroad. There are several widows among the Nattar community who collect widows' pensions.

The Paraiyar Dalits, the poorest of the communities discussed so far in this section, are differentiated along gender, generational and class lines. Of all the men in the paid workforce, a third are low-skilled factory labour, but a lot of Dalit women also work in the factories (in contrast to all other castes in Melpuram, and also in contrast to the village discussed in Benbabaali's chapter in this volume, where only Dalit men worked in the factory). My interviews, focus group discussions and observations consistently indicate that a much larger proportion of Dalit women work than Vanniyar, Gounder or Nattar women.[33] National Rural Employment Guarantee Act work is mostly done by women belonging to the middle and oldest generations, and men belonging to the oldest generation.

Generational differences are stark. The oldest generation of Paraiyar Dalits (aged 60+ in 2015) did not go to school and worked their whole lives as agricultural labour for the Nadar, the middle generation (40–59) mostly had very limited schooling and worked as low-skilled contract labour in the factories, and the younger generation (20–39) have pursued education beyond 12th grade. Several of them have secured government employment (men only) or tried to gain semi-skilled work in the private sector.

The success in acquiring government jobs has led to class differentiation among the Dalits. While my survey data (based on 91 out of 120 Dalit households) shows only nine Dalits with government jobs, there are actually 27 Melpuram Dalits with government jobs, over half of them in the police. Their success is visible in the construction of large, ornately decorated and brightly coloured houses that provide a striking contrast to the other Dalits' drab brick-and-thatch government scheme houses. These more wealthy Dalits have formed a kind of middle class among the Dalits and express desire to distance themselves from their poorer brethren. 'We wouldn't want our children to learn the ways of their children,' one of them said. Poorer Dalits speak bitterly of how the new middle-class Dalits have abandoned the community. Many unmarried men in their early twenties focus their energies on preparations for the next round of exams for entry into the police, either avoiding manual work entirely or engaging in low-skilled contract work that they view as a temporary job, filling in the time before they secure government employment. Case histories of Dalits who have secured government employment suggest selection may involve more 'who you know' than merit. Two brothers have three sons with government jobs (two on the railway, one teacher) and two other sons working as semi-skilled contract labour in Dubai. In another family, the grandfather drove the Nadar landlord family's bullock cart, the father is high up in the Dravida Munnetra Kazhagam party in Cuddalore (recall that a member of the Nadar family was the Member of the Legislative Assembly representing this party for Cuddalore), and the eldest son was the first in the colony to secure a position in the police, ostensibly through the sports quota. Shortly thereafter, 15 other Melpuram Dalits got police jobs.

The government jobs have, however, not translated into improved access to government services for the community. For example, and in contrast to the Nattar fishers, Dalit widows do not get widow's pension and they do not even try to claim it as they believe there is no chance they will get it.

The Irula Adivasi development trajectory is quite different. Only the younger generation have received any schooling, only two individuals have pursued education beyond 12th grade, and female education is much lower than that of males (see Figures 4.3 and 4.4). Across the generations *no one* has managed to secure work that moves them from the low-skilled to the semi-skilled category. Most Irulas do a combination of fishing, agricultural labour and construction, and many of them only work 10–15 days in a month, unlike the Paraiyar Dalits, most of whom work six days a week. Very few of them do low-skilled factory labour.

The refusal of the district collector to issue them with an Irula caste certificate means they cannot avail themselves of either government jobs or college seats reserved for Scheduled Tribes. One Irula woman, whose father was the leader of the Irula Caste Association for Cuddalore district and a former headman of Swami Nagar, succeeded in getting an Irula caste certificate (after a hunger strike and threatening self-immolation in front of the Collector's Office – see below for more details) and has completed a college course. Other Irula young people study up to 12th grade and then go into the same agricultural and construction labour and fishing that their parents do. The one exception to this is a small number of unmarried Irula women who go to work in the garment industry in Tiruppur (the youngest I encountered claimed to be 13 years old) but who return to the village when they get married.

No class stratification is visible in the Irula settlement, but the family of the Irula woman who managed to secure an Irula caste certificate has been ostracised by the community, apparently in the context of a power struggle between her father and the new headman of the settlement.

Several observations about the situation of women among the different caste communities in Melpuram can be drawn from the tables, figures and foregoing discussion. In line with Still's (2011) analysis of education among Dalit women in Andhra Pradesh, we see among the Paraiyars' younger generation men clearly receiving more education than women and the neglect of female education in comparison to that of males among the Irulas. Whereas in the past everyone in Melpuram apparently had full-time work in agriculture, my qualitative data indicates that now hardly any women have substantial paid employment except among the Paraiyar Dalits and Irula Adivasis, and while OBC (Vanniyar, Gounder and Nattar) women claim that this is because there is no work available, the more likely explanation is that these women have been withdrawn from the paid workforce for two reasons: their households can afford to forgo their participation in the paid labour market, and the agricultural labour they did in the past took place under conditions whereby they were under the continuous supervision of their peers and kin, within walking distance of their home. Today there *is* work available, but not under these conditions. I was told that among the Dalits and Irulas, where the women work, this creates tension within the household because men (and in-laws) are not comfortable with women working outside the village. In other communities women stay home, earning little or no money. Many OBC women do National Rural Employment Guarantee Act work, but this exception probably reflects widespread attitudes towards this work as 'socially acceptable' work for women more generally.[34] When the day's National Rural Employment Guarantee Act work is over, these women are picked up from the worksite (usually located across the highway on the interior road leading to the headquarters of the panchayat union to which Melpuram belongs) by their men on bikes and in cars, passing the long column of Dalits walking under the burning sun along the highway in the same direction.

The foregoing analysis paints a clear picture of caste-based labour market segregation persisting despite major socioeconomic change. In Melpuram's agrarian past, Nattars fished, Vanniyars and Paraiyar Dalits worked in Nadar paddy fields, and Irula Adivasis were bonded labour watchmen in Nadar coconut farms. In Melpuram's industrial present, the Nadar family is still on top, having successfully transitioned from village-based agricultural accumulation to varied non-agricultural accumulation (some connected to the local factories, some to projects elsewhere); the middle castes (Vanniyars, Gounders, Nattars) have been relatively successful in securing semi-skilled contract labour; Paraiyar Dalits are low-skilled contract labour in the bone factory; and Irulas engage in fishing and construction work locally and migrate for low-skilled contract work elsewhere. A significant number of Dalits have secured government employment, but this has not led to generalised better access to government services or money.

Interviews with Irulas reveal contradictory explanations for their absence from the factory workforce. Some say they are offered worse pay and conditions than non-Irula workers by contractors, some say they live a hand-to-mouth existence, cannot get credit on good terms, and therefore need work that pays daily rather than fortnightly like the factory does; others say they prefer work organised around short periods of intense work with several days or weeks of rest in between. The construction work Irulas do pays better than factory work (Rs.350 rather than Rs.250 per day for men) but is harder (twelve hours in the sun, sleeping by the roadside, in contrast to eight hours in the factory, sleeping at home). On the whole, the Irulas appear to do harder work that other members of the labouring classes won't do, including the work of cleaning septic tanks (a Dalit youth told me 'Vanniyars and Dalits won't do this because it's very low work'). Another factor may be the social-spatial separation of the Irula settlement, a point emphasised by one of the male line descendants of the Nadar landlord in an interview.

Vanniyar success at securing semi-skilled contract labour positions appears to be a combination of nepotism (which we might think of as 'discrimination for' or competitive altruism – 'I look out for my kin, I get them jobs') and *contemporary expressions of historical discrimination against* Dalits and Irulas.

Some examples of the advantages the Vanniyars have over the Dalits will help illustrate the diverse forms taken by contemporary expressions of historical discrimination. First, they have a numerical majority in both the panchayat to which Melpuram belongs and the region as a whole, with important consequences for their ability to access a wide range of legal and illegal benefits made available through both the panchayati raj system and local party-political organising efforts. The big landlord families of the panchayat (the Nadar landlord, whose centre of operations is Melpuram, and the family of the Naidu ex-village administrative officer who helped secure Swami Nagar for the Irulas) have extricated themselves from village-level politicking, leaving the way clear for the Vanniyars to move in, and over the past two decades almost all the panchayat presidents have been Vanniyars.[35] Second, the Vanniyars have been able to access the semi-skilled employment opportunities associated with industrialisation in a way that the Dalits have not. Third, and relatedly, some Vanniyar entrepreneurs have been able to access lucrative business opportunities in the private sector in a way that very few Dalits have. Fourth, many Vanniyar families own land whereas few Dalit families do. As land prices in India keep on rising as urbanisation and industrialisation in this region continues, this matters. Finally, a Nadar construction contractor explained that he employs Vanniyars not Dalits because he employs people based on recommendations from those who have already worked for him, and when he started he 'didn't know anyone from the Dalit colony or the Irula settlement'. It is in such circumstances that, despite the advancement of the Dalit community, the superior social and cultural capital of the Vanniyar community continues to enable them to position themselves to monopolise employment opportunities as semi-skilled contract workers.

In sum, the key element in the discrimination against Dalits and Adivasis in Melpuram is that they have historically been relegated to mainly low-skilled work, and this seems to be primarily a product of the fact that the resources to get better jobs have been captured by other groups. The one important exception is that young Dalits have been successful in accessing low-ranking government jobs, which they have been able to do because of policies of affirmative action for those jobs.

Examining the relationship between education, occupation and caste in Melpuram suggests that (in the context of the availability of posts through affirmative action), post-12th grade education helps secure better employment but does not guarantee it (see Table 4.1).[36] With the exception of the Irulas, all communities have seen a small number of people secure work that is better than low-skilled contract or daily wage labour; in some cases post-12th grade education may have helped, but many secured this kind of work through contacts alone and learned informally 'on the job' rather than through formal training. Many villagers explained that education had become more important over time as low-skilled work opportunities reduced or changed their requirements – crucially, many roles now require applicants to have attained a particular educational level, but did not have any such requirement in the past. Also revealed is a striking contrast between men and women: while education (sometimes) pays off for men (from all communities except the Irulas – who we must recall here do not have access to reserved college places or jobs as they do not have Scheduled Tribe certificates), education does not appear to translate into better work for women.

SEASONAL MIGRANT LABOUR IN MELPURAM

Moving on to the migrant workers, four such groups live in rented accommodation in Melpuram: 10 Tamil machine operators employed directly by the bone factory, 30–50 contract workers from Odisha, 30 contract workers from West Bengal, and 10 contract workers from Bihar and Jharkhand. The workers from Odisha and West Bengal work in the bone factory as low-skilled labour and are employed by contractors from their home state, while the Jharkhandis and Biharis work in another factory as security guards and are employed by an Indian-owned multinational security company. The workers from Odisha and West Bengal ended up working in the bone factory because they were searching for job opportunities outside the village and were referred to their present contractor by a friend who worked for him. In contrast, the Jharkhandis and Biharis responded to poster advertisements in their villages, went through a selection process in Ranchi and were then offered several options for postings; based on higher rate of pay they chose to work in 'Chennai' (in fact the factory they work in is 200 km from Chennai).

Although there may be many reasons for migrating,[37] the migrant workers in Melpuram came to make money, and did not intend to stay longer than necessary. Many of the workers from Odisha, Bihar and West Bengal shared a similar story: as the second or third son in a family with a small plot of agricultural land in Odisha, Bihar or West Bengal, they need to find work outside agriculture to provide for their family. Some are married, their wives living with their parents back in their home village; many are unmarried, having left school at age 16 to find work. All the younger migrant workers from Odisha claim they are age 18 or older, but some look younger than this. Without exception, they would prefer to work somewhere they can speak the local language – they are separated by language from almost everyone around them. At the same time, some of them have reasons for working in this part of Tamil Nadu that extend beyond the simple economic fact that the daily wage work they can find here pays better than the work opportunities they encounter elsewhere. For example, one Odia worker explained that he chose to come to this village in Tamil Nadu because there were others from his village here; during an earlier stint in Gurgaon (near Delhi) he had no one from his home state for company.

While local Tamil contract workers in the bone factory usually do one eight-hour shift, six days a week, the Odia and Bengali migrants regularly work between one and four shifts in a row, seven days a week. They achieve this seemingly impossible feat by means of an informal understanding with other workers and supervisors, in which workers take turns to sleep in a corner of the factory. They explain this practice by saying 'We are here to work' (implying it is their choice rather than something imposed on them). Some of them only stay in Tamil Nadu for a few months at a time, returning home to help their family with cultivation during the monsoon; others have been here for years, returning home only for festivals.

While there does not appear to be a big discrepancy in pay between the local Tamil contract workers and the Bengalis, the Odia workers face substantially inferior pay and conditions. The Tamil and Bengali contract workers believe their contractors take Rs.5–10 per worker per day as his or her cut, and it seems likely this is accurate. The Odia contract workers believe their contractor, Krishna, takes more than this, but he claims this money goes to pay for their food and accommodation.[38] The Tamil and Bengali contract workers buy and prepare food for themselves, and accommodation for the Bengali workers is provided by their contractor. As migrants, the Bengalis and Odias have no access to the important Public Distribution System ration shops for basic ingredients (rice, flour, sugar, oil) that Tamil Nadu is rightly famous for having subsidised more than nearly all other states. In 2015 a male Tamil Dalit coolie would receive Rs.220–250 for an eight-hour shift, while a male migrant worker from Odisha would receive Rs.200 for a twelve-hour shift plus food (three meals of dal and rice), accommodation (a sleeping mat on the floor in a crowded, windowless room with mosquitos and no fan) and 'medicine' (Krishna gives them paracetamol if they get a fever). Siva Nadar's wife – referred to as 'Amma (Mother) Contractor' by her Dalit employees – claimed that a few years ago several Odia workers under Krishna succeeded in temporarily leaving him to work for her. I was told that Krishna responded by getting these workers drunk so they missed their next shift, after which he convinced the factory to ask Amma to terminate their employment (which she did) and agree that only he would supply Odia workers to the factory.

CONTROLLING LABOUR: DIVIDE-AND-RULE, DISCRIMINATION AND LABOUR CONTRACTORS

This section discusses labour relations in the village, and relations between the bone factory and Melpuram villagers as workers and contractors. It looks at three ways that labour is controlled in relation to the bone factory: divide-and-rule, discrimination and through intermediaries. I argue that these elements result in the production and maintenance of a cheap, reliable and docile workforce for the bone factory.

As a strategy, 'divide-and-rule' is often seen as utilising one or both of two elements: dividing a potentially hostile group into smaller (and thus weaker) groups, and pitting those smaller groups against each other. Employment at the bone factory is *de facto* divided into five categories: permanent staff, three types of contract workers (semi-skilled, low-skilled local, low-skilled migrant) and labour contractors. Each category has different terms and conditions of work, and so it seems plausible to suggest that each category would have different interests as a result. In the bone factory, permanent employees receive training, can join unions, are hard to fire, and get salary increments, pensions, insurance, safety equipment and access to the canteen. Contract workers do not get these things. In a 69-day strike initiated by bone factory contract workers in 2008 (see below for more on this), the core demand was that they should be made permanent. One might safely assume that contractors were pleased that the factory refused this demand. The bone factory began using non-local, non-Tamil low-skilled contract labour in order to break the strike, with the Odia contractor Krishna being awarded his contract at that time.

There are three significant types of discrimination involved in how the bone factory controls labour – understood here as treating a particular group of people worse than other groups, which amounts to looking at divide-and-rule practices from a different angle. First, management's unofficial policy of refusing to employ locals as permanent staff is discriminatory. Second, unjustifiable differential treatment of particular categories of worker is discriminatory and includes the following: benefits for permanent staff that are unavailable to contract workers; masks and shoes given only to permanent staff but not contract labourers, despite the fact that the latter group of workers come into more frequent contact with the highly toxic substances being processed in the factory;[39] different shift length and pay for Odia and non-Odia contract workers. Third, there are indications of discrimination by the factory in how it treats its contractors, to the detriment of some contractors. Allegedly, one Dalit contractor initially had six contracts with the bone factory, but later the company took all except one of these and gave them to new, non-Dalit contractors because they had successfully exerted political pressure. The one contract left to the Dalit was cleaning bones and packing waste material. The company insisted that this particular contract would be the one he retained.

The benefits management accrues from the first two types of discrimination (but would almost certainly disavow) can be understood in the following terms: it is advantageous for the factory to look after its permanent staff because they are hard to fire, disadvantageous (because costly) for the factory to look after its contract workers who are easy to fire and easily replaceable, advantageous to recruit Madurai Nadars as permanent employees because they can be vouched for and controlled through the Madurai Nadar CEO's kinship networks, and disadvantageous to recruit local villagers as permanent staff because this would increase the potential for formation of effective worker–resident alliances. Management and the Odia contractor Krishna would almost certainly deny that differential pay for Odia and non-Odia contract workers is discriminatory on the basis that the two cannot be compared, since Krishna provides food and work whereas other contractors provide only work. However, it is hard to see what justification could be offered for the difference in shift length, and indeed Krishna denied his workers did twelve-hour shifts when I asked him.

Labour contractors play a core role in labour control. Each labour contractor has one or more contract with one or more factories. Each contract specifies a task in the production process, and how much the contractor will be paid to cover all the costs associated with getting that task done. This serves the interests of the companies admirably. It enables the companies to create a flexible workforce to whom they have few long-term commitments because many items of labour legislation do not apply to contract workers. In addition, the manner in which particular individuals are awarded labour contracts by the company means the labour contractor system disciplines the workforce and the local villages in a number of ways. Many contractors are influential residents of one of the villages inside or adjacent to the industrial estate, and can (and do) act as the 'eyes and ears' of the company, letting the company know about (and frequently dealing with) potential troublemakers. Others are well-connected individuals awarded contracts to 'stop their mouth', as one Dalit put it, after they threatened to make trouble for the company. Others again were previously low-skilled contract workers and were awarded contracts in recognition of their loyalty to the company. Finally, some workers became contractors as they sustained injuries in the factory and were unable to do manual work any longer. By law, the company and/or contractor is supposed to provide compensation to such individuals, and it seems possible that the company provided an alternative livelihood in the form of one or more labour contracts because it costs the company nothing and means the company can avoid admitting responsibility for the injuries.

The SIPCOT companies have good reasons for actively seeking to protect themselves against potential troublemakers. The Industrial Complex in Cuddalore is not hidden away in a remote district; it is close to Pondicherry and Chennai, and known as a global toxic hotspot. Since the 1990s environmentalists and communist labour organisers have had some success generating media coverage and pursuing cases against specific companies as well as against SIPCOT and the Tamil Nadu Pollution Control Board (who stand accused of covering up incidents, failing to investigate properly, and failing to penalise acknowledged wrongdoing sufficiently).[40] SIPCOT companies are sensitive to the threat of negative media exposure. The labour contractor system is an important element in the companies' efforts to combat this threat. Other elements include a close relationship between the companies and local police and village-based police informers.

Siva Nadar's wife, referred to by her Dalit employees as 'Amma (Mother) Contractor', occupies a unique position. Apart from the fact that she is probably the only female labour contractor in the industrial estate, she has shrewdly made use of her position as both an affine of the big landlord family and a labour contractor to create methods of accumulation that are not open to others. Her nickname is suggestive of a particular familial, caregiving relation; more importantly, 'Amma' is the name used across Tamil Nadu to refer to Jayaram Jayalalitha, who was Chief Minister of Tamil Nadu at the time of my fieldwork. At that time Jayalalitha's image could be seen everywhere in villages and towns in northern Tamil Nadu; Guerin et al. note how this use of her image functioned 'as a recurring reminder of her generous support to the working poor' (2015: 15).

In an interview, 'Amma Contractor' explained to me that she supported the Dalit community of the village in a number of ways, including through donations to the colony's temple festivals and, during the period of my fieldwork, a large financial contribution to a family in which the head of the household had committed suicide. But there is more to Amma than care.

Several Dalit contract workers explained that while other contractors pay their workers on the same day they receive payment from the company, Amma is sometimes up to a month late in paying, and while their money is with her she invests it in ways that give her a significant return.

It appears that the main obstacle preventing Amma's coolies from shifting to another contractor is debt bondage based on the advance of Rs.5000 she openly admits that she paid many of them in order to ensure their loyalty, and has never asked them to pay back. This ongoing debt makes it possible to describe the labour arrangement between Amma and her workers as 'neo-bondage'.[41] As with historical, rural forms of bondage, neo-bondage is a form of oppression that remains embedded in the caste hierarchy even if it 'obey[s] capitalist rules'.[42] Amma's debt bondage is embedded in the historical relation between her affines and the Dalits she now employs, and reliant on her ability to bring her family's wealth to bear in this way (none of the other contractors have the capital to do anything similar on a long-term basis), but it also incorporates other practices of subordination. Many Dalits told me that they preferred work in the factory to work in the landlord's field because factory managers treated them with dignity and respect, as workers, not Dalits; and yet I also witnessed some Dalits removing their slippers and approaching Amma's house barefoot, the way their fathers would have done when seeking an audience with the old landlord, Amma's father-in-law. Amma's apparently familial relationship with her workers is in fact a particularly tight form of labour control based in the historical dependence of the Dalit community on her family.

To conclude, the bone factory provides a range of employment opportunities, but the factory labour force is segregated insofar as each role is allotted to one particular social group, with little scope to move 'up' to roles with better pay and conditions. Locals recognise the company will not recruit them as permanent employees. Paraiyar Dalits recognise they are unlikely to get semi-skilled contract work, a role cornered by the Vanniyars. Some Dalit contract workers may harbour dreams of becoming a labour contractor, but recognise this too is highly unlikely.

COLLECTIVE ACTIONS AND SITES OF STRUGGLE

This section describes the variety of ways the labouring classes in Melpuram have engaged in collective actions to challenge the circumstances in which they live. First, the possibilities and limits of collective action by industrial labour in Melpuram will become clear through the following discussion of the role of unions in the industrial estate, two major disputes between industrial labour and the factories, and a number of minor incidents.

Many of the factories in the Industrial Complex do have unions. According to the organiser for the Central Indian Trade Union (CITU)[43] for the industrial estate, the reason there is no union in the bone factory is that the company's management actively recruits managers and administrators who will not demand a union; villagers explained to me that many of the managers and administrators are Nadars from Madurai, which is where the Nadar CEO comes from. As factories here and elsewhere are replacing permanent staff with contract workers wherever possible, one might expect the bargaining power of the unions will also reduce; at present they still have some significance within the industrial estate and are involved in the most visible labour disputes that take place.

If a contract worker tries to join or form a union, the company will request the worker's contractor to dismiss that worker; if the contractor refuses, the company will terminate the contractor's contracts. Consequently, the union affiliated to the Dalit Liberation Panther Party only has a presence in the four factories with Dalit permanent staff, and is only strong in the two factories where Dalit permanent staff are in senior positions. Unions are able to intervene on behalf of contract workers, but unless the union threatens legal action against the company there is no incentive for the companies to take their pleas seriously; threats of legal action sometimes lead to a settlement without a case being initiated.[44]

Some environmental activists claim that in the past unions in the SIPCOT estate refused to take up environmental issues because they saw this as detrimental to their primary objective of protecting jobs; the environmental activists claim that CITU changed its stance on this matter with the bone factory strike in 2008. The strike was initiated by contract workers, who, without external leadership, came together to demand permanent jobs and higher wages. They succeeded in recruiting some permanent employees, who demanded higher salaries. When CITU became involved, the central demand made by the union was for the company to stop illegally discharging untreated effluents into the river. One environmental activist associated with the SIPCOT Area Community Environmental Monitors claimed that this was strategic: the union recognised that the risk of negative publicity about pollution might be the most effective way to force the company to accept the union. After 69 days, the strike was called off when management agreed to recognise the union. The company invited the workers to return to work. Once they were back inside the company compound, police charged the workers with *lathis* (batons) injuring at least 15 including 5 women. Contract workers identified as strike organisers lost their jobs, some contract workers who had encouraged their colleagues to call off the strike were made permanent, and other contract workers were not made permanent. The company took on 30–40 workers from Odisha during the strike, who continued to work there afterwards.

Photo 7   Anti-pollution activists in the SIPCOT Industrial Estate near Melpuram,
Tamil Nadu
Photo by Community Environmental Monitoring.

The role of the police in the strike was firmly on the side of the company,
and this is consistent with accounts of other conflicts between the
companies and workers and between the companies and residents of nearby
villages. At the end of February 2016, a community meeting in a village
near Melpuram was lathi-charged by police. The residents had complained
to the police and Tamil Nadu Pollution Control Board about a very bad
smell coming from a factory close by, and had demanded the closure of the
factory, and the police and Pollution Control Board did nothing. When the
police arrived uninvited at the start of the meeting and spoke rudely, the
assembled residents surrounded the police. More police came in vans and
lathi-charged the crowd. A closure order for the factory was issued by the
Pollution Control Board in November 2016.

These disputes illustrate some of the limits on collective action in relation
to the factories. There are, however, also possibilities for 'micro' collective
action. One example was narrated to me by a migrant worker from Odisha
who lives in Melpuram. He explained that in the past, the water in the bone
factory filtration tank was very hot, so that those loading the tank were
exposed to hot water and steam, and those at the bottom had to hold a very
hot 'cake' in their hands. The Odia workers in the filtration department spoke

to their Tamil supervisor about the problem. One day when the managing director was in the factory, their supervisor told them 'Sit down and don't work.' The director said: 'Why are they not working?' When they explained, the director held the cake, agreed it was hot, and changed the process so the tank water was less hot.

The factory is not the only area of contestation for the Paraiyar Dalits. Within Melpuram, they think of their individual and community futures in relation to three 'Others': the Nadar landlord family, the Vanniyars, and other residents of the Melpuram Dalit colony.

The Dalits of Melpuram feel that as a result of the long-term socioeconomic changes described in this chapter, as well as the mobilisation efforts of the Dalit Liberation Panther Party over the past decade, they have now attained an equal status to the Vanniyars and Nattars in the village but, they say, members of those communities refuse to accept this. The Dalits also emphasise that the coming of the factories ended their community's total dependence on the Nadar landlord, and they argue that because several Dalit men now have well-paid government jobs, soon the Dalit community will have total financial independence from the Nadar big landlord family. At the same time, class divisions have emerged within the Dalit colony (between those households with government jobs and those without) and the new middle-class Dalits express a desire to distance themselves from poorer Dalits ('We wouldn't want our children to learn the ways of their children') and poorer Dalits speak bitterly of how new middle-class Dalits have abandoned the community.

With these distinct categories of 'Others' in mind, it is possible to distinguish between two categories of actions aimed at improving the position of the Dalit community: actions involving self-improvement of the community's capacity and standing, and actions involving assertion of the community *against* the Nadar landlord family and the Vanniyar community. In the first category are the ongoing commitments to the Dalit temples in the village and to the colony's tuition centre. Set up ten years ago by an enlightened headmistress of the government school in the village, the tuition centre provides a space – adorned with images of Periyar, Bhagat Singh and other figureheads of Dravidian, Dalit and class-based struggles for liberation – where educated Dalit youths supplement the school-based education of Dalit children on a voluntary basis. The centre is a highly impressive sign of community solidarity, especially when compared with the practices of youths in the Vanniyar, Nattar and Irula communities, where there seems to be little community solidarity.

Assertions *against* the Nadar landlord and Vanniyar community take different forms, reflecting the difference in relations. Today, Dalit assertion in relation to the Nadar takes fairly low-key, 'micro' and often individualised forms. Explaining the changing relationship between Dalits and the Nadar, both Dalits and the Nadar emphasised that those Dalits *not* employed by the Nadar now refer to him to his face as *annan* (older brother) rather than as boss (which is how they referred to members of his family in the past). Dalits also emphasised the fact that they no longer have to go shirtless and barefoot in front of his house as in the past. I also witnessed Dalit men insulting members of the lesser Nadar family to their faces and, in one case, threatening a Nadar man with physical violence. In contrast, recent assertions against Vanniyars have often taken the form of potentially violent face-offs between youths and leaders of the two communities, reflecting the competition between them, in which they are spurred on by the Vanniyars' Pattali Makkal Katchi party and the Dalits' Liberation Panther Party – in a region where deadly riots between Vanniyars and Dalits have been a fairly regular occurrence for decades.[45] There is a contrast here between wanting to escape dependency on the Nadar and to establish equality with the Vanniyars; both struggles are about dignity and respect, but one is the struggle of a subordinate against those they depend on, and the other is competition between caste groups where the Dalits feel in a position to reject their historically inferior position.

Unlike the Paraiyars, the attention of the Irula Adivasis is focused on a set of 'Others' who have nothing to do with the historical caste hierarchy of Melpuram – reflecting the fact that they successfully broke with this hierarchy in the 1980s. The key 'Others' of the Irulas include the two benefactors who allowed them to escape the caste hierarchy (the ex-village administrative officer and the Chennai-based activist mentioned above, both of whom are considered to be 'like gods' by many of the Irulas), the Nattars, and the district collector.

The significance of the Nattars in the Irulas' narrative is the result of competition over fishing. At the time of the tsunami, one of the livelihood activities of the Irulas was fishing in the river. After the tsunami, a Chennai-based activist secured funds from an international charity to buy boats, motors and nets for the Irulas. These were kept by the riverside in Melpuram, which is half an hour's walk from Swami Nagar, where the Irulas live. The motors were stolen and boats and nets destroyed. The Irulas believe the fishers were responsible and although they say they do not know which fishers, the Nattar river fishers of Melpuram seem the most likely suspects.

At the time of my fieldwork, the focus of the Irulas of Swami Nagar was on getting a Scheduled Tribe certificate as the next step to securing a better life for their community – getting recognition as Irula Adivasis, as a Scheduled Tribe community eligible for reservations in education and employment. In Tamil Nadu, a Scheduled Tribe certificate is more desirable than other caste certificates because there is less competition for Scheduled Tribe reservations. Government officers are under pressure to refuse to give a Scheduled Tribe certificate unless there is clear evidence that the individual is from a Scheduled Tribe. Many residents of Swami Nagar have blood relations in other settlements who have the Irula Scheduled Tribe certificate, but when some of these individuals tried to get the certificate from the district collector they were refused on the basis that two key sources of caste identification suggest they are either Scheduled Caste or Kattunayakan Scheduled Tribe, not Irula. Most households in Swami Nagar have a title deed (*patta*) for the land their house is built on, but these documents are stamped by the Adi Dravida Welfare Department and the collector claims this is evidence that the residents are Scheduled Caste, even though this welfare department is for Scheduled Castes *and* Scheduled Tribes. The stamp is on the title deed because the welfare department purchased the land on their behalf (while the ex-village administrative officer had allegedly promised to give his land to the Irulas for free, after his death his sons allegedly refused to do so). The school records of the younger generation of Irulas (the older generation did not go to school) state that they are Kattunayakan Scheduled Tribe people because when parents took their children to the school for the first time, the teacher wrote this as their caste in the school record book – because at that point they were illiterate and did not know their caste, all they knew was that they lived in the forest ('Kattu' in Tamil).

There is probably more to this story, however. Swami Nagar is the largest Irula settlement in Cuddalore *taluk* (district sub-division); most other sizeable Irula settlements are further south, in Chidambaram taluk, and the Irulas in those settlements *do* have the Irula Scheduled Tribe certificate. The high-caste, middle-class, Chennai-based activist claims that this is because, during the period after the tsunami when she was actively mobilising the Irulas of Cuddalore district, the sub-collector responsible for Chidambaram taluk was a man sympathetic to the Irula cause, and that he made sure the Irulas got the certificate. An alternative explanation has been offered by two communist Irula organisers who belong to an Irula mass-membership organisation that is, in some sense, a competitor to the Chennai-based activist. The communist Irula ex-professor-turned-social-worker who leads this organisation claims that the Irulas of Swami Nagar repeatedly self-sabotaged his attempts to help them, in contrast to the Irulas of Chidambaram taluk, who successfully mobilised collectively at election time to withhold their votes in order to get the caste certificate. A local organiser (who is also headman of one of the Chidambaram villages) explained that in villages south of Swami Nagar the Irulas told politicians canvassing for votes that 'If you give us the certificate we will vote for your party'; the politicians replied 'Vote first, then certificate,' the Irulas said 'Certificate first,' and got the certificate. 'The Swami Nagar Irulas did not do this because they do not know the value of their certificate, they're looking only at their everyday livelihood, not thinking about their children's future. Dravida Munnetra Kazhagam and All India Anna Dravida Munnetra Kazhagam will go to Swami Nagar, both will say "put vote for us" and give money, and will do nothing.' It may be relevant that the two major parliamentary communist parties – the Communist Party of India and the Communist Party of India (Marxist) – both have a strong presence in Chidambaram taluk and a weak presence in Cuddalore taluk.

In order to gain places in college, a couple of Irula youths have accepted either the Scheduled Caste or Kattunayakan Scheduled Tribe certificate the district collector is willing to give, and a single Irula woman has been able to get an Irula Scheduled Tribe certificate; other residents of Swami Nagar have either requested an Irula Scheduled Tribe certificate and been refused, or made no attempt to get any caste certificate at all. The community believes the youths who have taken Scheduled Caste or Kattunayakan certificates have made it harder for others in Swami Nagar to get an Irula certificate – which, they say, remains their goal because 'We are Irulas.' The woman who got an Irula Scheduled Tribe certificate claims to have done so by petitioning the district collector for days, accompanied by her father Murali – who was at the time leader of the Irula Caste Association for Cuddalore district and headman of Swami Nagar – and the Chennai-based activist. On the final day, the woman bought a can of kerosene and threatened to set herself on fire outside the Collector's Office: this threat secured the certificate. However, the woman and her father have been ostracised by the Irulas of Swami Nagar, who accuse them of looking out for themselves rather than for the community as a whole. This appears to reflect a view that the best way to get the certificate for the whole community is through petitioning the collector as a collective rather than as individuals. Their ostracisation has helped Murali's main rival for leadership of the settlement, who is now headman in his place, and this is perhaps indicative of something several communist organisers say, which is that the Irulas of Swami Nagar are unable to move forward because they get mired in factionalism.

Unlike the Melpuram Paraiyars, the Swami Nagar Irulas' Others are individuals or groups to whom the Irulas are connected in a relation of non-reciprocal giving or taking: long ago the government took away their forests and made it illegal for them to hunt snakes (their traditional occupation), later the god-benefactors gave, then the Nattars allegedly took away, and now the Irulas hope the district collector will give. It is this posture of petitioning that frustrates the communist Irula organisers, who see it as passive; the communist organisers believe it is possible and necessary for the Irulas to actively demand rights and resources, and believe the Swami Nagar Irulas are fundamentally unwilling to do this: 'They want people to do things for them, but they are unwilling to do things for themselves,' one organiser complained.

While the Irulas' attention is focused on Others *outside* Melpuram, and while their spatial, economic and political distance from Melpuram means that they are often seen as being 'outside of the village' by other residents of Melpuram, they are still occasionally the target of stigmatising comments by other residents of Melpuram.

CASTE-BASED SEGREGATION AND LABOUR CONTROL

Through an empirical account of the village of Melpuram, this chapter has foregrounded a 30-year transition from a village agricultural economy dominated by a single Nadar landlord family to a village economy dominated by a single factory. In both, dominance is mediated by a shifting constellation of actors and institutions. Under industrialisation, dominance is in some sense more dispersed and yet, when examined as a system, both agrarian and factory-dominated periods function to control labour, producing a docile and reliable workforce that meets the needs of the single dominant actor at the 'top'. Caste relations are central to labour control in both the village agricultural economy and under industrialisation.

In Melpuram, industrialisation, urbanisation and changes in agriculture transformed social relations, but the hierarchies of the old agrarian order persist in an ongoing caste- and class-based division of labour. In the new factories Dalit landless agricultural labourers get low-skilled jobs; OBC Vanniyar smallholders and Nattar fishers get semi-skilled jobs; and members of the Nadar big landlord family become labour contractors or salaried professionals. Thus, socioeconomic change in this region has led to *absolute* mobility but not *relative* mobility:[46] all castes now have better opportunities for education and work, but only within strict structural confines so the position of castes *in relation to each other* has not changed. Relations between castes are key to understanding the processes that have enabled this to come about. The Vanniyars' structural position based on land, political strength and access to better jobs helps them retain the upper hand in their ongoing competition with the Dalits; continuing economic dependence and clientelism in relations between the Dalit community and the land-lord-contractor family produce a docile, reliable workforce for the factory; and, paradoxically, the Irulas' relative isolation (in their spatially segregated settlement of Swami Nagar) plays a role in their continuing dependence on 'god-benefactors'. A number of studies in Tamil Nadu have described landlords moving from agriculture into non-agricultural accumulation,[47] but have not investigated the extent to which they have reinvented themselves as labour market intermediaries, and the implications of this for patterns of inequality and dominance. In my field site, local landlords have been able to become labour contractors, converting power they exerted in the old agricultural economy into new forms of power in a new economy centred on industry.

If there was a time when caste and class mapped neatly onto each other that is no longer the case in Melpuram. Nevertheless, there continues to be a strong *correspondence* between caste and class relations. Against the predictions of modernisation theory, the shift from agriculture to industry for Dalits and to other precarious jobs for Adivasis has not brought emancipation, but instead has created mechanisms for reproducing dis-crimination in new ways. If we focus on livelihoods, as the chapters in this book do, the key element in the discrimination against Dalits and Adivasis in the study village is not that they get paid lower for identical work, but that they are significantly under-represented in all categories of work except low-skilled work. This seems to be primarily a product of the fact that castes above them monopolise the resources needed to secure better jobs (contacts and networks, in particular). To an extent, the pollution-based logics of caste remain, so that in agricultural work it will be Dalits and Adivasis rather than Vanniyars who are offered the dirtiest tasks, and the contract workers labouring in close contact with animal bones in the smelly, unhygienic heart of the bone factory are overwhelmingly Paraiyar Dalits and migrant workers, most of whom are Dalit and Adivasi. Although the Paraiyar Dalits do not experience the migrants' presence as a threat, on some level it is, insofar as the bone factory brought them in precisely because of characteris-tics that make them more attractive than the Paraiyars as low-skilled labour.

At the same time, however, Melpuram's story is not exclusively a story about industrialisation. Rather, a complex causality characterises the way in which the transition from landlord dominance to factory dominance took place alongside major changes in landownership, agricultural production and government intervention, with differing implications for different castes and classes, who have travelled very different trajectories. The Vanniyars and Gounders bought land as the Nadar landlord family moved towards non-agricultural accumulation. The Paraiyar Dalits moved from dependency on the landlord as low-skilled agricultural labour to dependency on the factories as low-skilled industrial labour, and are now benefiting from government reservations. The Irula Adivasis escaped bonded labour for the Nadar to take up 'free' agricultural labour opportunities and now seek a Scheduled Tribe caste certificate. The decline in village-based agricultural labour opportunities has led to the withdrawal of OBC women from the workforce and increased tensions within Paraiyar Dalit and Irula Adivasi households: just as industrialisation has not freed Melpuram's labouring classes from the yoke of caste, neither has it freed Melpuram's women. With all these changes, it is possible to see that while industrialisation has played a major role in Melpuram's story, many of these processes would have taken place in a similar form anyway even if the industrial estate had not been built here.

Moreover, the factory has been adroit in making use of existing power structures, in particular through its intricate linkages with dominant caste actors. To an extent the factory has been able to simply let existing patterns of discrimination do the rest: regardless of what the factory does or does not do, certain caste groups will not easily be offered high-level opportunities.

The factories of the industrial estate – and, in particular, the bone factory – have come to exert a powerful influence over Melpuram through a range of interconnected mechanisms that limit scope for challenging their control, and yet, nevertheless, the labouring classes do find ways to pursue improvements. The Paraiyar Dalits and Irula Adivasis have both engaged in struggles specific to social relations shaped by their caste identity and the history of their recent ancestors. Some approaches are individualised and lead to divisions within the community: in particular, government jobs have led to new class divisions in the Dalit colony, and one Irula woman's attainment of an Irula caste certificate has led to the ostracisation of her and her father. Other approaches are also individualised but, because they lead to less dramatic socioeconomic advancement, do not lead to divisions in the same way: Dalit life chances improve a bit, rather than a lot, through education if they also have powerful connections, and in general if they try to move away from the village.

While other approaches are collective, it is possible that part of the reason their efforts seldom take them very far is that in these struggles they are, once again, divided by caste and class, and are often met with violent repression. Those doing low-skilled contract labour within the bone factory have struggled to improve their conditions of work and life, but the bone factory (and the other factories of SIPCOT) has been successful in preventing an effective coalition of labour and villagers, not least because contract workers have little leverage. One of the key reasons they have so little leverage is that, for many of them, contract work in the factories is still the best employment available. Perhaps, then, direct struggle against the factories will always be less rewarding than struggles for upliftment – within the village and more widely – that would challenge the conditions that tie them to the factory.

5

Bhadrachalam Scheduled Area, Telangana

Dalel Benbabaali

This chapter examines the processes of dispossession and marginalisation faced by Adivasis and Dalits in Bhadrachalam tribal belt, located on the banks of the Godavari River in Telangana. To explore this issue, it analyses the two main factors that have impacted the lives and livelihoods of these historically disadvantaged groups. The first is the migration of dominant caste farmers from Coastal Andhra into the Godavari valley to acquire the easily accessible, cheap and fertile lands in the forested territories where Adivasis traditionally practised shifting cultivation for their subsistence. The second is the expansion of a paper factory run by the Indian Tobacco Company near Bhadrachalam town. It uses water from the Godavari for the paper production process, coal from the nearby mines exploited by Singareni Collieries, and it used bamboo from the surrounding forests till it was exhausted and replaced with imported wood from Southeast Asia and local eucalyptus plantations. The story here relates to some of the same processes that we explored in Cuddalore district in Tamil Nadu in the preceding chapter. In both cases a dominant farming caste group moved in and took over the agrarian lands, and in both cases this was followed, later, by processes of industrialisation. But here, near Bhadrachalam, all this took place in spite of the formal protection of Adivasi lands and forests under the Fifth Schedule of the Constitution.

The Bhadrachalam tribal belt is endowed with plenty of resources but its Adivasi population has become increasingly resource poor. The various laws that guarantee tribal land and forest rights in Scheduled Areas are not properly implemented by the state. It has abandoned its protective role to embrace a predatory one, leading to the expropriation of Adivasis in favour of private companies. Tribal land alienation in Bhadrachalam started with the arrival of Kamma settlers from the Godavari delta who introduced commercial agriculture, employing the local Koyas to clear the forests and local landless Dalits to work on the fields. Following this exploitation of their natural resources as well as their labour, Adivasi autonomy has been progressively eroded and their customary rights undermined, while the dependence of Dalits on dominant castes has increased. The two main Dalit groups in Telangana are the Madigas, traditionally leatherworkers and agricultural labourers, and the Malas, who used to practise various occupations, including weaving and agricultural labour.

This chapter focuses on the power relations between the dominant Kammas on the one hand, and Adivasis and Dalits on the other. It is based on ethnographic research conducted between October 2014 and August 2015 in Bhadrachalam area, comprising a study of a village located near the Indian Tobacco Company paper factory. The quantitative data generated through the village survey were used to compare the socioeconomic status and inequalities between and within these groups, while the qualitative interviews tried to capture people's own analysis of power within the village and their assessment of external factors such as industrialisation and government interventions.[1] The first section presents the administrative history of the region to expose the dual role of the state in tribal areas. The second section analyses the results of the village study, while the last one goes beyond the village boundaries in order to look at the collective struggles around the paper factory.

PROTECTION OR PREDATION? THE AMBIGUOUS ROLE OF THE STATE IN ADIVASI TERRITORY

Telangana was carved out of Andhra Pradesh in June 2014 after decades of struggle. The proponents of this division argued that Telangana was a resource-rich region that remained underdeveloped because influential people from Coastal Andhra diverted its resources for their own benefit.[2] The formation of the new state created immense hopes for social justice and economic development, as promised by the Chief Minister K. Chandrashekar Rao, known as KCR, whose party, the Telangana Rashtra Samithi (TRS) came to power after the bifurcation.[3] However, as this chapter will show, the separation of the two Telugu-speaking states has not made much difference to people's lives, especially among the most oppressed sections of society.

The idea that 'development' would reduce poverty and inequality ignores the fact that it is precisely the neoliberal development model adopted in the mid-1990s by the united Andhra Pradesh that increased the social and regional disparities denounced by the Telangana statehood movement. The Telangana government has not challenged this model and its main objective is still to generate growth, not only through investments in Hyderabad, the capital city, but also through industrialisation of the most 'backward' areas, including Adivasi territories.[4] Telangana is home to a sizeable Adivasi population of around 10 per cent of the 40 million inhabitants of the state, most of whom are concentrated in Adilabad and Khammam districts. While the Gonds of Adilabad have attracted the attention of anthropologists since Fürer-Haimendorf (1948), little has been written about Bhadrachalam tribal belt of Bhadradri-Kothagudem district (part of Khammam district till 2016), which is mostly populated by Koyas.

The administrative history of the studied region is complex as Bhadrachalam used to be a *zamindari* estate falling partly under the Nizam's princely State of Hyderabad, and partly under British-ruled territory. From the colonial land settlement report, we learn that 'the estate of Bhadrachalam consists of 137 villages both on the left and right banks of the Godavari River. The Rani of Bhadrachalam traces her pedigree from Anapa Ashwa Rao, a Velama chieftain, who is said to have received the grant of the estate from the Emperor of Delhi in 1324.'[5] The lands of Bhadrachalam located on the left bank of the Godavari were ceded by the Nizam to the British in 1860, the river thus serving as a border between Hyderabad State and the Madras Presidency. According to the colonial administrators:

> the system of revenue collection previous to British occupation seems to have been both rude and oppressive. The Bhadrachalam zamindar always kept up a troop of Rohillas, who received very little pay for their services and lived chiefly by looting the surrounding country. The taluk was divided into 10 samutus, each of which theoretically contained 25 Koya villages and each of which had to supply for a month, without pay or batta, 100 Koyas to carry burdens, fetch supplies, etc. for the Rohillas, and 100 Madigas to act as horse-keepers. The Koya women were frequently stripped and then regarded as objects of ridicule.[6]

After being plundered by the Nizam's feudal regime, a portion of Koya territory was brought under paternalistic colonial rule. From the descriptions contained in the land settlement report, the indigenous people – men and women – continued to be regarded as 'objects of ridicule' needing the 'protection' of their new masters. Most importantly, they needed to be sedentarised so that revenue could be collected from their agricultural produce:

> Like all wild tribes, they are timid, inoffensive, and tolerably truthful; their restless habits however do not admit of their settling down as good agriculturists; generally speaking they move from one spot to another once in every three or four years, but on the banks of the river, there are numbers of them who have settled down and have accumulated some wealth, in flocks, herds and money. Where they can cultivate rice, they are

more attached to the soil, especially if a grove of *palmyra* be near, as like all Gonds they are fond of spirits.[7]

Rice could only be cultivated on the alluvial and black soils near the Godavari, while millets were grown in the forested areas using the slash-and-burn method. These sparsely populated and fertile lands attracted farmers from the high-density delta areas who had become expert rice cultivators after the British constructed two big dams in Coastal Andhra, on the Godavari in 1850 and on the Krishna in 1855. Most of those Andhra farmers belonged to the landowning Kamma caste that benefited tremendously from the introduction of canal irrigation in the Godavari and Krishna deltas, where they started producing a double crop of paddy annually. Intensification of agriculture enabled them to generate surpluses that could be marketed. With the commercialisation of agriculture, land itself became a valuable commodity and the demographic pressure prompted enterprising Kammas to sell their small plots in the deltas to acquire larger properties upstream in the non-irrigated tribal areas of the Godavari valley. Some of them were even invited by the Nizam to develop settled agriculture and introduce cash crops like tobacco and chillies in the forested areas of his state.[8]

However, both the British administration and the Nizam realised that the growing penetration of Andhra farmers, traders and moneylenders into tribal territories, for which they were responsible, was causing social unrest among Adivasis. To avoid the spread of tribal rebellions that were taking place elsewhere in India (Bates and Shah 2014), in 1917 the British enacted the Agency Tracts Interest and Land Transfer Act, which sought to limit interest payable by Adivasis and to restrict land alienation, which was often a consequence of indebtedness. As pointed out by the non-governmental organisation (NGO) Samata, the Simon Commission later justified the introduction of special laws in Adivasi territories:

> There were two dangers to which subjection to normal laws would have specially exposed these peoples, and both arose out of the fact that they were primitive people, simple, unsophisticated and frequently improvident. There was a risk of their agricultural land passing to the more civilized section of the population; and, secondly, they were likely to get into the wiles of the moneylenders.[9]

Similarly, the Nizam's government enacted the Hyderabad Tribal Areas Regulation in 1948 to protect Adivasis from land alienation and exploitation from non-tribal settlers. Anthropologist Fürer-Haimendorf, who was appointed Advisor on Tribal Affairs in Hyderabad State, prescribed the allocation of land deeds to the Gonds of Adilabad for the forest patches they were cultivating.

After Telangana was merged with Andhra in 1956 to form Andhra Pradesh, the first linguistic state of Independent India, the influx of capitalist farmers from the delta areas to acquire cheap lands in interior Adivasi territories became uncontrollable. The Bhadrachalam tribal belt, which was notified as a Scheduled Area under the Fifth Schedule of the Constitution, was particularly affected by this phenomenon because of its abundant resources and its accessibility. As a consequence, in 1959 the Andhra Pradesh government passed the Scheduled Areas Land Transfer Regulation, known as LTR. Regulation 1 of the Land Transfer Regulation Act, which was amended in 1970, prohibits land transfer from members of Scheduled Tribes to non-Scheduled Tribe people. What became known as the 1/70 Act is one of the most stringent pieces of legislation in India protecting tribal territories, as it presumes that in Scheduled Areas all lands belonged originally to Adivasis and should ultimately be restored to them by ensuring that immovable property be transferred only to members of a Scheduled Tribe or to cooperative societies composed solely of Scheduled Tribe members. Non-Adivasis living in Scheduled Areas bear the burden of proof and need to provide evidence that they acquired their lands before the act came into force.

There remained an ambiguity in this progressive legislation about whether the government could allocate land in Scheduled Areas to private companies. According to the Samata judgment delivered by the Supreme Court of India in 1997, in a case opposing the Government of Andhra Pradesh to an NGO contesting a mining lease, the government cannot transfer land notified under the Fifth Schedule or even lease it to private investors, unless the shareholders are Adivasis.[10] Despite this clarification by the Supreme Court that reiterated the constitutional safeguards relating to Scheduled Areas, the state continued to assign government land to industries that were attracted to the resource-rich Adivasi territories, in the name of 'development of backward areas'. A top manager of the Indian Tobacco Company paper factory used this expression when I asked him to explain the choice of location of this industry. According to him, it was the government of Andhra Pradesh who encouraged industrial development in Bhadrachalam because of the 'backwardness' of this 'so-called' Scheduled Area. By not acknowledging that the factory was indeed located in an Adivasi territory protected by the Fifth Schedule of the Constitution, he brushed away accusations regarding the illegality of the establishment of this industry *ab initio*, as it was set up after the Land Transfer Regulation Act was adopted.

The Indian Tobacco Company was founded in 1910 as the Imperial Tobacco Company and took its present name after Independence. Its headquarters are still in Kolkata and it is now a major private conglomerate operating diverse businesses such as cigarettes, paper and packaging, stationery, agro-industry, hotels, information technology, personal care and other consumable goods. In 1979, it took over and privatised Bhadrachalam Paperboard Limited, which had been established in Sarapaka village of Burgampudu *mandal*[11] two years before. The government had allotted 220 acres of reserve forest and 290 acres of agricultural land to the company. In 1997, the Kamma Chief Minister Chandrababu Naidu, known for introducing neoliberal policies in Andhra Pradesh, alienated another 90 acres of land for the factory. This was challenged in court by the communist member of the Andhra Pradesh Legislative Assembly Kunja Bhiksham, a Koya elected from Bhadrachalam constituency, which is reserved for Scheduled Tribe candidates. Against his own party (the Communist Party of India, which was then allied with Naidu's Telugu Desam Party), the Koya leader accused the state government of being in collusion with industrialists 'with every likelihood of crores of rupees changing hands'.[12] In spite of the suspension of the High Court order due to these allegations of corruption and the unconstitutional character of the land transfer, the Indian Tobacco Company continues to illegally occupy that land to grow eucalyptus plantations.

To denounce this situation a tribal organisation called the *Adivasi Chaitanya Samithi* approached the government officer in charge of Bhadrachalam Integrated Tribal Development Agency (ITDA), a civil servant from the Indian Administrative Service, who decided to take action against the company. In April 2015, in her counter-affidavit to a petition filed by the company contesting her instructions to Burgampudu's mandal revenue officer to repossess the encroached land, she wrote that 'the management of ITC [Indian Tobacco Company] is trying to misrepresent the case by creating litigation being fully aware of the legal and constitutional violations involved in taking over possession of land by private non-tribal companies in Scheduled Areas'. Since it was unlikely that the company would close down its Bhadrachalam unit and vacate the site, the Integrated Tribal Development Agency officer asked the management to compensate for the 'historical blunder' of choosing a Scheduled Area for the establishment of this factory by providing employment to the local Adivasis. Unlike the public sector industries located in Bhadrachalam (like the Singareni Collieries coal mines and Kothagudem Thermal Power Station), Indian Tobacco Company is a private company and therefore does not have reservations for Scheduled Tribes. However, the Tribal Development Agency officer tried to put pressure on the company to implement a quota policy on the grounds that the presence of the factory was responsible for the in-migration of outside labour that was providing most of the manpower, at the cost of work for local people.

According to the management, 17 per cent of the factory's casual labour force are Adivasi. Workers themselves put this figure much lower.[13] They argue that out of the 4000 casual labourers (skilled, semi-skilled and unskilled) currently employed by the factory, only 8 per cent are Adivasis (200 Lambadas, 100 Koyas and 20 Konda Reddis), and 25 per cent are local Dalits (Madigas and Malas). There are also migrant Dalits from Odisha (Doms) who do not have Scheduled Caste certificates. Among the permanent labour force, the proportions are even lower: out of 1575 employees, 5 per cent are Adivasis (45 Lambadas and 30 Koyas) and 8 per cent are Dalits (70 Madigas and 60 Malas). The rest are castes of the Other Backward Classes (OBC) group, as well as dominant castes (mostly Kammas and Reddis), a majority of whom are from Coastal Andhra. Finally, among the 700 managers, none are Adivasis or Dalits, most of them being upper caste and outsiders. To understand this under-representation of local Adivasis and Dalits, it was important to interview the workers themselves, as well as the people living in a nearby village who could not find jobs at the factory or did not want to work there. When the government justifies industrialisation of tribal areas in the name of development, the question that needs to be asked is 'Whose development?' Similarly, the claim that industries provide employment needs to be qualified with questions such as 'Employment for whom? What kind of employment? At what cost?' The next section, based on understanding in-depth a multi-caste village located 7 km away from the factory, tries to explore these issues by looking at inequality and power relations among the villagers.

LAND, WORK AND POLITICS IN A
KAMMA-DOMINATED TRIBAL VILLAGE

Located on the right bank of the Godavari, the village studied was under Nizam rule until 1948, and was part of Bhadrachalam estate, a portion of which, on the left bank of the river, was controlled by the British. According to the colonial land settlement report, the system of tenures in that estate was complicated because, 'in addition to the superior landholders, a distinct class of inferior holders have been found, on whom sub-proprietary rights have been conferred'.[14] Though the successive zamindars of Bhadrachalam were local Velamas, some of the landholders just below them were Kammas from Andhra who had been called in by the Nizam to bring the forests under cultivation. One of those agricultural colonists was given 1800 acres on the right bank of the Godavari to collect revenue from. To clear the forests, he used local Koyas as manpower and brought Madigas from the surrounding villages outside the forest area to work as agricultural labour, as well as service castes (now classified as OBCs, like carpenters, washermen, barbers and so on). The village was first established just next to the Godavari, but after a major flood in 1953, it was shifted 1 km away from the river bank.

An indirect descendant of the original Kamma landlord, Mr Rao, who is now 90 years old, still controls the whole area. Born in a neighbouring village, his father moved to the current one with his five sons in 1942. Rao has always been active in politics and as the village leader he occupied the *sarpanch* seat for more than three decades till 1977, the year when *panchayat* elections were introduced and reservations for Scheduled Tribe candidates enforced. With new waves of Andhra migrants, the village now counts 84 Kamma households and 14 Reddy households, mostly from the Godavari and Krishna deltas. Population-wise, these groups are dwarfed by Adivasi villagers (210 Koya households and 100 Lambada households), Dalits (Madigas [30]) and OBC castes (185) (see also Table 5.1).

In terms of landholdings, even though Adivasis form 60 per cent of the village population, they own only 26 per cent of the land, while the dominant Kammas and Reddis, who are 12 per cent of the population, own 53 per cent of the village land. The Dalit Madigas constitute 5 per cent of the population and own 1 per cent of the land. The OBC castes constitute 23 per cent of the population and own 20 per cent of the land, which is almost proportional to their demographic weight. For the quantitative survey, I have excluded the OBC castes since my focus was on Adivasis and Dalits in comparison to the dominant Kammas (only four Reddy households were present in the village at the time of the study since most of them are absentee landlords living in the cities). I selected 100 Dalit and Adivasi households, including all 30 of the Madiga households, as well as a sample of 40 Koya and 30 Lambada households. Added to these were 50 Kamma households, which includes all those present in the village at the time of investigation. A total of 508 individuals (275 male and 233 females) were thus surveyed in the 150-household multi-caste sample.

The survey reveals that most of the land and wealth is concentrated in the hands of one Kamma family: Rao and his four brothers. All of them inherited 50 acres from their father, but Rao, the eldest, now controls 300 acres, even if on paper he only owns 80. He recently took over the land of his deceased brother, an anaesthetist practising in Bhadrachalam town who died heirless in February 2015. Before that he had grabbed the property of another brother who was away in the United States working as a paediatrician. Rao's children are also working in the USA: one son as a software businessman, one daughter as a neurologist and another son as a cardiologist. Rao was proud to tell me that the latter owns six hospitals and a private jet to fly between them, while showing me his family albums in his mansion (Photo

8) – with ten rooms, marble floors, teak furniture and crystal chandeliers, on which he spent 15 million rupees (1.5 crore). Though he studied only up to 7th grade, Rao dominates his brothers as well as the rest of the village because of his political power. Most of the lands he accumulated over the years – forest, government or Koya-owned – were encroached on after 1970, the year when the Land Transfer Regulation Act was enacted. The 300 acres he now occupies amount to 100 times the average landholding of a Koya farmer in the village, a clear example of 'accumulation by dispossession'.[15] Unlike Rao's brother, who returned from the USA to recover his stolen land by filing a case in court, ordinary villagers find it difficult to fight injustice due to Rao's highly placed contacts in the police, the administration and even the judiciary.

Photo 8   Rao's village mansion, Bhadrachalam
Photo by Dalel Benbabaali.

The Land Transfer Regulation Act explains why 40 per cent of the Kamma households do not own land, since they settled in the village after 1970 and were not allowed to acquire property. However, some of those who migrated recently managed to occupy tribal land which they cultivate without official titles (*pattas*). They can do so by informally taking land on lease from Adivasis through an oral contract (since even tenancy is illegal for non-Adivasis), lending them money at usurious rates, sometimes up to 6 per cent per month (72 per cent per annum), and then acquiring the property as collateral when the indebted owners cannot repay their loans. Another way to circumvent the law is to buy a testament from an Adivasi landowner, since a will does not enter in the definition of transfer. Some Kamma men even marry Adivasi women as first or second wives, or just keep them as concubines, and in return for their maintenance, the women allow land to be held in their names and cultivated by the upper caste men. I have not come across such cases in the village but they are reported in official documentation about land alienation in the Scheduled Areas of Telangana.[16]

The average property size of a Kamma landowning household, excluding the 300 acres controlled by Rao, is 10 acres, which provides a sufficient annual income without having to work on other people's fields (see Table 5.2). Even the landless Kammas, thanks to other forms of ownership (like livestock, mostly buffaloes whose milk they sell), and thanks to caste status and privileged access to Rao, fare much better than the landless Madigas, who represent 85 per cent of the total Dalit households. The remaining 15 per cent own only half an acre per household after subdivision of marginal holdings, which cannot ensure their subsistence, and even less a marketable surplus. Few possess animals, and those who do use them for their own consumption of meat or milk.

More than 90 per cent of the Madiga men work as daily wage labourers, either in agriculture (47 per cent) or in industry (44 per cent), while the rest could either secure permanent employment in the paper factory or semi-skilled jobs (construction workers, tractor drivers) (see Figure 5.1). By contrast, 20 per cent of the Kamma men can rely on farming their own lands, and only 8 per cent work as agricultural *coolies*. Fourteen per cent of them work as casual labourers in the paper factory, and more than half are engaged in various businesses and professions, including Indian Tobacco Company contractors and permanent employees. Among the Adivasi groups, Koyas have remained much more agrarian than the Lambadas, who only acquired land in the area from the 1970s onwards: more than 90 per cent of the Koya men still depend on agriculture for their living (8 per cent on their own lands, 40 per cent as wage labourers, and 44 per cent combining both). Only 4 per cent of them are casual workers in the paper factory, against 31 per cent of the Lambada men. The Lambadas came to the village in different rounds, the first in the 1970s and the second in the 1990s. The second group came mostly for jobs in the paper factory so own less land.

Among the women, 57 per cent of the Kamma women are housewives, a traditional status symbol for upper caste women, while 12 per cent are agricultural labourers, and the rest work as tailors, beauticians, teachers, or sell vegetables and mangoes from their gardens in the market. On the other hand, three-quarters of the Madiga women work as farm coolies and one-quarter stay at home. While most of the Koya and Lambada women work in the fields (their own, for a small number, and/or other people's farms), two Koya women in the sample are tailors, another two have private jobs, and three could benefit from Scheduled Tribe reservations: one is the village sarpanch, and two are government employees working as a school cook and a crèche (*anganwadi*) teacher (see Figure 5.2).

The correlation of occupation and education data from the survey points to the fact that, for the same number of years of schooling, Kamma men and women are more likely than Dalits and Adivasis to access non-farm employment, whether in the private or public sector, in spite of reservations, due to their social and financial capital. Kammas have the highest literacy rate in the village (around 70 per cent for both men and women), followed by Lambada men (66 per cent), whereas around half of the Madigas and Koyas have never been to school. Among Kammas, 26 per cent of the men and 18 per cent of the women have a degree, a much higher proportion than among Koyas (7 per cent of the men, 5 per cent of the women), Lambadas (7 per cent of the men, 2 per cent of the women) and Madigas (4 per cent of the men). The most common degrees found in the sample are BTech, BCom and BSc (including BSc nursing for girls). Less than 10 per cent of the boys across caste groups underwent vocational training in Industrial Training Institutes (see Figures 5.3 and 5.4).

Among Kammas, the younger generation is better educated as the children are generally sent to the Indian Tobacco Company English-medium school in Sarapaka and then study in private colleges, mostly engineering, medicine and commerce. By contrast, there is still a large proportion of school dropouts among Dalit and Adivasi youths. The village government school doesn't offer teaching beyond 7th grade and few Adivasis are willing to move to *ashram* residential high schools in the towns, even though they are fully funded by the state's tribal sub-plan. Koya girls are generally married off at an early age (around 18) and then work as agricultural coolies. Though reservations have helped Dalits and Adivasis to access higher education, very few in the village could get a government job, and those who have are now living in nearby towns. Some Koyas complain that the benefits of the Scheduled Tribe quota are cornered by the educationally more advanced Lambadas, though this is not confirmed by my village survey. At a larger scale, however, it is true that Lambadas are over-represented among government employees in Bhadrachalam Scheduled Area. For example, 80 per cent of Adivasi teachers in the Integrated Tribal Development Agency are Lambadas, though they form less than 50 per cent of the total Scheduled Tribe population.[17]

Lambadas are nomadic people from the plains who were included in the Andhra Pradesh Scheduled Tribe list by the Congress Chief Minister Channa Reddy in 1976, during the Emergency, in order to get their votes and win the elections. Many Lambadas were subsequently elected from Scheduled Tribe reserved constituencies as Congress MPs and Members of the State Legislative Assembly. They are thus politically powerful and well connected.

Since the late 1970s an important influx of Lambadas from Maharashtra (which classifies them as OBC) has been observed in Bhadrachalam Scheduled Area, where their population has doubled since the 1991 Census. They came to benefit from various government schemes offered to Adivasis by the Integrated Tribal Development Agency and were allowed to buy land, unlike other settlers. Many Koyas resent their inclusion in the Scheduled Tribe list and consider competition with them to be unfair since they are more exposed to the outside world, which gives them an advantage in terms of knowledge of the mainstream economy and culture. To protect Koyas' interests, a circular was issued in 2010 by the Andhra Pradesh commissioner for tribal welfare, making it compulsory to provide evidence of living in Bhadrachalam Integrated Tribal Development Agency since 1950 to obtain Scheduled Tribe certificates. One should be able to prove that one's name was on voting lists, or in land or school records since that year. However, as the officer heading the Tribal Development Agency explained to me, the Koyas who never went to school, have no land deeds, and have never voted, are not able to provide such evidence. The irony is that many Lambadas are able to fabricate evidence thanks to their connections in the administration, but not the Koyas for whom this circular was issued and which is in fact making their lives more difficult, as they now have to struggle to get Scheduled Tribe certificates.

The Koyas are still better off than the Madigas as two-thirds of them own land, for which some received pattas a decade ago when the Forest Rights Act was implemented in the state by then Congress Chief Minister Y.S. Rajashekar Reddy. Pushed by Indian Tobacco Company, a few Koyas have started to plant eucalyptus, though they generally hesitate to accept the saplings sold to them by the company because one has to wait four years for the trees to grow enough to generate an income from selling the wood to the factory. Rao and other rich Kamma farmers have always been the biggest eucalyptus planters in the village for Indian Tobacco Company, including on encroached tribal lands where Koyas were employed as wood-cutters, but as the company is planning to increase the capacity of its pulping unit, it is also encouraging small farmers to practise intercultivation. As an Indian Tobacco Company manager explained to me:

We need more wood supply but we cannot expand our own plantations since we can't buy land here, so we have to convince the local farmers to plant eucalyptus by selling them the saplings cloned in our nurseries at subsidised prices and by teaching them intercultivation: between two rows of eucalyptus, they can grow cotton which will provide them with a yearly income, and after four years, the income from eucalyptus comes as a bonus.

The Koyas' first encounter with the Indian Tobacco Company, more than three decades ago, was when the company was laying a pipe in their village to bring water from the Godavari to the factory. At that time, some Koya men were offered permanent jobs by the company to compensate for the loss of land, since the pipe went across their fields. Many of them were not interested in taking up such jobs and preferred to be given financial compensation. Among the few who accepted, only one is still in the village, as others either died or moved to Sarapaka, closer to the factory. He is the wealthiest in his community, with a monthly salary of Rs.25,000 two years before retirement and an attractive four-bedroom house. His son, one of the few educated Koyas from this village, works as a mechanical engineer in Bangalore. This family's upward social mobility alienated them from other Koyas who disapprove of the way the paper factory employee left his widowed mother, now 80 years old, to live a miserable life in a hut just next to his house. Her only possessions consist of a few utensils and one sari, and she mostly wears towels over her blouse (Photo 9).

Photo 9   Koya permanent Indian Tobacco Company employee's mother
Photo by Dalel Benbabaali.

This case apart, there is a strong cohesion among the 1000 Koyas of the village, even if they are not all related like the 30 Madiga households, whose genealogies show that they are all relatives, and that their marriage patterns often involve the typical Dravidian cross-cousin or uncle–niece alliances. The Koyas are divided into exogamous clans and generally seek alliances from neighbouring Koya villages. Though Koyas and Madigas do not intermarry and live in different 'colonies', they often work and eat together in the fields. Madigas feel that the Koyas look down on them, but when asked about it, the latter deny it. Untouchability against the Madigas used to be practised mostly by the Kammas, but also by some Koyas who would not enter their houses. Interestingly, it is the only Brahmin in the village who told me so, the retired headmaster of the village government school who lives half of the year with his software engineer son in Bangalore since his wife died. In his criticism of untouchability, he seemed oblivious that this practice was a consequence of the penetration of Brahminism into Adivasi territory, conveniently putting the blame on the 'uneducated Kamma nouveau riche':

> I have no words to describe how the Madigas were treated when my father, a priest from Tirupati, came here in the 1940s to buy land. Everybody, including the Koyas, considered them Untouchables, and that continued till the 1980s. I'm an educated person, so I don't believe in caste, and as the village school headmaster, I am friendly with everyone. I am not into politics like this Rao who tells everyone that his children are earning millions in America but who doesn't give a single rupee to the poor except to buy votes.

Since the sarpanch seat is reserved for Scheduled Tribes, the Koyas can contest elections, unlike the Madigas. Their sheer numbers also give them political weight. Till recently, the condition for being elected was to be a member of the Telugu Desam Party, 'Rao's party', as the villagers call it. The current sarpanch is a Koya woman from this party whom Rao helped to win with his financial support and whose decisions he now commands. Telugu Desam is a regional party dominated by the Kammas at the state level, whereas the Reddis control the Congress. Rao, the president of the Telugu Desam farmers' union, has erected in the centre of the village a golden statue of 'NTR', the Kamma founder of the party and ex-chief minister of the state, before his son-in-law Naidu took over. However, since the formation of a separate Telangana State, Telugu Desam is perceived as an 'Andhra party', currently in power in Andhra Pradesh, with no chance of winning in Telangana. Rao is therefore thinking of supporting the Telangana Rashtra Samithi party, which is currently in power in Telangana. Although he has not left Telugu Desam yet, he is supporting his younger relatives Prasad, Ramesh and Prakash, three cotton traders living in the village, who have already joined Telangana Rashtra Samithi in anticipation of the next elections. The ex- Member of the Legislative Assembly of Khammam, Tummala Nageswara Rao, is also a Kamma who switched to this party in 2014 when the state was formed in order to become a minister in the new Telangana government. Its pink flags are now flying at the centre of the village.

According to my village survey, 95 per cent of the Madigas support Telugu Desam, but only 45 per cent of the Koyas, the majority of whom vote for Congress since they received pattas for their forest lands under Y.S. Rajashekar Reddy's regime. Another reason for this political difference is that the Koyas can afford to disobey Rao's voting instructions as they are less dependent on him than the landless Madigas, who work on his fields and seek his help to get employment in the paper factory. The paper factory labour contractors in the village are all Kammas related to Rao and therefore select the workers he recommends, based on their political loyalty. This partly explains why very few Koyas work as casual labour in the factory, but they are also not interested in industrial labour. As they say, 'it stinks in the factory' – a foul smell that reaches even Bhadrachalam town and that everyone complains about – and the three-shift system is not to their liking either. Working during the night and being regimented through fixed schedules infringes heavily on their sense of freedom. In fact, some of them were fired because they attended work according to their own timings or took leave without asking for permission. Among the younger generation, the few educated Koyas in the village do aspire to jobs in the paper factory, but probably due to lack of alternative employment opportunities in the vicinity. When I asked Shanta, a 20-year-old Koya studying BTech in Bhadrachalam Government College, 'What do you think of Indian Tobacco Company?' He replied: 'I don't like it, it created so many problems in our village'. Then I asked: 'Do you want to work there?' He said: 'If I get a permanent job, yes, because it is close to our village.' He was worried about not finding a job after completing his degree because he couldn't afford the Rs.10,000 industrial trip organised by his college to facilitate recruitment in various factories: 'My dad borrowed from relatives who gave up to Rs.200 each, but at the end he could gather only Rs.2000, which is not enough for the trip.'

The sarpanch of Sarapaka, an influential Lambada with corruption cases pending against him, is instrumental in Indian Tobacco Company's expansion projects since they need the approval of the *gram sabha*, as per the Panchayat (Extension to the Scheduled Areas) Act known as PESA. As the Lambadas of the village cannot expect much help from him, they seek favours from Rao, who generally obliges since 95 per cent of them vote for the Telugu Desam. Like for the Madigas, the Kamma leader's authority over them is strong due to the material conditions in which they find themselves. Though two-thirds of them own land, their plots are small (2 acres on average) and the soil of bad quality as they arrived relatively late in the village, when the best land had already been occupied. The first wave of

Lambadas settled in the Koya colony in the late 1970s and interact with the Koyas on a daily basis. A second wave came in the 1990s in search of employment in the paper factory and now live in a separate street, at the entry to the village, quite far from the other Adivasis.

In spite of the 'divide-and-rule' strategies used by Rao, who thinks of Koyas as rebellious and of Lambadas as obedient, hence preferentially employing the latter in his fields or helping them to get contracts in the paper factory, there is no enmity between the two Adivasi groups. The rivalry around reservations is not important in the village, as very few of them are educated enough to even aspire to government jobs. Intercaste marriages between them are rare (only two cases), but cultural differences are no obstacle to their daily interactions, especially while working together in the fields. During the cotton plucking season I spent time with the coolie women who enjoyed singing songs in their own languages while harvesting, some in Koya, some in Lambadi, and others (the Madigas) in Telugu (Photo 10). They communicate with each other in Telugu, and the younger Koyas have even stopped using their dialect due to schooling in Telugu-medium, since the Koya language does not have a script. Twenty-five per cent of the village Koyas have recently been converted to Christianity by the Indian Evangelical Mission, while others continue to worship their own deities or tribal saints like Saramma and Sarakka, the legendary female warriors who became martyrs fighting the imperial forces of the Kakatiya monarchs (a Telugu dynasty the Kammas claim to be descended from).

Photo 10   Koya, Lambada and Madiga women plucking cotton on Kamma land
Photo by Dalel Benbabaali.

Only one Madiga man has a permanent job with Indian Tobacco Company which he obtained 20 years ago, 'after working hard as casual labour for ten years', and now earns a monthly salary of Rs.20,000, just a year before retiring. While everyone in the Madiga street, the last street of the village, has a concrete house from the Indiramma scheme,[18] he built himself a bigger house with an extra room, where his deserted married daughter lives, and has a two-wheeler to go to the factory. Despite these visible signs of class differentiation, he shares a common trait with the paper factory casual workers of the Madiga colony – who earn Rs.3000 to 5000 per month and travel to the factory in auto rickshaws – which is a heavy tendency to drink bad quality country-made liquor after work to the point of being semi-conscious during all the time spent at home. It was difficult to interview these men as they were almost never awake, which I first thought was a consequence of their sleep deprivation due to the paper factory's three-shift system. I spent most of the time with their wives who did not seem to suffer from their husbands' alcoholism as is sometimes assumed (in terms of domestic violence for example – although, of course, the men's potential contribution to household income was diverted to drink), and were totally in control of the households since the men were always 'absent'. Their agricultural wages, of around Rs.130 per day, are almost similar to those of the men who do unskilled casual labour in the factory for Rs.200, from which they have to deduct Rs.50 for travel. Though extremely low, these wages give the Madiga women some degree of independence vis-à-vis their husbands, who, as said, spend most of their income on drinking, while the women provide for the household's expenses.

The gender-based division of labour that is found among Madigas and Lambadas does not exist among the Koyas since most of the men do agriculture just like the women. Couples and their teenage children often work together on their *podu* fields,[19] growing rain-fed rice or Bt cotton, a genetically modified cash crop introduced in this village in the late 1990s by the Kammas, who occupied the best black cotton soils with lift irrigation from the river, where they could also grow tobacco, chillies and a double crop of paddy. The Koyas not only get less yield due to lack of irrigation facilities and mediocre soil quality, but the average size of their landholdings is only 3 acres, which is just enough for their subsistence.

Compared to other groups, the Koyas have maintained a higher level of economic and cultural autonomy, which is slowly being eroded by processes of land alienation and incorporation into mainstream society as wage labourers. Even the landless among them prefer to work as coolies on other Koyas' fields to avoid being dependent on the dominant Kammas, towards whom they feel more suspicion than respect. While everybody else in the village calls Rao '*pedda*', a Telugu word that literally means 'big' or 'elderly', but which expresses deference (it can also be translated as 'important' or 'powerful'), the Koyas see him as a 'cheat' (they use the English word). When all the villagers attended Rao's brother's funeral to express their condolences, the Koyas ignored the ceremony and stayed at home. They would rather live on the little they have than do a job they dislike or ask Rao for favours. During the agricultural lean season, Koya men and women would sit idle outside their houses and drink palm wine (toddy) or *mahua* liquor together, with their children playing around. Gender relations are more egalitarian than among other groups and their way of sharing natural fermented drinks is very different from the alcoholism observed among the paper factory workers, whether Madigas or Lambadas. However, their progressive loss of land is forcing some of them to take up industrial work at the risk of alienation, or to become wage-earners by cutting eucalyptus in the Indian Tobacco Company plantations on cleared forests which used to be theirs. The expansion of the company is the major threat they will have to face in the coming years, but this will probably not happen without resistance, as the current struggles already show.

SOCIAL, HEALTH, AND ENVIRONMENTAL STRUGGLES AROUND THE INDIAN TOBACCO COMPANY PAPER FACTORY

In February 2015, a major protest united the villagers against the Indian Tobacco Company, whom they accuse of taking water from the river near their village without connecting taps to the pipe for the people to drink. They only have hand pumps from which the water often comes out brown, mixed with mud, which gives the children fever and diarrhoea. Only the Kamma street has a tap for almost every house and a concrete road, built by the company with which Rao has excellent relations, since the company's executives used to stay in his house when the factory was under construction in the late 1970s. The pumping station by the river was built at that time, but recently the company started raising a water tower outside the village, barely 100 metres away from the Madiga street. As a Madiga woman complained: 'ITC is building its water tank right here, but it is not for us. ITC has done nothing for the village.' In a rare show of village solidarity, Madigas, Koyas, Lambadas, OBC castes and even Kammas without water access decided to march to the tower and to occupy the construction site. Some camped there for many days to prevent the work continuing. 'No party led the agitation', an OBC man assured me. 'We were all having the same feeling: it is going to be summer and we will have no water, while ITC is here on the village land, building a tank for uninterrupted water supply.' The company asked the police to intervene when some villagers went to the pumping station in order to force the gates open and stop the pump machinery. There was no violence as the police threatened to arrest the protesters if they destroyed anything but allowed them to camp near the gates. The agitation came to an end after a week, when the company signed a commitment in the presence of bureaucrats and politicians, which included providing drinking water to the villagers and building roads for the Adivasi and Dalit colonies.

When asked about this victorious outcome, Rao claimed that he was the main negotiator behind the agreement. Sensing that his traditional authority is declining (this was a village where the police never came as he used to settle every dispute), he knows that he can't just dictate rules and command people's votes without 'delivering' by keeping his promises of 'developing the village'. However, people are not duped any more and the success of their protest clearly showed that the village development is not a favour to be expected from Rao's bargaining power with the Indian Tobacco Company and the government, but a right that can be demanded through collective mobilisation. The agitation also helped the Madigas, Lambadas and Koyas, no longer divided into two categories of 'obedient' versus 'disobedient' subjects as perceived by the Kamma landlord, to realise the importance of unity to achieve common goals. Even the OBC groups, who are better off, were in solidarity with them and accepted that roads should be built in their colonies since the mud paths there were flooded every monsoon, whereas the majority of these groups live on the main street connecting the village to the paper factory, which is a metalled road. The most ardent opponent to Rao is an OBC leader from the Congress, a retired teacher who recently opened a marriage bureau in Sarapaka. When he was teaching in the village school he tried to convince the government to extend the classes to 10th grade, but was stopped in his endeavour by Rao who filed a fake case against him, as he didn't want the Dalits and Adivasis to be more educated than he was and to study beyond 7th grade.

Another major protest took place during one whole year starting from July 2014, on a stretch of bushy terrain belonging to the Forest Department, located midway between the village and the paper factory. Around 300 plastic tents were set up there and occupied by people from Sarapaka and other nearby villages who wanted this land to be given to them to build their houses on. Their argument was that the rents in Sarapaka had become unaffordable for the poor due to the rising demand for accommodation by people working in the factory, as it does not provide housing facilities, except for its managers. The average rent for a one-bedroom house in Sarapaka is now (2015) Rs.2000, while it was Rs.500 ten years earlier. Before the establishment of the paper factory, back in the 1970s, Sarapaka used to be a tiny village of a few hundred inhabitants. It has now become a small town with a population of nearly 20,000, even if it is still considered a panchayat and not a municipality, just like Bhadrachalam that has now reached 50,000. Only 3 per cent of the population in Sarapaka are Koyas, as many were displaced by industrialisation. The rest are Dalits, Lambadas, upper castes, but also people from outside the state, mostly Tamils, Bengalis and Odias, who came to work for the company. This dramatic change in the demography of a tribal village was accompanied by rapid socioeconomic transformations, which mostly affected the poor, despite the company's claim of having 'developed' Sarapaka by making it a 'bustling town'. One of these adverse consequences is the rise in rents which pushed homeless people to participate in the protest camp asking the government for house sites. Many of them are from neighbouring villages and came to Sarapaka in search of work in the factory.

When I conducted a survey of the camp in June 2015, only 60 households were left of the original 300. Most of them had abandoned the fight due to the unbearable heat in the month of May, as it was hardly possible to live in plastic tents under 50° Celsius (Bhadrachalam area is one of the hottest places in India due to the coal mines and heavy deforestation). The following month, heavy rains totally washed away the ramshackle tents as the monsoon arrived unusually early. Their huts had already been destroyed several times by the Forest Department officials who wanted the protesters to vacate the land on which they were illegally camping. Their last intervention was particularly violent, as men, women and children were beaten up, which prompted a Koya woman to file a case under the Scheduled Caste/Scheduled Tribe Atrocities Act that was dismissed because the Forest Department officer she accused, a Lambada, was himself from a Scheduled Tribe. After this brutal intervention, the officer heading the Integrated Tribal Development Agency asked the Forest Department to allow the protesters to stay there until she finds a solution for them. She asked the mandal revenue officer of Burgampadu to list the names of all Adivasi people camping there and promised to give them house sites on government land if it was verified that they didn't own any property.

At the time of my survey, there were 17 Adivasi households (13 Koya and 4 Lambada), 24 Dalit (16 Madiga and 8 Mala), 14 OBC (11 Hindu and 3 Muslim), and 5 general castes (3 Reddy and 2 Komati). It rapidly became apparent that many of them were not eligible for allocation of a house site, not only because they were not from a Scheduled Tribe, but because they already had a house and were just taking advantage of the protest in the hope of getting more land. Most of them were from Sarapaka or other villages of Burgampadu mandal. Among the men, only six were casual workers in the paper factory, and others were agricultural coolies, drivers (auto rickshaw/ taxi/ tractor), construction workers, or old people living on pensions. Most of the women were also coolies, or non-working widows who were apparently abandoned by their families. Apart from the harsh climate, the living conditions in the camp were appalling: no toilets, no electricity and no water (they drank from a leak in the Indian Tobacco Company pipeline). Some children were not attending school, while others were sent to their grandparents in their native villages to be able to go to school. However, the better off among the protesters, especially the upper caste ones, didn't sleep in the camp as they had other places to stay and turned up only during the day.

The protesters formed two separate groups: one small group organised by a Madiga leader from the Telangana Rashtra Samithi, and a bigger group organised by an OBC leader from the Communist Party of India (Marxist-Leninist) (CPI (ML))-New Democracy (Photo 11). In July 2015, after one year of occupation, the protesters were asked to vacate the camp as the Integrated Tribal Development Agency allotted house sites to 65 households (44 Koya and 21 Lambada) who didn't own any property and who had annual incomes of less than Rs.48,000. However, the CPI (ML) leader refused to give up his demands for Dalits and OBC castes. Since the officer in charge of the Tribal Development Agency was promoted as joint collector of Khammam district, he asked her to provide house sites to non-Scheduled Tribes as well, in nearby towns that were not notified as Scheduled Area, like Palvoncha and Kothagudem. When I interviewed him, he argued that most of the people he was fighting for were casual workers in the Indian Tobacco Company and that he would help them get a wage rise, thanks to which they would be able to afford to commute from those towns if they could

Photo 11   CPI(ML)–New Democracy's organised protest for house sites
Photo by Dalel Benbabaali.

build their own houses there. To date, his demands have not been satisfied and it is quite unlikely that the company will increase the workers' wages anytime soon.

According to a manager of Indian Tobacco Company, one of the reasons why the company wants to expand its Bhadrachalam paper unit, rather than its West Bengal one, is that 'people never go on strike here'. It is true that this factory does not have a particularly remarkable history of labour struggles, but this is not due to distinctive traits of Telangana workers, supposedly 'less combative' than their Bengali counterparts. The explanation most probably lies in the corrupt character and upper caste leadership of the factory unions. The four main unions are the TNTUC (Telugu Nadu Trade Union Council), affiliated to the Telugu Desam Party and headed by a Kamma who won the last elections; the INTUC (Indian National Trade Union Council), affiliated to Congress and headed by a Reddy; the AITUC (All India Trade Union Council), affiliated to the Communist Party of India and headed by a Kamma; and the CITU (Central Indian Trade Union), affiliated to the Communist Party of India (Marxist) and headed by an OBC leader. The Kamma and Reddy union leaders are known for interfering in the job selection process by recommending people from their caste in exchange for a sum that can go up to Rs.1 million (10 lakhs). Without caste-based patronage and money it is now impossible to get a permanent job in the paper factory, since employment opportunities have become scarcer. The managers are aware of these practices, but, by turning a blind eye to the unions' corruption, they ensure that no strike will be organised and no wage rise will be demanded. This is how social peace is bought.

On 12 June 2015, during the launch of the Telangana government's new industrial policy which promised 'zero tolerance to corruption', Y.C. Deveshwar, the CEO of the Indian Tobacco Company, announced an investment plan of Rs.8000 crores in Telangana, half of which will increase the production capacity of its Bhadrachalam paper unit (the other half will go to luxury hotels and a 'world class' food processing plant in the chief minister's home district of Medak, from which he was elected). Deveshwar justified his company's investments by mentioning the competition with China in the domestic market: 'We are doubling the paper mill capacity to one million tonnes. But in China one single machine produces one million tonnes of paper.'[20] The Bhadrachalam unit has seven machines producing half a million tonnes of paper per year, and the plan is to build an eighth machine which will be fully automated in order to allow 'rationalisation' of the manpower. In other words, the factory will occupy more land in the Scheduled Area without creating new jobs for the people who will be affected. According to one employee:

We are around 1500 now and they want to reduce the permanent workforce by 200 in the next two years. They won't fire us, but they will not replace the people who retire. They are saying: if you're going to invest, invest in new technology, not in workers. For technology, you pay only once, for an employee you must give promotions and salary increments, so it becomes very expensive after a few years.

While the Telangana chief minister agreed to sanction the diversion of 1300 acres of forest land in Sarapaka for the Indian Tobacco Company, in spite of a petition filed by an Adivasi organisation, the expansion has not happened yet because the clearance was denied by the Ministry of Environment and Forests in Delhi as it goes against the Conservation of Forest Act. The ministry also argued that the planned eighth machine was not site-specific and could be built elsewhere. Moreover, the company had offered compensatory afforestation in Anantapur district, which is now part of Andhra Pradesh, and Telangana will therefore be losing forest land without it being replaced in the state. Not discouraged by this temporary setback, the company is now trying to convince the government to consider 'tree cover' instead of 'forest cover', arguing that the company is promoting plantation of eucalyptus, which are TOF ('trees outside forest'). While tree cover is often shown as afforestation through satellite images, the plantation ecosystem on the ground is much poorer than that of a forest.

To increase its production, the factory will require more and more raw material, hence the intensified campaign to convince local farmers to grow eucalyptus, even if this has proved disastrous for the environment. The Indian Tobacco Company benefited from the farm forestry programme introduced at the national level in 1988 as part of the National Forest Policy, which aimed at increasing the forest cover to reach 33 per cent of the total land area. With their insatiable demand for wood fibre, the paper mills were seen as responsible for the fast-depleting forest cover and were encouraged to take up farm forestry, where small growers supply wood in the open market, instead of the mills using forest land for raw material sourcing. But eucalyptus plantations created a new ecological problem as they are highly unsustainable: they quickly deplete underground water and exhaust fertile soils, leaving them sterile in the long run. The leaves, bark and fruits of eucalyptus trees are useless for Adivasis and their animals, unlike other local trees that are traditionally used for various purposes. Eucalyptus does not provide shade, and repels birds, butterflies and bees, causing pollination stoppage. Its slim trunk and narrow leaves are incapable of resisting wind, so the soil becomes eroded due to direct exposure to sun and wind. During the monsoon, the exposed sandy upper level of the soil gets washed away into the river and the accumulation of sand keeps widening the river bed, thus increasing the risk of floods.[21]

The company took advantage of Telangana's *Haritha Haram* ('Green Belt') reforestation scheme to offer 10 million eucalyptus saplings to farmers at Rs.1 each as part of corporate social responsibility. Not only will selling those saplings bring 1 crore to the company, but this massive plantation will make the price of eucalyptus wood fall. It is therefore a clever strategy to cheat the farmers who will ultimately sell the wood to the company at a low rate due to increased supply. The Haritha Haram scheme is threatening Adivasis practising agriculture on forest land without pattas, as the Telangana government has decided to recover those cultivated plots from anyone who is unable to show land titles. In the studied village, 25 Koya households are concerned and are going to lose their only means of livelihood because of the scheme. In 2008 the previous Congress Chief Minister Y.S. Rajashekar Reddy decided to implement the Forest Rights Act and organised a massive programme of forest patta distribution to attract Adivasi votes before the State Assembly elections. However, the allotment of pattas was done in an arbitrary manner and was probably influenced by political connections and corruption. Shanta, the Koya BTech student who was one of my main informants, told me that his father could not get a patta for his 3 acres of forest land on which the whole family depends, 'because he doesn't have money and connections'. According to him, 'Koyas are innocent, but Lambadas are shrewd, so they all got land titles in our village.' The only solution for him and the other 24 Koya households in the same situation, is to apply for a fresh patta under the Forest Rights Act, but the chief minister has instructed the state's administration not to deliver any new land titles under that act, arguing that Telangana has to achieve the 33 per cent mandatory forest cover.

Paradoxically, the Indian Tobacco Company is praised by the Telangana government for its efforts in planting trees, notwithstanding the fact that eucalyptus is harmful, while Adivasis are blamed for deforestation on the grounds that many continue to practise shifting cultivation. The government is especially targeting the Gutti Koyas, who are displaced Adivasis from the conflict-torn neighbouring Chhattisgarh and who are treated as illegal encroachers on government forest land.[22] They are denied Scheduled Tribe status and the benefits of the Forest Rights Act, and they are constantly harassed by the Forest Department as well as the police, who accuse them of being Maoist sympathisers since they fled the Salwa Judum, an anti-Maoist militia. At the same time, the Telangana government gave away to Andhra Pradesh seven tribal mandals of Bhadrachalam Integrated Tribal Development Agency that will be submerged by the Polavaram dam on the left bank of the Godavari, so that the rehabilitation and resettlement of the displaced people becomes the responsibility of Chandrababu Naidu, whose state will get irrigation from the dam, as well as water for the industrial coastal corridor. By not opposing the construction of the dam, the Telangana government is *de facto* agreeing to the loss of 4000 hectares of forests and to the displacement of 400,000 people, two-thirds of whom are Adivasis and Dalits. The Indian Tobacco Company has been prompt to see an opportunity there: since the dam will not be completed within the next five years, the company is planting eucalyptus on the lands of the expropriated Adivasis living in the submergence area, who were given compensation to resettle elsewhere.[23] Various Adivasi organisations are trying to build a resistance movement against the dam, some of them even advocating the creation of a separate tribal state where Adivasis would reclaim their autonomy through self-rule instead of being the perpetual victims of the Telugu States' development and industrialisation projects.[24]

The last form of mobilisation observed around the company concerns health and pollution issues. According to the Delhi-based Centre for Science and Environment (n.d.): 'most of the Indian paper mills do not have adequate technology to recycle their wastes. Effluent treatment plants (ETPs) are capable of handling discharges and emissions emerging from single-product paper plants only. With an increase in the types of paper produced, the efficiency of the ETPs plummets.' Though the company claims that the effluents it releases into the Godavari are treated and therefore 'clean', this is not the perception of the people living in the village by the river, where an open canal carrying industrial waste runs through the fields, just a few kilometres away from Sarapaka. Not only is their drinking water contaminated, but also the paddy they cultivate on the riverbank. They realised that the rice they were eating had become so dangerous for consumption that it was safer to grow eucalyptus instead of paddy. The sarpanch of that village, a Lambada woman, fought back against the company by making a list of demands under its corporate social responsibility obligations, which included drinking water taps for every house. She also approached the Tribal Development Agency officer who instigated a civil suit on public nuisance against the company and asked the company to provide a clearance from the Telangana State Pollution Control Board, which the well-connected managers were able to obtain within two days.

In Sarapaka the Dalit colony called Gandhi Nagar and the Odia Camp, where migrant workers from Odisha live, are the most affected neighbourhoods. Although the factory has its main outlets releasing effluents into the Godavari, there are pipes releasing dirty water into residential areas as well. The people I talked to complained that it is a major problem during the monsoon, leading to flooding of their streets and a high incidence of dengue and malaria. Their only source of drinking water is open wells, which also get polluted and give the children diarrhoea. The Odia camp dwellers are the most marginalised people in Sarapaka, and no politician is listening to their complaints. They are mostly Doms, a Dalit community of Odisha that is not on the Scheduled Caste list of Andhra Pradesh/Telangana. The administration refuses to deliver caste certificates for their children unless they provide proof with proper documentation from their district of origin (Malkangiri). Since most of them left their native villages 30 years ago, none of them can provide such evidence. They first crossed the Odisha/Andhra Pradesh border to build the Sileru dam, and then moved to Sarapaka to build the paper factory. They are considered to be 'hard workers' who can do any kind of heavy construction work, unlike the local Koyas. Since they didn't have land back in their villages they were forced to migrate and do this type of work, whereas the local Koyas can survive on their forest lands. Even today, the Doms do all kinds of manual labour, but most of them are casual workers in the paper factory. The younger generation is still mostly uneducated, and the lack of Scheduled Caste certificates hasn't helped. The school dropouts are now working as labourers or auto drivers.

The Integrated Tribal Development Agency has conducted a health survey in the villages surrounding the paper factory and has identified an unusual number of cancer cases and of lung diseases due to air pollution, though many people are hesitant to declare their illnesses as they are afraid of losing their jobs in the factory. During my fieldwork, I met the family of Nagaraju Koppula, a Madiga journalist from Sarapaka who was treated in Hyderabad for lung cancer and whom I visited several times in the city before his death in April 2015, at the age of 32. A non-smoker, he himself alerted me to the probable connection between his cancer and industrial pollution. Some of his activist friends intend to file a Public Interest Litigation to enquire about health issues related to the paper factory. The 'Justice for Nagaraju Koppula' campaign is also denouncing what many perceive as a case of caste discrimination by the newspaper for which Nagaraju was working, since he was fired as soon as the management came to know about his cancer and was not given any financial assistance to pay for his chemotherapies. Nagaraju comes from an extremely poor family in Sarapaka. He was the first Madiga in Telangana to be offered a job by an English-language newspaper, in a country where Dalits are severely under-represented in the media, and totally absent from the newsrooms' key posts.[25]

Nagaraju's personal trajectory of upward social mobility against all odds is quite exceptional. He was born in Gandhi Nagar, the Dalit colony of Sarapaka located just next to the factory. His father went missing when he was a child; he was brought up with his four siblings by his mother, a daily wage labourer who took part in the construction of the paper factory in the 1970s. She was a casual labourer in the paper factory even as she was pregnant with

Nagaraju, and he himself worked there for five years as a board painter to pay for his studies. He studied in Bhadrachalam Government College in Telugu-medium. He wanted to become an Indian Administrative Service officer but ultimately received a scholarship to complete a Master's in journalism at Hyderabad University. The most educated Madiga of his village, he was the pride of his family, and the main breadwinner. His funeral in Sarapaka was attended by a huge crowd of people from neighbouring villages, who came to pay their respects to the 'English Sir' (as some called him because of his command of the English language). I attended the ceremony that was organised in his memory in Sarapaka community hall, built by the Indian Tobacco Company as part of its corporate social responsibility work.

UNEQUAL LIVES, POWER RELATIONS AND STRUGGLES OF DALITS AND ADIVASIS

The four groups I have studied in this chapter – Koyas, Lambadas, Madigas and Kammas – have distinct histories and social trajectories. As original inhabitants of Bhadrachalam area, the Koyas have been the most affected by processes of dispossession through the loss of their lands, forests and water, which progressively undermined their economic and cultural autonomy. Latecomers, the Lambadas benefited from their inclusion in the state's Scheduled Tribe list, which allowed them to buy land to some extent and take advantage of various government schemes under the tribal sub-plan. As Dalits, the Madigas living in this tribal area have mostly been landless and cannot claim rights over immovable property since land transfers to non-Scheduled Tribes are prohibited in Adivasi territories. Because of their landlessness, they are even more marginalised than the Adivasis in that area. At the other end of the social hierarchy, the Kammas became the most dominant group after acquiring vast properties at the cost of the original landholders, and continued to prosper even after the protective legislations were enacted.

With the setting up of the Indian Tobacco Company paper factory the main landlord and other Kamma landowners became part of a new, wider process of capital accumulation – just as the Nadar landlords in Cuddalore district, analysed in the preceding chapter did with the arrival of the bone factory. It is also striking how, both in the Bhadrachalam area and in Melpuram in Cuddalore, local Dalits became informalised, insecure workers in the factory while Adivasi groups did not do so, although in Bhadrachalam the Lambadas, whose Scheduled Tribe status is recent, have also joined as workers. But while the processes of dispossession and industrialisation have similarities in Bhadrachalam and Cuddalore, they also played out in different ways. For example, the fact that the Koyas have some land has enabled them to maintain a degree of autonomy unheard of in Cuddalore. I have shown how, in Bhadrachalam, the protection offered by the Fifth Schedule in many instances has been brushed aside by powerful landed groups and industrialists, but it nevertheless provides some defence for the Adivasis compared to what is available to Adivasis and Dalits in Cuddalore.

As with the rest of the chapters in this book, looking at unequal lives and power relations in a particular setting has provided empirical evidence for the arguments made in this chapter. I have tried to explain how the Adivasis and Dalits living in a resource-rich territory have become increasingly poor. Their impoverishment is primarily a consequence of wealth capture and capital accumulation by the dominant castes who migrated to that area. This chapter also illustrates how corporate interests under the patronage of the state plunder natural resources in a collusive alienation of Adivasis from their lands. In this sense, resource capture is a euphemism for the theft of the commons. Historically, it is the quest for resources and cheap labour that has led to the penetration of Adivasi territories by the state, industries and agricultural colonists belonging to the dominant castes, whose feudal oppression progressively gave way to capitalist exploitation. The government's rhetoric about economic development and job creation purposefully ignores the human, environmental and social costs of such 'progress' that benefits only a small section of the population while others pay a heavy price for it, thus deepening the gap between rich and poor. The constitutional safeguards that are supposed to protect Scheduled Areas remain a dead letter when huge industrial investments are at stake. This is why the people who are deprived of their means of livelihood and deliberately kept at the bottom of the social and economic hierarchy need to resort to collective struggles to assert their rights.

6

Chamba Valley, Himalaya, Himachal Pradesh

Richard Axelby

Prakaso and Mussa disagree on what it means to be nomadic. The Hindi word *'ghumantu'* – roving, mobile, wandering – also translates into English as 'itinerant' – a word with considerable negative connotations. The stereotypes that attach themselves to the term, however, have not stopped both Gaddi and Gujjar Adivasis in Chamba district from laying claim to it. Prakaso – who is from the Gaddi tribe – says ghumantu means 'people who travel' whether this be families who move from a summer to a winter home or nomadic shepherds who travel year-round with flocks of sheep and goats. Mussa – a member of the Gujjar tribe disagrees; according to him only his people are ghumantu as they, unlike the Gaddis, travel as family groups alongside the herds of buffalo they own. He says the difference is that while Gujjars 'look to our buffalo', the Gaddi 'look first to their land'. In fact, neither Mussa nor Prakaso migrate with their animals in the manner that their grandfathers did. Yet both men, and many others like them, now must leave their homes in Chamba district of Himachal Pradesh and travel in search of work building roads or labouring on hydro projects. Moving beyond nomadism, these new forms of migration have become an increasingly important – though often precarious – component of household livelihood strategies that combine agriculture and livestock rearing with local and non-local wage labour. In the foothills of the Himalayas the families of formerly ghumantu Gaddis and Gujjars face considerable obstacles in their search for new forms of upward mobility.

This chapter takes us to the Himalayas, to the district of Chamba in Himachal Pradesh. It concentrates on two Adivasi groups, the Gaddis who are Hindus and the Gujjars who are Muslims. Confronted by high mountains, cold winters and thick forests, Gaddi and Gujjar livelihoods traditionally depended on combinations of settled agriculture and nomadic pastoralism. Though culturally distinct from one another, I show how these two ethnic groups share a common class position which distinguishes them from the wider non-tribal population. Against the backdrop of booming India, I investigate how Gujjars and Gaddis struggle to negotiate the obstacles which block paths to economic and social mobility.

In the mountains of Chamba there are no large factories dominating new informal labour relations like those found in the villages in Tamil Nadu and Telangana discussed in the two preceding chapters. Nor is there a single dominant landowning caste such as those that rule in Cuddalore, the tribal belt of Khammam district or the plains of Nandurbar in Maharashtra. Yet there are significant points of similarity concerning the mundane processes of historical marginalisation and their present-day effects. This chapter presents an account of how, though their lives have changed in significant ways, Chamba's tribal families remain trapped at the bottom of the socio-economic hierarchy. Examining the contrasting paths taken by Gaddis and Gujjars helps to unpick forms of 'residual' poverty caused by isolation and marginality from new types of 'relational' poverty rooted in processes of social exclusion and adverse inclusion.

I show how Gaddis and Gujjars historically occupied precarious ecological and social niches of pastoralism and settled agriculture in the hierarchically organised princely state of Chamba in the Himalayas. The decades following Independence have seen a steady shift towards sedentarisation, in part due to government control of grazing land. At the same time, some Gaddi and Gujjar families gained access to small plots of relatively good agricultural land which cemented their transition into farming. But the Gaddis' and Gujjars' shift out of their customary pastoralism did not have much impact on the domination by local 'caste' Hindus and 'general' Muslims of government employment, private service and urban business. In the last decades, these groups have also found good high-status jobs in the new industrial belt in southern Himachal and elsewhere, and invested in high-value agriculture. In comparison to the Adivasi Gaddis and Gujjars, it is apparent that local rural Dalits have had more success in getting government jobs and moving into semi-skilled occupations. The Gaddis and Gujjars, on the other hand, have been left behind: unable to continue to live off the land, unable to invest seriously in their land, and unable to gain significant access to anything but informal, seasonal work. As in the other cases covered in this book, the migration of labour is important. Here I contrast the Gaddis' and Gujjars' limited experiences as unskilled, migrant workers going to work elsewhere, against those of incoming labour drawn from the states of Bihar, Uttar Pradesh and Rajasthan.

Today, Himachal Pradesh is known for its strong human development record and high levels of economic growth and it has long been argued that caste relations in the Himalayas are more egalitarian than elsewhere in India. However, it is still a state which is economically and politically dominated by high caste Rajputs and Brahmins. Gaddis and Gujjars of the valley I studied have little political clout and only a few of them have been in a position to benefit from the neoliberal reforms and the growing market economy.

I also show that the historical and social differences between the Gaddis and the Gujjars, and how they have been integrated into the wider economy, have led to different social and economic strategies for the two groups. The kinds of networks they have been able to forge, including along religious lines, differ and this has had an impact on the degree of class differentiation within the two groups. These are important nuances but, overall, both groups still find themselves at the bottom of society.

CHAMBA DISTRICT IN HIMACHAL PRADESH

Himachal Pradesh would, in many ways, appear to have benefited from processes of economic liberalisation and political decentralisation since the early 1990s. Having lagged behind its more prosperous neighbours the state has, over the last two decades, enjoyed rapid and sustained growth. Economic development in Himachal Pradesh has been driven by a combination of tourism (especially trekking and adventure sports), floriculture and commercial horticulture (as the 'fruit bowl' of India), hydro projects (which involve damming along the five major river basins of the state) and industrial development (through a central government-supported programme of incentives, subsidies and infrastructure provision designed to attract businesses to the southern districts of the state). With its low levels of corruption and responsive institutions Himachal Pradesh is now described as 'a leader of hill area development' (*Divya Himachal* 2013). Significantly, in Himachal economic development has been achieved alongside improvements in education (Jean Drèze and Amartya Sen rate Himachal Pradesh's progress as the most impressive in India [2013: 91]) and its Multidimensional Poverty Index is among the best in India (see the chapter by Kannan).[1] Himachal Pradesh also has a much higher proportion of households with salaried government jobs than other Indian states.[2]

However, this is not to say that the benefits of growth have been shared equally. Located in the foothills of the Himalayas, the overwhelming majority (nearly 90 per cent) of Himachal Pradesh's population live in rural areas. For various reasons – not least the mountainous terrain – its agricultural growth rates have lagged far behind other sectors. Typically, agricultural holdings are small and labour is drawn from within the household. Small fields on steep hillsides are unsuited to mechanised production. Being dependent on the monsoon rains, yields vary from year to year. Geographically, certain districts have poverty levels that are significantly higher than others.

The old princely state of Chamba was ruled for more than a millennium by the same family. After Independence in 1947, the area was transformed into a district of the embryonic state of Himachal Pradesh. Despite this change, Chamba's developmental performance remains among the least impressive in the state. Chamba district has the state's lowest income per capita with the majority of the population classified as being below the poverty line or only marginally above it.[3] It also has the highest illiteracy rates and levels of life expectancy are far below the average. Adivasi families in Chamba are over-represented among those living below the poverty line and among the poorest of the poor. Here, two groups – the agro-pastoral Gaddi and Gujjar – have long suffered from disproportionately low income per capita and perform poorly on multidimensional human development indicators, including child mortality and literacy.[4]

Confronted by high mountains, cold winters and thick forests, the livelihoods of Gaddis and Gujjars traditionally depended on combinations of settled agriculture and nomadic pastoralism. For generations Gaddi shepherds and Gujjar herdsmen have driven their goats and buffalo along steep mountains trails from the winter grazing grounds close to the neighbouring state of Punjab up to alpine pastures high in the Dhauladhar and Pir Panjal mountain ranges. In 1950, on account of their unique cultures, their geographical isolation and the 'backwardness' of their traditional nomadic occupation, the Gaddis and Gujjars of Chamba district were both granted Scheduled Tribe status. But there has always been a degree of ambiguity over the official 'tribal' status of both Gaddis and Gujjars. The 1965 Lokur Committee Report recognised Gaddis and Gujjars in Himachal Pradesh as nomadic shepherds and herdsmen but recommended that they be excluded from the list of Scheduled Tribes on the grounds that 'these communities do not possess any tribal characteristics'.[5] In neighbouring Kangra district (which was part of Punjab at the time of Independence), Gaddis and Gujjars were only awarded Scheduled Tribe status in 2002.[6]

The shared Scheduled Tribe status of Gaddis and Gujjars in Chamba masks significant differences: buffalo-herding Gujjars are Muslim while shepherding Gaddis straddle the border between nominal mainstream Hinduism and animism. Gaddis are a majority community in particular areas of Chamba district while Gujjars being both Muslim *and* tribal are a minority within a minority. Furthermore, Gaddi identity is connected to a clear sense of geographical belonging, which enables them to make a claim to indigeneity in a way that Gujjars cannot. It is important to recognise the role of different categories in construction of identity markers at the intersections of community, state, religion and politics. With Gaddis like Prakaso and Gujjars such as Mussa making the transition from nomadic pastoralism to migration in search of work the related but distinct ideas of being nomadic (ghumantu) and being tribal (Adivasi) have played out in contrasting ways.

A slice of the Saal valley

Chamba town is the sole urban centre in the Chamba valley, the former capital of the Chamba Rajas, and the district headquarters of Chamba district. Into the hills to the north of the town a mountain road runs parallel to the River Saal for 15 km before passing through a narrow gorge. On the far side, as the valley widens out, we find Badagaon[7] – a village which, with its 50 households, is considered large in these parts, with schools, daily needs stores, a chai-shop and the *panchayat* office. Set amid extensive fields, the concrete houses of Badagaon appear more prosperous than their neighbours that occupy the steep slopes that rise up from the valley bottom. With a few notable exceptions, the main part of Badagaon village is occupied by high caste Hindus, Muslims and some Dalit families. The surrounding villages have terraced fields that are smaller and narrower; the scattered houses are built of wood, mud and stone. This is where most of the Gaddis and Gujjars live – Prakaso with his wife, son and daughter in a single room with additional space for their animals downstairs, Mussa in a neighbouring Gujjar village, where he has built a single storey house with two small rooms for his wife and five young children.

I have been a regular visitor to this part of Chamba since 2002, when I spent a year in the Saal valley. The fieldwork from which this chapter draws was mostly carried out between September 2014 and August 2015. My ethnographic research is based on participant observation complemented by quantitative household surveys (recording assets, landholdings, access to government and private sector jobs and education) and lengthy formal and informal interviews. The eleven villages I selected for my study contain a total of 138 households and a population of 735. Of these households 88 are Adivasis (48 Gujjar and 40 Gaddi), 21 are Dalits (Hali and Jogi), 8 are Muslim and 21 high caste Hindu (15 Rajput, 6 Goswami). The household survey I carried out covered all these households.

A comparison of living conditions reveals a clear divide between the Adivasi and the 'general' population of these villages. Families that are high caste Hindu, Muslim or even Dalits typically live in '*pukka*', two-storey, multi-room houses with separate bathrooms and attached latrines. Gaddi and Gujjar households are more likely to be one- or two-room affairs in which the whole family lives, eats and sleeps. Despite government efforts to prevent it, in these villages open defecation remains the norm. The holding of household assets presents more evidence of an ethnic divide. Gujjar and Gaddi households own less land on average than other households and what land they do own is less productive. Some non-Adivasi families now employ tractors for ploughing and many own mechanised wheat-threshers and corn-shellers. Some of these families draw on a limited amount of paid agricultural labour at harvest time in their fields or when fruit must be picked and transported from apple orchards. Over the last decade, polytunnels have become a feature of the fields around Badagaon and an irrigation scheme is under construction that will free the farmers there from the uncertainties of rain-fed agriculture. In contrast Gaddi and Gujjar households rely on family labour and use teams of oxen to plough their hillside terraces. Though a limited amount of mechanisation is under way, many families continue to use traditional methods to thresh wheat and shell corn and go to water-powered mills to grind these crops into flour. The gulf between Adivasi and non-Adivasi families is even starker when comparing educational attainment and access to secure employment. Of the 'general population' adults surveyed, fewer than 30 per cent had less than five years of education while 54 per cent had studied past 9th grade. For the Dalit population, these figures are reversed: 70 per cent had either not attended school or had not progressed beyond grade 5; 22 per cent reached high school. More than 70 per cent of non-Adivasi households have one or more family members in permanent government or private sector salaried employment against just 16 per cent of Gaddi and Gujjar households. Out of the 88 Gaddi and Gujjar households, 64 revealed themselves to be officially classified as living below the poverty line.

Recognising that Gaddi and Gujjar households are markedly different from all other groups with respect to assets, education and employment we must ask how these differences can be explained. The following sections examine first the relationship of Gaddis and Gujjars to land and agriculture, and second the relationship of Gaddis and Gujjars to employment and labour markets. To illustrate changes in the conditions of these households I focus on a slice of land that rises from Badagaon and the fast-flowing Saal River, through villages between 1000 and 2000 metres above sea level, and up through mixed coniferous forest before reaching a chain of mountain pastures that mark the top of the valley. In the first sub-section, I look at changes in the ability of Gaddis and Gujjars to access forest resources; the following two sections cover the Gaddis' shift into agriculture by looking first at villages on the upper slopes of the valley, and second at their move to new villages lower down and closer to the road. A fourth sub-section compares Gujjar landownership in terms of quantity and quality against both Gaddis and the high caste Hindu population of the area. By looking at the different households living in this cross-section of the Saal valley we can start to unpick the forces and relationships that shape lives and through which opportunities are determined and denied.

Photo 12   A slice of the Himalayan Saal valley showing Badagaon (bottom) and forests and pastures (top)
Photo by Richard Axelby.

FROM PASTORALISM TO AGRICULTURE

To understand the differences between Gaddis and Gujjars and the wider population, and to understand why the Adivasi families are noticeably less well-off, I begin with the social history of the area. For the Gaddis and Gujjars, this means starting with pastoralism and, topographically, starting at the top. The tree-covered ridges that mark the edge of the Saal valley look down upon Badagaon village and the Saal River two vertical kilometres below. The meadows that top these ridges remain under snow until late April. In the months that follow, groups of Gaddis and Gujjars, many with home villages in the valley below, come to the pastures with their animals and stay for five or six months. By November the ridges that crown the Saal valley are snowbound again.

   Gaddi shepherds have been visiting the grazing pastures above the Saal valley for many hundreds of years as part of their annual cycle of migration. The 1904 *Gazetteer of Chamba State* describes the Gaddis as being 'indigenous to the Bharmour *wizārat* of the Chamba State' (1904: 137). Reconstructed histories suggest that Gaddis initially migrated to the upper parts of the Chamba valley (present-day Bharmour *tehsil* [administrative sub-district]) before the eleventh century. Centred on the sacred Kailash peak, this area is known as Gaddern and is considered to be the Gaddi homeland. In this remote and inaccessible area, the Gaddis developed their own culture, a distinctive dress of *chola* and *dora* and *launchari* (for women), and a language – Gaddi boli – which is as different from Chamiali (the language of the Chamba valley) as it is from Hindi. Alternative narratives of Gaddi origins set out their intimate connection with shepherding. Oral accounts[8] begin with a tale of a procession of gods trying to cross the ice-bound Himalayas. Finding their way blocked by snowdrifts, Shiva created a flock of sheep, which walked ahead and cleared a path through. Shiva then took a pinch of dirt from his skin and out of it created the first Gaddi man and woman to ensure the flock were properly cared for. Gaddi shepherding involves travelling with flocks of sheep and goats from winter pastures in the Punjab, up through home villages on the slopes of the Dhauladhar and Pir Panjal Ranges, and spending the summer sheltering from the monsoon rains in the upper parts of the Chamba valley or in neighbouring Lahaul. For Gaddi shepherds the meadow and forests above the Saal valley are intermediary locations on this long bi-annual journey. Whatever their origins the shepherds have been visiting these pastures for a very long time.

By comparison Gujjars are newcomers. By most accounts they arrived with their buffalo sometime late in the nineteenth century when the Raja, hoping that a regular supply of milk would be brought to his palace, invited them to settle in Chamba state. As place of historical origin, colonial-era ethnographies suggest Gujarat though others point to Afghanistan, Punjab and Central Asia. What is generally agreed is that by the late nineteenth century migratory Gujjar buffalo herders could be found across a broad swathe of the western Himalayas from Jammu and Kashmir, through Himachal Pradesh and on to Uttarakhand.[9] Living in forests and taking their buffalo to graze in the mountains, Gujjars maintained a separation from the wider community. Tall and thin, with the men wearing turbans and the women in embroidered *kurtas,* the appearance of Gujjars is recognisably distinct, as is their Gojari language. Gujjars are Muslim and, admitting to origins elsewhere, they, unlike the Gaddis, are unable to make claims to being indigenous to this section of the Himalayas.

Although their buffalo do not travel as far or as high as the Gaddi flocks, Gujjar herders exploit a similar ecological niche. Whole families start to arrive at these pastures from late April and they stay with their buffalo through the summer. This journey takes only one or two days and there is much back and forth between the pastures, home villages and Chamba town, where milk is taken daily to be sold. After summers on these meadows the Gujjars return to their more permanent homes in the valley where the Raja granted them land beside the river. Here they are able to feed their buffalo with grass cut from local hillsides in the autumn and stored to last through the winter.

Looking beyond the determining influence of the seasonal change, the pastoral production system is determined by political and economic conditions as much as environmental and climatic ones.[10] The Raja granted hereditary rights to individual Gaddis and Gujjars to graze their animals on particular alpine grazing *dhar*, and the relationship of pastoralists and the Chamba state was formalised through a system of taxes levied according to the number of animals they were permitted to graze there. These rights are retained today and are now administered by the Forest Department of Himachal Pradesh. Despite these rights, there has been a decline in the viability of traditional nomadic pastoralism in the Saal valley. Permits issued by the Forest Department set a limit to the number of animals that can be taken to the pasture and, in spite of an exponential increase in the requirements of the shepherds and herders due to demographic change, this limit has never been increased. Mussa's father's father's father[11] was one of the three brothers who were first granted permits to take a fixed number of buffalo to the meadows at the head of the Saal valley. Four generations down the line these three grazing permits are, in legal terms, the divided inheritance of over 100 individuals.

Photo 13   A Gaddi shepherd and flock
Photo by Richard Axelby.

While many accounts suggest processes of state-enforced sedentarisation as linear and unvarying, the situation in the Saal valley is more complex than a narrative of simple decline.[12] Gujjar families especially have shown greater tenacity in maintaining their nomadic occupation (though, as I will show, this is the result of not being able to access suitably rewarding alternatives). Of the 48 Gujjar families included in my survey of households, 32 own buffalos. Of these there are 11 families that continue to visit the summer pastures bringing their own buffalo and those of their neighbours also. From the 40 Gaddi households only 3 send men with their flocks to the upper parts of the Chamba valley as part of their year-long migratory cycle. Nevertheless, the rearing and sale of livestock and animal products remains an important part of the household economics of Gaddi families: almost all continue to keep sheep and goats which they shear for wool and periodically sell for meat.

With academic attention focused on the Gaddis' and Gujjars' activities as pastoralists, and their historical and contemporary alienation from forests and grazing meadows, other aspects of the household economy of Gaddis and Gujjars have been overlooked. Alongside the *push* towards sedentarisation brought about by state restrictions on nomadic movement, we need to consider the *pull* of new opportunities and occupations. For Gaddi and Gujjar families in the Saal valley, declining engagement in nomadism needs to be understood together with their integration into wider economic systems and deepening interaction with various facets of the state.

The Gaddi villages of the upper slopes of the Saal valley have a distinct social history. The second half of the nineteenth century saw a wave of out-migration from the Gaddi heartland around Bharmour at the head of the Chamba valley. Some – including Prakaso's great-grandfather – moved to the hills above the Raja's capital. The land below the forest on the upper slopes of the Saal valley was first farmed in the early decades of the twentieth century, when Gaddi families moved down from the Bharmour area and took up residence there. In order to do so they had to seek permission from the Raja. Prakaso tells the story of his shepherding great-grandfather passing through the area on migration and learning that the land was available to anyone who was prepared to convert the waste to agriculture. Being above 2000 metres above sea level, it is possible only to eke one crop from this land each year but, in comparison with the remote home villages in upper Chamba, it represented an upgrade. Continuing to combine nomadic shepherding (providing meat, wool and cash) and agriculture (for basic subsistence), pioneers such as Prakaso's great-grandfather were able to establish themselves in the area.

During the Kings' time, all the land in Chamba – both cultivable and forest – was owned by the Raja.[13] The people of Chamba were required to request permission from the Raja's officials if they wanted to open up a new area to agriculture. Though vested with the right of use, they were not permitted to buy or sell the land they cultivated. Those who farmed were taxed on their production (*theka*); other taxes were also levied on grazing animals (*trini*) and each family was periodically expected to provide free labour (*begaar*) at the request of the Raja or his representatives. The rule of the Rajas was hierarchically directed through the personage of the Sovereign; intermediaries might *collect* various forms of taxation and rents but they did so in the king's name only. This was to change with Independence in 1947, when the princely state of Chamba was merged as a district into the embryonic state of Himachal Pradesh.

With Independence and the end of Chamba as a princely state, the people of the valley went from being the subjects of the Raja to citizens of democratic India. This had profound implications for arrangements governing landownership in Chamba. Between 1947 and 1952 a *bandobast* (land settlement) was carried out in the newly created Chamba district. The exercise had two aims: first to identify those with claims to the land to whom direct titles could be transferred; and, second, to determine the value of the revenue that should be paid according to the productivity of the land. Typically, this meant that the upper caste elites who had formerly gathered taxes on behalf of the Raja were vested with title to the best land regardless of who actually farmed it. The Gaddis of the upper villages and the Gujjars down by the river were also now formalised as independent owners of land. But, located on steep slopes or above 2000 metres, the Gaddi land provided barely enough for subsistence living. It was the high caste Hindu families that owned the most productive agricultural land around Badagaon village who benefited most from land settlement.

Despite the changes that followed Independence, for the Gaddi and Gujjar inhabitants of the Saal valley life continued to be a hardscrabble existence. Winter snow and freezing temperatures limited agriculture in the upper villages to one crop each year. Many of the older people recall instances of hunger during which the thick forests that cloak the upper slopes of the Saal valley provided a vital lifeline. At times of shortage people would enter the forests in search of herbs, berries and the roots of certain trees that could be eaten. From the forest they were also able to collect timber for fires and cut fodder for their animals. The Gaddis living in the upper villages were able to eke out a living by cutting timber which could be transported to Chamba town and sold as firewood. At Independence, in parallel with the Revenue Department's land settlement, the newly created Forest Department of Himachal Pradesh carried out a settlement of Chamba's forests and brought them more firmly under its control. While use rights to agricultural land had been converted into full rights of ownership, access rights to forest resources and grazing remained strictly at the discretion of the state. That there was no parallel transfer of ownership of forest land disproportionately disadvantaged Gaddi and Gujjars. Access to the forests to collect minor produce might continue, though only under a strictly regulated system of permits, quotas and taxes; the option to supply timber for sale in the city was blocked altogether and, more recently, the right to request timber for housebuilding has been similarly curtailed.

Unlike the higher villages, the land nearer the river (around 1200 metres above sea level) can manage two crops each year – typical staples are maize, which is harvested in September, and wheat, which grows through the winter months and is harvested in April. At first sight, the 'tribal' villages of the Saal valley give the appearance of timeless simplicity: small terraced fields which depend on rain-fed irrigation are ploughed by teams of oxen, with family farms almost entirely reliant on their own labour. However, on closer inspection a more complicated picture begins to emerge: these villages are both newer and more closely integrated into wider economic systems than they initially appear.

Until the late nineteenth century the area around Badagaon was relatively unpopulated. Aside from the agricultural land next to the main village the hillsides were covered by jungle and forest. Then, as a series of progressive Rajas sought to modernise and expand Chamba town, urbanisation brought a rising demand for food and labour. At the same time as Gaddis were moving to the higher village, Gujjars were allowed to clear the jungle beside the river (see below). But the best land – on wide plateaus above the river – was secured by members of the royal court. Up to 1947 sections of land owned by the Raja were awarded to members of the court and wealthy business families who, in turn, leased them out to tenant farmers. This status quo was maintained in the first bandobast land settlement, which formalised landownership in the names of these members of the former king's court – known as 'city men' to the rural population. Thus the most productive land remained under the control of these wealthy, urban families, who rented it out to tenant farmers and continued to take a half-share of the produce. After Independence, eight Gaddi families living in the *ek-faisli* (single-crop) land at the top of the mountain were invited down to the good *do-faisili* (two-crop) land to work as tenant farmers for two of these wealthy, urban 'city men'. Though it meant handing over half the crop they cultivated to the landowning city men, they accepted.

Prakaso's father and his two brothers were among those Gaddis who moved down to establish new lower villages. Of these three brothers, one is still alive: Prakaso's uncle. He told me that they had little option but to move as the land around the upper villages couldn't be further subdivided. Though this change of residence opened up a new niche for pastoralism – shepherds in the lower villages could shift their flocks up to their upper villages each summer – the ability to produce two crops from the land near the river allowed for the beginning of the move away from agro-pastoralism and into straightforward agriculture. The sedentarisation process was further accelerated in the early 1970s when the Himachal Pradesh Tenancy and Land Reform Act (1972) forced owners to hand over their land to the families who farmed it.[14] A small amount of compensation had to be paid to the city men; the simplest way for shepherds to find this sum was by selling their flocks.

Village life during the post-Independence decades was made less precarious and more attractive with the provision of subsidised food through the Public Distribution System in the 1970s, the delivery of piped water in the 1980s and the arrival of electricity in the 1990s. But the most significant change was the availability of new sources of income. While previously agriculture as practiced by Gaddi families was carried out on a subsistence basis, the metalling of roads and improved communication links now allowed for the transportation of produce for sale at market. The shift towards commercial agriculture was further promoted by the distribution of government-sub-sidised rice which replaced maize as the dietary staple allowing a greater share of the crop to be sold. These were happy days for the Gaddis in the Saal valley as they made the transition from nomadic shepherds to settled farmers. In spite of the problems arising from the withdrawal of forest access, this phase of integration into wider systems of market exchange was softened by the pro-poor welfare provisions of the Indian state. The stated aim of government policy was that these marginal tribal people should be encouraged to engage with the mainstream of economic and political life.

In 2015 the Gaddi families derived a greater share of their household income from agriculture compared to the other inhabitants of the Saal valley. Agriculture in the villages of the Saal valley is very much a family operation. Though ploughing is the exclusive domain of men, women and children will join in with all other aspects of sowing, weeding and harvesting. Though there is no strict division of activities it usually falls to women to collect fodder and firewood from the forest, and to children to watch over a family's animals as they graze. The summer crop of maize provides Prakaso's family with fodder stalks to feed animals and husks which are burnt for heat in the cold winter months. A share of the maize is retained to provide enough of the staple maize bread to last for six months; but the bulk is sold. Once de-shelled, the corn kernels are carried down to the river where the miller will grind them into flour in return for a 10 per cent cut. This flour can then be sold on to Gujjar shopkeepers next to the road: cash payment may be requested but most prefer an arrangement by which the sum is recorded in a book and offset against purchases of dal, rice, tea, sugar, tobacco and other necessities through the year. The shopkeepers who buy maize flour usually store it until they have a sufficient amount and then sell it on to Mahajan and Rajput businessmen from the town who transport it to the Punjab border. Purchased by commission agents, the final stage of the corn's journey is on to poultry farms where it is processed into chicken feed. In winter, the fields are turned over to wheat and to a lesser extent to vegetable crops; the former is retained, most of the latter is sold. Though heavily dependent for their livelihoods on their crops, Gaddis struggle to negotiate a fair share for their sale. I asked Prakaso why Gaddis like him didn't get into the trading business: he said that their villages were away from the road, they couldn't drive, didn't own pick-ups and being 'too simple' would be cheated by sharp-witted merchants.

Almost without exception, every household – Gaddi and Gujjar – in my study villages owns some land; for the most part the land they own they cultivate themselves. On average both the Gaddis and Gujjars and the rest of the population have small landholdings (0.72 acres against 0.9 acres) but there is a sizeable group of high caste Hindus with larger holdings (see Table 5.1).

In addition to inequality in land amount, it is the *kind* of land to which people have access that shapes their livelihoods. The quality and value of land varies very significantly – that is, Gaddi-owned land on the higher parts (above 2000 metres) of the shaded north-facing slope is ek-faisli (single cropped) but lower down is do-faisli (the River Saal is around 1100 metres above sea level at this point) with broad terraces. In contrast, Gujjars own land on both the south and north faces of the slope, though in all cases this tends to be close to the river and the road (below 1300 metres). When they first arrived in Chamba, this rough and well-grassed waste ground would have appealed to buffalo-herding Gujjars for the fodder it provides post-monsoon. However, the agricultural potential of much of the Gujjar-owned land is limited, either because it is on the dry side of the valley most exposed to the sun or because it is harder to plough than the wide terraced fields that Gaddi families gained after the bandobast. This explains why most Gaddis living in this area have been able to abandon their migratory traditions while many Gujjars continue to keep buffalo and travel with them each summer up to their grazing dhars.

On the land beside the river several Gujjar families claim long-standing residence dating back more than a hundred years. This is confirmed by their possession of grazing permits that were given to them prior to Independence. Interestingly, this means that Gujjars have lived in this part of Chamba for as long, if not longer, that their Gaddi neighbours. New households were established in the late 1970s and early 1980s when a short-lived land redistribution (*nautor*) policy handed an area of forest to a number of landless Gujjar families – this was how Mussa's father got his land. Other Gujjar houses have been built on government land without permission; the families living there hope that in ten years or so they will be given title to the land they illegally cultivate but know they could be evicted at any time. A few Gujjar families got lucky – the most valuable land in the whole area is that on the right bank of the river which lies next to the road. Others were less advantaged – the steep slopes of the former forest land are prone to landslips that have taken with them fields full of crops and destroyed houses. When compared with their Gaddi neighbours, the average Gujjar family has less land and what they have is often set aside for grazing and growing fodder. On the land that they do cultivate, Gujjars have been quick to turn their fields over to cash crops – peas, chilli, cabbages – which are sold in their entirety. Mussa grows peas that he takes to Chamba town to sell to wholesalers.

Gaddis and Gujjars are differentiated from the non-tribal population not just in terms of the quantity and quality of the land they farm but also in the relationship to farming. Most of the high caste Hindu families in Badagaon are also involved in agricultural production to some extent and this typically takes one of two forms: for those with secure salaried employment farming is done as a sort of leisure activity ('hobby') and is entirely self-consumed ('for the taste'); others specialise in commercial agriculture, investing in polytunnels and selling their crops to urban centres as far away as Delhi. Orchards of apples, pears and kiwi fruit have become a popular investment around Badagaon – expected profits per acre may be not more than if wheat or maize were grown instead, but fruit requires less year-round labour and thus can be more easily combined with permanent employment (see below). 'Progressive' farmers in Badagaon are able to access government subsidies to construct polytunnels or to establish orchards. In contrast to these high caste Hindu farmers, the Gaddis and Gujjars struggle to attract the attention of government extension agents. Dismissed as 'lazy' and 'uneducated', they rarely possess the capital to benefit from government-secured loans or crop insurance schemes.

In summary, the three decades that followed Independence saw a radical reconfiguration of the relationships that Gaddis and Gujjars had with land and natural resources. State policies and new institutional arrangements provided fixed property rights to cultivated land for the first time while simultaneously restricting access to forest resources and grazing pastures. This allowed some families ownership of good agricultural land for the first time. However, the benefits of these changes have not been evenly shared: Gaddis and Gujjars lost most through the closure of the forest; compared to non-Adivasi households they have gained least from the granting of rights to land and subsequent agricultural extension efforts. The next section moves out from these farms and forests to see how Gaddis and Gujjars have fared as they have become more firmly integrated into rural and urban labour markets.

MOVING TO WORK

In the Saal valley agriculture is important – all families own some land which they cultivate. But few families – whether Adivasi or not – have enough land to be able to satisfy all their needs. The benefits of land redistribution and passing ownership to the tiller have, over time, been diluted by population growth, and, with holdings divided between sons, other sources of income are required. In the past that meant pastoralism; but with the decline in access to pasture and education and links to town, new forms of work have been pursued. Again, the distribution of new opportunities is differentiated by ethnicity.

The most significant difference between Gujjar and Gaddis and all other groups is in access to more or less secure salaried employment. Of the 88 Gujjar and Gaddi households of the 11 villages surveyed only 9 had family members in government jobs (10 per cent); this compares with 27 out of 50 non-Adivasi households (54 per cent). This is in spite of seven decades of affirmative action policies supposed to open up government jobs to Dalit and Adivasi communities.[15] The sorts of government posts that Adivasis are able to access tend to be low level and unskilled – it's unusual to find a Gujjar or Gaddi who has risen above the level of a Forest Department *mali* or Public Works Department *bheldar*. Many non-Adivasi families, on the other hand, have benefited from secure government employment – with the police, army, health or education departments – that has been passed down, in many cases, from father to son or arranged through family connections. And there is more – while previous generations of high caste Hindus used their connections to access government jobs, their children are now finding their way into higher status opportunities in private service – moving away to work in factories near the border with Punjab or as computer engineers, call-centre workers or hotel receptionists in Amritsar, Chandigarh and Delhi. Part of the reason these jobs in the private sector have risen in status is because they are considered 'caste-blind', with recruitment supposedly based on merit rather than bound by reservation quotas. In our survey, general population men are over-represented in semi-skilled government jobs, managerial /white-collar government jobs, and private sector salaried jobs, Dalits dominate semi-skilled work, while Gaddis and Gujjars are confined to farming their own land, coupled with agricultural and non-agricultural manual labour (see Figure 6.1).

How might the command of secure salaried jobs by all other groups but the Gaddis and Gujjars be explained? The importance of historical advantage cannot be ignored – over many generations the non-tribal population of Badagaon have accumulated stores of social and cultural capital. This continues to regulate new opportunities to the detriment of Gaddis and Gujjars. Carefully cultivated connections ease well-placed individuals into private sector jobs or gift families the soft loans and government-subsidised trees that assist the development of horticulture. Social stigma also plays a part as demonstrated by the example of a government official who described his fellow high caste Hindus as 'hard-working' and 'progressive' in contrast to the 'ignorant and lazy' Gaddis and 'dishonest' Gujjars.

Here it is instructive to compare the position of the Adivasi population against that of low caste Dalits in the area. Compared with the Gaddis and Gujjars, my survey revealed less of a divide between Dalit families and their high caste Hindu neighbours. Though some academic accounts describe social discrimination on the basis of caste in the western Himalayas, this goes against a general perception that hill society is more egalitarian than that of the plains.[16] Pointing to the 'Hali' village of Dadaru, one Gaddi informant told me that caste has not mattered in Chamba 'since 1947' when it was 'abolished by Gandhi'. This is confirmed, he went on to say, by the good footpaths that lead to the Dalit settlement, the well-maintained village temple and the newly built primary school in the middle of the village. These remarks may have been meant flippantly – certainly studies from elsewhere in Himachal Pradesh point to a high caste domination of state-level politics, which persists despite the 26 per cent of the population classified as Scheduled Castes.[17] But, at least at the local level, Dalit political under-representation is not apparent in Badagaon, where a member of the Panchayat Samiti (and former two-term Pradhan of Badagaon panchayat) boasts of having brought government services and jobs for his fellow Dalits. Though it could be argued that Gaddis and Gujjars also have the chance to benefit from the reservation of political seats, so far they have not shown the same wherewithal to secure and direct government programmes to their own advantage.

It is also noticeable that many Dalit men have come to be employed in the sorts of skilled and semi-skilled professions that Gaddis and Gujjars have struggled to enter. Talking to Dalit families they described how, in the past (and as elsewhere in India), the castes which are now covered under the 'Scheduled' administrative category encompassed a wide variety of social situations and occupational niches – from respectable shoe-makers (who considered themselves to be artisans) to barbers, drivers of ploughs and removers of night-soil. What was specific for the Chamba Dalits in the Saal valley was that low caste families were given land by their high caste patrons, which was formalised under their ownership following Independence. Crucially, this provided these families with a small amount of capital and allowed them to combine farming with the traditional services they performed. Second, in the kings' time these families – in common with high caste Hindu and Muslim families from Badagaon – were likely to be tied to the Chamba court and to businessmen and public officials in the town for whom they provided services. These relationships – and the accompanying knowledge of the urban milieu – have developed since Independence and ensured that the children of non-Adivasi families were equipped to access education, training and employment. As the traditional services performed by these castes declined, they had the capital, the connections and the cultural know-how to recognise and move into new areas. Buttressed by a sideline in agriculture, Dalit families have been able to translate the specialised services they once performed into semi-skilled and service occupations – from ploughing as a Hali to being a mason, painter or plasterer, from a Sipi musician to Irrigation and Public Health Department fitter, from a Chamar leather-worker to a taxi driver or electrician. From a starting position at the bottom of the social order, Dalit individuals have been able to leverage contracts spanning the urban and the rural into better employment opportunities. For Gujjars and Gaddis, whose 'specialisation' was animal husbandry, it has proved harder to make the leap into service and semi-skilled work.

Although occupations are clearly differentiated by ethnicity, across communities there are also similarities in the ways that activities and occupations are gendered. At home women of all groups do most of the cooking, cleaning and childcare (though there is no bar on men doing these things when required). The main divide between the Gaddis and Gujjars and the rest of the population is how common it is that women do such reproductive work only (see Figure 6.2). This is predominant among the general category households whereas nearly all Gaddi and Gujjar women combine reproductive work with working on their own fields – and only their *own* fields – taking animals to pasture and cutting wood from the forest. As described earlier, Gaddi women are fully involved in farming work and grazing animals; this is also true for many Gujjar families. Non-Adivasi-household women are far less likely to work in their fields; partly because of a higher degree of mechanisation, partly because they are more likely to hire in labour (often Gujjar and Gaddi men) at busy times, but mainly because for women to work outside of the house is seen as being low status. Out of the 42 'general category' women included in the household survey, 7 did salaried work, 11 assisted the family in agricultural activities, and 24 were confined to household work. This is in marked contrast with Gaddi women (of 59 there were 52 who worked in their fields) and Gujjar women (of 50 there were 2 in salaried jobs and 41 were involved in agriculture). Of the 138 households surveyed, only 17 reported having female family members in paid private sector or government employment – two Muslim women work as tailors while several high caste Hindu women are employed to teach in schools or as *anganwari* assistants.

As we have seen, social and cultural identities are crucial to the way an individual manoeuvres around labour markets. Those from non-Adivasi backgrounds – including Dalits – are likely to be able to deploy extended social networks and connections spanning rural and urban locales in order to access new employment opportunities. Though there is no obvious local 'dominant caste' in the Chamba area in the sense that is identified in the chapters by Thakur, Benbabaali and Donegan, it is apparent that there is a clear line of division which separates those who are tribal from those who are not. In this section, I examine how education accompanies ethnic and social differentiation in ways that underpin this economic divide.

Labour market segmentation is often assumed to relate to levels of skill, training and education. Figures 6.3 and 6.4 show a stark distinction in levels of education between Gaddis and Gujjars and all other groups, whether men or women: the average number of years schooling for Adivasi adults is 4.2; for the rest of the population it is 7.6. The differences are particularly stark with regard to female education, with more than 50 per cent of Gaddi women and 80 per cent of Gujjar women not having any formal schooling. While the educational attainments of Gujjars, and especially Gaddis, have improved they continue to play catch-up in comparison with all other groups.

Those teachers whom I asked explained to me that the lower levels of educational attainment are a legacy of the Gaddis' and Gujjars' migratory background. Sometimes they would also mention the lack of schools in remote areas (and higher up in the hills) as a contributing factor. A primary school opened in high caste Badagaon in 1962, but until the 1980s the nearest high school was 5 km away in Saho and the nearest senior secondary school and college was in Chamba town. As elsewhere in India, it seems that government schools were built not according to population size or need; rather their location both illustrates and also reinforces existing patterns of exclusion and privilege. In the 1970s and 1980s, government primary schools were opened around the higher reaches of the valley to cater mainly for Gaddi students. Yet these were still hard to reach for students coming from the upper villages. And students wishing to study beyond 10th grade continue to make the long walk down to the road before catching the bus into Chamba town. The journey times – sometimes up to two hours – are frequently given, especially by girls, as a reason for quitting school early.

While (as Table 6.2 reveals) there has been some progress in levels of education, new divides are opening up. With increasing numbers of Gaddi and Gujjar children attending government schools, high caste Hindu and Muslim families are starting to look for alternatives. A private school was established in Badagaon in 2011, though (for those who can afford it) similar establishments in Chamba town are considered more attractive options.

But geographical remoteness and segregation into different schools is only part of the problem: we should not ignore the importance of social distance between Adivasi and non-Adivasi families. The teachers who make up the staff of rural schools are almost without exception town-born high caste Hindus. 'Tribal' children suffer the stigma of being stereotyped as 'incapable of learning' and many complain of being beaten by their teachers. The domination of school teaching by upper caste Hindus, the Hindi medium of instruction and the general ambience of 'banal Hinduism' that characterises schools leave many Muslim Gujjars feeling doubly excluded.[18]

Many Gaddi and Gujjar families continue to question the value of education, especially with good government posts in short supply. And indeed, whereas for the general category the better educated men get relatively good jobs, a much higher proportion of well-educated Gujjars and Gaddis are stuck in unskilled or, at best, semi-skilled jobs. Again, Dalits fare somewhat better (see Table 6.3). There clearly is a social divide with, on one side, those who have good connections and feel comfortable in the culture of the town, and, on the other side, Gaddis and Gujjars who struggle for acceptance and are unable to approach intermediaries from the state and private sector on an equal basis. Education is not a very effective remedy against this.

We now turn to the sorts of low-status, low-pay work that is available to those living at the bottom of the social hierarchy.

Increasingly restricted in their ability to exercise their traditional nomadism and unable to gain entry to new forms of government and private employment, Gaddis and Gujjars are forced into combinations of income-earning activities which, being temporary and precarious, they label 'petty work'. Though (as shown in Figure 6.1) some families from all groups are solely dependent on combinations of farming and unskilled labour, it is Gaddi and Gujjar families who are most likely to be restricted to this kind of work. From 138 households surveyed, 61 households were solely dependent on combinations of agriculture and daily-wage labour; of these 8 were not Adivasis (16 per cent of non-Adivasi households), 28 were Gaddi (70 per cent of Gaddi households) and 29 were Gujjar (60 per cent of Gujjar households). To survive, these households combine a range of activities that might include agricultural and non-agricultural labour, work that may be waged or unwaged, in the formal and informal sector, sometimes self-employed and sometimes working for others. Wages are typically paid on a daily basis and range from Rs.160 and Rs.250 per day for local 'mazdoori' labour, up to Rs.400 per day for 'project work'. A crucial component of 'petty work' is employment on National Rural Employment Guarantee Act schemes (Rs.154 per day in 2014),[19] though no households were able to obtain the full 100 days of labour supposedly guaranteed to them each year. The balance of work will vary from person to person, family to family, and from year to year. None of these activities can be guaranteed and none of them are likely to last for long. Though both Gaddis and Gujjars depend on finding work as unskilled labourers there are important differences in the balance of their activities and the forms of work they engage in. Here I describe the routes into work taken by Gaddis residing in villages on the upper and lower slopes of the Saal valley before going on to show how this differs from Gujjars.

As we have seen, a major problem facing the Gaddis living in the Saal valley is that there simply is not enough land to go around. This was the driving factor that brought their grandfathers down from Bharmour to Chamba and their fathers down from the upper villages to be sharecroppers for city men. Land reform eased this problem for a time but now, as families increase in size, landholdings become fragmented and increasingly they must find work outside of their own fields. Following the land reforms of the 1970s Prakaso's father assumed ownership of 2 acres of land, which was enough to feed the family with some spare to sell. Those 2 acres are now divided between Prakaso and his brothers and are not nearly enough to feed three families. In the past, the solution would have been shepherding, but, beginning in the early 1970s, they started to shift towards daily-wage labour and government employment projects.

The Gaddis' move into 'petty work' started with the upgrading of the road to Chamba town. The Public Works Department offered this work on a temporary basis, only lasting so long as funds were available. In the villages where I conducted my research many of the older Gaddi men – Prakaso's father included – had for some years been engaged by the Public Works Department to provide labour to build roads. Typically, this had involved spending a maximum of 18 days each month breaking rocks, and clearing debris. Rates of pay were comparatively low but slightly more than could be obtained as agricultural labourers. As 'daily-wage' labourers they worked alongside 'regular' (permanent and full-time) Public Works Department employees who used heavy machines to cut the route and lay tarmac. Once the road was completed, the work would finish and the temporary workers would go back to their fields until further funds were made available. Men from these villages were also able to obtain daily-wage labour mending fences and digging holes for the Forest Department, or laying pipe with the Department of Irrigation and Public Health. Significantly this daily-wage local labour was rarely taken up by Gujjars.

In the late 1990s the opportunity arose for daily-wage labourers to be made into regular government employees. This would mean increased pay, good pensions, sickness cover plus 'full facilities – uniforms, shoes and umbrellas'. Those people who were at the time engaged as labourers for the Public Works Department, the Department of Irrigation and Public Health or the Forest Department were able to take advantage of the policy to become 'regular'. However, in those panchayats where no work was being undertaken at the time, people who had previously served on a temporary basis were not offered the chance to take up these permanent positions. This was the case in the villages around Badagaon. Around the same time a major shift took place in the balance of public and private involvement in road construction in Himachal Pradesh; the Public Works Department put out to tender the work that had previously been the sole responsibility of the state and since then no new recruits have been taken on. Lucrative tenders to build or repair stretches of road are usually won by officially registered contractors with political connections. Stretches of road are then separated into sections and different tasks – cutting, cage work, metalling – are passed down to be undertaken by local subcontractors.

Many of the people who had previously been employed as 'daily-wage' labourers for the Public Works Department were re-employed to fulfil the same tasks but this time working for private contractors (*thikedars*). Though rates of pay have increased, the chances of local men finding such work have declined as we see below. Now they are instead compelled to seek work as seasonal migrant labour elsewhere, and roadbuilding projects, which primarily employ unskilled labour, form a major part of this. The example of local Gujjar road building contractors indicates the employers' preference for seasonal migrant labour. As they expanded their operations into other districts of Himachal Pradesh they stopped employing fellow Gujjars and Gaddis from the Saal valley and, instead, began to employ seasonal migrant labour from elsewhere – predominantly Jammu and Nepal – which they described as 'more reliable' – and, as one case I found demonstrated, less likely to damage the contractor's local social status if they are found to have cheated those that work for them.

There is, in fact, a long history of labour migration into the Himalayas for road construction. The border roads were constructed by gangs of labour from Jharkhand, Bihar and other states, and presently a seasonal migrant labour force of around 70,000 works for the border road constructing government agencies. But in the Saal valley seasonal labour in-migration is a relatively recent phenomenon.

In 2005 work began on a hydropower project that would generate electricity from the River Saal close to Badagaon village. The contract for the overall project was won by a company from Andhra Pradesh which then subcontracted out to smaller operators. Some contractors drew labour from the local area; others employed seasonal migrant labour from other states (Jammu and Uttar Pradesh). With the hydropower project now operational and ongoing and road building increasingly handed over to seasonal migrant labour, the chances of local men finding labouring work close to their homes have largely dried up. They are also unable to get a foothold in local technically skilled work, such as in mechanised specialised tile making (done by Bihari seasonal migrant tile makers), or technical and machinery-intensive roadworks jobs (which two Rajasthani families have specialised in, as subcontractors). The lack of multi-generational experience of migration means Gaddis and Gujjars do not possess the connections and forms of knowledge that would enable them to gain employment in such jobs requiring technical training.

Increasingly it is left to the young local men – Gujjars as well as Gaddis – to travel elsewhere to find employment as seasonal migrants. Though now a vital source of income for many families, this 'project work' is temporary, precarious and irregular. Local Adivasis seek project work, which is generally done through labour contractors who recruit for work on hydropower projects and road building programmes elsewhere in Himachal Pradesh. The daily-wage rates for 'project work' are high – as much as Rs.350–400 per day – and there is the promise of extra for overtime. Against this, the work can be difficult and dangerous and the living conditions rough. Those labourers who leave Chamba to work on projects often live in very basic accommodation – parachute tents or shepherds' huts – especially when making roads in remote mountainous areas. Those involved in project work elsewhere in Himachal will typically sleep in a labourers' camp where they may be 10–20 people sharing a room. No advances are given for travelling to the site and it is necessary for men to stay away from home for several months at a time, which prevents them from working on the family fields. Wages may be withheld until after the work is finished and payment rarely meets the advertised amount. Those who do not find work have to return to their fields and a dependence on the uncertain and irregular provision of National Rural Employment Guarantee Act work as a way to earn. In these ways, through bringing in cheaper seasonal migrant labour from other states, the livelihoods of the local Adivasi households have been made more precarious and uncertain.

When I arrived back in the Saal valley in September 2014 I found that Prakaso was engaged in contract work road building on the route up to the Sach Pass in the remote north-west of Chamba district. It took me three buses and the best part of the day to reach Kalaban, where Prakaso and his fellow workers were stationed. Prakaso had got the job through his brother-in-law who worked as a driver for the Rajput thikedar that had won the tender to repair the road. With Prakaso were his brother, two of his cousins, two nephews and several of his friends from the village neighbouring his own. Prakaso had been elected to be the camp cook but the others spent the day breaking rocks with hammers and then carrying loads to fix a buttress. At night, they struggled to keep warm: the high-altitude chill given a further edge by the knowledge that at this same place in the late 1990s a group of Pahari road-workers had been massacred by Jihadis from Kashmir.

Photo 14   Gaddis at work building roads
Photo by Richard Axelby.

Over the last decade the main source of non-agricultural employment has shifted from the state to private contractors and an array of subcontractors. This system functions in ways that distance contractors from the actual work in a manner that allows them to devolve responsibility for the pay and conditions of labourers. In the main, people work for registered subcontractors but in some cases this responsibility for organising labour is passed down to a local man who agrees a lump-sum payment or a cut of the wages of those he recruits. Labourers see the subcontractor as their formal employer – this is who they negotiate wages with, who supervises their work on a day-to-day basis, and who they argue with when the promised wages are not paid.

Prakaso worked at Kalaban for only a few weeks and then returned home as the maize crop had to be harvested. Though the Rajput contractor agreed to pay wages monthly it took until January before he came through with the money (he blamed late payment from the prime contractor he subcontracted from). Negotiations with the workers took place over the course of an afternoon, with the contractor reneging on his promise to pay for food and expressing doubt about the number of hours of overtime that Prakaso and his co-workers had recorded themselves as doing. Eventually an agreement was thrashed out – the basic daily rate of Rs.350 was handed over but without the additional overtime payments. Later I asked Prakaso if he was happy with what he was paid – 'fifty-fifty' he replied. Would he work for the same contractor again? 'Yes – if he asks us.'

Mussa seeks work as a seasonal migrant labourer more regularly than Prakaso and will travel further to find it. Every year he hopes to spend three or four months working away from home. During my fieldwork, there were two occasions when he and his co-workers came back earlier than expected – the first time after they had seen a man crushed by a wall; the second time because the workers were refused pay when construction had been held up for five days by heavy rain. The Centre of India Trade Union (CITU) says they would gladly represent daily-wage and contract workers but that they are rarely asked to do so. Unions such as CITU, while known to labourers, are not viewed as being relevant to the problems they face as temporary wage workers. Those able to find employment on projects consider themselves to be lucky – the pay is good compared to whatever else is available – and they are reluctant to rock the boat as future work is dependent on maintaining good relations with contractors. Trade union labour activism does not provide a solution to the problems of underemployment or insecurity faced by many Gaddis and Gujjars.

As in the Peermade tea plantations and the Cuddalore bone factory, the inflow of seasonal migrant labour brings a downgrading of labour in other ways. Employers seek 'reliable' labour and this means that migrants with whom there are no local social ties and who rely on the employers for shelter and food are preferable. The availability of a wider pool of labour in Chamba and across Himachal Pradesh also increases uncertainty about the provision of regular work, which helps in maintaining control over labour; withholding offers of employment and delaying payment ensure that workers are pliant and docile. The main problem for the Gaddis and Gujjars is to find work as seasonal migrant labour; and, while the examples above show that the terms and conditions can be quite extreme, workers respond through low-level bargaining, not high-profile collective action.

As we have seen, Gaddis are able to claim to be indigenous to the Chamba valley in a way that Gujjars cannot. Returning to Mussa's characterisation of Gaddis 'looking to their land', we can expand on their shift into agriculture to consider how their identity and their politics depend on association with a sense of place and, as such, are territorially bounded. In the Gaddi homeland around Bharmour they make up a majority of the population. As a reserved constituency, this area is represented by a Gaddi Member of the

Legislative Assembly (currently the Himachal Pradesh Minister for Forests Thakur Singh Bharmouri); while as a 'tribal' area it has, since 1975, received additional government funding for education and infrastructure through a tribal sub-plan. The ability of the Gaddis in this area to apply political pressure through elected representatives means that they enjoy advantages that are not available to those who live outside it, such as easier access to schools, greater availability of government jobs and enhanced wages for National Rural Employment Guarantee Act work.

Outside of this 'tribal' area the Gaddi community in the Saal valley did, nevertheless, for some time gain concrete benefit from state policies – through land redistribution, provision of wage labour and the promise of Scheduled Tribe reservations. However, the rebalancing of the relationship between state and citizens that accompanied the liberalisation of India's economy has left them feeling abandoned. Land redistribution was a one-off; government wage labour is no more; and in most cases Scheduled Tribe reservation was always an impossible dream. They struggle to exert influence in panchayat- and block-level politics where power is more likely to be vested in representatives of high caste Hindu, Dalit and even Gujjar communities. Poorly integrated into political networks, Gaddis in the villages around Badagaon lack the traction necessary to achieve influence through conventional party structures or the alternatives of union and non-governmental organisation (NGO) activism. Denied the economic benefits brought by the boom, for many Gaddi households the shift to a sedentary life now looks like a dead end.

Feeling left behind by development, the Gaddis in the area where I conducted my fieldwork describe themselves as having 'turned inwards'. Among these families there is a marked reliance on village community or *bhaichara*. People work together, socialise together, share resources and support one another with loans in time of shortage. If a new house needs building the community collectively lend a hand. Marriages require the bhaichara to cut wood from the forest as fuel for the fire on which they will cook the communal feast. When Prakaso's father became ill it was to their neighbours and relatives that the family turned for the money that funded his ultimately unsuccessful treatment. There is, however, a downside to the intense egalitarianism of these networks of community support: it separates Gaddis from the kind of patronage networks which (though unequal) Dalit families have benefited from. Turning inwards, the Gaddis reproduce the sense of egalitarianism and isolation which is seen as characteristic of tribal society. The closely bound bhaichara can be viewed as both a cause and a consequence of the political and economic weakness of the Saal Gaddis. In contrast to the Gaddis who live in the tribal sub-district around Bharmour, the Saal valley Gaddis are less able to draw on an outwardly directed history of collective mobilisation for political and economic change.

Owning land that has less agricultural potential than that of their Gaddi neighbours, the Gujjars in the Saal valley have sought out different routes to survival. But the new forms of work that have emerged are differentiated by ethnicity, including differentiation *within* as well as *between* Adivasi communities.

Though disadvantaged in Chamba district as a religious and ethnic minority, Gujjars have shown a greater capacity to reach out and make links with other places and people, be they Congress politicians, civil society activists or Islamic educational associations. Over the course of my fieldwork I found connections between Gujjars in the Saal valley and American missionary associations, tribal rights activists in Kashmir and Uttarakhand, and, perhaps most surprisingly, the All India Gurjar Mahasabha located in Nandurbar district, where Gujars are the dominant, politically influential, landowning caste (see the next chapter for a discussion of Gujars of Nandurbar). The most significant external actors, however, have proved to be the '*Ulemma*' (religious scholars) trained in Deobandi influenced madrasas. As well as providing a non-state source of education and welfare provision, their Islamic religious beliefs offer a new source of identity to the tribal Gujjars of Chamba. However, not all Gujjar households are able to draw benefits from these associations, and, as we shall see, the benefits are not distributed equally.

Unable to accommodate their herds of buffalo within the restrictions of Forest Department quotas, in the 1990s and early 2000s a significant number of Gujjars – perhaps as many as one family in five – opted to permanently move away from the valley. In search of new pastures, they moved to Punjab and, in doing so, lost their Scheduled Tribe status and their entitlements as citizens (though, as they point out, they rarely realised these rights anyway). Between the industrial-scale agriculture of Punjab and the expanding peri-urban space around Ludhiana, Jalandhar and Malerkotla, these Gujjar families have established a new form of pastoral nomadism that leaves them entirely reliant on the sale of buffalo milk and on the kindness of big Jat farmers to accommodate them in their search for fodder. In some respects – landownership, voting rights, official assistance – these Punjab Gujjars are disadvantaged compared to those that stayed in Himachal Pradesh. However, it is notable that few have reversed their decision and moved back to Chamba, and most feel better off than their relatives in the hills. The shift to Punjab can be viewed as a continuation of the Gujjars' historical movement out of Kashmir to Himachal and Uttarakhand. Demonstrating their continued commitment to 'buffalos' over 'land', opportunities in Punjab are shaped by old ties of Gujjar kinship networks and new affiliations with the educational infrastructure of Deobandi Islam. Those Gujjars who opted to remain in the Saal valley use similar connections to explore alternative avenues for advancement.

As a religious and ethnic minority, Gujjars throughout Chamba district have struggled to benefit from state programmes of affirmative action and official development schemes. As a result, they have tended to shy away from state-prescribed forms and institutions. Informal community courts operate separately from the official village panchayats, the more religiously inclined have opted to send sons to be educated in madrasas in Uttar Pradesh rather than local 'Hindi' schools. Significantly the daily-wage local labour – with the Public Works Department, Irrigation and Public Health Department, and Forest Department – that was attractive to Gaddis in the Saal valley was rarely taken up by Gujjars. Instead, those Gujjars seeking labouring work go to find it in Chamba town. Being familiar with the daily journey into town to sell their milk, Gujjars came to know private employers who could offer higher rates of pay – from Rs.200 to 250 per day – compared to that available around their village homes. Though some Gujjar men do travel alongside Gaddis to take up 'project work', they are more likely to work on a daily basis in the town, either helping in construction or in small-scale commercial activities – selling fruit and vegetables or peddling ice-creams to bus passengers. While agriculture is the primary income source for the typical Gaddi household, for Gujjars it is labouring and petty forms of enterprise.

SOCIAL DIFFERENTIATION IN THE SAAL VALLEY

The links between town and country also explain emergent processes of differentiation *within* the community of Gujjars living in the Saal valley. As mentioned earlier, Gujjars in this area typically own land close to the river which suffers most from flooding, or on steep hillsides which are difficult to cultivate. This land may be less agriculturally productive, but it lies next to the road and this has brought steadily accumulating benefits to families living there. Processes of differentiation within the Gujjar community started back in the late 1960s when the Public Works Department started upgrading the road to Chamba town. Better connections and the introduction of a bus service encouraged some Gujjars to establish roadside shops. These families benefited from rising land values and easier connections to urban areas, education and jobs. It was not, however, until the neoliberal reforms of the 1990s that these families – literate, with business knowledge, contacts and capital – were able to branch out and take advantage of new opportunities to establish themselves as businessmen and contractors. These families were well placed to work as local partners providing labour to the big thikedars who negotiate tenders for government contracts.

The construction of a series of hydropower projects along the length of the Saal River brought other forms of benefit to those Gujjars who lost land to the schemes. Compensation came in the form of generous lump-sum payments and guaranteed jobs with the power company. The Gujjar contractors who had cut their teeth organising labour to build roads were able to tender successfully for elements of powerhouse construction – one to clear the site, one to build the powerhouse, one responsible for the weir and one to build the pipeline that brought water from the Saal River. Although this business elite represents a minority among the Gujjar population, they wield considerable economic power and social influence. Initially these contractors drew labour from the local area but, as discussed above, this changed when they expanded their operations to other parts of Himachal Pradesh.

Not all attempts to move into commerce are successful – as is demonstrated by Mussa's endeavour to establish himself as a vegetable seller in the Chamba bazaar. Every morning Mussa would buy his day's stock from a wholesaler and hope to turn a profit. After a couple of months, he gave up, complaining of police harassment brought on as a result of not having the right permit. Mussa's brother Lalli had also tried to establish himself in business. Lalli was a driver for a shopkeeper but quit when he was offered a loan from the TATA company to buy one of their trucks. Things went well at first but then business dried up for a couple of months. Struggling to keep up with the repayments he first sold the truck's tyres and replaced them with old ones. With no upturn in sight he then was forced to sell the original engine. When the inevitable eventually happened and the truck was reclaimed he found himself deep in debt and trouble.

In the past Gujjars saw less benefit from government but, with increasing wealth, have shown a greater ability to self-organise and take advantage of wider linkages with a variety of welfare organisations, rights campaigns and NGO projects which are aimed at or cater exclusively for Gujjars. In the eyes of Chamba society – the wealthy Rajputs, Mahajans and Ashraf Muslims of the town – rural Gujjars are stigmatised as dirty, ill-educated and dishonest. However, as wealthy Gujjars in the Saal valley have achieved a degree of success in business, they have sought to transcend local discrimination by reaching out to actors and institutions at the regional, national and international level. The religious reform movement of Deobandi Islam has been enthusiastically adopted by some Gujjars, while others have made connections with secular political parties and social movements at the national level. Doing so requires taking on particular forms of identity – exaggerating their 'tribal-ness' on the one hand or emphasising a reformist Muslim identity on the other. The impacts of these contrasting forms of identity are especially apparent for Gujjar women. Those who take the former path emphasise the freedom that women enjoyed in traditional Gujjar culture where they were never required to wear the veil. On the other hand, in those families that have been attracted to reformist Islam, Gujjar women have largely been withdrawn from public life.

The new emphasis which many Gujjars are placing on religious identity – and particularly their association with the 'reformist' Islam of the Deobandi School – has seen a shift in approaches to education. As we have seen, many Muslim Gujjars express a reluctance to send their children, especially girls, to government 'Hindi' schools. The opening of a number of madrasas and Gujjar student hostels has encouraged some students to continue their studies, with a curriculum that combines religious studies, Urdu and Arabic language, and 'modern' subjects including maths and computer science. In contrast with the town-based teachers of the government schools, staff in these madrasas are mostly locally born Gujjars trained at Islamic seminaries in Uttar Pradesh and Punjab. These madrasas have contributed to a rise in education levels among Gujjars – as many parents argued and as Table 6.4 demonstrates – their establishment coincides with a rapid decline in the number of Gujjar children who received no education. The hope of parents is that their children will be better able to access opportunities through Muslim business networks or the enormous rewards they believe are available through migration to the Gulf. Against this, parents recognise that the shift into madrasa education is likely to prevent their children from accessing jobs in the government and high caste-dominated private sector.

Though upward mobility only involved a small proportion of Gujjar families it has an impact on the wider population. Where Gaddis talk of bhaichara, rich Gujjars tell you about the 'social work' they do – providing loans, giving jobs and funding building of mosques and madrasas. Social reform is at the forefront of such efforts but poor Gujjars often complain that 'rich Gujjars do nothing for us'. In the recent past, it was expected that each September all the members of a community would come together to assist one another with the annual cutting of grass reserves that would provide fodder for the winter months. In recent years this has changed: poorer Gujjars complain that their wealthy relatives try to buy themselves out of their communal activities by paying others to do the work for them. Mussa's sister is the current Pradhan of Badagaon panchayat. Her husband works for an NGO and is the president of a Gujjar welfare organisation. This does not seem to have been of much benefit to Mussa. Mussa's wife's brother teaches in one of the local madrasas but Mussa doesn't get on with him. Another relative is a contractor who found work for Mussa near Rampur in the east of Himachal Pradesh. When Mussa and his fellow workers (all from the Saal valley) discovered that this man pocketed 20 per cent of the daily wages paid by the company they quit their jobs and came home. Now this relative prefers to employ labourers from Jammu as they are less troublesome and more reliable. Upward mobility for the few has led to a social differentiation (see Table 6.5) in which the majority are left behind or forced to conform to reductive forms of tribal or religious identity as their only form of collective action, which, so far, has yielded few benefits to the many. Instead of the soft comfort blanket of egalitarianism found among the inward-looking Gaddi community, the economic and social diversification of the outwardly oriented Gujjars risks creating a degree of divisive polarisation.

NEW FORMS OF MOBILITY AND BARRIERS TO DEVELOPMENT

As shown in this chapter, marked differences exist between tribal and non-tribal households in the Saal valley with respect to assets, education and employment. Poverty among tribal populations is often explained by their geographical isolation. Secluded in remote Himalayan valleys and scratching a living from subsistence agriculture and pastoral nomadism, Gaddis and Gujjars of the Chamba valley lived self-sufficient lives in which survival could turn on the vagaries of nature. Much has changed – roads, schools and reservations brought these tribal people closer to the notional mainstream of Indian society. Gaddis and Gujjars have come a long way since the days when they depended on shepherding and buffalo herding. Though not absent altogether, the kinds of absolute poverty described by the older generations have largely disappeared. What has not changed is that they remain at the bottom of the social and economic hierarchies that order Chamba society. Relative poverty is persistent and the clear divide that existed between Adivasi and non-Adivasi families in the past has continued in the present, with the latter proving better equipped to benefit from the economic growth in Himachal Pradesh during the post-liberalisation era. Squeezed out of customary nomadism, most Gaddi and Gujjar families have struggled to gain access to secure employment and lucrative business opportunities. What remain are the kinds of insecure, precarious and dangerous work that represent the dark side of the boom. As the first chapter of this book argues, the use of potentially less quarrelsome and more malleable migrant labour that can be worked harder is a pattern emerging across our field sites. These may be Adivasis or Dalits from Bihar-Jharkhand or Odisha (see the chapters by Raj and Donegan) or Bhils from Nandurbar (see Thakur's chapter). The bringing in of this migrant labour force means that Gaddis and Gujjars have seen the local work opportunities at their doorstep disappear, in road building, hydroelectric projects and so on, and have had to become short-term labour migrants themselves.

Clearly the Gujjars and Gaddis of Chamba district face common obstacles that derive from more than the mountainous geography of the state.

Tracing the historical causes of inequality, a number of causal factors are identified – historical exclusion from natural resources, loss of traditional livelihoods, division of assets following demographic change, political marginalisation, lack of cultural capital, confidence, knowledge and contacts, and discriminatory barriers that stop Gaddis and Gujjars from accessing educational and economic opportunities. Some of these factors are long-standing, some of them are new. But none of these factors stands alone: the causes of persistent poverty overlap and reinforce each other.

A return visit to Chamba in April 2016 allowed me to catch up with events in the Saal valley and the lives of the Gaddi and Gujjar families among whom I had lived. Prakaso and his fellow Gaddis were celebrating their success in the recent panchayat elections. They told me how the three wards which contained substantial Gaddi populations had agreed to unify behind a common candidate. This allowed them to defeat the other four wards whose votes were split. With their representative installed as Pradhan the Gaddis of these three wards could now expect an upturn in the number of development projects allocated to the area. Already they were getting the full guarantee of 100 days of National Rural Employment Guarantee Act work that previously had been denied to them: for a daily-wage of Rs.170 most of the men from Prakaso's village were now engaged in building a pukka path up from the river.

Walking up to Mussa's house, I found him complaining about the lack of decent jobs in Chamba district. He had briefly been employed to lay a water pipe but the contractor still had not given him anything for the work he had done. Project work had largely dried up and anyway, if it was offered to him, Mussa felt reluctant to leave his growing family for any extended period of time. Sitting on the terrace of his small house with its beautiful views over the whole valley, Mussa told me that he was thinking of selling his land and going to live with his uncles in Punjab. There were opportunities to be had in Punjab: he could work as a labourer to earn money. Once he'd saved enough he would buy more buffalo and live off the sale of their milk. When they grew up his sons might be able to find work in a factory or drive taxis for a living.

This chapter has shown how new occupations and opportunities are accessed and distributed unevenly between and within groups. As part of this process, ideas of traditional identity and community among Gaddis and Gujjars have been constantly updated to produce new forms of mobility, according to the changing political and economic contexts in which they live. It is useful to refer back to the two concepts – being 'ghumantu' (nomadic) and being *Adivasi* (indigenous) – to describe the ways in which tribal identify is articulated. Both concepts suppose a particular relationship with place – either moving through it or belonging to it. While the former depends on the establishment of new social and economic ties, the latter is a more politicised form of identity used to seek benefits from political representatives and the state. The degree and form of 'connectedness', and the ways in which identity is constructed around a sense of place, work to determine Gaddis' and Gujjars' limited capacity to access opportunities both within Chamba district and in the world outside the valley.

7

Narmada Valley and Adjoining Plains, Maharashtra

Vikramaditya Thakur

This chapter is concerned with the Bhils of western India, an Adivasi group who inhabit large stretches of land that now form part of Madhya Pradesh, Maharashtra, Rajasthan and Gujarat. It focuses on Bhils in north-western Maharashtra, bordering Gujarat, in areas of what was historically known as 'Khandesh': a territory that used to be densely forested, stretching from the Satpura Hills in northern Maharashtra and adjacent areas in Gujarat and Madhya Pradesh, to the plains of northern Maharashtra in the south.[1]

The chapter explores Bhil integration into the present-day Indian capitalist economy and how this has been shaped by processes of oppression and exploitation from the colonial period onwards, including by the Sardar Sarovar Project dam on the Narmada River and their struggle against this. It focuses on three villages of Nandurbar district in northern Maharashtra: Bhils who are still living in the Satpura Hills; Bhils, including some of the main local leaders of the Narmada dam struggle who have been resettled on the plains south of the Satpura Hills; and Bhils who have been part of the landlord-dominated agricultural villages of the plains for generations. The fate of Bhils differs in a number of ways between those who remain in the hills and those who have moved to the plains, and also between different groups of Bhils on the plains. However, for all of them, the integration into present-day economic relations has reinforced their disadvantaged position compared to the general caste groups in the region. The means through which this is happening might have changed but their overall position in society remains the same.

Historically, the oppression of the Bhils can be traced back to early colonial days. In the pre-colonial period, the Bhils had been integrated with the plains but the colonial regime turned the balance of power against them. After the colonial rulers took control of the area in 1818 they either 'pacified' or deposed the various Bhil rulers. The Bhils of the hills became confined to their local area where they were policed, like many other Adivasi groups in eastern and central India, by the government's Forest Department. The Bhils also inhabited the southern plains of Khandesh but, especially from the latter half of the nineteenth century on, this area was taken over by in-migrating farming groups such as the Gujars. Though the Gujars who immigrated from Gujarat settled largely in one part of Nandurbar district, particularly Shahada *taluka* (administrative district), their role is pertinent for this study as they became a dominant caste group. These in-migrants were early capitalist farmers. They had the economic and political muscle to dispossess the Bhils of the plains of their land and turn them into agricultural workers and tied farm servants. They also used the modern system of contracts and courts towards this end.

The disadvantaged position of the Bhils culminated, for the hill Bhils, with the construction of the Sardar Sarovar Project dam on the Narmada River in the Satpura Hills from the 1980s onwards. Swathes of the hill valleys were submerged and thousands of Bhils were resettled on the plains, while the lives of those who could stay on also changed. As this chapter shows, the Bhils still living in the Satpura Hills at the edge of the new Narmada reservoir lake cannot eke out a proper living from their non-irrigated fields in the now deforested hills.[2] In some cases local circumstances and conditions created by the Sardar Sarovar struggle have enabled additional local means of survival, but for most households, seasonal migration to the Marathwada region of Maharashtra or to neighbouring Gujarat's plains has become a necessity. Here, they find work at the bottom of the sugar production chain, doing back-breaking sugar cane cutting in the fields of the landed castes.

The resettled Bhil community that I studied was relocated to a new, independent, Bhil village on the plains and given unalienable agricultural land. The long-running anti-dam social movement had fostered values of unity, the importance of education and a sense of hope coming from their success in dealing with the state over their resettlement. The resettled Bhils are trying to emulate the model of economic success of the local dominant farming group, the Gujars, but I show that their future may be risky and uncertain, both in farming and in potentially more prosperous non-agricultural walks of life.

The third group of Bhils studied have been living on the plains for generations, in precarious conditions. They have experienced long-term integration at the very bottom of the society of the plains, in a Gujar-dominated village. The century-long Gujar hegemony has loosened as Gujars have sought livelihoods outside the village and these Bhils now survive through seasonal labour migration. They find work at the bottom of the regional labour hierarchies in sectors that feed the Indian economic boom: the brick kilns of Gujarat and Maharashtra that produce bricks for the construction sector which is rapidly expanding its employment to millions of precarious workers across India; and they undertake the arduous work of cutting sugar cane in the fields of the landed dominant castes in Maharashtra. Compared to the other groups of Bhils studied here, these are the ones most directly integrated into precarious capitalist labour relations, without other options available to them and with little ability to carve out their own space.

Although all three categories of Bhils find themselves at the bottom of the pile of today's capitalist social and economic relations, it is also clear that their integration into these relations is uneven and differs from case to case. Moreover, the Bhil category is not homogeneous but is comprised of various *jatis* (endogamous social groups). To give an idea, the 1991 Dhule *District Census Handbook* lists 13 sub-tribes of Bhils.[3]

The first study village is Ambegaon. It is located in the midst of the Satpura Hills in Akrani taluka and had a population of 77 households in 2013, divided into six hamlets bordered by the Narmada River and scattered across a large area, as is typical of hill villages. The study also draws on data from ten nearby villages on seasonal migration. As is common in this area, all the villagers are Bhils. The two other study villages, Mankheda and Anand Nagar, lie in the plains of Shahada taluka. Anand Nagar is a resettlement colony settled in 2004 by the government. It houses 255 Bhil families from eight hill villages of Akrani taluka that were resettled in the plains when displaced by the Sardar Sarovar Project dam, on land from the neighbouring village of Mankheda a couple of kilometres away, and other neighbouring villages. Mankheda, the third study village, is a multi-caste village with a population of 390 households. Of these, 220 are Bhils while 83 belong to the dominant peasant caste of Gujars.

The fieldwork for this chapter was conducted over a 14-month period of August 2014–15, and March 2016, living in these three villages. In addition to participant observation, I undertook a household sample survey and other minor surveys in each village. Notes from my earlier fieldwork during the period 2001 to 2012 supplement this work. Except for social movement groups, their leaders and other public figures who have been extensively documented in published literature, the names of all persons and village names have been changed to protect their identity.

Four aspects of socio-political and economic changes from colonial times onwards are crucial for our analysis. The first is the agrarian boom ushered in by dominant peasant castes that took root in the colonial period. It peaked with the Green Revolution in the three-decade period from the 1960s to the early 1990s and has since been in a decline. Farmers are now trying to offset the decline by venturing into newer cash crops. The second aspect is linked to the colonial census and consolidation of various dominant caste groups from the early twentieth century via pan-India associations that marked the formal beginning of their social mobility.[4] It has translated into electoral hegemony and control of state resources to largely serve the interests of these dominant castes in the postcolonial period. The third impact arises from the building of the Sardar Sarovar Project dam on the Narmada River and the struggle against this, which triggered major changes both in the hills and, obviously, for the Bhils who were resettled. The fourth aspect has been the exit of people from the dominant farming groups from the agriculture-based rural setting to government and business jobs in towns and cities, achieved through a combination of education and powerful connections. Other less wealthy and less politically influential groups have also moved away from agriculture but, as elsewhere in India, their options have been limited mainly to low-paid informalised seasonal labour. The rest of the chapter, after a historical overview, focuses on each of the three study villages.

HISTORY

The present-day Nandurbar district is part of the historical Khandesh region. A rich and prosperous area before the ascendancy of the Marathas, large parts of Khandesh, including the present-day Nandurbar district, were largely depopulated due to long internecine battles between the various Maratha local rulers (*satraps*). It was overgrown with dense forest when the British took control after defeating the Marathas in 1818.[5] Deforestation for agriculture took place earlier in the plains, during the colonial period, but the inaccessible hills had forest cover till the 1970s.[6] Khandesh became part of the Central Division of Bombay Province, with the Satpura Hills governed by various Bhil chieftains under the control of colonial 'political agents' or, in cases such as that of the Rana of Akrani, the ruler was deposed and their area brought under direct British rule.

The Bhils continued to subsist on a mix of shifting agriculture, cultivating one crop during the monsoon, along with hunting and gathering. Forest produce, including timber, also played an important role. Shifting cultivation slowly gave way to the farming of fixed plots of land, spurred on by progressive deforestation and population growth in the most recent three decades.[7] Except for a few who were granted land titles during the colonial period itself, most Bhils did not have formal land rights.[8] Revenue settlement did not take place in these villages even during the postcolonial period, till the Sardar Sarovar Project dam construction commenced in 1987.[9]

With the coming of the Forest Department from the late nineteenth century, the Bhils technically became encroachers on government land. They were fined on an annual basis by the Forest Department guards for farming on government property, but the guards often simply pocketed the money and did not even provide receipts for it. Confiscation of cattle, being ill-treated and demands to be entertained with chicken and liquor were problems commonly faced by the Bhils for over a century under the regime of the Forest Department. Inaccessibility due to absence of roads, and the absence of other parts of the state and its welfare arms, exacerbated the socioeconomic marginalisation of Bhils in most parts of the hills. This continued until the coming of the dam in the 1980s.

The plains of Nandurbar, on the other hand, were completely transformed. By 1852 the East India Company had undertaken the first revenue survey along with land settlements.[10] Settled agriculture was vigorously pursued in the plains to maximise revenue and tillage was pushed right up to the Satpura Hills.[11] Modern means of transportation and communication –railways, roads, bridges and telegraph – along with courts, hospitals and schools, were established in large numbers.[12] The dramatic changes in the plains heightened the isolation of the hills, which were left practically untouched except for the periodic visits of the Forest Department and occasional visits by the police.

The plains of Nandurbar witnessed the rise of a vibrant cash crop economy, first by way of a cotton boom of 1860s.[13] From the onset the peasant proprietors were able to take advantage of this. This was facilitated by the fact that, in contrast to the *zamindari* system of Bengal that strengthened landlordism, the British introduced the *ryotwari* system here, a system where the peasant proprietor held land titles and paid the revenue directly to the state.[14] The first agrarian boom in Khandesh was intertwined with the immigration of Gujars from Gujarat who took control of most of the farmland in Shahada taluka.[15] Other Gujar groups already inhabited the eastern and north-eastern parts of Khandesh but the immigration in the north-western parts including Nandurbar and Shahada taluka took place from the third decade of the nineteenth century.[16] Business castes also arrived, like the Parsees from Gujarat and Marwaris from Rajasthan, 'almost all since the establishment of British rule'.[17] These peasant and business castes reaped the benefits of the new British system. This, though, had a deleterious effect on existing peasant groups like the Bhils and Malis (a peasant caste group), by causing indebtedness and loss of agricultural land.

As agriculture expanded and the demand for labour increased, the immigrant Gujars of north-west Khandesh and Shahada in particular, described as 'capitalists, not peasant proprietors' by the colonial gazetteer, used the Bhils' 'ignorance and carelessness' in combination with new institutions like civil courts to 'have them at their mercy' as a source of cheap labour.[18] The gazetteer gives a vivid account of how a small sum of money borrowed by a Bhil couple for their children's marriage or for buying a bull led the Bhil husband to become a lifetime slave along with his wife, as serfs who could be even transferred to another Gujar owner. This system was called *saldari* and the Bhil a *saldar*. Large-scale alienation of agricultural land by Gujars and moneylending castes, hand in hand, continued.[19] It was on the foundation of this exploitation that Gujar agrarian prosperity developed in the postcolonial period.

The conditions of the Bhils in the plains remained miserable for over a century until the rise of a Bhil leader, Ambarsing Suratwanti (1940–74), educated up to 10th grade, a rare feat among the Bhils back then, who had earlier worked in the Gandhian institution of Sarvodaya.[20] A group of young, upper caste, middle-class, urban youth from cities like Mumbai and Pune, dissatisfied with the mainstream communist political parties joined Ambarsing to set up a group called Shramik Sanghatana in 1970.[21] After Ambarsing's untimely death, the external activists, in alliance with local Bhil leaders, continued to lead landless and marginal landowners, particularly Bhils, in successful strikes against big landlords and dominant Gujar farmers and their armed private militias of '*Peek Saunrakshan Samitis*' (Crop Protection Societies), opposing the working conditions of the near-slavelike practice of saldari (which, at this point in time, involved being tied as a wage labourer on an annual basis while it often continued for the person's entire life).[22] Issues of exploitation of women, including sexual assaults, were also taken up and local women played an important role in the group.[23] The Progressive Democratic Alliance that gained power in Maharashtra, in the wake of the National Emergency (1975–77) imposed by Prime Minister Indira Gandhi, had strong socialist inclinations. It outlawed the saldari system besides appointing special *mamledars* (magistrates) to take *suo motu* notice of land grabs by all parties, even by Bhils from other Bhils, as well as household goods taken away in lieu of pending debts, and brought such cases to courts and resolved them within days.[24] From the middle of the 1980s, the Shramik Sanghatana started losing support among the Bhils as the coercive power of the Gujars and other exploiting sections declined to a substantial extent.[25]

BHILS OF THE HILLS:
FROM BACKWATER TO BORDER VILLAGE AT THE LAKE

The recent history of the Bhils of the Satpura Hill village Ambegaon is closely linked to the construction of the Sardar Sarovar Project dam on the Narmada River and the fight against this. The dam submerged 33 villages in Maharashtra, including 24 villages in Akrani, either fully or partially. The submergence area rises right up to the village of Ambegaon, which now finds itself located on the bank of the new lake-sized river, while their kinsmen from the neighbouring, now submerged, villages have been resettled on the Nandurbar plains, including in the second fieldwork village of Anand Nagar.

The construction of the Sardar Sarovar Project dam transformed Ambegaon. Road construction integrated the Bhils into the market-based economy of the plains. This integration also meant access to health and education. The long-running national and international movement against the dam led by the Narmada Bachao Andolan (Save Narmada Campaign) from 1985 onwards added to the changes,[26] not least because the leading Bhil activists were from the neighbouring villages. The Bhils became trained activists, the outside world opened up to them, and this put them on a stronger footing vis-à-vis government officials. Since the Narmada Bachao Andolan, government and the Forest Department harassment has been conspicuous by its absence, which, among other things, has enabled the Bhils to keep cultivating any forest land that they have encroached on over time, even if they are not formally registered as owners. At the same time, the local Public Distribution System ration shop is now properly supplied by the government, providing subsidised grain, vegetables, oil and so on to all households.

Today the main income source of practically all Bhils of Ambegaon is farming their own land. In the absence of irrigation facilities, given the hilly terrain that makes it practically impossible to transport water using pipes, they can only grow one crop a year, and only 'dry' crops such as *jowar* (sorghum) or maize. The standard of living is basic for most, but given that land has been readily available for all households (the average landholdings are around 3.8 acres),[27] and given the Public Distribution System rations as well as access to forest produce and fishing, there is little abject poverty. This makes this a comparatively egalitarian village, like many other Adivasi villages in interior India.

The household survey undertaken for this chapter confirms that practically everyone lives off farming and also does occasional paid agricultural labour for each other (see Figures 7.1 and 7.2).[28] Most households appreciate the importance of '*jod dhandha*' (allied activities). Fortuitously, the new lake provides good opportunities for fishing, which many households undertake on a seasonal basis. The fish caught is both for own consumption and for sale in the nearest market town, Dhadgaon, accessed by road. Other border trade with Gujarat also provides a good income for some households. Only a few of the households – three in all – have members with government jobs, all low-ranking local ones (for example, as police *patil* [village-level police officer] and village *sarpanch*) and one of them has been able to invest in minor business activities. A few other Bhils also have businesses such as a basic village shop or, at best, a jeep plying the dirt road to the nearest market town (see Table 7.1). This may indeed provide the basis for further economic differentiation but for now this is still only incipient. The seeds of socioeconomic differentiation lie in the ability to use the market in

Photo 15   Bhils farming in the hills near the banks of the Narmada River
Photo by Vikramaditya Thakur.

conjugation with the holding of formal authority by specific family lineages in every village. The traditional posts of *karbharis* (village managers) have often later translated into formal government posts such as police patil and elected sarpanch for the same set of families. I will return to the comparisons between the villages and between Gujars and Bhils below.

The absence of good government jobs, in spite of reservations of such jobs for Scheduled Tribes, is not due to lack of education among the Bhils. Illiteracy is common among the older generation but 14 per cent of the men from our sample – all from younger generations – are graduates or have diplomas (see Figure 7.3). However, from a job perspective this has so far been to no avail. In fact, the three government employees in our sample all have no schooling and none of the educated people have been able to get such jobs.

There is little difference in the gendered division of labour among the hill Bhils as agriculture involves all household members (see Figures 7.1 and 7.2). However, when it comes to education, illiteracy is more common among women and only 3 per cent of women have the highest level of education, showing that there are limits to gender equality also among the Bhils (see Figure 7.3). The lower degree of literacy among women is due to several factors. The primary one is that government schools (except for primary school) and colleges are away from the village and require students to reside at the place of the institution. The patriarchal aspect comes into play here as preference is given to the male child by their parents. The cost of education, too, becomes a factor. The increased mobility of men, who travel periodically outside the hills to the plains, also allows them to develop greater familiarity with Marathi, the medium of education, while women usually only speak the Bhili dialects. Finally, given that marriage in the hills take place at an early age, women usually are bearing children before they are out of their teens. All these factors have kept women's literacy low in the hills.

Given the harsh terrain and far-flung habitations, along with the relatively homogeneous nature of the groups in any given hamlet, the degree of cooperation is high among the hill communities. They have a tradition of *laha*, where an entire hamlet gets together to help with the harvest of one family's fields. This process is repeated for every family in turn. In the Bhil resettlement colonies in the plains, laha was however immediately discontinued. The larger size of agricultural plots, the availability of a paid local labour force in the neighbouring villages and access to mechanised equipment such as tractors obviated the need to persist with the hill tradition. However, the practice of the entire village coming together to help build the house of a newly married couple continued in the plains as well.

Poor rains in 2012 and the consecutive droughts of 2014 and 2015, among the most severe in recent history for large parts of India, left many Bhils with huge unpaid debts and mounting interest. The impact of the drought was universal and affected all the villages in the hills as well as the plains. Many were forced to forgo the kilos of silver jewellery, purchased from profits of the previous years for the womenfolk, the typical mode of saving among the Bhils of Nandurbar. The jewellery is used as collateral for loans from goldsmiths and moneylenders, a primary source of agricultural credit. Though stipulated by the Reserve Bank of India to charge no more than 18.5 per cent annual rate of interest, the actual lending rate was 3 per cent per month (36 per cent per annum).[29] The absence of cheap and readily available credit remains a problem for large parts of India and also for the Bhils. Obtaining loans from the government banks is a long, complicated and tedious process and requires literacy, familiarity with the process of paperwork and the possession of assets for collateral such as land. An example of the slow pace of government machinery is that the meagre government compensation for the drought of 2012 (Rs.1200–3000) came into the Anand Nagar Bhils' bank accounts only in late 2014.[30] In contrast, the courteous moneylender is keen to offer loans at a minute's notice if the creditor has collateral to offer and is known to his patron.

In drought years or in areas where the summer is particularly harsh in terms of water supply forcing people to temporarily migrate to nearby towns, the Government of Maharashtra runs an Employment Guarantee

Scheme (EGS) to provide work during the lean months. Maharashtra was one of the pioneers of such a scheme in the wake of the drought of 1971 and it continues to operate in hundreds of villages every year depending on the situation. In 2005, when the Government of India put the India-wide National Employment Guarantee Scheme in place, the Maharashtra Employment Guarantee Scheme became part of this. As per the national-level government's minimum wages act, the daily wage stands at Rs.168 and this is also the pay of the Employment Guarantee Scheme. In May 2015, the Ambegaon Bhils dug a well as part of the scheme but come the end of August 2015 they still had not been paid their dues. This delay in payment, often stretching to 4–6 months or even more after the work is complete, and in a drought context when money is desperately needed, makes it a failure in Nandurbar. Due to delayed payment, villagers often do not have money in the lean season to tide them over the meagre months or for buying the seeds and fertilisers for the next sowing season. Instead people resort to seasonal migrant labour, which involves an advance paid before the work is undertaken to those willing to sign up for it in July.

Seasonal labour migration became an option in the hills of Akrani following the building of new roads. Normally the Ambegaon villagers do not take part in this as they have alternative income sources on the spot, but in 2015 the failure of timely rains meant signing up for seasonal migration for cutting cane in the nearby districts of Maharashtra's Marathwada region. The move to Marathwada is much more common in the other hill villages next to Ambegaon with no fishing or border trade access. The complete absence of any alternative employment opportunities in the hills forces the Bhils to sign up for the seasonal migration trip. The outline below is based on conversations with three Bhil *mukardam* (labour contractors) and over 30 Bhil seasonal labour migrants.

A team of two persons, a man and a woman comprise a *koita*. The man's job is to cut the cane using a *darya* (machete) while the woman ties the bundles. A group of 15 koitas comprise a *tukdi* (group). Payment for cane is based on weight. Thus, for example the going rate for the 2014–15 season was Rs.190/ton of cane. On average, a tukdi can cut 17–20 tons of cane in a day, thus earning between Rs.107–126 per person per day. In addition, the labourers can earn in two more ways: cutting and selling the leafy crown at Rs.7–10 per kilo locally, as it is used as both cattle fodder and a fuel source, thus fetching an additional Rs.56–80 daily. The other is the bonus, ranging from Rs.500–1500 that a farm owner gives to a tukdi once all the cane has been cut from the field and loaded onto trucks headed for the mill. The labour can take advances for buying food articles and other daily needs, including condiments, cooking oil, soaps, candies and mobile-phone recharge vouchers among other items of basic need, as and when they want and it is deducted from their final payment. If needed, they can also take an advance to go back home to attend a sick relative or some important family life-cycle ritual and then return to resume work. Given that the mukardam is usually a relative or someone from the same or a neighbouring village who knows every member of his labour team intimately, and the fact that a labour group is comprised of people who are from the same village or hamlet and related to each other, the risk of the individual labourer not returning is very low. Most of the Bhils try to meet their expenses from the sale of the crown and the bonuses, letting the final payment remain untouched till it is paid via their mukardam at the end of the season. A team of two can save and bring back money ranging from Rs.20,000–45,000 at the end of a seven-month season lasting from late September to early April when the final settlement is made at the end of the season.

The koita need not necessarily be made up of a man and a woman. At times, two unmarried young men team up to save and bring back money for their marriages. Among the Bhils, it is the man who has to pay the bride price. Though the price is not standardised and varies depending on the village or the family, it has been going up at a rapid rate in each of the eight villages of the seasonal migrants. It ranged from Rs.35,000 to well above Rs.100,000. Besides household utility articles, clothes and jewellery, the seasonal migrants spend the money on building *pukka* houses and the purchase of mobile phones, television sets or motorcycles in some cases, along with making some savings (self-help groups for women and various saving schemes of private agencies). Most of these expenses have come into the picture less than a decade ago.

When seasonal migration began, locals of the area where the migrants went to work would own the shops selling everyday utilities. In the last decade, the mukardams have themselves ventured into this lucrative profession, the shop often being manned by a literate relative. The latest development is that other migrant Bhils set up shops in the place of work with close links to the mukardam. Larger advances and the relaxation in the terms of employment, allowing them to be back home temporarily, are other recent developments.

All the Bhils I spoke to gave the same set of reasons for undertaking the seasonal migration as those going to kilns from Mankheda. They had been undertaking this trip for four to five years. 'The population has shot up, there is little land left to bring under plough in the hills. Needs have increased and there is no work in the hills ... this is the only way out,' was a response I got repeatedly when I asked why they had started undertaking these journeys.[31] In addition, they pointed out how the advances for cutting cane allow them to get what they view as interest-free cash to grow the rain-fed crop in the hills. 'It is better to go out and make money once the crops are ripe by late September than sit home idle with no money and have petty fights with neighbours,' as one Bhil put it. The three Bhils who work as mukardams said the advances are transferred by the sugar mill owner through electronic bank transfers to their account that they pass on to the Bhils who have signed up for being part of a tukdi.

From the mukardam's perspective, unsurprisingly perhaps, seasonal migration is the best thing that could have happened to the hill people and is a boon. 'Yes, there are some minor problems and work is tough but it is manageable,' as they put it. This is understandable as the mukardams usually have a commission ranging from 15–20 per cent of the earnings per koita – which is a very high fee compared to what we came across elsewhere (see the chapters by Raj and Donegan)[32] – that is paid directly at the end of the season when the final accounting is done and the labourers paid. From the male labourer's perspective, an additional issue at times is that of their women's safety when the locals are hostile in an unknown setting. Under extreme circumstances, they have to stay awake at night, taking turns at guard duty while the others sleep. For the women, harassment is a regular occurrence, with the locals leering at them when they take their bath, as they have to, in the open. They have no alternative but to wash as best they can and then hastily get dressed, with lack of hygiene over extended periods causing health complications. Harassment and sexual innuendo from local farm owners, truck drivers and others, along with unwelcome physical contact, is equally common but the Bhil women have to take this in their stride. In any case, there is no formal redress mechanism in an alien setting. Cases of women being sexually assaulted by the locals and of teenage girls being enticed by other labourers or truck drivers only to be left after a time, often in a late stage of pregnancy or following the birth of a child were also related by the women I spoke to. These are the visible forms of exploitation. Other problems include extended working hours that are often uncompensated, poor housing and insanitary conditions. Given that movement of labourers from one field to another or the coming of the vehicle, usually a tractor, to collect the cane results in some gaps, the work time is not strictly regulated in terms of fixed hours.

The Bhils of the Satpura Hills benefit from the absence of direct oppressors and dominant classes exploiting them, including the near absence of the Forest Department, state police and so on. Their economic conditions and the manner in which they have been integrated into the wider economy have their variations but nearly everyone in this relatively egalitarian Adivasi area is shown in government records as being below the poverty line. The Ambegaon Bhils are in a slightly better position than other nearby hill villages due to the Sardar Sarovar Project dam and the struggle against it. However, while they have some degree of economic independence as petty producers and petty traders, seasonal labour migration is a very real option for many of them too, especially when nature plays its tricks on them as marked by failure of the monsoon.

Photo 16   Boats of seasonal migrants crossing from Maharashtra to go to the sugar
cane fields in Gujarat
Photo by Alpa Shah.

MANKHEDA VILLAGE OF THE PLAINS

The plains offer a different story of Bhil integration into the modern
economy – in fact, different stories. The village of Mankheda provides the
main storyline as, like many other villages of Shahada taluka, its history is
one of Gujar dominance and oppression of the Bhils. Its tale begins with two
Bhil brothers, Lakira and Fakira, at around the beginning of the twentieth
century. They supposedly got many acres of land from the British but most of
it was not fertile.[33] Two Gujar brothers Ramu and Shyamu, both unmarried,
moved to Mankheda with their widowed mother after the untimely death of
their father to farm 5 *partan* (a local measure equivalent to 3 acres) owned
by their paternal grandfather.[34] Shyamu (1911–76), the younger sibling,
had studied till the 4th grade, staying with his grandfather. Over time, the
two brothers bought an additional 45 partans (135 acres) using their own
savings and with help from their kinsmen, and dug a well to irrigate a large
part of their land. Ramu died issueless and Shyamu's six sons inherited all
the land, about 25 acres each, at the death of their father. Many Bhils served
them as saldars for generations, including Jaysing Sonawane's grandfather,
named Ripa, for 25 years (1945–70), and later his father from 1970 to 1979.

In 1979, Ripa and his several family members were awarded 14 acres by the government from Shyamu's vast landholdings, which were divided among his three sons and a second wife. The Sonawanes, like the other Bhils, lacked capital to improve the land or provide irrigation. Ripa's efforts ensured his son was educated and he became the first Bhil to reach 10th grade. The son, however, failed to pass the 10th grade exam, never managed to secure a government job despite being highly educated for his times and instead replaced his father as a saldar. Many other Mankheda Bhils have been landless labourers for generations. The empirically grounded absence of trust in education's emancipatory potential and resignation to one's fate as a daily wage labourer are reflected in Figures 7.3 and 7.4, where not a single Bhil from a sample of 15 randomly chosen families has managed to make it to college.

While the Bhils in the Gujar-dominated plains villages live in poor thatched mud huts even today, the Gujars, on the other hand, went from strength to strength. The Green Revolution boosted their income dramatically. The first tractor was bought in the 1980s and today every household owns at least a small tractor. Gujars with landholdings of 7–10 acres, small by their standards, have been able to build big concrete houses, and to take loans, either from banks or from private moneylenders, to invest in newer bore wells, ensuring further expansion first into Bt cotton and nowadays into even higher value cash crops such as papaya, and to install drip irrigation systems.

The long history of solidarity among the Gujars has been an important source of prosperity. The Gujars of Nandurbar, also known as Leva Patidars, formed a caste association with a list of published rules for guiding the conduct of all its members in 1939.[35] Till a decade back they systematically control every aspect of local administration, capital and knowledge in Mandheka, Shahada taluka and beyond.

Bada-bhai, a Gujar and one of the sons of Shyamu, is a strapping man despite touching 70 in age. A close associate of P.K. Anna, the Gujar leader,[36] and a member of the board of trustees on many of the cooperative institutions, he recalled him fondly as we walked through his papaya plantation on a humid afternoon of August in 2014:

He had the vision to start schools, colleges with residential facilities offering many technical courses, a cooperative bank, a large cooperative sugar mill, a distillery to produce alcohol from the waste generated, a cotton ginning and textile mill in a planned manner using the cooperative model and also funded by donations from other Gujars. The cooperatives ensured that we farmers controlled the market instead of the trading caste who hold sway otherwise. The huge shopping complex he set up in Shahada town stocks all the agro-products and is mostly owned by our fellow Gujars. Like him, I am wary of communists – they are divisive – but subscribe to the idea of socialism. Hence I was the first to welcome the Anand Nagar Bhils and taught them how to profit growing cash crops. Ask them and not one of them will deny.

The reference to communists was an oblique reference to the pro-Bhil Shramik Sanghatana that had to counter a P.K. Anna-led repressive hegemonic phase of the Gujars in Bada-bhai's youth. Bada-bhai also failed to add that the cooperative bank started by P.K. Anna had to shut down due to corruption and mismanagement and a few other ventures too had shut down by the early 2000s. They had, however, helped the Gujars prosper for three decades in the interim period.

In spite of their dominance of agriculture and allied agribusiness, for the last decades the objective of the Gujars – as of other landed classes across India – has been to get their offspring educated and moved into salaried jobs.[37] In Mankheda, as is true for large parts of rural India, those with non-irrigated land, marginal landholders and the landless are not even eligible to enter the fray for this transition. As Mota-bhai, the sexagenarian from Mankheda recalled:

We were a large family of six brothers and one sister as was typical of that time. Our father Shyamu could only afford to invest in the higher education of one son, my brother who went to college and retired as a government teacher. Most other Gujars too could afford to pay for one or two children at most, usually sons – getting the daughters educated was more common among the Maratha caste if they did not have sons or the sons were no good. The idea was that the other sons will look after the farm so the one usually not good in studies would drop out by middle school or after failing 10th grade. It ensured lesser fragmentation of land to maintain some sort of viability while assured monthly income instead of returns once or twice a year from the sale of crops allowed for capital investment for improvement of land. Back then, land was plentiful and there was limited motivation for working hard to pursue education for many of us. But now, it is only education and jobs or the situation is bad. Thankfully, not a single Gujar is landless or has to work as a seasonal labour migrant. We are an enterprising group. Education allows us to at least start some business even if a job does not work out. Several of our youth got educated and have opened various shops that sell agricultural equipment such as pumps, seeds and similar assorted wares. Without education, one cannot even understand the quality and working of their own wares. The preference of course is for technical courses and salaried jobs.[38]

Engaged in social mobility via agricultural accumulation for several generations, the Gujars are reaping the fruits of institutional infrastructures they now control, such as agricultural cooperatives and educational centres created half a century back. A retired Gujar college teacher residing in Shahada town explained: 'My grandfather was barely literate, my father studied till 7th grade, I did an MA in literature to get a job in the college established by P.K. Anna while both my sons are now software engineers in the US. In fact, Shahada taluka has the maximum number of US green-card holders of any taluka in Maharashtra.'[39] Of our small survey of a sample of ten randomly selected Gujar households (65 adult men and 48 adult women), more than 40 per cent of the men and 21 per cent of the women have graduated or have a diploma. In addition, most Gujars who have managed to get a government job or entered into business have moved away from the village and thus do not form part of this survey.

Gujars of Mankheda village often used to maintain undivided households for up to three generations but this system has largely collapsed in the last decade. Thus, while Shaymu's six sons including Bada-bhai and Mota-bhai stayed with their father along with their wives and children and split only after their father's death to build their own houses, their own sons in turn, each having two children, have moved out independently, over a decade since, to Shahada town for jobs or business and for educating their children. The Gujars left back in Mankheda (and the Anand Nagar Bhils, see below) are now cultivating the land of those that have left on the basis of *batai* (shared profit). While earlier it made sense to keep land consolidated within extended families, now there is an emphasis on living in nuclear families and investing in education, specifically technical courses like diplomas and degrees in engineering for boys, nursing and medicine for girls, along with English and computer classes for both. As the marriage market, too, demands qualified women who can live in urban centres and work, girls are also being allowed to pursue higher education.

The systematic control by the Gujars of every aspect of local administration, capital and knowledge till the 1990s resulted in a general atmosphere of resignation of the Bhils towards the future. The Bhils did not have the capital or guidance either to dig wells in the 1950s, to go for hybrid seeds and fertilisers in the 1960s, or to get motor pump-driven bore wells dug from the late 1980s. There is not a single tractor among the Bhils in Mankheda. While spending time with many Bhils in their agricultural fields from 2007 till 2015, I noted that instead of the minimum optimum requirement, it was the availability or lack of capital that decided how much and what kind of fertiliser or pesticide they used, and the question of affording more expensive nutrients has been a non-issue. Moreover, no Mankheda Bhils have succeeded in going to university or getting into vocational training, not to mention getting into government jobs. However, a few households have succeeded in setting up shops or investing in an auto rickshaw. Given that these ventures are only a few years old, their long-term implications can only be gauged in the times to come.

Though the dominance of the Gujars over the Bhils in terms of overt *violence* on an everyday basis, including beating and abuses, that was prevalent till the 1980s has almost become a matter of the past, it is still intact in terms of taunts and verbal abuse by Gujars hurled at their Bhil labourers in many villages. The disappearance of the violence and the diminishing dominance of the Gujars is due to several reasons, including the political struggles outlined earlier. Another reason is that the village is no longer at the heart of Gujar accumulation, nor Bhil labour relations in the way they used to be. The Gujar youths are largely missing from the farms, being away at schools and colleges. Many of them are either staying in hostels in Shahada or other nearby towns and cities, or have salaried jobs or businesses away from the village. The coming of alternative occupations for the Bhils through seasonal migration to cut sugar cane and to work in brick kilns, described below, has also had a deep impact on Gujar–Bhil relations. The related diminished sense of power, along with the uncertainty of agricultural output and market prices in the twilight of his life, was reflected in this lament of Mota-bhai, the Gujar of Mankheda:

> The son has moved away with his family to Shahada town as he wants to educate his two children in a private English-medium school. He himself studied in the local Marathi-medium only till 10th grade but that was a different time. There were few educated folks, job vacancies existed; he got employed as a clerk in the neighbouring cooperative factory. It is the same story in most other Gujar houses with the sons out of the village for jobs, now even our daughters are following the same path. The villagers don't follow our word as they did back in my father's time, and nor does this fickle weather. Farming or life in the village is just not what it used to be.

The condition of the Bhils of Mankheda is a stark contrast to their Gujar counterparts. Though there are several Bhil households that make a living solely out of agricultural land, most of the others, including those with land, also work as farm labourers in the farms of the Gujars within their village or the neighbouring ones. Nearly all Bhil households are labouring households but of a different kind to what they used to be. Land fragmentation over the last generation has ensured that very few Gujars, only around 8–10, can afford (or need) to maintain a saldar. Most Gujars hire daily wage labourers as per their requirements. The going rate for a saldar was Rs.30,000–35,000 per year in 2014–15. This could include advances of a few thousands as well as other periodic advances as per the needs of the individual saldar. Saldari, presently, could include one individual Bhil or additional members working in the households of the Gujars on certain clearly defined tasks. Saldari is still an annual association with a single farmer, but after the 1980s mobilisation and anti-bonded labour legislation, it has become like other verbal contract systems and the Bhils can and do change masters frequently. That said, by far most Bhils prefer to work as daily wage labourers within the village or the neighbouring ones – and a big chunk of them undertake seasonal migration and work elsewhere for 6–8 months of the year.

All but a few Bhil households are marginal landowners or landless so have little choice but to find some wage income. Today, seasonal migrant labour is the preferred option. The process of seasonal migration by the Bhils of Shahada taluka to work as cane cutters in neighbouring Gujarat from the late 1970s played a crucial role in weakening the grip of the Gujars. It also helped improve the working conditions as well as push up the daily wage rate for six to nine hours of work sowing, weeding or harvesting, over time. The Bhils of Mankheda, however, work in brick kilns, a vocation in which the Gujars paradoxically played an initiating role.

Labour migration as cane cutters began from the early 1980s when mukardams (subcontractors or recruiting agents, usually Bhils themselves who began as seasonal migrants) got in touch with some of the Bhils from this village and a few went to work in Gujarat to cut cane. It did not pick up much given that in 1979, a person of kumbhar (potter) caste leased some land from Shyamu Gujar and started a brick kiln, thus providing a source of income right within the village. Following his lead, two of Shyamu's sons started their own respective kilns in 1982, having observed how the process worked. These kilns closed down by 1987 when the soil types required for bricks were exhausted on the land owned by them. Given that the Bhils had gained expertise in the technique of mixing the correct proportions of ingredients for making bricks and in baking them, they were contacted by kiln owners from neighbouring districts. By 2007, when I first visited the village, migration for about seven months to work on kilns was a major source of income for most families. As many as 110 out of the 220 Bhil households have at least one, or usually two or three persons, including teenage boys and girls, who work in kilns in the neighbouring districts of Maharashtra and Gujarat.

Through the process of advances and payments, the work is similar to that of the cane cutters, described above, but the contract system and the work differ on some counts. Each family works as a unit, dividing the various tasks, including kneading the soil and other ingredients in the correct proportions, adding water, using the metal cast to make bricks; stacking them for drying, making arrangements to get them baked and ensuring the proper baking of all the bricks. During the last ten years, the owners have increasingly dealt directly with a particular family via cellular phone. Advances are negotiated during the rains and the male member goes to collect it from the owner or, at times, the owner or his contact person comes to deliver it. The amount ranges from Rs.15,000 to Rs.20,000 but can go up depending on the special needs of the individual. The family makes a temporary shack next to the kiln where they reside for the period of work. They take money from the kiln owner on a regular basis for provisions and this is deducted from their final settlement at the end of the season. Payment is linked to every 1000 bricks made by a family and is guaranteed irrespective of whether the bricks are sold. For the 2014–15 season, the rate was Rs.350–500 for every 1000 bricks prepared for the kiln. Jaysing Sonawane of Mankheda, along with the other two members of his family, said they prepared around 1300–1500 bricks working the entire day. At the end of the previous season, he had brought back about Rs.50,000. The average amount of money brought back ranges from Rs.45,000 to 65,000 for a family of 2–4 members for one season.

Though a worker usually returns to work for the same kiln owner year after year, there are hundreds of brick kilns to support the burgeoning expansion of cities in south Gujarat as well as smaller towns in every district of Maharashtra including Nandurbar. The competition among the kilns and the need for a reliable labour force ensures that there is minimal interference in the day-to-day work by the owner. The labourers who are away from home, and the owner who is usually a medium-sized farmer trying to get prosperous using the profits from kilns, have the shared goal of producing the maximum number of bricks, albeit the advantages of this are heavily skewed towards the owners.[40]

As Jaysing put it, 'But for kilns, our homes would have continued to remain rickety shacks. There is a definite material improvement in our lives due to working in the kilns.' Every Bhil family of Mankheda village I spoke to looked at the job of working in brick kilns positively. From mobile phones to television sets, motorcycles for a few and concrete houses for all of them, they pointed out the tangibles created from working in kilns. Their responses also reflected how there is an unspeakable magic about the thick wad of notes running into thousands that one collects at the end of the season when leaving. That compensates for the harsh working conditions that they face for months. The flexibility to avail themselves of advances as and when needed is another plus. Being part of a team comprising one's family or fellow relatives provides both emotional and physical support during emergencies and a sense of home even though they are away from the village. This also speaks volumes about how extreme the situation of the Mankheda Bhils was before they found employment that took them away from the grip of the local Gujars, and how extreme the lives of previous generations as saldars were.

Given that there is a direct relation between a team and the owner, relationships are often close and personal. Though there is a conscious decision to send children who are left behind with their elders or grandparents to school, I found that the youth dropped out by 6th or 7th grade at the age of 12–14 to join the kilns. Our small survey (Figures 7.3 and 7.4) also shows this. In any case, even when in school, they have to contribute to the family budget by working as farm labourers on many days after school. Most of the Bhil youth dream of a better mobile phone, hopefully a second-hand motorcycle and will be headed for the kilns in the times to come. Once married, they look forward to having their wives join them in the migration.

The Mandheka Bhils are structurally in a position which has clear similarities to Dalit groups across the plains of India, in terms of their integration into the agrarian economy as assetless and powerless agricultural workers and in terms of having broken the worst of the dominance of the local farmers by taking up work outside the village at the bottom of the informalised economy (see also chapters by Donegan and Benbabaali on the breakdown of village-based work and dominance relations in Coimbatore and Bhadrachalam). They have less in common with the landed Bhils or those in the Satpura Hills and their everyday freedoms.

ANAND NAGAR: THE RESETTLEMENT VILLAGE

There is a considerable literature on the struggle of the Bhils against the Sardar Sarovar Project dam, and the poor condition of the resettlement colonies in the initial phase where the Bhils were moved.[41] Beginning from 1991, after a prolonged struggle, the government offered a comprehensive resettlement package that included a housing colony and agricultural plots for every displaced family. Groups of hill Bhils affected by the Sardar Sarovar Project dam accepted this resettlement offer over time. The resettlement took place in two phases; the first one, from 1991, involved the setting up of five resettlement colonies with the hill Bhils moving to an area that was previously under the Forest Department. In the second phase, beginning from 2004, the Bhils moved into another set of resettlement colonies that were settled by the government purchase of private land from farmers in the plains to create a land bank. One such resettlement colony is that of Anand Nagar, where the Bhils from hamlets just below Ambegaon in the hills, including the main local leaders of the struggle, were resettled. This resettlement colony consists of a housing colony, with houses built in the classic manner of the hill Bhils, and individual agricultural plots scattered across several villages in a radius of 0–10 km.

Practically all the resettled Bhils live solely off agriculture. They have put in a lot of effort to adapt their life and agricultural practices to the new setting. But the state's resettlement package, though apparently highly beneficial on paper, was a mixed bag on the ground. The adult Bhils got an agricultural plot of either 2.5 or 5 acres depending on their categorisation of landholding in the submergence village by the government. This land cannot be sold or mortgaged, as per the Government of Maharashtra's resettlement policy, to ensure that a dominant host community cannot pressurise a resettled group into parting with its land.[42] However, though promised irrigated land by the government, only a few plots were given irrigation facilities. Dry land yields only one crop a year during the monsoon agricultural season of *kharip* and even that crop is dependent on the vagaries of nature.

The land allocated to the Bhils in 2002 came from the local Gujar dominant landowning caste in Mankheda and other villages in the vicinity. They sold it to the state for the Sardar Sarovar Project resettlement on the back of two consecutive years of poor rains in 1999–2001, resulting in rising debt and poor market rate for agricultural produce.

However, by 2004–05, genetically modified Bt cotton appeared on the scene, giving respite from the Bollworm cotton pest which had decimated the income from cotton in previous years. The Gujars of Mankheda say that, aided by assured irrigation from bore wells, the cotton yield now went up three to four times from 300–400 kg to 1200–1600 kg per acre.[43] It helped that the market prices for cotton offered by the local ginning firms, in turn dependent on global cotton demand, were decent. In the first three years the Bhils stuck to the dry crops jowar (sorghum) and maize before learning cotton growing and cash crop agriculture more widely from the Gujars of Mankheda, with people like Bada-bhai actively integrating them into this cash crop economy. They invested in tractors beginning from 2007 (see Table 7.1) and from 2008 onwards many began using the profits from agriculture to pay for digging of bore wells. At that point in time this cost Rs.50,000–60,000; by 2014–15 the cost of boring had gone above Rs.120,000.[44] Those with irrigation facilities shared water with their neighbouring farms for free, ensuring that around 150 of the 255 households had irrigation. From 2013, some Bhils have begun installing drip irrigation systems. Now every resettled Bhil household cultivates cotton – which can also be grown on non-irrigated plots although this is a good deal more risky – on almost all their land, along with some coarse grains for own consumption.

From 2010–11, cotton prices have stagnated and hovered around Rs.3800–4400 per 100 kg and constantly changing crop has become a new strategy of farmers with irrigated land as, since 2008, a new set of cash crops such as papaya and banana, have been inroduced. Traders from Rajasthan and north Gujarat have started doing business with the farmers of

Nandurbar, mostly with Gujars but also with those Bhils who own irrigated land and have the capital to invest. These Bhils include around 50 farmers from Anand Nagar (and none from Mankheda). The papaya saplings cost Rs.7–8 each if booked in advance but upwards of Rs.11 closer to the season. Gujars may be able to pay this upfront but the Bhils have to take out loans or advances. The traders offer advances ranging from Rs.12,000–16,000 per acre for the cost of inputs. They keep inspecting the crops and choose the time to bring in their trucks with hired local labourers, Bhils from nearby villages, for plucking, weighing and loading operations. The produce is dispatched to north Indian cities like Delhi. The farmers are paid on the spot. 'In 2008 and 2009 the prices were great so I invested in papaya in 2010. The return was fine, the same was the case in 2011–12 as well,' said Balram Vasave. He was one of the first from Anand Nagar to attempt this expensive experiment. 'But things turned bad in 2013–14 season, the first output got Rs.8–9 per kilo but prices thereafter kept falling to dip below Rs.5 when most of the crop was ripe.' By February 2015, in the subsequent season, when the traders offered Rs.2 per kilo, the Gujars along with a few Bhils began an agitation, refused to let the trucks be loaded and blocked the roads forcing the police to intervene. From 2011–12, newer crops like banana have been introduced as a few big planters from the neighbouring districts started offering the same advances with similar arrangements to the papaya traders. With falling papaya prices, a few Bhils of Anand Nagar started booking banana for the coming season from March 2015 onwards by paying an advance of Rs.15,000–20,000, only to withdraw and move back to papaya when they found that those who had planted bananas the previous year saw their crops rot in the field as there was no timely collection by the merchants.

Those of the resettled Bhils who were in a position to invest in agriculture were thus trying to be adept at the high-risk game of cash crops where one failed season could be potentially fatal. Agriculture is inherently a risky venture primarily due to the vagaries of nature. The risk of serious economic losses increases many times over with cash crop production as the cultivation cost is much higher. The higher cost is for seeds, fertilisers and pesticides along with constant attention in the form of weeding and irrigation. Despite all the investment and care, a few unexpected showers when the cotton pods are ripe and ready or the papaya saplings small in size can result in huge financial losses. Still, unlike most other Bhils of Nandurbar district, including their kin in the hill village of Ambegaon, many cash crop Bhil farmers of Anand Nagar have been making a handsome profit, despite fluctuating prices and unpredictable returns (see also Table 7.2).

But the cash crop agrarian economy has not benefited everyone in equal measure in Anand Nagar. About 100 households only have non-irrigated land. They are able to make a decent living in years with a good monsoon growing cash crops such as cotton but when the monsoon fails, as in 2014 and 2015, they are in a bad position. Still, all households can make a living from a combination of farming their own land and some agricultural labour within the village itself, even in the absence of the forest produce, fishing and so on that they used to be able to rely on in the hills. As of now, unlike in the neighbouring villages of the plains and the hills, there is practically no seasonal migration from Anand Nagar. During my visit in March 2016 I found that a few Bhils had gone to work outside for short periods but, as they themselves pointed out, it was on account of the unprecedented drought over the last two years. According to the national newspapers, this natural calamity has seen widespread rural-to-urban migration as agriculture has been badly affected, forcing families to move to urban centres in order to feed themselves.

At the other end of the income scale, some Bhils have been able to invest in petty businesses. In the absence of any industries or other employment opportunities in Nandurbar district (the cooperatives controlled by the Gujars are for doling out favours to their own fellow caste men), this is the one outlet for Bhils with a bit of agricultural profit to invest. They may open a small retail shop, including groceries and mobile-phone recharge coupons, and a few have taken nationalised bank or private finance company loans to purchase and operate auto rickshaws connecting the various villages to the nearby town (see Table 7.1). Though small in number, these kinds of petty business initiatives are more common here than among the landless Bhils of Mankheda and those with dry land in Ambegaon, reflecting that a degree of accumulation is more common here – and, related to that, that the business opportunities are better. There is however a limit to these ventures in terms of demand, as only a finite number of auto rickshaws and shops can be economically viable in a village with a relatively small and fixed number of potential consumers. Some of those who have succeeded in capitalist agriculture and petty business were from the group of leading anti-dam activists; they had the connections and ability to gain access to government programmes and capital for agricultural investments. Others are from large households having several adult children, each of whom fitted the eligibility criteria of the state to qualify as a 'project-affected person' – the official term for the Sardar Sarovar Project and other project displaced people – ensuring, jointly, over 15–25 acres of fertile agricultural land as compensation that is farmed by pooling resources under the direction of the respective patriarch. And yet others were simply lucky to be among those who were given irrigated land, or later managed to strike water when they paid to sink their own private bore well.

However, it is government employment that is the dream of every Bhil youth.[45] They are accumulating degrees, all in 'Ar-tas' (Arts, referring to humanities and social sciences), Bachelor's and Master's degrees with additional diploma certificates. Besides a Bachelor's degree in arts, Bolya Vasave, a youth leader in his early thirties, also holds a diploma in agriculture and another in computers. A member of the first generation of learners in his community, he had aspired to a government job that continues to elude him, despite many applications over the years. Undaunted, he continues to apply for every government job going and also networks with government officials and local politicians in the hope of finally landing one soon. Thus far, only two youths of Anand Nagar have the permanent 'naukri' that Jonathan Parry refers to in his study of Bhilai steel city, both outstanding athletes who got into the entry rank of the police service as constables.[46]

The Anand Nagar youths are well educated compared to the Mankheda Bhils (see Figures 7.3 and 7.4). Many of them, including women, below the age of 40 were the first to sit in functional primary schools, thanks largely to the initiative of the Narmada Bachao Andolan (NBA)-run *jivanshalas* back in the hill villages before resettlement. Post resettlement, they have continued their formal education, attending schools and later college. A few of their hill cousins from Ambegaon too have followed the same route. Balram Vasave would periodically remind me during conversations:

In my generation, I was the sole educated Bhil for many villages in the Narmada valley because of a fortuitous coincidence when the great leader Vinoba Bhave visited the hills in my childhood.[47] One of his activists stayed back for a while and sent me to a plains school where I studied till 7th grade. From among the eight hill villages that are part of Anand Nagar, not one person above the age of 40 ever saw a functional school. I, however, chose to serve our people through the NBA-led movement instead of opting for a government job. I have been pushing the youngsters to study and get salaried jobs.

The quest for government jobs is a relentless search. It is the middle of August of 2015, the peak of agricultural season. Bolya, the youth leader is in an elated mood for a different reason. He, along with his fellow youth leaders of Anand Nagar, have managed to secure admissions for over 20 of their fellow villagers' kids in a new set of governmental residential schools across Maharashtra for Adivasis that will provide free education from 1st to 10th grade: 'The best part is it will be in *ingraji* [English] medium. This will change their lives! Many of us tried to send our kids to the private English schools in Shahada town where the Gujars send their children. A few are still persisting but most others had to withdraw their kids as they could not afford it. There however is no point sending children to a "Marathi-medium school" [vernacular], however good the teachers,' he added at the

end, perhaps anticipating my question about the decent teachers in Anand
Nagar's government primary school. I wondered about the fate of the
hundreds of other Bhil children who were studying at the village's vernacular
medium school.

However, for this first generation of literates, the strategy of college
education has thus far failed to yield dividends in terms of jobs. There are
thousands of unfilled posts both at the central as well as state government
levels including those reserved for Scheduled Tribes even as the cash-
strapped state government of Maharashtra has banned the creation of new
posts.[48]

Some Bhil parents did not want to continue sending their children to
school if they did not show keen interest to study. 'I am illiterate, so are all my
family members. I notice that the other children who went to Ashramshalas
[vernacular residential schools run by the government for Adivasis] did not
even know how to hold the reins of a bull. If they can't plough, what will
they eat?' said Punya Vasave, the father of five children including four sons,
the eldest aged 12. He owns 4 acres of irrigated agricultural land given by
the government. The next generation would inherit only 1 acre for each
of the sons. If Punya's daughter goes on to demand her share (as is legally
enforceable though unheard of among Bhils and unusual in most of rural
India), it would reduce to less than an acre each. No wonder that many
others in Anand Nagar feel compelled to have faith in education as the
redeeming factor for the next generation.

The integration into the modern economy impacts on the Anand
Nagar Bhils in other ways as well. The older generation, many of them
battle-hardened from the Sardar Sarovar Project dam struggle, succeeded
in recreating an edifice of their way of life in the hills in the resettlement
colony. Large, traditional Bhil timber houses with wattle and daub walls
were painstakingly dismantled and reconstructed after they were relocated
from the hills by the state as part of the resettlement package. Useful trees
were planted all around the resettlement colonies, creating an environment
that was akin to that of the hill villages. The existing occupational, gender
and intra-household social relations were maintained as much as possible,
in spite of the changed environment. The young generations have other
values: education, mod cons such as motorbikes and so on matter more than
upholding hill-based traditions from what they see as another era.

BHIL TRAJECTORIES AT THE BOTTOM OF SOCIETY

As shown in this chapter, rural life in general and the lives of groups at the
bottom of society, including Adivasis, has always been precarious. The Bhils
of the three villages studied have been integrated into the capitalist economy

in different ways, but they all find themselves at the bottom of the modern economy. In income terms, the hill Bhils of Ambegaon are poor but the Sardar Sarovar Project struggle means that today they are freed from the daily harassment of the Forest Department and either have use rights or outright ownership of the lands in their vicinity; and a functioning Public Distribution System (and a dysfunctional National Rural Employment Guarantee Act programme) have been introduced. They are also probably a bit better off than those in the neighbouring villages, who have had to embark on arduous seasonal migrant labour to the sugar cane fields of the plains. At the same time, while economic difference within their community is taking root, they are yet to be riven by major internal economic fault lines.

The Mankheda Bhils who reside in their village with Gujars are in many ways their exact opposite, even if in economic income terms their position may not be that different. They have been directly oppressed and exploited by their Gujar landowners for generations and have little economic autonomy. For them seasonal migrant labour, primarily in the brick kilns across the region or cutting cane in neighbouring Gujarat, represents the best they can hope for in income terms and, along with the political mobilisation of the plains Bhils in the mid to late twentieth century, this has meant a degree of liberation from the oppressive relations to their old masters, the Gujars of their village.

The resettled Bhils of Anand Nagar, with their roots in the Sardar Sarovar Project struggle, are the only group who have seen a decent share of their households doing a good deal better in economic terms. Still, without much capital and no economic buffers to speak of, their engagement in the cash crop economy is high risk and precarious. When it comes to growing cash crops or to finding ways to conduct themselves 'properly' in public, they have looked up to the Gujars of Mankheda as their role models – while also looking down upon the existing plains Bhils and keeping them at arm's length. However, they remain much worse off than the Gujars as they do not have any access to the lucrative jobs in the non-agricultural economy which, locally at least, is dominated by Gujars. Their attempts to get into government jobs have not been successful. The Gujars accumulated agricultural surplus and invested it to move into business or private white-collar as well as government jobs over a period of three or four generations spanning nearly a century. The resettled Bhils are playing catch-up with this model in a span of just over a decade; they can only do too little, too late, compared to the more powerful groups in society. Generational cultural change and some economic differentiation are also taking place, changing the character of this community. A fair few among them will probably join the army of seasonal migrants within a generation or two. Besides those involved in activities such as running a shop or an auto rickshaw, perhaps the only ray of hope in the long run for those with some irrigated land is that, in some good years, they can generate sufficient surplus to tide themselves over the bad years and still have something to invest in the future of the coming generation by funding their education.

The fate of the Bhils compared to that the dominant Gujar farmers reflects historical processes of generational accumulation, dispossession and exploitation. For now, in the hills they get by through low-profit dry agriculture combined with migrant seasonal labour and various other activities; in the resettlement village, risky cash crop production and small business activities for some; and in the Gujar multi-caste village roaming seasonal migrant wage labour while at least some of them are hoping against hope the that the strategy of 'reading' for government jobs will yield some results. They did not win the Sardar Sarovar Project struggle, in the sense that the dam was indeed built and some of them were forced into resettlement, but the struggle did provide measurable results for them, as did the earlier mobilisation of the plains Bhils against Gujar oppression. For the Bhils to improve their lives now, again, either through individual attempts at social mobility or jointly through political action will be a new uphill struggle.

Photo 17   Migrant colony of Bhil sugar cane cutters
Photo by Vikramaditya Thakur.

8
The Struggles Ahead
Alpa Shah and Jens Lerche

In *Ground Down by Growth* we have shown that with economic growth, not only income inequality but also social inequality has become entrenched rather than erased in India. The spread of capitalism has used social divisions to its own ends, in processes we have explored here as 'conjugated oppression' which, crucially, involve the inseparability of class relations from caste, tribe, gender and region. These processes explain how and why the marginalisation of India's low castes and tribes – its Dalits and Adivasis – persists.

We also hope to have shown the value of a systematic and comparative ethnographic approach to exploring the processes of socioeconomic transformation that inextricably link identity-based oppression to class relations and power. In exploring the continuities and changes in relations of power between Adivasis and Dalits and all other castes, as well as within the Dalit and Adivasi groups, we hope to have established the significance of enquiries into the transformation of forms and sites of discrimination, exploitation and oppression between and within different social groups in the belly of capitalism.

What emerges clearly across all our sites is how the most vulnerable and most exploited of the Indian workforce are Adivasis and Dalits. With almost no protection of any kind, nor any social security, and under exploitative conditions, they enter into multiple strategies of livelihoods that combine agricultural labour with hard manual labour, mainly in manufacturing and construction. They typically occupy the most precarious rung of the occupational ladder and do the jobs no one else wants. Also striking is that the locally dominant caste groups have now become major or auxiliary players in the new economy, controlling access to jobs, resources and the state, thus shaping the processes of inequality beyond the village context and in the new economy, leading to the continued powerlessness and oppression of Adivasis and Dalits and keeping them firmly at the bottom of Indian society. Seasonal casual labour migration is a crucial part of the ways in which ethnically and regionally different groups of labour are being pitched against each other to create a super-exploited and divided workforce. More than any other social group across our sites in India, Adivasis and Dalits are being disadvantaged by the kind of capitalist development that is taking place. Their oppression as castes and tribes, through regional differences and gender relations, takes place through the forms of class relations in which they are enmeshed in an overall process that, following Philippe Bourgois (1988, 1997), we have called conjugated oppression.

What is to be done to challenge this 'grinding down by growth' in India? The most formidable obstacle seems to be ideological in nature: a firm belief in the benefits of growth and the unfettered market to address poverty – a belief that has been promoted relentlessly globally as well as in India. There are no easy answers and the challenges are many fronted.

FROM TAXATION TO SOCIAL WELFARE

Globally today there are several proposals as to what must be done. The one which has received the most attention in recent years – boosted by the widespread attention gained by the work of Thomas Piketty (2013) – has been the recommendation to increase taxation on wealth for redistribution. In India, where the richest 1 per cent now hold 58 per cent of all wealth,[1] taxation of the elite is particularly important if we are to consider any form of redistribution for the public good. However, the Indian elite is notorious for evading taxes and not much is done to clamp down on this evasion. Only 1 per cent of the population pay income tax[2] and most of India's wealthy evade corporation tax.[3] Moreover, Piketty (2013) only proposes taxation as a means to cut back growing inequality, not to challenge inequality per se.

Also, quite how taxation could mitigate India's inequalities of caste, tribe, region or gender when the state itself is being rolled back is manifestly unclear. India spends disproportionately little of its budget on essential welfare measures such as health and education, and even what little provision there is has been cut back in recent years. For instance, in 2015 India's healthcare budget shrank to 1.2 per cent of GDP and has been described as one of the 'stingiest in the world'.[4] In a climate of increasing austerity and where budgets for basic welfare have shrunk, there is clearly a need to fight against these cutbacks.

India has in fact seen vibrant struggles pushing an agenda for basic human development, livelihood security and social inclusion. These social protection measures have been a major focus for pro-poor politics in India. Kannan (2010, 2014) and Srivastava (2013), for instance, have both argued for the need to create a 'social floor' for the poor – as a defining characteristic of the welfare state in the modern world – that incorporates a minimum of basic social security such as food entitlements, education, health and shelter as well as provision for sickness, old age and accidents/death. Many such programmes for social security have been backed by international players such as the International Labour Organization. Though there is not yet a truly national social security scheme in India,[5] there has been a series of initiatives – many through the new rights agenda – including the work entitlements of the National Rural Employment Guarantee Act (2005), the Forest Rights Act (2006), the Unorganised Workers Social Security Act (2008), the Right to Education Act (2011), and the translation of a national food distribution scheme to a National Food Security Act (2013). These are ambitious programmes and the proponents of the social security strategy, in the current Indian context, see them as the hopeful future, some even arguing that mobilisation around demands for social rights will provide a broad base for wider unity and mobilisation.

However, all of these measures come with their own problems and regional differences, with social programmes in states such as Kerala, Tamil Nadu and Himachal Pradesh having a stronger reach than elsewhere. Severe delays in implementation, along with corruption and co-optation by local elites are common problems.[6] Though schools are being built across the country, their quality is questionable and in many parts of the country even the rural poor prefer to send their children to private schools if they at all can. In many states, the Forest Rights Act is being diluted by other acts which work against the protection it offers. The National Rural Employment Guarantee Act, the flagship of these kinds of programmes, reached its peak back in 2009–10 and since then it has reached fewer people.[7]

India is now also considering direct cash transfers akin to the Brazilian Bolsa Familia programme, which proponents sell as a 'basic income' initiative (Standing 2017). Critiques, however, point out that such a programme would have very different implications in India (to Brazil or Finland for instance), potentially leading, on the one hand, to the wholesale demise of state-led provision of welfare in general and, on the other, to dependence on the market for what ought to be public services (such as hospitals) and the inevitability of profit orientation of these services (Lerche 2012). Social security measures such as these are, moreover, no substitute for proper secure employment – unless the direct cash transfers are to be a real significant universal basic income such as the scheme Finland is currently experimenting with. There is no sign of this taking place in India (Lerche 2012), where its proponents are going so far as to argue that the amount of money given is not the important issue.

Radical critiques of social welfare measures in India suggest that any kind of targeting of the poor with services is misplaced because, unless they are to serve everyone, they will prove to be universally bad. Jos Mooij, for example, introduced a welfare regime approach to the analysis of social welfare in India. She argued that there are three trends within the Indian

'welfare' context: a collective rights-based trend, an individualising marketisation trend and, related to that, a state policy targeting approach. Her work
showed the ways in which market-based provision of basic welfare, such as
education, removed protections from the state sector and encouraged those
who could afford it to leave. Mooij (2014) argued that the overall effect is
that the state has become *for* and *of* the poor: creating poor provision for the
poor.[8] What India ought to focus on, the sociologist Dipankar Gupta (2014)
has argued, is high-quality services for everyone, and he says the country
can now afford these. These, though, seem utopian propositions given that
even the basic social security measures discussed earlier are so difficult to
fight for.

TACKLING SOCIAL DISCRIMINATION

Yet none of these efforts specifically address India's caste- or tribe-based
discrimination. As Jonathan Parry (2014) asks, why would the elite of India
want to foot the bill for their poor or rub shoulders with Dalits and Adivasis
in state schools and hospitals? In this sense, India's affirmative action policies
– through reservations, through land and forest protection of Adivasi areas
in the Fifth and Sixth Schedules, and through the Prevention of Atrocities
Act targeted at Scheduled Castes and Scheduled Tribes – were a radical
departure to address social inequality.

However, the protection that has existed for Adivasi land and forest rights
has been under consistent threat, often superseded by land acquisition bills
and illegal purchases or encroachment on Adivasi land by non-Adivasis,
as shown in the chapter by Benbabaali. Use of the Prevention of Atrocities
Act is fraught with problems of implementation but, in some places, it has
helped nurture a climate in which Dalits have at least something with which
to fight back against the caste violence they face.[9]

Reservations have resulted in heated public debate on a range of different
issues. The criteria for Scheduled Caste and Scheduled Tribe status rely on
disputed colonial classifications[10] that are fiercely contested, with ever more
groups seeking classification.[11] Key questions are whether job reservations
are incompatible with institutional well-being, and whether they pose a threat
to the principle of equality of individual opportunity. Acrimonious debate
persists over the question of whether reservations benefit only the better off
among the communities they are set aside for, that is, the 'creamy layer'.[12]
Social movements have even developed for 'reservation within reservations'
to differentiate castes and tribes who have fared worse than others in the
same groups.[13] Indeed, critiques have argued that in many senses caste has
been enabled to gain a new lease of life through reservations.

While new groups may be accommodated into spheres they were previously left out of, crucially there are no guarantees that this 'politics of recognition',[14] as found in reservations, contains the possibility to fundamentally challenge material inequalities. In none of our sites do we have evidence that the overall structures of inequality have been challenged through affirmative action. It is not just that reserved jobs, where they have been acquired, have been only on the lowest rungs of state sector positions (such as low-ranking posts in the police) but also that, by comparison, the higher castes in the same sites have continued to monopolise access to jobs, resources and livelihoods that will ensure they are better off than the Adivasis and Dalits.

Moreover, the greatest number of Adivasis and Dalits across our sites are working in the informal economy of the private sector, in which there are no reserved jobs, and they are working in jobs that most higher castes would avoid doing. Though some scholars and activists have advocated extending reservations to the private sector,[15] it is hard to see how private sector employers will run with this idea; Jodhka and Newman (2010) argue that employers are convinced there is no problem of caste or religious prejudice in modern India. It is also the case that while reservations will indeed improve conditions for some individuals, their impact on the wider community is less clear.[16]

It has been argued that if Dalits or Adivasis were to become small-scale or even large-scale capitalists, with or without government support, this would solve the issue of caste discrimination.[17] Our field evidence does not support this idea. Moreover, the literature shows that even where Dalits and Adivasis have access to capital they tend to face discriminatory practices;[18] and special government programmes for Dalit and Adivasi entrepreneurs have only benefited few, and in a limited manner.[19] More importantly, perhaps, as argued by a number of Dalit scholars, Dalit and Adivasi capitalism will not emancipate the Dalit and Adivasi masses as it will not address social discrimination nor, in fact, will it address capitalist oppression.[20]

UNIONS AND LABOUR STRUGGLES

Perhaps the greatest hope among the challenges to the conjugated oppression that we see in these chapters is that which emerges in the various social struggles from below. Some scholars argue that India has seen an increase in struggles from below during the last decade.[21] These have included the continued reach, with economic liberalisation, of India's half-century-old Maoist-inspired armed guerrilla Naxalite movement fighting for a communist society. These struggles from below include campaigns for proper implementation of pro-poor legislation, especially the Employment

Guarantee Act, struggles against land grabs, for labour rights, struggles against discrimination, oppression and mass rape and killings of Adivasis and Dalits.

Classically, the challenge to capitalism was to come from working-class struggles. But in the sections which follow we argue that trade unions in India have only really addressed the concerns of an aristocracy of labour, leaving aside most workers in the informal economy.[22] We also argue that, historically, left struggles have generally ignored the specificities of oppression based on race, caste, tribe, ethnicity or gender, and, fearful of fragmenting 'the base', the workforce, have treated such oppression as aspects of an ideological 'superstructure'. This has undoubtedly alienated many Dalits (and perhaps increasingly Adivasis) who started off in leftist movements, and has encouraged instead a representational identity politics away from material concerns. Given the central messages of this book, we also propose here that this failure of the Indian left, and the resultant turn away from the left by Dalits (and Adivasis), is a great tragedy for the working poor of India given that within left thought internationally there is now a rich tradition that sees race/indigeneity as a central feature of how class relations are lived, and serious work explicitly bringing together race/ethnicity/gender/class into a common focus (as was also explored in our opening chapter).

That trade unions tend to represent an aristocracy of workers is shown sharply in Jayaseelan Raj's, Brendan Donegan's and Dalel Benbabaali's chapters. Moreover, in Telangana the unions of the paper factory were more interested in exercising caste-based patronage than in fighting for the rights of any workers. In Tamil Nadu contract labourers who tried to join a union were likely to get the sack. Worse still, in the Kerala tea plantations the unions were so close to management that when the workers struck back, as the Tamil Dalit women tea workers did with their strike (analysed by Raj and to which we will return), they did so not only outside of the union context but also against the unions.

Barring a few exceptions (such as *bidi* workers), India's Naxalite revolutionaries have also found it difficult to mobilise workers in their workplaces in the informal economy. It is true that in the last decade new campaigning organisations such as the New Trade Union Initiative have brought some of the concerns of informal workers to the fore, but in general both unions and revolutionary parties have made very little impact among informalised workers in the workplace (Lerche 2010). Seasonal migrant workers are of course left out of almost all mobilisation efforts – whether in the fight for welfare or for better terms and conditions from the employers. This is as true of the left union initiatives as it is of the Naxalites (Shah 2013; Navlakha 2010), and also of the Tamil Dalit women workers' strike in our site.

That unions have left out informal workers does not, of course, stop workers from fighting back. Struggles organised outside the unions have sometimes bridged the formal–informal divide by successful cross-cutting labour action, resulting in informal labour being formalised, or in improved pay and conditions of these workers.[23] The best-known case is that of the Maruti factory in Manesar in the industrial belt south of Delhi where several years of struggles for the right to organise and for pay and conditions culminated in 2012, and involved joint action by formal sector regular workers and contract workers.[24]

At the bone factory in Tamil Nadu such joint action also occurred, though the outcome was disastrous for the informalised workers. Not only were they – and only they – beaten up after the end of the strike, their leaders were also sacked while those among them who had sought to end the strike were given permanent jobs. In addition, the factory management brought in seasonal migrant workers from Odisha as strike breakers and have kept them on at the factory ever since, potentially serving a disciplining role to keep the local contract labour from taking action again. Creating permanent jobs is often at the heart of factory-related conflicts. At the paper factory in Telangana, an upright government officer sought to get the factory to put in place a caste/Adivasi quota policy but to no avail. Everyday struggles and negotiations protecting the rights of labour are also commonplace, as for example in the shape of negotiations between Gaddi labour and labour sub-contractors of the Saal valley and their end-employers, seeking – not always successfully – to ensure that they are paid as agreed at the end of a road building contract.

It has been argued that for informal labour in India today the primary struggles are – and should be – those targeted at the state for the provision of social welfare rather than against employers for better terms and conditions of work, and that these state-level struggles have been successful under certain political conditions (Agarwala 2013). However, this ignores the difference between local workers and seasonal migrant workers and the fact that the latter rarely benefit from social welfare programmes. So far, these struggles are rarely for them. Moreover, we find that in most of our sites informalised labour does try to mobilise for labour rights at their workplaces, although it is much harder for their stories to be heard as they are also likely to face the silencing that results from the violent repression which follows.

Significantly, unless focusing on a labour issue which relates to a particular caste group (for instance the Dalit Sanitation Workers and their strikes), it is rare that labour struggles in India address the specific concerns of Adivasis or Dalits; these latter are most often left out in the desire to focus on the universal idea of the proletariat. In thinking through the interrelations between class, caste, gender and region, perhaps the most remarkable struggle in our sites was that of the Tamil Dalit women tea pluckers in Munnar highlighted in the chapter by Raj. Led by the Tamil Dalit women themselves, it stands out as a struggle not only for labour rights and against corrupted trade unions but also against the discrimination, infantilisation and vilification of Dalits, Tamils and Dalit women in particular.

WIDER SOCIAL MOVEMENTS

Many Dalits who may once have been close to left parties have been alienated by the casteism they feel they have faced within the parties. Dalit activists in particular have legitimately questioned the dominance of upper castes in leadership positions in Marxist and Naxalite organisations (see Rawat and Satyanarayan 2016) and the failure of these Communist parties to adequately theoretically account for caste (Srinivasulu 2017). Similarly, the tensions between class struggle and indigeneity in relation to the Maoists (in India but also Nepal) have also been brought to light (Ismail and Shah 2015; D'Mello and Shah 2013). Elsewhere in the world, critiques have argued that the Cuban revolution failed to take into account racial inequality within Cuba (Dominguez 2013). They showed that black American workers becoming the 'dirty laundry' of the white American working class (Roediger 1991). And they pointed to the tensions that have long existed between working class and indigenous liberation movements in Latin America (Becker 2008). Similarly, it is easy in the Indian context for the specific oppressions of Adivasis and Dalits to be reproduced – and thereby intensified – by other workers in the labour hierarchy above them.

India, though, has a long and rich history of social struggles, some of which have emerged from Adivasis and Dalits. In the nineteenth and twentieth centuries Adivasis in eastern India launched some of the most remarkable resistance campaigns against outsiders brought in to take over their land and forests for colonial revenue collection,[25] and in 1927 in Mahad, Maharashtra, Dalits led a struggle against upper caste dominance and chicanery in what has been called the making of the first Dalit revolt.[26] In more recent years emulation of the African-American US Black Panthers by the Dalits in Tamil Nadu[27] and the resurrection of Dalit heroes by the Bahujan Samaj Party (a Dalit party) in Uttar Pradesh[28] have attracted much attention. Equally, so too have Adivasis – hugging trees in the Himalayas to prevent deforestation,[29] resisting their displacement by big dam projects in the Narmada valley (as Thakur's chapter here has shown) and elsewhere, such as the Koel Karo in Jharkhand,[30] or by mines,[31] and fighting for the rights of indigenous people in international fora.[32] Conversion to religious sects,[33] Hindu right-wing movements[34] or Christianity[35] have run parallel to the spread of the Maoist-inspired Naxalites.[36]

The chapters of this book report on many such struggles. The struggle against the Sardar Sarovar Project dam forms the backdrop to Thakur's chapter on the Adivasi Bhils of Nandurbar. Attempts to stop expropriation of Adivasi land are a major issue in central and eastern India (such as the states of Jharkhand and Odisha), the source of the seasonal migrant labour in several of our sites. There are also cases of Dalits organising. Raj details the story of Sundaram, a Dalit plantation worker. Returning to the plantation after having worked as migrant labour elsewhere, he found caste discrimination unbearable and this led him to join Viduthalai Chiruthai Katchi (the Dalit Panthers) and become a community leader for the Paraiyar caste group. In Melpuram in Tamil Nadu, images of figureheads of Dravidian, Dalit and class-based struggles for liberation line the walls of the Dalit-run voluntary educational centre for Dalit youth. The Dalit women tea pluckers in Kerala are another case in point. Finally, in Telangana, Benbabaali reports on a broad, mainly low caste and Adivasi protest alliance leading to signed promises from the paper factory to provide drinking water to the village and build roads for the Dalit and Adivasi colonies. She also details a year-long struggle for housing near the paper factory by mainly low caste people, which split along Dalits vs leftists line as protesters formed two separate groups: one small group organised by a Madiga leader from the Telangana Rashtra Samithi, and one bigger group organised by an Other Backward Classes leader from the Communist Party of India (Marxist Leninist)-New Democracy. The Indian Evangelical Mission is also active in the village where she worked and one quarter of the Adivasi Koyas recently converted to Christianity. The remaining Koyas continue to worship deities like Saramma and Sarakka, female warriors who fought the forces of a Telugu dynasty of which the Kammas, including their own dominant landlord, claim to be descendants. Meanwhile, in the Saal valley the Muslim Gujjars, disadvantaged both as an ethnic and a religious community, have reached out and made links with other places and people, not the least through the 'reformist' Islam of the Deoband School. This has led to a rise in education levels through madrasas and to the hope that the wider Muslim business network now available and, potentially, migration to the Gulf will benefit the next generation.

In considering such movements we should, though, be wary of a solely identity-focused politics that is devoid of a concern for material transformations and alliances across groups and segments of society facing similar problems. Whatever the form of the struggle, the relationship between inequality, growth and poverty analysed in our book suggests that any analysis must 'explore whether that struggle is progressive and whether it benefits capital or not. It must consider both people's subjective conception of the struggle they are involved in and develop an analysis of that struggle that contextualises it within a wider analysis of class relations' (Ismail and Shah 2015: 112).

In India, Anand Teltumbde has warned the Dalit movements, for example, against turning Ambedkar into a god-like figure and against growing as a 'reactionary stratum of self-seeking Dalit elites' (Teltumbde 2013: 10). More generally, critics of identity-based politics have pointed out that it is the structures of neoliberal capitalism that have created an 'identity machine' (see Leve 2011; also Hale 2002) or an 'ethnicity Inc.' (see Comaroff and Comaroff 2009). As Leve has said:

> the current profusion of identity talk and also the political compulsion for states to recognize citizens' sub- and supernational identities are at once parts and products of this global assemblage, which works by extending a particular style of thought and social organization in which identity proliferates and identities proliferate and in order to do certain kinds of politics, you have to represent yourself in certain terms and make your claims in certain ways. (Leve 2011: 9)

These authors have indicated that such identity-based struggles can rely on a kind of authenticity or purity of identity that is often far removed from the everyday lives of those it claims to represent (see Shah 2010 in the case of indigeneity and Adivasis). Yet the 'self-racialisation' of the working class, as Balibar (1991a: 214) calls it, can also be an attempt to turn the signifiers of class racism back against elite society, or here class-, caste- and tribe-based oppression. Indeed, both the Indian left and Dalit and Adivasi movements may have much to gain by thinking about the debates bringing together class relations and social oppression based on race/ethnicity/gender in other parts of the world. As E.P. Thompson (1963) long ago pointed out, class consciousness is the way in which class experiences (determined by the productive relations into which people are born or enter) are 'handled in cultural terms: embedded in traditions, value-systems, ideas, and institutional forms' (Thompson 1963: 9–10) and may thus result in 'class struggle without class' (Thompson 1978). Class struggle, as E.P. Thompson argued, is people's struggles around antagonistic points of interest when they find themselves in structurally different positions in relation to their experience of exploitation, and – crucially – may be expressed in a range of different idioms (including caste or tribe/indigeneity).

Jeffery Webber (2011) has called the interweaving of politics/class struggle and indigenous liberation 'combined oppositional consciousness', to capture the interpenetration of class and indigenous identity and how working-class identity and organising was constituted in and through rich traditions of indigenous resistance.[37] As David McNally (2015: 144) puts it, 'racialized workers, women workers, queer workers, disabled workers must all be able to determine, in and through their own activities and aspirations, the very meanings of working-class identity and struggle'.

In India, the shape of class struggle is indeed likely to be different for Adivasis and Dalits. Prathama Banerjee (2016) has recently argued that while Dalits have articulated themselves as political subjects in India through representation, Adivasis have done so through autonomy. Whether this is empirically the case remains a question, but the conclusions of our work do suggest that the struggle for land and forest rights is as important as the struggle for labour rights if we think not just about Dalits but also about Adivasis. As we see in our sites, low caste and tribal labour from less developed tribal-dominated regions (such as in eastern India) is brought in as a seasonal casual migrant labour workforce to undercut the power of local low caste workers. While the fight to provide them with better terms and conditions of work in their sites of migration is important, equally important is the protection of the historic land and forest rights that have enabled these seasonal migrant workers a small degree of autonomy over their lives away from their total exploitation and oppression. This is the very autonomy that is now being dismantled in the race to harvest the mineral resources that lie under their lands and that is now being undermined by the various state measures to erode the historic land and forest protection that Adivasis fought for. The struggle to protect land and forest rights – especially under the new regimes of dispossession for mines and industries and special economic zones accompanied by land acquisition acts – is as significant as more classical labour struggles and social welfare struggles to ensure the prevalence of multiple livelihood strategies and hence the autonomy of Adivasis and Dalits in the belly of the Indian boom.

REPRESSION OF PROGRESSIVE STRUGGLES

We must caution, though, against overly optimistic readings of struggles from below – just as Michael Burawoy did against the 'false optimism' of global labour studies (2010). The Maoist-inspired armed struggles, and the increase in actions taken by Dalits, Adivasis and other sections of the informalised classes of labour are often rearguard actions against increased oppression, and generally do not meet with success but rather with increased oppression, smart counter-tactics and counterinsurgency.

India's working poor are up against strong enemies. Informal contract workers can easily be sacked and replaced by others. They do not even have the formal right to unionise at their workplace since, technically, they are employed by a contractor, not by the *de facto* end-employer. This also means that while we should not belittle the achievements of the Munnar Dalit women tea pluckers, we should recall that they did take action from what, in one respect, was a position of strength – being permanently employed gave them a degree of security – and also notice that they were eventually co-opted and divided by the political parties.

Moreover, employers can normally manage united action of formal sector regular workers and informal labour by letting the regular workers benefit disproportionally from such action while the informal workers face their full wrath, as reported by Donegan from Tamil Nadu.[38] At the Maruti factory in Manesar the recent labour unity is now undermined by an increase in regular workers' pay, thus creating a bigger divide between them and contract labour (Barnes et al. 2015). Moreover, the state ruled with a heavy hand, arresting 148 workers and, in March 2017, convicting 31 workers and even handing down life imprisonment to 13 of them. Elsewhere radical organisations for informalised labour – as in the case of the remarkable Chhattisgarh Mukti Morcha – had to face the concerted hostility of employers, police and less radical unions (Parry 2009).

Workers face open and brutal collusion between capital, state justice, the police system and elected politicians, and languish in jail for years on trumped-up charges (Ness 2016: 100–06). Moreover, the vilification and oppression of Dalits, Adivasis and the informal labouring classes is, if anything, increasing across India. The everyday disregard of labour rights is being legalised by the rolling back of labour laws; land protection legislation is being watered down and political actions by Dalits and Adivasis and their organic intellectuals are branded as 'anti-national', with all that entails of very real threats of ending up in prison or of extra-juridical killings. All this is on top of the persistence of the most brutal forms of everyday violence against Adivasis and Dalits, often targeted at their women, as in the case of rape, murder and burning in the village of Khairlanji in Maharashtra in 2006, when dominant caste members killed four Dalits, two of whom were women, who were paraded naked in public and were raped before being murdered (Teltumbde 2010).

The Maoist struggle against inequality is also being met with the full repressive strength of the Indian state. Since 2010 we have seen entire areas of central and eastern India militarised in counterinsurgency measures to hunt down guerrillas and, in the process, the clearing of Adivasis from the lands that are rich in mineral resources that are wanted for mining. As part of this campaign, Adivasis have been branded as terrorists or terrorist supporters and have been subject to the most brutal acts of vigilante and police action, whereby entire villages have been burnt and displaced, women raped, and thousands arrested, tortured and killed, under the guise of the 'civilising' mission of development (Shah 2011; Sundar 2016).

The complicity of the Indian state in human rights abuses has attracted increasing criticism from international organisations such as the UN Human Rights Council (UNHCR), the European Union and national governments.[39] At the 2017 UNHCR meeting, a number of governments (including the Netherlands, Germany, Switzerland, the UK and the US) criticised the use of excessive force by India's security personnel (such as army and policing outfits), its non-ratification of Convention Against Torture, and its imposition of restrictions on civil society, among other things.[40]

Clearly there are many challenges ahead, not least for the Indian state in keeping alive the spaces of democracy. There are no easy answers. But at this current juncture we do see hope in all the various forms of social struggles arising across the Indian landscape fighting for better models of development, fighting for basic human rights and dignity, challenging the structures of power and current forms of capitalist growth – growth that makes some people wealthy while at the same time increasing income inequality, entrenching social inequality and oppressing others.

Appendix
Tables and Figures

TABLES AND FIGURES FOR CHAPTER 3

Table 3.1 Types of contracts of tea plantation workers, Hill Valley estate, Kerala

Permanent	Temporary	Casual
Minimum wage	Minimum wage	Minimum wage
Work is guaranteed throughout year.	Work is not guaranteed. Any work in addition to that done by permanent workers goes to temporary workers.	Work is not guaranteed. Work when the supply of permanent and temporary workers is below the demand.
Eligible for provident fund.	Eligible for provident fund.	Not eligible for provident fund.
Eligible for medical care outside the plantations. The company will refund medical bill if the company doctor approves it. Eligible for paid medical leave.	Not eligible for medical care outside the plantations. Can use local medical facilities within plantations, if available. No paid medical leave.	Not eligible for medical care outside the plantations. Can use local medical facilities within the plantations, if available. No paid medical leave.
Housing guaranteed.	Housing is not guaranteed. Temporary workers will be considered for housing if houses are available after permanent workers are provided for.	Housing is not guaranteed. Casual workers will be considered only if houses are available after providing for permanent and temporary workers. In most cases, they must share with other casual worker families.
Eligible for annual bonus.	Not eligible for bonus.	Not eligible for bonus.
Eligible for retirement benefits (Gratuity).	Not eligible for retirement benefits.	Not eligible for retirement benefits.
Eligible for weather protection including blanket and umbrella. Also eligible for free work tools, including bamboo basket and plucking machine.	Not eligible for weather protection and tools.	Not eligible for weather protection and tools.

Table 3.2   Relationship between education and occupation, Hill Valley estate, Kerala: occupational categories for each educational group, caste-wise (%)

Caste category	Occupational category	0/Illiterate	*Years of education:* Less than 6	6–8	9–12	13+
Dalit men	Unskilled	100	90	63	27	13
	Semi-skilled	0	10	35	64	13
	Service and business	0	0	2	9	75
General caste men	Unskilled	100	80	67	63	0
	Semi-skilled	0	20	33	25	0
	Service and business	0	0	0	13	100
Dalit women	Unskilled	100	91	76	50	0
	Semi-skilled	0	9	24	50	25
	Service and business	0	0	0	0	75
General caste women	Unskilled	100	100	71	67	0
	Semi-skilled	0	0	29	33	100
	Service and business	0	0	0	0	0

Table 3.3   Ten case histories of tea worker households, Hill Valley estate, Kerala

---

1. (Pallar): Jacob (1948) = Yesamma (1950). Children: Prema (f) 1969; John (m) 1971; Arul Mary (f) 1975.
Prema married a photographer in neighbouring estate and works as tea plucker. Arul Mary married a relative of Prema's husband in the same estate. Arul Mary stitches clothes for women and children. John left for Coimbatore in 1996 after the crisis. Yesamma lives with John. Jacob died in 1998. Persons still in plantations: 2 of 5.

2. (Paraiyar): Sunderraj (1950) = Thayamma (1952). Children: Selvam (m) 1971; Ilaiyaraja (m) 1974; Kumari (f) 1975; Divya (f) 1983.
Kumari married a relative in Chennai. Kumari studied to 8th grade, and works as sales girl in textile shop in Chennai. Divya studied to 10th grade. She is unmarried and stays with the family of Ilaiyaraja. Ilaiyaraja moved to Chennai with parents. Selvam stayed back as permanent worker. Sunderraj and Thayamma died in 2006 and 2010. Persons still in plantations: 1 of 6.

3. (Nadar): Varghese (1952) = Selvi (1952). Varghese's parents: Prakasam Nadar (m) 1932; Susaiyamma (f) 1935. Children: Francis (f) 1974; Stella (f) 1977; Makson (m) 1979; Nikson (m) 1984.
Selvi died in 2014 at the estate. Varghese lives with son Makson who stayed in the plantation but works outside. His wife is a tea plucker and permanent since 2012. Nikson is a schoolteacher in private school in Munnar. Francis married a Pallar caste women, a permanent worker, and lives in the plantation. Stella married and lives with husband in Mysore and is general nurse. Persons still in plantations: 3 of 6.

4. (Paraiyar): Periya Pandian (1946) = Lekshmi (1948). Pandian's father Sudalai (m) 1925. Children: Karuppasamy (m) 1960; Valli (f) 1966; Sundaram (m) 1970; Ramesh (m) 1980; Robin (m) 1984.
Sudalai died in 1992. Karuppasamy stayed back in Hill Valley. Valli married a permanent worker in neighbouring estate, and is a permanent tea plucker there. Rest of household moved to native village in Tamil Nadu in 1998. Ramesh is now a tailor in Tiruppur, Robin is assistant to a mason in native village, and Sundaram worked in dyeing unit in Tiruppur but returned to native village. Persons still in plantations: 2 of 8.

5. (Paraiyar): Gomas (1948) = Muthumma (1951). Children: Sekhar (m) 1969; Kamalam (f) 1970; Lekshmi (f) 1972; Parvathy (f) 1975; Elango (m) 1977; Thangaraj (m) 1980.
Sekhar is permanent worker in Hill Valley. Muthamma lives with Sekhar after her retirement. Gomas passed away in 2008. Kamalam and Lekshmi married men from Koodalur, Tamil Nadu. Parvathy married her cousin in Hill Valley, so stayed back. Elango moved to another town with his wife. Thangaraj is a manual labourer in the construction industry in Dubai. His wife is a housemaid there. Persons still in plantations: 3 of 8.

6. (Arunthathiyar): Arumainayagam (1932) = Sornam (1935). Children: Rasaiyya (m) 1952; Malaiyarasi (f) 1953; Ganesan (m) 1957. Malaiyarasi's children: Muniyandi (m) 1973; Pazhani (m) 1977; Thanam (f) 1977.
Arumainayagam and Sornam died in 1998 and 2001. Rasaiyya and Ganesan are permanent workers and live in Hill Valley. Malaiyarisi retired from Hill Valley as tea plucker in 2006. Her daughter is married to a barber in Kumily, a plantation town. Both Muniyandi and Pazhani moved to Tamil Nadu with their wives. Persons still in plantations: 3 of 8.

7. (Paraiyar): Chinna Pandian (1946) = Vellaiyamma (1952). Children: Murugaiah (m) 1968; Samuthiram (f) 1969; Ravi (m) 1970; Ghanam (f) 1972; Sasikumar (m) 1974.
Chinna Pandian moved to native village in Tamil Nadu after retirement, died in 2004. Vellaiyamma and son Sasikumar live in their native village in Tamil Nadu. Samuthiram and Ghanam married men from native village in Tamil Nadu and live in villages neighbouring this. Ravi and Murugaiah stayed in Hill Valley. Murugaiah is a permanent worker. Ravi was a temporary worker and since the crisis works in a stone quarry outside the plantation. Ravi's wife became a permanent worker in 2012 and they continue to live in same house where Ravi's parents lived in Hill Valley. Persons still in plantations: 2 of 7.

8. (Paraiyar): Sudalai (1946) = Lekshmi (1949). Child: Madasamy (m) 1968.
Sudalai and Lekshmi died in 1998 and 2001. Madasamy was permanent worker but left the plantation, and went back to his ancestral village in 2004 when his wife deserted him. Persons still in plantations: none.

9. (Paraiyar): Chinna Sudalai (1948) = Parvathy (1950). Children: Saraswathi (f) 1968; Vellasamy (m) 1970.
Chinna Sudalai is younger brother of Sudalai (house 8). Chinna Sudalai died in 2007. Parvathy and son Vellasamy (temporary worker in the estate) moved to the ancestral village in Tirunelveli district in Tamil Nadu. Saraswathi married a manual labourer in Koodalur village near Cumbum valley, Tamil Nadu. She died in 2008 in mysterious circumstances. Persons still in plantations: none.

10. (Paraiyar): Velliyappan (1951) = Masanam (1954). Children: Selvi (f) 1970; Mallika (f) 1974; Murugesan (m) 1976.
Velliyappan died in 2008 in Hill Valley. Masanam then moved to Tamil Nadu to live with a relative. Murugesan lives outside the plantation with his family. He is an assistant to a mason. Mallika and Selvi married men from Tamil Nadu. Both of them work as agricultural labourers in their village in Tamil Nadu. Persons still in plantations: none

---

Note: Houses are all from Line 2 of Hill View estate. The figure traces the families from 1980. Years listed are the years of birth of each family member. For those who were born before 1950 this is the year registered for plantation work but this may be imprecise. f = female, m = male.

Table 3.4   Caste wise distribution of skilled/semi-skilled jobs, Hill Valley estate, Kerala

Job category	Dalits	Others	Total
Supervisor	5	3 (2 Vellalar, 1 Nadar)	8
Driver	1	1 (Vellalar)	2
Chief security guard	0	1 (Nepali Brahmin)	1
Watchmen of fields	3	0	3
Office assistant grade one	0	1 (Maravar)	1
Mechanic	0	1 (Maravar)	1
Plumber	1	0	1
Office assistant at medical clinic	0	1 (Maravar)	1
Cook	1	0	1
Crèche worker	1	0	1
TOTAL	12	8	20

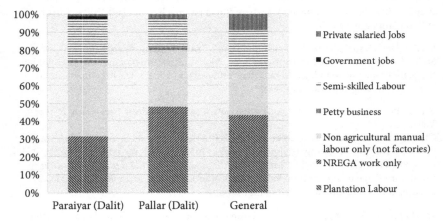

Figure 3.1   Occupations of men by caste group, Hill Valley estate, Kerala

Note: 'General' refers to high caste and OBCs; NREGA – National Rural Employment Guarantee Act.

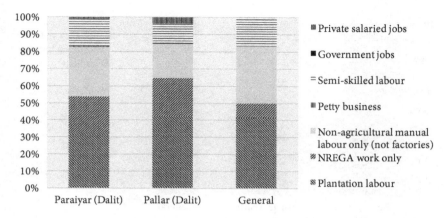

Figure 3.2   Occupations of women by caste group, Hill Valley estate, Kerala

Note: 'General' refers to high caste and OBCs; NREGA – National Rural Employment Guarantee Act.

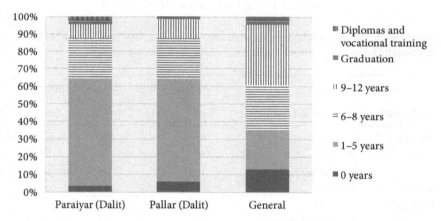

Figure 3.3   Years of schooling of men by caste group, Hill Valley estate, Kerala

Note: 'General' refers to high caste and OBCs.

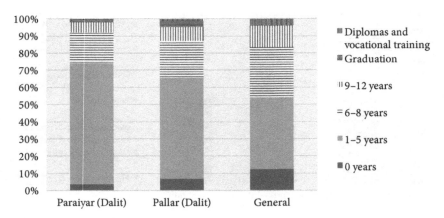

Figure 3.4   Years of schooling of women by caste group, Hill Valley estate, Kerala

Note: 'General' refers to high caste and OBCs.

TABLES AND FIGURES FOR CHAPTER 4

Table 4.1   Relationship between education and occupation, Melpuram, Tamil Nadu: cccupational categories for each educational group, by caste and tribe (%)

Caste, tribe	Occupational category	Years of education: men		Years of education: women	
		9–12	13+	9–12	13+
Paraiyar	Unskilled	67	74	100	91
(Dalit)	Semi-skilled	16	8	0	9
	Service and business	18	17	0	0
Irula	Unskilled	100	100	100	67
(Adivasi)	Semi-skilled	0	0	0	0
	Service and business	0	0	0	33
Vanniyar	Unskilled	14	33	14	67
	Semi-skilled	28	0	28	0
	Service and business	57	66	57	33
Nattar	Unskilled	50	82	50	100
	Semi-skilled	50	0	50	0
	Service and business	0	18	0	0
Nadar	Unskilled	33	0	33	0
	Semi-skilled	33	0	33	0
	Service and business	33	100	33	0

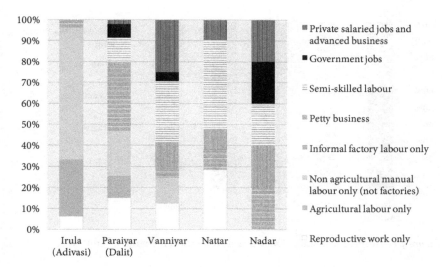

Figure 4.1 Occupations of men by caste and tribe, Melpuram, Tamil Nadu

Note: 'Reproductive work' refers to unpaid labour relating to maintenance and reproduction of the household, that is, what is referred to in political economy literature as social reproduction of labour.

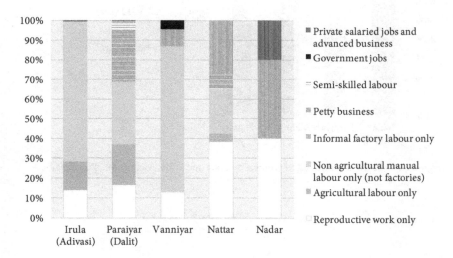

Figure 4.2 Occupations of women by caste and tribe, Melpuram, Tamil Nadu

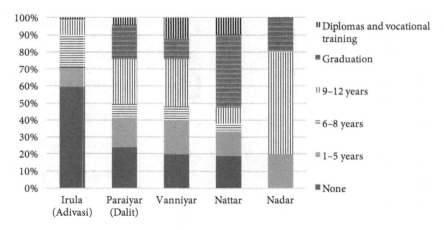

Figure 4.3   Years of schooling of men by caste and tribe, Melpuram, Tamil Nadu

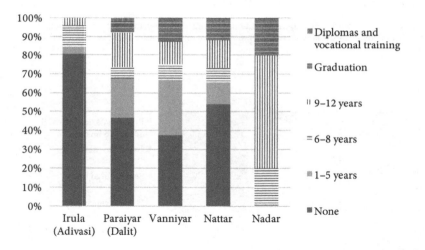

Figure 4.4   Years of schooling of women by caste and tribe, Melpuram, Tamil Nadu

TABLES AND FIGURES FOR CHAPTER 5

Table 5.1 Population and landholding profile of a Bhadrachalam village, Telangana, by caste and tribe

Caste, tribe	Population			Land	
	Households	People	%	Acres	%
Madiga (Dalit)	30	122	5	12	1
Koya (Adivasi)	210	1055	43	273	23
Lambada (Adivasi)	100	425	17	42	3
OBCs	185	561	23	235	20
Kamma	84	252	10	262	22
Reddy	14	56	2	374	31
Total	623	2471	100	1198	100

Note: OBC: Other Backward Classes.
Source: Mandal Revenue Office, Burgampadu, 2015.

Table 5.2 Distribution of landownership by caste and tribe (%) in a Bhadrachalam village, Telangana

Caste, Tribe	Land-less	Less than 1 acre	1–2 acres	2–3 acres	3–5 acres	5–10 acres	Above 10 acres
Kamma	40	0	14	4	12	18	12
Madiga (Dalit)	85	15	0	0	0	0	0
Koya (Adivasi)	33	5	25	15	19	3	0
Lambada (Adivasi)	33	8	8	17	30	4	0

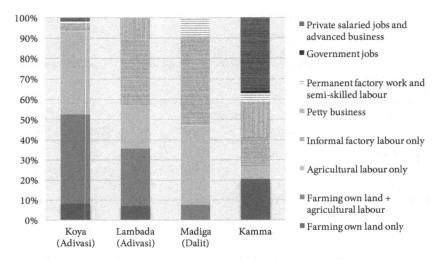

Figure 5.1   Occupations of men by caste and tribe in a Bhadrachalam village,
Telangana

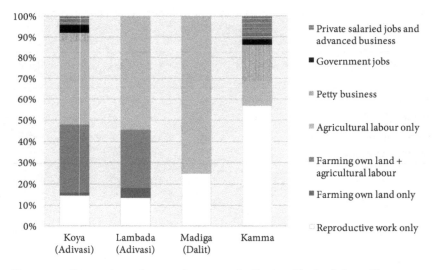

Figure 5.2   Occupations of women by caste and tribe, in a Bhadrachalam village,
Telangana

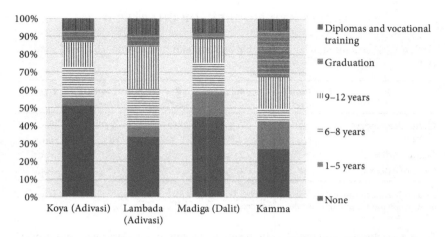

Figure 5.3   Years of schooling of men by caste and tribe, in a Bhadrachalam village, Telangana

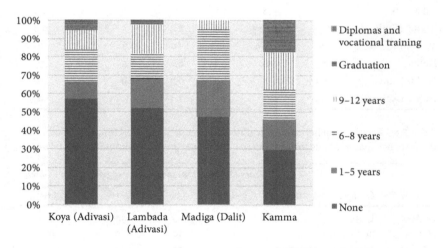

Figure 5.4   Years of schooling of women by caste and tribe, in a Bhadrachalam village, Telangana

TABLES AND FIGURES FOR CHAPTER 6

Table 6.1 Distribution of landownership by community, Badagaon, Himachal Pradesh (%)

	Less than 0.4 acres	0.4–0.8 acres	0.8–1.2 acres	More than 1.2 acres	Total
General category*	21	28	17	34	100
Dalits	19	57	5	19.5	100.5
Gaddi (Adivasi)	7.5	42.5	25	25**	100
Gujjar (Adivasi)	48	27.5	16.5	8	100

Notes: General category: * 21 'caste' Hindu households and 8 Muslim households. ** This is land above 2000 metres that only produces one crop each year.

Table 6.2 Average number of years schooling by community, age-range and gender, Badagaon, Himachal Pradesh

	Average years education	Males aged 20–39	Males aged 40–59	Males aged 60+	Females aged 20–39	Females aged 40–59	Females aged 60+
All adults	5.38	8	5.6	4	5.8	2	0.2
'Caste' Hindu	7.75	11.75	7.9	8.4	9.5	3.8	0.8
Muslim	8	10.6	10.2	10	10	4.8	0
Dalits	7.5	10	9.4	6.2	8.5	1.8	0
Gaddi (Adivasi)	4.3	8	2.7	0.7	4.9	0.9	0
Gujjar (Adivasi)	3.9	5.9	5	2.1	3	0.8	0

Table 6.3 Relationship between education and occupation, Badagaon, Himachal Pradesh: occupational categories for each educational group, community-wise (%)

		Years of education: men		Years of education: women	
Caste, Tribe	Occupational category	9–12	13+	9–12	13+
Gujjar	Unskilled	25	0	50	0
(Adivasi)	Semi-skilled	8	50	0	0
	Service and business	67	50	50	100
Gaddi	Unskilled	33	33	100	100
(Adivasi)	Semi-skilled	20	0	0	0
	Service and business	47	66	0	0
Dalits	Unskilled	19	0	78	50
	Semi-skilled	52	0	0	50
	Service and business	29	100	22	0
General	Unskilled	5	9	77	0
Category	Semi-skilled	9	0	0	50
	Service and business	86	91	23	50

Table 6.4   Schooling of Gujjars by generation, Badagaon, Himachal Pradesh

	Age 5–19	*Age 20–39*	*Age 40+*
No schooling	23%	50%	59%
Government school	40%	44%	36%
Madrasas	22%	6%	5%
Private school	15%	–	–

Table 6.5   Differentiation within the Gujjar and Gaddi communities, Badagaon, Himachal Pradesh

	Gujjars doing 'petty work'	*Gujjars in commerce or salaried employment*	*Gaddis doing 'petty work'*	*Gaddis in commerce or salaried employment*
Number of families	35	13	29	11
Number of people	179 (5.1 per HH)	70 (5.4 per HH)	158 (5.4 per HH)	78 (6.8 per HH)
% of children in full-time education	66.6%	96.5%	92.4%	95%
Average years of education (men aged 20–59)	3.9	10.7	4.5	8.4
Literacy rate among adult men	58.5%	90.5%	55.5%	78.2%
Literacy rate among adult women	19%	47%	36%	59%
% with electricity	60%	100%	90%	100%
% with latrine	37%	92%	45%	91%
% with vehicle	0	46%	0	45%
Land owned (bighas)	2.9	2	4.7	3.3
Average number of animals per family	6.7	1.9	7.3	3.3
% of families owning buffalo and/or cattle	97%	77%	90%	73%

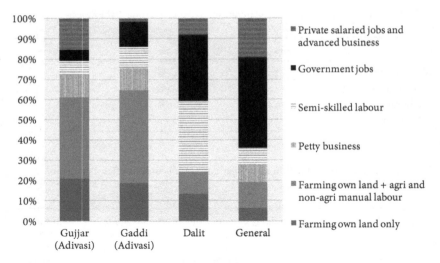

Figure 6.1   Occupations of men by community, Badagaon, Himachal Pradesh

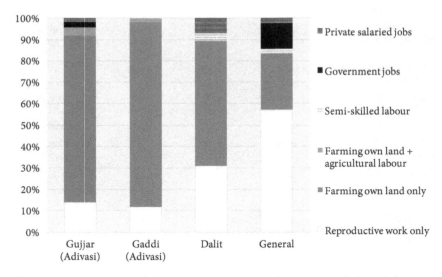

Figure 6.2   Occupations of women by community, Badagaon, Himachal Pradesh

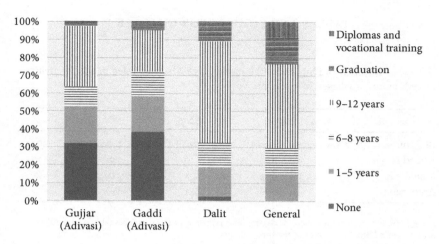

Figure 6.3 Years of schooling of men by community, Badagaon, Himachal Pradesh

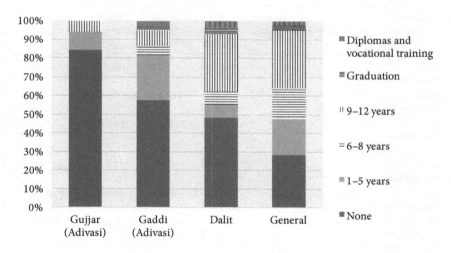

Figure 6.4 Years of schooling of women by community, Badagaon, Himachal Pradesh

Table 7.1 Numbers of Bhil (Adivasi) households that have invested in allied activities, three Nandurbar villages, Maharashtra

	Auto rickshaw			Shops			Tractors		
Bhils of:	2004	2010	2015	2004	2010	2015	2004	2010	2015
Anand Nagar	1	4	9	1	6	8	0	5	17
Mankheda	0	1	5	0	1	4	0	0	0
Ambegaon*	–	–	–	0	1	3	–	–	–

Note: * Hill village, terrain not conducive for auto rickshaw or tractors. This table covers allied activities of *all* Bhil households of the three villages.

Table 7.2 Average household income and expenditure from agriculture for Gujars and Bhils (Adivasi) of three Nandurbar villages, Maharashtra

Category of households	No. of households	Average land holding (acres)	Type of land holding	Annual gross income, Rs.	Annual expenditure, Rs.	Annual net income, Rs.
Gujar (Mankheda)	5	13.1	Irrigated	1,277,216	325,935	951,281
Bhil (Mankheda)	7	2.5	Non-irrigated	42,995	Not available	-
Bhil (Mankheda)	3	–	Landless (daily wages)	115,112	Not available	-
Bhil (Anand Nagar)	10	3.7	Irrigated	330,767	78,170	252,597
Bhil (Anand Nagar)	9	3.75	Non-irrigated	54,974	25,621	29,353
Bhil (Ambegaon)	15	3.8*	Non-irrigated	22,776	20,690	2086

Note: * Rough estimate, claims made under Forest Rights Act 2006 pending cadastral survey.

This table is based on a detailed survey of income and expenditure of selected households throughout one year, during the period October 2014–September 2015. This was a drought year so incomes from non-irrigated landholdings were significantly below normal.

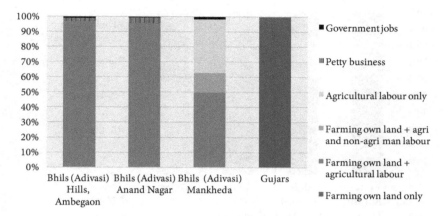

Figure 7.1   Occupations of Gujar and Bhil (Adivasi) men of three Nandurbar villages, Maharashtra

Note that secondary income sources such as fishing and border trade are not included in these figures while shops and rickshaw ownerships are.

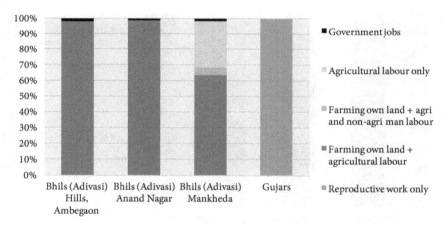

Figure 7.2   Occupations of Gujar and Bhil (Adivasi) women of three Nandurbar villages, Maharashtra

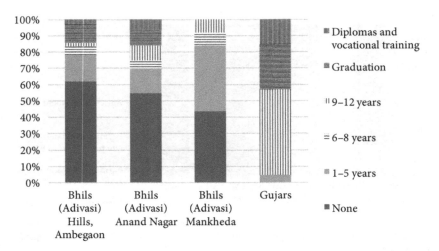

Figure 7.3   Years of schooling of Gujar and Bhil (Adivasi) men of three Nandurbar villages, Maharashtra

Notes

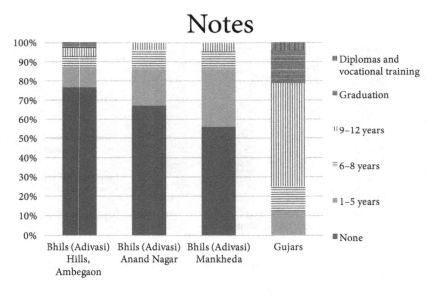

Figure 7.4   Years of schooling of Gujar and Bhil (Adivasi) women of three Nandurbar villages, Maharashtra

PREFACE

1. The 2017 Forbes list shows India to have 90 dollar-billionaires.
2. Harvey 2005 provides a useful brief history of neoliberalism.
3. See for instance Dollar and Kraay 2002, 2004.
4. Cardoso and Faleto 1979.
5. See also Saad Filho 2011.
6. The World Bank has reacted to the dismay over extreme inequalities with an apparent *volte-face* and, since 2013, it has promoted 'shared prosperity' and labour policies for job creation, arguing that high levels of inequality and the absence of good jobs will impede economic growth in the long run. However, perhaps unsurprisingly, this realisation has not led to changes in its economic policies. It still adheres to the same kind of market-led development that has led to the present-day inequalities (World Bank 2012: 3).
7. Between 1990 and 2005, the Indian economy grew at an average of about 6 per cent annually and poverty reduction was less than 1 per cent a year (Kannan 2011). Even though poverty reduction increased in the next periods (2004–05 to 2009–10: 1.5 per cent and 2009–10 to 2011–12: 2.2 per cent), this was still woefully below the annual economic growth rate of this period of 8.3 per cent (Anand et al. 2014: 9).
8. This is comparable to the global poverty line of US$2 PPP (Purchasing Power Parity), see chapter 2.
9. See also Bhaduri 2009.
10. Both schemes do reach wide sections of the poor even though they suffer from funding shortfalls and interference by powerful rural classes. Other important programmes include old age pensions, provision of free mid-day meals to primary school children, supplementary nutrition to pre-school children through the Integrated Child Development Scheme; and additional measures by some state governments (additional pensions, wider coverage of school children for mid-day meals, etc.). Loans to farmers have also been waived to mitigate the economic distress of small and marginal farmers; the last time this happened was in 2008.
11. Kannan and Breman 2013.
12. The National Commission for Enterprises in the Unorganised Sector webpages were reinstated in 2015: http://nceuis.nic.in/
13. See also Kannan 2011.
14. Galanter 1984 is the classic text.
15. Rajshekar 1979; Narula 2007; Setalvad 2004 [2001]; Teltumbde 2010.
16. Guru and Chakravarty 2005; Thorat 2010; Desai and Dubey 2011; Deshpande 2000, 2011; Thorat and Newman 2007; Nathan and Xaxa 2012.
17. Gopal Guru and Anuradha Chakravarty have said there is a 'Dalitisation of poverty in India' (2005: 136).
18. Kannan 2011; Gang et al. 2008.
19. Bhalla 2003; Patnaik 2007; Deaton and Drèze 2002; Mehta and Venkatraman 2000.
20. See also Thorat and Newman 2007.
21. Gang et al. 2008, 2011; Bhaumik and Chakrabarty 2006; Kijima 2006; Boorah 2005.
22. For instance, Deshpande 2011; Madheswaran and Attewell 2010; Thorat et al. 2010.
23. Nayak and Prasad 1984; Saggar and Pan 1994; Kannan 2011.
24. Varshney et al. 2013; Harriss-White et al. 2014.
25. Gang et al. 2008; Kijima 2006; Boorah 2005; Kannan 2011.

26. The problems are well documented in Deaton and Drèze 2002; Palmer-Jones and Sen 2003; Patnaik 2007.

27. Exceptions include the work of 'field economists' such as Barbara Harriss-White and Judith Heyer.

28. We were able to do so thanks to the award of an EU European Research Council (ERC) Starting Grant and a large research grant from the UK Economic and Social Research Council (ESRC) to Alpa Shah as Principal Investigator (ERC-2012-StG_20111124 'The Underbelly of the Indian Boom: Adivasis and Dalits' and ESRC ES/K002341/1 'An Ethnographic Investigation into the Persistence of Poverty among Adivasis and Dalits in India'). We were also able to do so thanks to the help of many colleagues and friends, including economist Barbara Harriss-White, anthropologist Jonathan Parry and anthropologist Clarinda Still as Co-Investigators alongside geographer Jens Lerche.

29. The five researchers had three-year postdoctoral fellowships in the Department of Anthropology at LSE to pursue the research.

30. See Mines and Yazgi 2010; Sorge and Padwa 2015; Simpson et al. forthcoming.

31. To present a book as multi-authored is rare in anthropology where most work is done by lone researchers who, if they come together to work on an idea, usually do so through edited works. Recent years have seen more efforts at research that is collectively prepared and executed, spurred in part by changes in funding, but the standard is still to work on edited collections and present single-authored books even where research has been done by others. There is of course a fear that multi-authored works will not be as recognised as single-authored ones when it comes to job appointments or promotions. However, where appropriate and where researchers agree to write together, we hope that we are here setting new ethical standards for anthropology and pushing the discipline to value equally, alongside the product of writing from the lone researcher, those research endeavours that have genuinely tried to work collectively and comparatively from the preparation and throughout the research and the writing process.

1   TRIBE, CASTE AND CLASS – NEW MECHANISMS OF EXPLOITATION AND OPPRESSION

1. Scheduled Caste and Scheduled Tribe are government categories, the basis on which groups are officially classified and eligible for various specific benefits – such as quotas of reservations. These categories are inevitably contested. Several groups have ongoing mobilisations to try to claim Scheduled Tribe status (see Middleton 2016; Moodie 2015; Kapila 2008). Moreover, while some groups have Scheduled Tribe status in some states, where they have migrated to other states they have lost that status (the classic case is Adivasis from Jharkhand, who were taken to the tea plantations of Assam and who are not recognised as Scheduled Tribes there; see Ananthanarayanan 2010). And some groups are classified as Scheduled Tribes in some states but as Scheduled Castes in other states. In this book we prefer to use the popular terms Adivasi and Dalit, as these are terms which have emerged from activism mobilised within those communities (for the development and use of these categories see Charsley 1996 for Dalits and Shah 2010 for Adivasis). Of course, the use of the terms Adivasi and Dalit is not straightforward either. In areas where their political mobilisation as Adivasis and Dalits is weak, those whom others may call

Adivasis and Dalits may not recognise themselves as such. So, although not always emic categories, for analytic purposes we use the terms Adivasi and Dalit instead of Scheduled Castes and Scheduled Tribes – except when discussing government policies such as reservations, where the bureaucratic categories are the most appropriate.

2. See e.g. Breman 1974, 2007; Vishwanath 2014.

3. Habib 1995a: 106, 1995b: 251.

4. Dumont 1970.

5. Habib 1995c: 166.

6. See Omvedt 1994: 45–6, 69–79. However, whatever minor land rights they had were conditional and different from land rights of other castes, and dependent on the will and might of the landowning community (see, for example, Vishwanath 2014: 23–39). Rawat (2011) points out that some Chamars in Uttar Pradesh had landownership rights, not the least in agrarian frontier areas, but the social characteristics of these rights are unclear.

7. Omvedt 1994: 68–9.

8. Bailey 1961.

9. Shah 2010.

10. Skaria 1997.

11. As Breman 1974 does the Dublas of Gujarat.

12. Habib 1995c: 166; Kosambi 1956; Kumar 1992; Ludden 1989: 91.

13. Breman 1974; Prakash 1990.

14. A range of tribal rebellions across the country, from the Santhal Hul of the 1850s to the Birsa Rebellion of the early 1900s, forced the colonial administrators to consider protective land rights policies that made it increasingly difficult for outsiders to grab Adivasi lands and forests, though there were always ways in which these regulations were breached (see for instance Damodaran 2013; Bates and Shah 2014; Munshi 2012; Singh 1982; Shah 2010, 2014; Sundar 1997).

15. See for instance Breman 2007; Cohn 1987; Omvedt 1994; Robb 1993; Teltumbde 2016; Vishwanath 2014; Zelliott 1992.

16. See, for example, Singer 1972.

17. Fuller 1996.

18. Parry 2007.

19. Though Donegan's chapter does not go into this, there is a long history of Jesuit mobilisation of Dalits in the wider region (see especially Mosse 2012; Vishwanath 2014).

20. The Gujar farmers of Maharashtra have little in common with their near-namesake, the Gujjars of Chamba valley except, perhaps, a shared past as pastoralists.

21. The move away from agriculture to a non-farm economy is echoed in many studies, including the seven decades of re-studies of Palanpur in Uttar Pradesh by Nicholas Stern and his team of economists (Stern 2017) but also in the Slater re-study (Harriss et al. 2010), the Jodkha (2011) re-studies in Haryana, the re-studies based on the earlier work of Pradhan Prasad in Bihar (Rodgers and Rodgers 2001), the collection of re-studies in Himanshu et al. 2016, in Judith Heyer's work (2014) and of course Jan Breman's long-standing work in western India (1996). See the review of overall trends in Shah and Harriss-White (2011) and Lerche (2011).

22. Marx 1867.

23. See Harriss-White 2006.

24. Davis 2006; Bernstein 2007; Breman and van der Linden 2014; Breman 2016.

25. See Li 2010: 68 and Breman 2016: 21–23.
26. From 2000 to 2012, employment grew at 2.2 per cent per year. This small growth came especially from the construction sector, which grew in terms of jobs by 17 per cent per year from 1999 to 2012. Jobs in trade, hotels and restaurants, which includes all petty shopkeepers, hawkers, roadside food sellers, etc., as well as jobs in 'other services' (like cooks, maids, guards, washermen) also experienced some increase. Agriculture, which still employs most Indians (48 per cent), was stagnant in employment terms and manufacturing grew very modestly (4 per cent per year) (Varma 2014).
27. More than half of all workers in the formal sector (58 per cent) are informal, including 34 per cent who are employed through labour contractors (in 2010–11) (Institute for Human Development 2014: 56, 58).
28. For an overview of labour laws, see NCEUS 2007: 154–71.
29. Fifty-two per cent were self-employed, i.e. working in household enterprises, in 2011/12. For the non-agricultural economy, the figure was 40 per cent (Government of India 2013). This includes industrial outworkers/ homeworkers (see Srivastava 2012: 80) and also disguised wage labour.
30. Breman 2003: 13, here from Bernstein 2007: 8.
31. Davis (2006: 202), here from Bernstein (2007: 8). Marxist analysis sometimes equates capitalism to a society which, empirically, is divided between a capitalist class and a proletarian working class. However, Bernstein argues that while capital today is so dominant that it shapes class relations, this has not led to the dominance of the 'classic' capital–labour relations. His concept, 'classes of labour', encompasses all those social groups who 'have to pursue their reproduction through insecure and oppressive – and typically increasingly scarce – wage employment and/or a range of likewise precarious small-scale and insecure, "informal sector" ("survival") activity, including farming; in effect, various and complex combinations of employment and self-employment' (Bernstein 2007: 6). 'Classes of labour' thus includes everyone who is in a relation of exploitation – including those who alternate between being wage labourers and small-scale petty commodity producers, seasonally or throughout their lifetimes.
32. For a brief review, see Scully (2016: 162–65) but see also Pun and Huilin (2010) for the view that a proletariat is, slowly, emerging in China.
33. We will return to the importance of social reproduction later in this chapter.
34. This is a pattern which has also been shown by other in-depth studies in recent years (e.g. Carswell et al. 2010; Carswell et al. 2017; Heyer 2014; Picherit 2009).
35. Institute for Human Development 2014: 79–80, 83.
36. Crenshaw 1989 is the classic.
37. See also McNally 2015: 143.
38. See Anderson 2010; Shanin 1983.
39. See Reed 2002; McNally 2015; Camfield 2016.
40. See the reviews by Reed 2002 and Camfield 2016.
41. See e.g. Grosfoguel 2016.
42. Fletcher 2016: 46.
43. For instance, Habib 1963; Kumar 1992; Vishwanath 2014; Kosambi 1956.
44. For the capitalists, Barbara Harriss-White (2003), among others, has highlighted the significance of what she calls the 'social structures of accumulation' in relation to the significance of their gender, race, caste and religion. More recently, Grace Carswell and Geert De Neve (2014) have shown how neoliberalisation in a major industrial cluster of Tamil Nadu does not lead to linear transformations of caste relations and

social inequalities but transforms the relevance and meaning of caste in uneven and contrasting ways.

45. See *Economic & Political Weekly* (2016) for a brief outline with several empirical similarities.

46. See also Jodhka and Newman (2010) and Deshpande and Newman (2010).

47. See Cross 2014.

48. See also Roberts 2016.

49. Government of India, 2017 and see e.g. UNESCO 2015 for earlier estimates.

50. See also Rogaly et al. 2002; Mosse et al. 2002; Shah 2006; Breman 1996.

51. Ministry of Housing and Urban Poverty Alleviation 2017: 14–17. Note that all figures are for male migrants in non-primary sectors only.

52. In the Bhil case, the oppressive *saldar* (bonded farm servant) relations and violent oppression from the Gujars.

53. While local construction workers have won rights to Welfare Board Schemes, seasonal migrants are overwhelmingly excluded from these (Srivastava and Jha 2016).

54. Carswell and De Neve (2014: 118) report similar instances in Tiruppur.

55. The research field evidencing such caste discrimination – what economists call labour market discrimination – is growing in India. Shah et al. (2006), drawing on an ActionAid study, shows how Dalits were denied wage employment in agriculture, faced discrimination in payment, received wages that were less than the market rate and less than wages paid to other workers, and also showed the persistence of practices of untouchability. Madheswaran and Attewell (2007) claim that 15 per cent of the difference in earnings between Scheduled Castes and non-Scheduled Castes in National Sample Survey data was due to labour market discrimination. Thorat and Newman (2010) highlight the discrimination against Dalits and Muslims at the stage of job selection, showing that caste favouritism and social exclusion of Dalits and Muslims was prevalent in the most dynamic sectors of the Indian economy.

56. According to official figures, in the period 2004–5 to 2011–12, poverty fell by 28 per cent for Adivasis, 42 per cent for Dalits and 45 per cent for other groups (Panagariya and More 2013: 7). See also chapter 2.

57. Centre for Equity Studies 2014: 47.

58. Xaxa 2001.

59. In 2011–12, the percentage of Adivasis in private sector regular formal employment was 2.2 per cent, out of an Adivasi workforce making up 10.2 per cent of the total Indian workforce. For Dalits the figure was 10.2 per cent out of a Dalit workforce of 19.3 per cent of the total Indian workforce. The extremely low Adivasi figure was in fact boosted by very high regular formal worker employment of Adivasis in the north-east of India where, in most parts, Adivasis constitute the majority (Institute for Human Development 2014: 80, 90).

60. Within the rural population, 35.5 per cent of Adivasis are landless, compared to 56 per cent of Dalits and 37.8 per cent of non-Dalits/Adivasis. In Adivasi 'heartland' states such as Chhattisgarh and Jharkhand, Adivasis' landlessness is even lower, 18–19 per cent, while Dalits are around twice as likely to be landless (Bakshi 2008: 10). That said, landlessness is increasing among Adivasis (Karat and Rawal 2014).

61. See also Shah forthcoming for this argument. According to poverty statistics, also in central and eastern India – including in Telangana – poverty is less prevalent among Dalits than among Adivasis (Panagariya and More 2013). There is clearly a need to delve deeper into the relationship between the poverty data and the lived experiences of Dalits and Adivasis. One aspect of this, as Breman has suggested and

as pointed out by Benbabaali in relation to the Telangana factory workers, is that taking up work outside the village as informalised factory workers involves new unavoidable expenses, which means that an increase in income does not always lead to an actual increase in standards of living.

62. Present-day case studies show the adverse conditions of groups of Adivasi workers (e.g. Mosse et al. 2005; Roesch et al. 2009) but comparative studies of Adivasis and Dalits are rare.

63. Neff et al. 2012.

64. A recent example is the lynching of beef eaters. The extreme beating of four Dalit men for allegedly killing a cow in Uni in Gujarat in 2016 was even uploaded onto social media by the perpetrators (*Economic & Political Weekly* 2016). During the five-year period 2009–14, reported crimes against Scheduled Castes increased by 40 per cent and against Scheduled Tribes by 118 per cent, reaching 47,064 and 11,451 incidents respectively in 2014. The conviction rate, meanwhile, was a mere 28 per cent against a rate of 48 per cent for all Indian Penal Code cases (Ghosh 2016).

65. See also Cross 2014.

2   MACRO-ECONOMIC ASPECTS OF INEQUALITY AND POVERTY IN INDIA

1. Between 1991 and 1992 (when economic liberalisation was initiated) and 2009 to 2010, India's national income more than tripled in real terms. In comparison, during the previous 18 years it had increased by 2.3 times only. On a per capita income basis, the increase was more than double – 2.4 times – compared to just 1.6 times or a mere 60 per cent during the preceding 18 years. If one takes a longer period of almost a quarter century between 1991 and 2015, then the increase in national income (GDP) is 7.1 times (or 710 per cent) and per capita income 4.7 times (or 470 per cent).

2. Incidence of informality of course does not always mean poverty. Informal work also encompasses economic activities where earnings are comparable to, or at times more attractive than, those associated with formal work status or work in the formal sector. The common examples are the work of educated professionals (such as doctors, architects, legal practitioners, artists and so on) or those engaged in trading of various kinds. A small section of farmers with large landholdings may also belong to this group, as well as those engaged in informal credit markets such as moneylenders.

3. See for instance the symposium in *Indian Journal of Human Development* 2010. Adjustments in 2010 and 2012 – the first major ones since 1973 – revised the normative poverty line somewhat upwards. But this still left it below the international definition of 'extreme poverty' of PPP$1.25 (Purchasing Power Parity dollars) per capita per day, let alone much below the standard 'international poverty line' of PPP$2 per capita per day, and the methodology adopted also came in for severe criticism (see Raveendran 2016).

4. Some clarification is necessary about the aggregation of socio-religious groups (castes, tribes and religious communities) into four broad groups. From a social point of view, the Indian caste system consists of innumerable castes and sub-castes. The two social groups included in the special schedule of the Constitution, Scheduled Castes and Scheduled Tribes, are grouped together here as Adivasis and Dalits. At the top of the caste hierarchy are the various Hindu upper castes with a common historical experience of access to assets, education and a superior social status. The official policy recognises them as not suffering from social disadvantage and hence

not entitled to any official positive discrimination. The minority religious groups other than Muslims (Sikhs, Christians and Jains) are wealthier than upper caste Hindus (Kannan 2016) so they have been included in the 'Others' category together with upper caste Hindus, except for those among them reporting as Scheduled Castes/Scheduled Tribes. The innumerable caste groups such as artisans, tenants/ small cultivators and others are placed between the top and the bottom regarding caste status. Officially they are classified as OBCs. Large sections of Muslims have been classified officially as OBCs and others as upper classes. We have ignored this and kept Muslims as a separate social group for the purposes of this analysis since the share of the non-poor category among them is closer to that of Adivasis and Dalits than to the two other social groups.

5. Elsewhere we have probed this social hierarchy in not only income/consumption poverty but also its close correlates, such as informal work status and education, and monthly per capita consumer expenditure, and found a 'systemic and hierarchical segmentation' in income poverty and other forms of deprivation (Kannan 2014), underlining the fact that poverty as an outcome is a manifestation of basic endowments and capabilities (Kannan 2016).

6. It is also important to acknowledge the many inadequacies in the implementation of such schemes.

7. Had the scheme been implemented to ensure 100 days of employment this share would have doubled and brought about a bigger decline in the incidence of the poor, howsoever measured.

8. For simplicity, the table does not include data for Muslims and OBCs.

9. The seven north-eastern states are grouped together under the acronym NEA (North East except Assam).

10. Jammu and Kashmir has a 65 per cent Muslim population, followed by 33 per cent in Assam, 26 per cent in West Bengal and 12 per cent in Jharkhand. It is puzzling that in the Muslim-majority state of Jammu and Kashmir, Muslims find themselves at the bottom of the social hierarchy as far as poverty and vulnerability is concerned, but it may relate to disadvantages in terms of access to assets such as land and education. In the case of Assam, the lowest rank of Muslims could be due to their being poor migrants without the advantages of assets and social networks. However, in the case of West Bengal, with a sizeable Muslim population of about 26 per cent, the finding here raises more questions than answers, although the difference in the incidence of poverty and vulnerability between Muslims and Dalits/Adivasis is quite small (around 3 per cent).

3   TEA BELTS OF THE WESTERN GHATS, KERALA

1. Daniel 1996.

2. I have used pseudonyms for the estates and the plantation companies to protect the identities of my informants.

3. This covered all 136 labour households of the tea lines: 123 Dalit households (82 Paraiyar, 37 Pallar, 4 Arunthathiyar) and 13 general caste households.

4. Government of India 2011.

5. The district of Idukki where Peermade is located has one of the highest 'deprivation index' scores of all districts in Kerala (13th out of 14 in 2001) (Government of Kerala 2006: 62).

6. Beckford 1983; Hoerder 2002.

7. Guilmoto 1993.
8. Cf. Mayer 1961; Jayawardena 1963; V. Lal 1993.
9. Chatterjee 2001; Macfarlane and Macfarlane 2004.
10. Guilmoto 1993; Hoerder 2002.
11. Lovatt 1972.
12. *Kangani* is a Tamil term meaning 'supervisor', equivalent to the north Indian *'sardar'*. The Kangani system, as it became known, was a form of recruitment and labour control that was common in plantation belts across the world, as Tamil workers were some of the earliest colonial recruits to coffee/tea plantations in Sri Lanka, Malaysia, South Africa, Mauritius, Myanmar, Fiji and the Caribbean islands. For a detailed analysis of the Tamil migration cycle, see Guilmoto (1993).
13. Baak 1997.
14. Raman 2002.
15. Guilmoto 1993.
16. Heidemann 1992; Hollup 1994.
17. This Act was only repealed in 1935 following pressure from international agencies, especially the League of Nations.
18. Breman 1989.
19. Andrews and Pearson 1916.
20. Tinker 1974.
21. Quoted in Baak 1997: 172.
22. Raman 2010.
23. Kumar 1965; Pandian 1990.
24. See Franke and Chasin 1989; Heller 1999.
25. Baak 1997.
26. The transition of the tea market from a state-regulated to a free market was part of larger transformations in the international political economy of trade; similar changes occurred in other major agricultural commodities such as coffee and cocoa.
27. Neilson and Pritchard 2009.
28. India Today 2013.
29. This new plantation tourism is in effect a rediscovery of a colonial connection between tea plantations and tourism (Jolliffe 2007).
30. Sara Besky has reported similar developments in north-eastern India, where the powerful planters' associations evade state control and earn fair trade certifications even when basic conditions for fair trade are not met, such as safe working conditions and decent wages (2008: 126–28).
31. That is, the minimum weight of tea leaves to be plucked by the workers to qualify for the daily minimum wage of Rs.216.
32. The retirement benefits include two key components: the gratuity amount and provident fund. The gratuity amount is calculated by multiplying half of the salary of the last three months by the number of years of labour. A person retires on completing 40 years of labour or when they reach 58 years of age, whichever comes first. The provident fund is a combination of employer and employee contributions, both contributing 12 per cent of workers' daily wage.
33. Those who left the plantations entirely usually had siblings or other relatives staying back in the plantations and so retained their ties with the plantations through, for example, attending ceremonies.
34. The survey included (number of men/women) Dalit Paraiyar 160/214; Dalit Pallar 81/85; high caste and OBC 23/24. A group of Dalit Arunthathiyar plantation

workers was also surveyed but are not included in the figures due to their small numbers (six males and six females). The significant difference in the number of Paraiyar women to men is the result of a combination of factors. First, many Paraiyar men who moved out of the plantation got married earlier than the women in their family, and therefore formed separate families while the women remained as part of the family back in the plantation. Second, there were also a few Paraiyar men who left permanently as they migrated to towns in search of jobs. Third, there are a few Paraiyar women whose husbands had died in their early forties. Fourth, more Paraiyar men migrated out for work compared to Pallar men, possibly because landownership (although less than 1 acre in most cases) was more common among Pallars.

35. As mentioned earlier, the Arunthatiyars have not been included in the figures as they consisted of only four families, but their life situation was the worst of all the Dalit groups.

36. *Times of India* 2016.

37. This trend seems to be the case for all the social groups irrespective of caste identity, and the partial suspension of the caste system in the class order of the plantation could be a reason behind that (Raj 2014). It must be noted that the move into semi-skilled work is more common among educated Dalit plantation women than among educated Dalit women from the other sites of this volume.

38. Chari 2004; Carswell and De Neve 2013.

39. Hindu BusinessLine 2011.

40. While there was no difference in the terms and conditions of work between other workers and plantation Dalits, the plantation Tamils had less choice in terms of changing their employers (or stitching/dyeing units). This is because of their lack of the networks and functional literacy that other groups were able to accumulate over years of association with the units. Furthermore, the plantation Tamils are sceptical of contractors in general. Therefore, they prefer to find job opportunities through their 'plantation network' of the 100 families.

41. There are more than 3000 small textile and garment manufacturing units that rely on contract work from larger companies (http://www.knitcma.com/KNITcMA_HtmX/Vision.htm).

42. The tailors are specialised in stitching different elements of clothing. For example, if it is a shirt, one will stitch the cuffs, one will stitch the neck and another person will stitch the rest.

43. A fact-finding team of Delhi university students found that more than 800 workers committed suicide between 2008 and 2011 in the entire Tiruppur garment industry (Sanhati 2011).

44. See Carswell and De Neve 2014.

45. It is possible that second and third generations of Dalit migrants from the plantations to the cities will benefit more from greater economic mobility, as they may be able to access better education than those who stayed in the plantations.

46. Houses 1, 2, 3, 4, 5, 6 and 7.

47. Different waves of migration of Tamils to Kerala took place in the modern period. The Tamil Iyers settled in Palaghat and Travancore regions; in Palaghat they became a major landowning community whereas the Travanacore Iyers were high officials of Travancore princely state. The landowning higher caste of Vellalas and Tamil Muslims from the Madurai region migrated to the valleys of the high ranges, mostly in and around the present districts of Idukki and Pathananthitta. Another group

of migrants is the Tamil Dalits who were brought as manual scavengers (night soil workers), in the first half of the twentieth century, to central and southern Kerala. This migration continued in the postcolonial period. While Kerala was declared a 'scavenger-free state' in early 1980s, the descendants of these migrants were incorporated into comparable occupations, often as cleaners/sweepers. The plight of these Dalits is detailed in a famous Malayalam Novel, *Thottiyude Makan* (Scavenger's Son) by the well-known novelist, Thakazhi Sivasankara Pillai.

48. The contract posts are not covered by affirmative action.
49. Raj 2014.
50. In Dumka 93 per cent of the population remains rural, average literacy stands at 61 per cent in 2011; for Godda these figures stand at 95 per cent and 56 per cent.
51. In 2006 the Indian government listed Godda and Dumka as amongst the country's 250 most backward districts (out of a total of 640).
52. The Lohras, although landless, do engage in rice cultivation in the role of paid wage labourers for the Santalis and Mundas.
53. Drèze and Sen 1989.
54. Kannan 1988; Nair 2006.
55. Rammohan 1998.
56. Viswanathan and Saqaf 1999.
57. Raj 2014.
58. The TATA group used to be a major tea producer in Munnar and is now a major trader/buyer of tea worldwide. It is often used as synonymous with the plantation companies in Munnar.
59. While the marginal position of tea plantation workers in West Bengal and Assam was made visible, this had not happened for their counterparts in Kerala, largely due to the very good development indicators of Kerala and the higher wages of the workers here. But the tea plantation workers are a low-paid workforce in Kerala. The worsening of the conditions of tea workers in Kerala made Bhowmik (2015) note that the difference of the quality of living of tea workers across India is now insignificant.

4   CUDDALORE, CHEMICAL INDUSTRIAL ESTATE, TAMIL NADU

1. Ghani et al. 2012.
2. In 2009–10, manufacturing employed 17 per cent of the workforce in Tamil Nadu, with only West Bengal and Delhi employing a larger proportion (18 per cent and 27 per cent) (Planning Commission n.d.).
3. Harriss et al. 2010: 61.
4. See also Harriss 2013.
5. Carswell and De Neve 2014.
6. I surveyed 91 Paraiyar Dalit households (414 individuals, 289 of them aged 20+) out of a total of 120, all 126 Irula Adivasi households (488 individuals, 290 of them aged 20+), 17 Vanniyar and Gounder households (which are effectively a single inter-marrying community in this village) out of a total of 120, 20 Nattar households out of a total of 60, and 3 out of 4 Nadar households.
7. Cross 2014.
8. Adnan 2013: 96.
9. Chakravarti 2014.
10. Hexa Research 2016.

11. Pandian and Kalaiyarasu 2013.
12. Ibid.
13. Government of Tamil Nadu n.d.
14. See chapter 2 of this book and Shrinivasan 2016.
15. Bugge 1994: 33–34.
16. This related to the decline in the *mirasi* rights of the Mirsidars over land and labourers during the nawab rule (Bugge 1994: 35).
17. Bugge 1994: 154; Amrith 2011: 32–38.
18. Hjejle 1967: 101, 122.
19. Garstin 1878: 399.
20. Hjejle 1967: 122.
21. Different government documents provide different numbers of operational units in the estate.
22. Community Environmental Monitoring 2013. Doubts have been raised as to whether further industrialisation and urbanisation in the region is wise. The November–December monsoon of 2015 saw millions of people in Chennai and Cuddalore affected by the highest rainfall in 100 years. In the aftermath, it has been suggested that Cuddalore should be 'zoned' as a region particularly prone to freak climate events (Dominique 2015), having also been badly affected by the tsunami in 2004, severe floods in 2005–06 and Cyclone Thane in 2011.
23. All Dalit households in the village are Paraiyar with one exception: a 60-year-old Arunthathiyar man (or, in the pejorative language of the Paraiyars, a 'Chakkiliyan'), his 30-year-old son and his 90-year-old mother. He serves the Paraiyar community, ironing laundry and carrying the firestick in temple processions. In the past, he washed clothes for the Paraiyars, but stopped doing this long ago.
24. The exception here is the street where the Nattars live, known as Meenavar Nagar (literally 'Fisherman Street'), which was tarmacked after the 2004 tsunami (when much humanitarian aid intended for tsunami-affected communities went exclusively to fisher communities).
25. Hardgrave 1979.
26. Gorringe 2012.
27. Ibid.
28. Kumar et al. 2013.
29. Heyer 2012: 94.
30. Heyer 2012: 95. It should be noted that agricultural labour in this area was never unionised and that this contrasts with Nagapattinam and Thanjavur districts (adjacent to Cuddalore district, barely 100 km south of Melpuram), which, as the old Tanjore district, saw the rise and repression of a district-wide communist Kisan (peasant) movement between 1947 and 1948 (Gough 1973: 236–40).
31. Guerin et al. (2015) recently suggested that 1 million people from these parts of South Asia currently work in Tamil Nadu.
32. Vanniyars and Gounders are discussed together under the label 'Vanniyar' because these two communities intermarry and consider themselves to be a single community. Note that the survey does not capture the number of Vanniyar households who work on their own land because those who do so also do other types of work (which are captured here as their 'main' work). The survey also under-represents the number of Paraiyar Dalit households in which one or more person has government employment (more on this below).

33. This distinction between Dalit/Adivasi women and Vanniyar and Gounder women is not visible in my survey data. The most likely reason for this is that the sample of Vanniyar/Gounder households surveyed is small (14 per cent) compared to the sample of Dalit (76 per cent) and Adivasi households (100 per cent).
34. Carswell and De Neve 2013: 87.
35. The Irulas have the least access to the panchayat of anyone: whereas the Dalits have one ward member, the Irulas don't even have that as the ward to which they belong is their settlement plus another settlement.
36. Note that Table 4.1 underestimates the proportion that has been able to access government jobs, at least among the Dalits.
37. Mosse et al. 2005; Shah 2006.
38. The labour contractors for the Adivasi Bhil seasonal migrant agricultural labourers in Nandurbar, Maharashtra, charged a whopping 15–20 per cent of the daily earnings (see chapter 7) whereas the Adivasi migrant labourers in the Kerala plantation managed to get rid of the contractor's fee altogether (see chapter 3).
39. In 2014–15 safety equipment was given to contract workers in the bone factory for the first time.
40. Indian People's Tribunal 2003.
41. Breman 1996.
42. Guerin et al. 2015: 15.
43. The Communist Party of India (Marxist) union.
44. The legal 'case' here is in fact a First Information Report submitted to the Workers' Welfare Department.
45. Vincentnathan 1996.
46. See also Osella and Osella 2000.
47. Harriss 2013.

5   BHADRACHALAM SCHEDULED AREA, TELANGANA

1. I surveyed 150 of the 623 households in the village (508 individuals): 100 households from the three Dalit and Adivasi groups, Madiga (Scheduled Caste), Koya (Scheduled Tribe) and Lambada (Scheduled Tribe), and 50 from the dominant Kamma caste. See Tables 5.1 and 5.2 for details.
2. Simhadri and Rao 1997.
3. His rival Chandrababu Naidu's Telugu Desam Party (TDP) won the elections in the residuary State of Andhra Pradesh.
4. Benbabaali 2016.
5. Hemingway 1907: 259.
6. Hemingway 1907: 260.
7. Glasfurd 1868: 26.
8. Benbabaali 2017.
9. Simon Commission Report 1930, quoted in Samata 2000.
10. Samata 2000.
11. A mandal in Telangana is a district subdivision.
12. *The Hindu* 1997. One crore is 10 million.
13. It was not possible to obtain a list of employees from the unions.
14. Hemingway 1907: 175.
15. Harvey 2004.
16. Girgliani 2005.

17. Bhadrachalam Integrated Tribal Development Agency has a total population of around 1 million, two-thirds of whom are Adivasis. The main Adivasi groups are Koyas (314,000), Lambadas (329,000), Yerukulas (20,000) and Konda Reddis (10,000).

18. The Integrated Novel Development in Rural Areas and Model Municipal Areas (INDIRAMMA) is a mass housing scheme introduced by the Government of Andhra Pradesh in 2006 when the late Congress Chief Minister Y.S. Rajashekar Reddy aimed to make the state 'hut-free'.

19. In Telugu, the term *podu* normally refers to shifting cultivation, but *podu bhoomi* (*podu* land) in the village simply means forest lands that were cleared many years ago when the Koyas used to practise shifting cultivation and are now used for settled agriculture.

20. *Business Standard* 2015.

21. Devi 1983.

22. *The Hindu* 2015.

23. Umamaheshwari 2014.

24. Interview with Sondu Veeraiah, convenor of the *Girijana Rastra Sadhana Committee* and state convenor for the *Adivasi Samkshema Parishad*.

25. Jeffrey 2012.

6 CHAMBA VALLEY, HIMALAYA, HIMACHAL PRADESH

1. For a nuanced evaluation of improvements in human resource development see Sanan (2004).

2. The proportion of rural households with salaried government employment in Himachal Pradesh is 23 per cent, compared to the Indian average of 5 per cent (Government of India n.d.). This is most likely due to Himachal being a traditional recruitment base for the Indian army.

3. In Chamba district, 54.1 per cent of households are below the poverty line against a Himachal Pradesh average of 23.9 per cent (Department of Economics and Statistics Himachal Pradesh 2013: 162).

4. Government of Himachal Pradesh 2002.

5. Government of India 1965: 61.

6. Kapila 2008. Six per cent of Himachal's population is categorised as Scheduled Tribes. This includes the trans-Himalayan district of Lahaul and Spiti, where the whole population is listed as Scheduled Tribe.

7. Badagaon is a fictitious name and pseudonyms are also used for individuals and other villages.

8. As recorded by Noble (1987) and Kaushal (2001).

9. Gooch 2004.

10. Axelby 2007, 2016.

11. Though legally rights are inherited by all children, in practice they are passed down the male line.

12. Saberwal 1999; Chakravarty-Kaul 1997.

13. *Gazetteer of Chamba State* 1904: 267.

14. Bhatnagar 1981.

15. Elsewhere in Himachal Pradesh access to government jobs has been better for Adivasis, while other groups have attained above the state average in the villages of

this research. The Himachal figures are: All 23 per cent; Scheduled Castes 18 per cent; Scheduled Tribes 24 per cent (Government of India n.d.).

16. Jodhka 2015; Berreman 1963.

17. *Divya Himachal* 2014.

18. See Jeffery et al. (2007). Sikand (2005: 97–98) also records the suspicions which many Muslim parents hold, with good reason, about government schools.

19. In 2016 this rose to Rs.170 per day in non-tribal areas and Rs.213 per day in tribal areas (including the tribal sub-tehsil of Bharmour).

7 NARMADA VALLEY AND ADJOINING PLAINS, MAHARASHTRA

1. Maharashtra state is made up of diverse regions, including India's financial centre Mumbai, major industrial areas, commercial agricultural regions as well as rain-fed, less economically developed areas. Nandurbar is the least developed district in the state, with the lowest human development indicators (YASHADA 2014: 11ff).

2. On the deforestation of the hills, see *Gazetteer of India* (1880: 297) and Thakur (2014a: 228–51) for more details.

3. Census of India 1991: 25–26. The relation of these sub-tribes to each other is not standardised and the interpersonal relations vary from one village to another. There is a sense of hierarchy among the various jatis but that too varies every few kilometres. Many of them also have their own specific dialect and often tend to be endogamous, and all these distinctions again have numerous variations. For further details on this topic see Thakur (2014b).

4. For the impact of colonial processes see Cohn (1996). The decennial census and detailed ethnographic studies resulted in the formation of various caste groups. Regarding the social mobility of the Kanbi peasant caste of south Gujarat (kin of Gujars across the Narmada River), see Breman (2007: ch. 3).

5. For further information on the pre-Maratha period, see Quddusi (2002), for the pre-Mughal period, see Husain (1963) and for the British settlement, see Deshpande (1987).

6. *Gazetteer of India* 1880: 297; Thakur 2014a: 228–51.

7. Ibid.

8. For details of their subsistence model and reasons for the changes in it over time, see Thakur (2014a).

9. Claims made under the Forest Rights Act, 2006 are pending with the government.

10. Deshpande 1987.

11. *Gazetteer of India* 1880: 297.

12. Ibid. 210–11.

13. This boom was closely related to the American Civil War that disrupted the supply of US cotton to the mills in England.

14. For the variable impact of the ryotwari system in Bombay Presidency, see for example Charlesworth (1985) or Guha (1985).

15. For further information on the Gujar–Bhil relations, see Paranjape (1981).

16. Brahme and Upadhyaya 1975: 366.

17. *Gazetteer of India* 1880: 57. For the deleterious impact of the Parsees see Hardiman (1987). On the question of the Baniyas see also Hardiman (1996).

18. *Gazetteer of India* 1880: 197–98.

19. Symington 1938.

20. Manohar 2001.

21. The details of his work along with the Shramik Sanghatana activists were covered in various Marathi periodicals by the group itself. See for example, Shramik Sanghatana (1973, 1979). I thank Vikram Kanhere, a founder member of the group, for sharing these.

22. Shramik Sanghatana 1973, 1979.

23. Basu 1992. For the tactics used to organise disparate marginal groups, see Kulkarni (1979).

24. During my archival work in the District Record Room of Nandurbar, I noted case files pertaining to hundreds of such cases. I later verified some of these claims on the ground and in interviews with former Shramik Sanghatana activists as well. There was significant state action for restoration of Bhils' property, while the grip of the Gujars was also diminished.

25. Conversation with Vikram Kanhere and Ranjana Kanhere, founder members of the group. They have run a non-governmental organisation (NGO) called Janarth since the late 1980s in Shahada and Akrani talukas working on education, health, community forestry projects and self-help groups among other initiatives.

26. Nilsen 2010.

27. Rough estimate, claims made under Forest Rights Act 2006 pending cadastral survey.

28. The survey covered 30 (39 per cent) of the 77 Bhil households in Ambegaon; 35 (15 per cent) of the 225 Bhil households in Anand Nagar; and in Mandheka, 15 (7 per cent) of the 220 Bhil households and 10 (12 per cent) of the 83 Gujar households. The difference in sampling sizes reflects a main focus on the hill Bhils and the resettled Bhils. While the samples are relatively small except for Ambegaon, the picture emerging is in line with what I observed during the fieldwork.

29. Though the two goldsmiths and one moneylender I spoke to refused to divulge the interest rate they charged, many Bhils and Gujars confirmed the interest rate they pay.

30. The compensation was only for the Bhils of the plains, for those with formal land titles who also filed written petitions to the government. The Bhil hill village hardly has any formal land titles, made no claim for agricultural losses and got no compensation.

31. See Thakur (2014b) for the interlinked phenomena of population growth, expansion of agriculture and deforestation in and around the Narmada Valley that took place from the middle of the twentieth century.

32. The contractor's fee of the Odia seasonal migrant workers in Cuddalore might have been equally extortionate although the exact size of this fee is not known (see chapter 4).

33. Description based on the genealogy of the Bhil families made during January–August 2015. Conversation with Moti, Fakira's 90-year-old son, and four other Bhil relatives on 31 July 2015.

34. Description based on the genealogy of the Gujar families made during January–August 2015.

35. A copy of this Marathi booklet was provided by Dilip N. Patil, a resident of Shahada and a Gujar, an academic who has also published a book on the history and folk stories of Gujars. The Gujars of Nandurbar and the Gujjars in Chamba (see chapter 6) have little in common except, perhaps, a shared past as pastoralists. See chapter 6 for a discussion of the history of Gujars/ Gujjars in India and beyond, and for present-day moves to create India-wide Gujar-Gujjar networks.

36. Purshottam K. Patil (1923–2014), popularly called 'P.K. Anna', was a leader of the Shahada Gujars from the 1950s to the 1990s. He set up many cooperative institutions from 1969 onwards and consolidated the solidarity within the Gujar community (Sawant 2002).

37. Gujars are an 'Other Backward Class' caste in Maharashtra and are eligible for reservations in educational institutions and government jobs.

38. See also Gidwani (2008). For unemployment and the resultant inability of Gujar men to get married, see Tilche (2016).

39. Interviewed on 9 May 2015 at his residence in Purshottam Nagar, Shahada.

40. Breman argues that kiln owners use advance wages as a mechanism of attachment and 'the recipient has to pay the provider in labour … for a price lower than the going market rate' (2010b: 49). While this is no doubt the case, still the Bhils return to work at the kiln every year voluntarily by availing themselves of fresh advances. Given the absence of real alternatives they see this as their best, or least bad, option.

41. On the topic see for example Nilsen (2010), Baviskar (2005) and Whitehead (2010). For more information on the poor condition of the resettlement colonies in Maharashtra during their first few years, see *Economic & Political Weekly* (1991, 1993, 1999).

42. Maharashtra Resettlement of Project Displaced Persons (Amendment and Validation) Act, 1985.

43. Herring (2012) shows that Bt cotton merely means the ability of the breed to resist bollworm while a lot of informants in my field also attributed the seed with faster growth and maturing of cotton plant. My guess is that going for Bt also resulted in switching to better varieties of seeds that made the Gujars think all the benefit was due to the Bt aspect of the seed.

44. The government has started reimbursing the Bhils for the cost of digging bore wells at the rate of Rs.145,000 starting from 2016, with 13 cases approved as of June 2016 and others in the process of being cleared.

45. Their situation is different, for instance, from the unmarried Jat youth of Uttar Pradesh in their early thirties (see Jeffrey et al. 2008: 31) as the Bhils get married and become fathers by the time they are 20.

46. Parry 1999: 107–40.

47. Vinoba Bhave was anointed by Mahatma Gandhi to lead his social reform movement. He was founder of the Sarvodaya movement and visited the Satpura hills in the 1930s (*Swatantra Bharat* 1958).

48. Over 27,000 posts were unfilled in 2013 itself (*Global Gujarat News* 2013). For Maharashtra, see the *Times of India* (2015).

8   THE STRUGGLES AHEAD

1. Credit Suisse 2016: 148.

2. *Indian Express* 2016.

3. See Kumar 1999. Between 2000 and 2015, 80,000 Indians who had wealth of more than US$30 million each left India to take up domicile in Singapore and the UEA, where income and corporate tax are very low. India also has no inheritance tax.

4. http://economictimes.indiatimes.com/industry/healthcare/biotech/healthcare/indias-disproportionately-tiny-health-budget-a-national-security-concern/articleshow/49603121.cms

5. Kannan and Breman 2013.

6. See for instance Kannan and Breman 2013; Mooij 1999; Ruud 2014.
7. IndiaSpend 2016. In 2017 a proclaimed 25 per cent fund hike only amounted to a 1 per cent raise. See http://timesofindia.indiatimes.com/city/jaipur/nrega-fund-hike-only-1-not-25-claims-aruna-roy/articleshow/56928831.cms. Last accessed on 7 June 2017.
8. See also Higham and Shah 2013b.
9. See Lerche 2008; Carswell and De Neve 2015.
10. See Cohn 1987; Dirks 2001; Pinney 1990; Fuller 2016.
11. Kapila 2008; Mayaram 2007; Middleton 2016; Moodie 2015.
12. See Béteille 1983, 1991, 1992 for the key issues.
13. Balagopal 2000; Teltumbde 2009.
14. Taylor 1992.
15. See Madheswaran 2017.
16. As shown by Donegan in Melpuram, access to government jobs has not improved access to government services and rights for the Dalit Paraiyar community. Moreover, the educated Dalit Paraiyar youth play an important role in educating and possibly also in politicising other young Dalit Paraiyars, but the new income and status differences among the Dalits arising from the fact that only a minority have gained access to the coveted government jobs has also riven the community with new divisions.
17. See Kapur et al. 2014.
18. Prakash 2015; Harriss-White et al. 2014.
19. Pai 2014.
20. Guru 2012; Teltumbde 2011; see also Kalva 2016.
21. Pratap and Bose 2015; Ness 2016; Sundar 2012.
22. See also Parry 2009.
23. Barnes et al. 2015: 366–67; Sundar 2012.
24. AngryWorkersWorld 2015.
25. Guha 1999; Bates and Shah 2014.
26. Teltumbde 2016.
27. Gorringe 2005.
28. Jaoul 2006; Pai 2000.
29. Guha 1991.
30. See also Baviskar 2005 [1995]; Nilsen 2010; Whitehead 2010; Ghosh 2006.
31. Padel and Das 2010.
32. Karlsson 2003; Karlsson and Subba 2006.
33. Hardiman 1987; Desai 2010.
34. Froerer 2007.
35. Mosse 2012; Roberts 2016.
36. Shah 2014.
37. This is in the context of the Gas Wars of El Alto in Bolivia.
38. See AngryWorkersWorld (2015) for similar cases.
39. These criticisms have a 20-year-long history (Lerche 2008) but they have intensified since 2016.
40. https://thewire.in/132165/india-unhrc-universal-periodic-review/. This followed the UNHRC Report of the Special Rapporteur on Minority Issues which first highlighted – in 2016 – the significance of caste discrimination as a human rights concern on par with other forms of discrimination. The report highlighted 'caste-based violence, particularly sexual violence' against Dalit women and girls, and

how 'atrocities against women from marginalized castes' are used as a punishment 'to teach the woman and her community a lesson' (UNHCR 2016: 19). Meanwhile the European Parliament stated that it is 'deeply concerned by the alarming rate of caste-based violent attacks on Dalits and of institutionalised discrimination with impunity' (European Parliament 2016).

Bibliography

Adnan, S., 2013. 'Land grabs and primitive accumulation in deltaic Bangladesh: interactions between neoliberal globalization, state interventions, power relations and peasant resistance'. *Journal of Peasant Studies*, 40(1): 87–128.

Agarwala, R., 2013. *Informal Labor, Formal Politics, and Dignified Discontent in India*. Cambridge: Cambridge University Press.

Alkire, S. and M.E. Santos, 2010. *Acute Multidimensional Poverty: A New Index for Developing Countries*. Oxford Poverty and Human Development Initiative, Working Paper 38. Oxford: OPHDI.

Ambedkar, B.R., 1989. 'Untouchables or the children of India's ghetto'. In *Dr. Babasaheb Ambedkar Writings and Speeches*, vol. 5, compiled by V. Moon. Bombay: Education Department Government of Maharashtra.

Amrith, S., 2011. *Migration and Diaspora in Modern Asia*. Cambridge: Cambridge University Press.

Anand, R., V. Tulin and N. Kumar, 2014. *India: Defining and Explaining Inclusive Growth and Poverty Reduction*. IMF Working Paper 14/63. Washington, DC: IMF.

Ananthanarayanan, S., 2010. 'Scheduled Tribe status for Adivasis in Assam'. *South Asia: Journal of South Asian Studies*, 33(2): 290–303.

Anderson, K., 2010. *Marx at the Margins: On Nationalism, Ethnicity, and Non-Western Societies*. Chicago: University of Chicago Press.

Andrews, C.F. and W.W. Pearson, 1916. *Report on Indentured labour in Fiji: An Independent Enquiry*, http://dspace.gipe.ac.in/xmlui/handle/10973/24936 (accessed 19 June 2017).

AngryWorkersWorld, 2015. 'Struggles "Made in India": on the series of factory riots, occupations and (wildcat) strikes in Delhi's industrial south, 2014', http://tinyurl.com/zzbr4t8 (accessed 16 December 2016).

Axelby, R., 2007. 'It takes two hands to clap: how Gaddi shepherds in the Indian Himalayas negotiate access to grazing'. *Journal of Agrarian Change*, 7(1): 35–75.

Axelby, R., 2016. 'Who has the stick has the buffalo: processes of inclusion and exclusion on a pasture in the Indian Himalayas'. *SAMAJ* 13(1).

Baak, P.E., 1997. *Plantation Production and Political Power: Plantation Development in South-west India in a Long-term Historical Perspective*. New Delhi: Oxford University Press.

Bailey, F.G., 1961. '"Tribe" and "caste" in India'. *Contributions to Indian Sociology*, 5: 7–19.

Bakshi, A., 2008. 'Social inequality in land ownership in India: a study with particular reference to West Bengal'. *Social Scientist*, 39(9/10): 95–116.

Balagopal, K., 2000. 'A tangled web: subdivision of SC reservations in AP'. *Economic & Political Weekly*, 35(13): 1075–1081.

Balibar, E., 1991a. 'Class racism'. In *Race, Nation, Class: Ambiguous Identities*, eds E. Balibar and I. Wallerstein. London: Verso Books, 204–216.

Balibar, E., 1991b. 'Racism and crisis'. In *Race, Nation, Class: Ambiguous Identities*, eds. E. Balibar and I. Wallerstein. London: Verso Books, 217–227.

Banaji, J., 2003. 'The fictions of free labour: contract, coercion, and so-called unfree labour'. *Historical Materialism*, 11(3): 69–95.

Banerjee, P., 2016. 'Writing the Adivasi: some historiographical notes'. *Indian Economic and Social History Review*, 53(1): 1–23.

Bardhan, P. (ed.), 1989. *Conversations between Economists and Anthropologists: Methodological Issues in Measuring Economic Change in Rural India.* Oxford: Oxford University Press.

Barnes, T., K. Shekhar, L. Das and S. Pratap, 2015. 'Labour contractors and global production networks: the case of India's auto supply chain'. *Journal of Development Studies*, 51(4): 355–369.

Basu, A., 1992. *Two Faces of Protest: Contrasting Modes of Women's Activism in India.* Berkeley: University of California Press.

Basu, K., 2008. 'India's dilemmas: the political economy of policymaking in a globalised world'. *Economic & Political Weekly*, 43(5): 53–62.

Bates, C. and A. Shah (eds), 2014. *Savage Attack: Tribal Insurgency in India.* New Delhi: Social Science Press.

Baviskar, A., 2005 [1995]. *In the Belly of the River: Tribal Conflicts over Development in the Narmada Valley.* New Delhi: Oxford University Press.

Becker, M., 2008. *Indians and Leftists in the Making of Ecuador's Modern Indigenous Movements.* Durham, NC: Duke University Press.

Beckford, G.L., 1983. *Persistent Poverty: Underdevelopment in Plantation Economies of the Third World.* Morant Bay: Maroon Publishing House.

Benbabaali, D., 2016. 'From the peasant armed struggle to the Telangana State: changes and continuities in a South Indian region's uprisings'. *Contemporary South Asia*, 24(2): 184–196.

Benbabaali, D., 2017. 'Caste dominance and territory in South India: understanding Kammas' socio-spatial mobility'. *Modern Asian Studies.*

Bernstein, H., 1992. 'Poverty and the poor'. In *Rural Livelihoods: Crises and Responses*, eds H. Bernstein, B. Crow and H. Johnson. Oxford: Oxford University Press.

Bernstein, H., 2007. 'Capital and labour from centre to margins'. Keynote address at Living on the Margins: Vulnerability, Exclusion and the State in the Informal Economy conference, 26–28 March, Isandla Institute, Cape Town, http://tinyurl.com/lqp6vxz (accessed 16 December 2016).

Berreman, G., 1963. *Hindus of the Himalayas.* Berkeley: University of California Press.

Besky, S., 2008. 'Can a plantation be fair? Paradoxes and possibilities in fair trade Darjeeling tea certification'. *Anthropology of Work Review*, 9(1): 1–9.

Béteille, A., 1983. 'The backward classes and the new social order'. In *The Idea of Natural Inequality and Other Essays*, ed. A. Béteille. New Delhi: Oxford University Press.

Béteille, A., 1991. 'Distributive justice and institutional well-being'. *Economic & Political Weekly*, 26(11/12): 591–600.

Béteille, A., 1992. 'The future of the backward classes: the competing demands of status and power'. In *Society and Politics in India: Essays in a Comparative Perspective*, ed. A. Béteille. London and Atlantic Highlands, NJ: Athlone Press.

Bhaduri, A., 2009. *The Face You Were Afraid to See: Essays on the Indian Economy.* New Delhi: Penguin.

Bhagwati, J., 1993. *Indian in Transition.* Oxford: Clarendon Press.

Bhagwati, J. and A. Panagariya, 2013. *Why Growth Matters: How Economic Growth in India Reduced Poverty and the Lessons for Other Developing Countries.* New York: Public Affairs.

Bhalla, S., 2003. 'Recounting the poor: poverty in India, 1983–1999'. *Economic & Political Weekly*, 37(4): 338–349.

Bhatnagar, S., 1981. 'Politics of land reforms in India: a case study of land legislation in Himachal Pradesh'. *Asian Survey*, 21(4): 454–468.

Bhaumik, S.K. and M. Chakrabarty, 2006. *Inter-caste Differences in Formal Sector Earnings in India: Has the Rise of Caste-based Politics had an Impact?* Keele: Centre for Economic Research, Keele University.

Bhowmik, S., 2015. 'Living conditions of tea plantation workers'. *Economic & Political Weekly*, 50(46/47): 29–32.

Boorah, V., 2005. 'Caste, inequality, and poverty in India'. *Review of Development Economics*, 9(3): 399–414.

Bourgois, P., 1988. 'Conjugated oppression: class and ethnicity among the Guaymi and Kuna banana workers'. *American Ethnologist*, 15(2): 328–348.

Bourgois, P., 1989. *Ethnicity at Work*. Baltimore, MD: Johns Hopkins University Press.

Bourgois, P., 1995. *In Search of Respect: Selling Crack in El Barrio*. Cambridge: Cambridge University Press.

Bourgois, P., 1997. 'In search of Horatio Alger'. In *Crack in America: Demons, Drugs and Social Justice*, eds C. Reinarman and H.G. Levine. Berkeley: University of California Press.

Brahme, S. and A. Upadhyaya, 1975. *A Critical Analysis of the Social Formation and Peasant Resistance in Maharashtra*, vol. 2. Pune: Shankar Brahme Samaj Vidnyan Granthalaya (unpublished manuscript).

Breman, J., 1974. *Patronage and Exploitation: Changing Agrarian Relations in South Gujarat, India*. Berkeley: University of California Press.

Breman, J., 1989. *Taming the Coolie Beast: Plantation Society and the Colonial Order in Southeast Asia*. New Delhi: Oxford University Press.

Breman, J., 1996. *Footloose Labour: Working in India's Informal Economy*. Cambridge: Cambridge University Press.

Breman, J., 2003. *The Labouring Poor in India: Patterns of Exploitation, Subordination, and Exclusion*. New Delhi: Oxford University Press.

Breman, J., 2007. *Labour Bondage in India: From Past to Present*. New Delhi: Oxford University Press.

Breman, J., 2010a. 'India's social question in a state of denial'. *Economic & Political Weekly*, 45(23): 42–46.

Breman, J., 2010b. 'Shifting boundaries between free and unfree labor: neo-bondage: a fieldwork-based account'. *International Labour and Working-class History*, 78(1): 48–62.

Breman, J., 2016. *On Pauperism in Present and Past*. New Delhi: Oxford University Press.

Breman, J. and M. van der Linden, 2014. 'Informalizing the economy: the return of the social question at a global level'. *Development and Change*, 45(5): 920–940.

Bugge, H., 1994. *Mission and Tamil Society: Social and Religious Change in South India (1840–1900)*. Richmond: Curzon Press.

Burawoy, M., 2010. 'From Polanyi to Pollyanna: the false optimism of global labor studies'. *Global Labour Journal*, 1(2): 301–313.

Business Standard, 2015. 'ITC plans Rs 4000 crore investment to expand paper production', 15 June, http://tinyurl.com/l42m3jo (accessed 19 June 2017).

Camfield, D., 2016. 'Elements of a historical-materialist theory of racism'. *Historical Materialism*, 24(1): 31–70.

Cardoso, F.H. and E. Faleto, 1979. *Dependency and Development in Latin America*. Berkeley: University of California Press.

Carswell, G. and G. De Neve, 2013. 'Labouring for global markets: conceptualising labour agency in global production networks'. *Geoforum*, 44(1): 62–70.

Carswell, G. and G. De Neve, 2014. 'T-shirts and tumblers: caste, dependency and work under neoliberalisation in South India'. *Contributions to Indian Sociology*, 48(1): 103–131.

Carswell, G. and G. De Neve, 2015. 'Litigation against political organization? The politics of Dalit mobilization in Tamil Nadu, India'. *Development and Change*, 46(5): 1106–1132.

Carswell, G., G. De Neve and J. Heyer, 2017. 'Caste discrimination in contemporary Tamil Nadu: evidence from the Tiruppur textile region'. In *Waning Hierarchies, Persisting Inequalities: Caste and Power in 21st-century India*, eds J. Manor and S. Jodhka. Hyderabad: Orient Blackswan.

Carswell, G., J. Heyer and G. De Neve, 2010. 'Looking beyond the industrial cluster: the impacts of a South Indian garment cluster on rural livelihoods'. *Global Insights*, School of Global Studies, University of Sussex http://tinyurl.com/mfgpgq7 (accessed 16 December 2016).

Census of India, 1991. *District Census Handbook: Dhule Handbook*. Bombay: Government of India Press.

Centre for Equity Studies, 2014. *Indian Exclusion Report 2013–14*. Bangalore: Books for Change.

Centre for Science and Environment, n.d. 'Green rating project – key findings of pulp and paper sector'. *Centre for Science and Environment*, http://www.cseindia.org/node/286 (accessed 19 June 2017).

Chakravarti, S., 2014. *Clear. Hold. Build: Hard Lessons of Business and Human Rights in India*. New Delhi: HarperCollins.

Chakravarty-Kaul, M., 1997. 'Transhumance: a pastoral response to risk and uncertainty in the Himalayas'. *Nomadic Peoples*, 1(1): 133–149.

Chandavarkar, R., 1999. 'Questions of class: the general strikes in Bombay, 1928–29'. *Contributions to Indian Sociology* 33(1–2): 205–237.

Chari, S., 2004. *Fraternal Capital : Peasant-workers, Self-made Men, and Globalization in Provincial India*. New Delhi: Permanent Black.

Charlesworth, N., 1985. *Peasants and Imperial Rule: Agriculture and Agrarian Society in the Bombay Presidency, 1850–1935*. Cambridge: Cambridge University Press.

Charsley, S., 1996. '"Untouchable": what is in a name?' *Journal of the Royal Anthropological Institute*, 2(1): 1–23.

Chatterjee, P., 2001. *Time for Tea: Women and Post-colonial Labour on an Indian Plantation*. Durham, NC: Duke University Press.

Chevalier, L., 1981 [1973]. *Labouring Classes and Dangerous Classes: In Paris during the First Half of the Nineteenth Century*. Princeton, NJ: Princeton University Press.

Cohn, B.S., 1987. 'The census, social structure and objectification in South Asia'. In *An Anthropologist among the Historians and other Essays*, ed. B.S. Cohn. Oxford: Oxford University Press.

Cohn, B.S., 1996. *Colonialism and its Forms of Knowledge: The British in India*. Princeton, NJ: Princeton University Press.

Comaroff, J. and J. Comaroff, 2009. *Ethnicity, Inc.* Chicago and London: University of Chicago Press.

Community Environmental Monitoring, 2013. *Counter-mapping the Tamil Nadu PCPIR: A Report on the Preparation of Community Baseline Maps*. Chennai: Community Environmental Monitoring (unpublished report), http://tinyurl.com/jh9k8rf (accessed 15 December 2016).

Cox, O.C., 1970 [1948]. *Caste, Class, and Race. A Study in Social Dynamics.* New York: Monthly Review Press.

Credit Suisse, 2016. *Global Wealth Databook 2016*, http://tinyurl.com/h6pnrcp (accessed 6 May 2017).

Crenshaw, K.W., 1989. 'Demarginalising the intersection of race and gender: a black feminist critique of antidiscrimination doctrine, feminist theory and antiracist politics'. *University of Chicago Legal Forum*, 1(8): 138–167.

Cross, J., 2014. *Dream Zones: Anticipating Capitalism and Development in India.* London: Pluto Press.

Damodaran, V., 2013. 'Indigenous agency: customary rights and tribal protection in eastern India, 1830–1930'. *History Workshop*, 76: 85–110.

Daniel, V., 1996. *Charred Lullabies: Chapters in an Anthropography of Violence.* Princeton, NJ: Princeton University Press.

Das, A.N., 1984. 'Class in itself, caste for itself: social articulation in Bihar'. *Economic & Political Weekly*, 19(37): 1616–1619.

Davis, M., 2006. *Planet of Slums.* London: Verso.

Deaton, A. and J. Drèze, 2002. 'Poverty and inequality in India: a re-examination'. *Economic & Political Weekly*, 37(36): 3729–3748.

Department of Economics and Statistics Himachal Pradesh, 2013. *Statistical Outline of Himachal Pradesh 2012–13.* Shimla: Government of Uttar Pradesh.

Desai, A., 2010. 'Dilemmas of devotion: religious transformation and agency in Hindu India'. *Journal of the Royal Anthropological Institute*, 16(2): 319–329.

Desai, A. and A. Dubey, 2011. 'Caste in 21st-century India: competing narratives'. *Economic & Political Weekly*, 46(11): 40–49.

Deshpande, Arvind M., 1987. *John Briggs in Maharashtra: A Study of District Administration under Early British Rule.* New Delhi: Mittal Publications.

Deshpande, Aswini, 2000. 'Does caste still define disparity?' *American Economic Review*, 90(2): 322–325.

Deshpande, Aswini, 2011. *The Grammar of Caste: Economic Discrimination in Contemporary India.* Oxford: Oxford University Press.

Deshpande, Aswini and K. Newman, 2010. 'Where the path leads: the role of caste in post-university employment expectations'. In *Blocked by Caste: Economic Discrimination in Modern India*, eds S. Thorat and K. Newman. New Delhi: Oxford University Press.

Devi, M., 1983. 'Why eucalyptus?' *Economic & Political Weekly*, 18(32): 1379–1381.

Dirks, N., 2001. *Castes of Mind: Colonialism and the Making of Modern India.* Princeton, NJ: Princeton University Press.

Divya Himachal (newspaper), 2013. 'A march towards prosperous Himachal', http://www.divyahimachal.com/2013/04/a-march-towards-prosperous-himachal/ (accessed 1 August 2017).

Divya Himachal, 2014. 'Caste in Himachal politics', http://www.divyahimachal.com/2014/04/caste-in-himachal-politics/ (accessed 1 August 2017).

D'Mello, B. and A. Shah, 2013. 'Preface'. In the Indian edition of *Jose Carlos Mariategui: An Anthology.* Translated by Marc Becker and Harry Vanden. New Delhi: Cornerstone.

Dollar, D. and A. Kraay, 2002. 'Growth is good for the poor'. *Journal of Economic Growth*, 7(3): 195–225.

Dollar, D. and A. Kraay, 2004. 'Trade, growth and poverty'. *Economic Journal*, 114(493): 22–49.

Dominique, B., 2015. 'No lessons learnt from Thane cyclone, Cuddalore district continues to suffer'. *Times of India*, 12 November, http://tinyurl.com/kh62kq4 (accessed 15 December 2016).

Dominguez, E.M. (ed.), 2013. *Race in Cuba: Essays on Revolution and Racial Inequality*. New York: Monthly Review Press.

Drèze, J. and A. Sen, 1989. *Hunger and Public Action*. Oxford: Oxford University Press.

Drèze, J. and A. Sen, 2013. *An Uncertain Glory: India and its Contradictions*. Princeton, NJ: Princeton University Press.

Dumont, L., 1970. *Homo Hierarchicus: The Caste System and Its Implications*. London: Wiedenfeld & Nicolson.

Economic & Political Weekly, 1991. 'Blinkered vision', 26(29): 1708–1709.

Economic & Political Weekly, 1993. 'Sardar Sarovar project: review of resettlement and rehabilitation in Maharashtra', 28(34): 1705–1707 and 1705–1714.

Economic & Political Weekly, 1999. 'Narmada project: desperate measures', 34(22): 1304–1305.

Economic & Political Weekly, 2016. 'The Dalit question', 51(52): 8.

European Parliament, 2016. *Report on the Annual Report on Human Rights and Democracy in the World and the European Union's Policy on the Matter 2015*, Committee on Foreign Affairs, 28 November, http://tinyurl.com/yac2sva2 (2016/2219(INI)) (accessed 2 May 2017).

Federici, S., 2004. *Caliban and the Witch: Women, the Body and Primitive Accumulation*. New York: Autonomedia.

Fletcher, B. Jr, 2016. 'Race in the capitalist world-system: response to the symposium essays'. *Journal of World-Systems Research*, 22(1): 45–49.

Franke, R.W. and B.H. Chasin, 1989. *Kerala: Radical Reform as Development in an Indian State*. San Francisco, CA: Institute for Food and Development Policy.

Froerer, P., 2007. *Religious Division and Social Conflict: The Emergence of Hindu Nationalism in Rural India*. New Delhi: Social Science Press.

Fuller, C.J., 1996. 'Introduction: caste today'. In *Caste Today*, ed. C.J. Fuller. New Delhi: Oxford University Press.

Fuller, C.J., 2016. 'Colonial anthropology and the decline of the Raj: caste, religion and political change in India in the early twentieth century'. *Journal of the Royal Asiatic Society*, 26(3): 463–486.

Fürer-Haimendorf, C. von, 1948. *The Raj Gonds of Adilabad: A Peasant Culture of the Deccan*, London: Macmillan.

Galanter, M., 1984. *Competing Equalities: Law and the Backward Classes in India*. Berkeley: University of California Press.

Gang, I., K. Sen and M.-S. Yun, 2008. 'Poverty in rural India: caste and tribe'. *Review of Income and Wealth*, 54(1): 50–70.

Gang, I., K. Sen and M.-S. Yun, 2011. 'Was the Mandal Commission right? Living standard differences between OBCs and other social groups in India'. *Economic & Political Weekly*, 46(39): 43–51.

Garstin, J.H., 1878. *Manual of the South Arcot District*. Madras.

Gazetteer of Chamba State, 1904. New Delhi: Indus Publishing Company.

Gazetteer of India, 1880. *Gazetteer of the Bombay Presidency: Khandesh District*, vol 12. Bombay: Government of India Press.

Ghandy, A., 2011. *Scripting the Change: Selected Writings of Anuradha Ghandy.* New Delhi: Danish Books.

Ghani, E., A.G. Goswami and W.R. Kerr, 2012. *Is India's Manufacturing Sector Moving Away from Cities?* Harvard Business School, Working Paper 12–090. Cambridge, MA: Harvard Business School.

Ghosh, K., 2006. 'Between global flows and local dams: indigenousness, locality and the transnational sphere in Jharkhand, India'. *Cultural Anthropology*, 21(4): 501–534.

Ghosh, H., 2016. 'Why crime is rising against India's lowest castes and tribes'. *Indiaspend*, 4 July, http://tinyurl.com/l5a4ywm (accessed 21 December 2016).

Gidwani, V., 2008. *Capital Interrupted: Agrarian Development and the Politics of Work in India.* Durham, NC: Duke University Press.

Girgliani J.M., 2005. *Report on Tribal Land Issues in the Telangana Area.* Hyderabad: Government of Andhra Pradesh.

Glasfurd, C.L.R., 1868. *Report on the Land Revenue Settlement of the Upper Godavery District, Central Provinces.* Nagpur: Chief Commissioners Office Press.

Global Gujarat News, 2013. '27,488 govt posts for SC/ST/OBCS unfilled'. 18 September, http://tinyurl.com/nx28y2r (accessed 25 November 2016).

Gooch, P., 2004. 'Van Gujjar: the persistent forest pastoralists'. *Nomadic Peoples*, 8(2).

Gorringe, H., 2005. *Untouchable Citizens: Dalit Movements and Democratisation in Tamil Nadu.* New Delhi: Sage.

Gorringe, H., 2012. 'Caste and politics in Tamil Nadu'. *Seminar*, http://tinyurl.com/mrafmxv (accessed 15 December 2016).

Gough, K., 1973. 'Harijans in Thanjavur'. In *Imperialism and Revolution in South Asia*, eds K. Gough and H.P. Sharma. New York: Monthly Review Press.

Government of Himachal Pradesh, 2002. *Human Development Report.* Shimla: Government of Himachal Pradesh.

Government of India, n.d. *Socio Economic and Caste Census 2011* http://secc.gov.in/welcome (accessed 16 December 2016).

Government of India, 1965. *The Report of the Advisory Committee on the Revision of the List of Scheduled Castes and Scheduled Tribes* (Lokur Committee Report). New Delhi: Government of India, Department of Social Security.

Government of India, 2011. *Provisional Population Totals Paper 1 of 2011 India: Series 1.* New Delhi: Office of the Registrar General and Census Commissioner, India http://tinyurl.com/kr3xhvt (accessed 15 December 2016).

Government of India, 2013. *Key Indicators of Employment and Unemployment in India, 2011–12.* National Sample Survey 68th Round (June 2011–June 2012), Ministry of Statistics and Programme Implementation, http://www.mospi.gov.in/sites/default/files/publication_reports/KI-68th-E%26U-PDF.pdf (accessed 16 December 2016).

Government of India, 2017. *Economic Survey 2016–17.* Ministry of Finance, http://indiabudget.nic.in/es2016-17/echapter.pdf (accessed 30 April 2017).

Government of Kerala, 2006. *Kerala Human Development Report 2005*, http://tinyurl.com/mtjkxfm (accessed 2 April 2017).

Government of Tamil Nadu, n.d. *Adi Dravidar and Tribal Welfare Department*, http://www.tn.gov.in/department/1 (accessed 2 March 2017).

Grosfoguel, R., 2016. 'What is racism?' *Journal of World-Systems Research*, 22(1): 9–15.

Guerin, I., G. Venkatasubramanian and S. Kumar, 2015. 'Debt bondage and the tricks of capital'. *Economic & Political Weekly*, 50(26): 12–18.

Guha, R., 1991. *The Unquiet Woods: Ecological Change and Peasant Resistance in the Himalaya.* New Delhi: Oxford University Press.

Guha, R., 1999. *Elementary Aspects of Peasant Insurgency in Colonial India (1983)*. Durham, NC: Duke University Press.

Guha, S., 1985. *The Agrarian Economy of the Bombay Deccan, 1818–1941*. New Delhi: Oxford University Press.

Guilmoto, C.Z., 1993. 'The Tamil migration cycle, 1830–1950'. *Economic & Political Weekly*, 28(3/4): 111–120.

Gupta, D., 2014. 'From poverty to poverty: translating growth to development in India'. In *Persistence of Poverty in India*, eds N. Gooptu and J. Parry. New Delhi: Social Science Press.

Guru, G., 2012. 'Rise of the "Dalit millionaire": a low intensity spectacle'. *Economic & Political Weekly*, 47(50): 41–49.

Guru, G. and A. Chakravarty, 2005. 'Who are the country's poor? Social movement politics and Dalit poverty'. In *Social Movements in India: Poverty, Power, and Politics*, eds R. Ray and M.F. Katzenstein. Oxford: Wiley-Blackwell.

Habib, I., 1963. *The Agrarian System of Mughal India (1556–1707)*. London: Asia Publishing House.

Habib, I., 1995a. 'The social distribution of landed property in pre-British India: a historical survey'. In *Essays in Indian History: Towards a Marxist Perception*. New Delhi: Anthem Press.

Habib, I., 1995b. 'Forms of class struggle in Mughal India'. In *Essays in Indian History: Towards a Marxist Perception*. New Delhi: Tulika.

Habib, I., 1995c. 'Caste in Indian history'. In *Essays in Indian History: Towards a Marxist Perception*. New Delhi: Tulika.

Hale, C.R., 2002. 'Does multiculturalism menace? Governance, cultural rights and the politics of identity in Guatemala'. *Journal of Latin American Studies*, 34(3): 485–524.

Hall, S., 1986. 'Gramsci's relevance for the study of race and ethnicity'. *Journal of Communication Inquiry*, 10(5): 5–27.

Hardgrave, R., 1979. *Essays in the Political Sociology of South India*. New Delhi: Usha Publications.

Hardiman, D., 1987. *The Coming of the Devi: Adivasi Assertion in Western India*. New Delhi: Oxford University Press.

Hardiman, D., 1996. *Feeding the Baniya: Peasants and Usurers in Western India*. New Delhi: Oxford University Press.

Harriss, J., 2007. *Bringing Politics Back into Poverty Analysis: Why Understanding Social Relations Matters More for Policy on Chronic Poverty than Measurement*. Chronic Poverty Research Centre, Working Paper 77. Manchester: ChronicPoverty Research Centre.

Harriss, J., 2013. 'Does "landlordism" still matter? Reflections on agrarian change in India'. *Journal of Agrarian Change*, 13(3): 351–364.

Harriss, J., J. Jeyaranjan and K. Nagaraj, 2010. 'Land, labour and caste politics in rural Tamil Nadu in the 20th century: Iruvelpattu (1916–2008)'. *Economic & Political Weekly*, 45(31): 47–61.

Harriss-White, B., 2003. *India Working*. Cambridge: Cambridge University Press.

Harriss-White, B., 2006. 'Poverty and capitalism'. *Economic & Political Weekly*, 41(13): 1241–1246.

Harriss-White, B. and N. Gooptu, 2000. 'Mapping India's world of unorganised labour'. *Socialist Register*, 37: 89–118.

Harriss-White, B., E. Basille, A. Dixit, P. Joddar, A. Prakash and K. Vidyarthee, 2014. *Dalits and Adivasis in India's Business Economy: Three Essays and an Atlas.* New Delhi: Three Essays Collective.

Harvey, D., 2004. 'The "new" imperialism: accumulation by dispossession'. *Socialist Register*, 40: 63–87.

Harvey, D., 2005. *A Brief History of Neoliberalism.* New York: Oxford University Press.

Heidemann, F., 1992. *Kanganies of Sri Lanka and Malaysia.* Munich: Anacon.

Heller, P., 1999. *The Labor of Development: Workers and the Transformation of Capitalism in Kerala, India.* New York: Cornell University Press.

Hemingway, F.R., 1907. *Madras District Gazetteers. Godavari*, vol. 1. Madras: Government Press.

Herring, R.J., 2012. 'On the "failure of Bt Cotton": analysing a decade of experience'. *Economic & Political Weekly*, 47(18): 45–53.

Heyer, J., 2012. 'Labour standards and social policy: a South Indian case study'. *Global Labour Journal*, 3(1): 91–117.

Heyer, J., 2014. 'Dalit households in industrializing villages in Coimbatore and Tiruppur, Tamil Nadu: a comparison across three decades'. In *Dalit Households in Village Economies*, eds V.K. Ramachandran and M. Swaminathan. New Delhi: Tulika Books.

Hexa Research, 2016. 'Press release: Global gelatin market is expected to grow by 2020, Asia Pacific is estimated to grow at around 4% from 2014 to 2020'. AB Newswire, http://tinyurl.com/kykxpef (accessed 15 December 2016).

Higham, R. and A. Shah, 2013a. 'Conservative force or contradictory resource? Education and affirmative action in Jharkhand, India'. *Compare: A Journal of Comparative and International Education*, 43(6): 718–739.

Higham, R. and A. Shah, 2013b. 'Affirmative action and political economic transformations: secondary education, indigenous people, and the state in Jharkhand, India'. *Focaal*, 65: 80–93.

Himanshu, P. Jha and G. Rodgers (eds), 2016. *The Changing Village in India: Insights from Longitudinal Research.* New Delhi: Oxford University Press.

Hindu BusinessLine, 2011. 'Court order on dyeing units closure chokes Tirupur garment sector'. 3 February, http://tinyurl.com/lxz2qdf (accessed 2 April 2017).

Hjejle, B., 1967. *Slavery and Agricultural Bondage in South India in the Nineteenth Century.* Copenhagen: Scandinavian Institute of Asian Studies.

Hoerder, D., 2002. *Cultures in Contact: World Migrations in the Second Millennium.* London: Duke University Press.

Hollup, O., 1994. *Bonded Labour: Caste and Cultural Identity among Tamil Plantation Workers in Sri Lanka.* New Delhi: Sterling Publishers Private Ltd.

Holt Norris, A. and E. Worby, 2012. 'The sexual economy of a sugar plantation: privatization and social welfare in northern Tanzania'. *American Ethnologist*, 29(2): 354–370.

Husain, M., 1963. *Khandesh in New Light.* Bangalore: Mythic Society.

India Today, 2013. 'Tea: a cupful of woes'. 4 November, http://tinyurl.com/ls4aqw6 (accessed 7 December 2016).

Indian Express, 2016. 'Data shows only 1% of population pays income tax, over 5000 pay more than 1 crore'. 1 May, http://tinyurl.com/zektydu (accessed 28 December 2016).

Indian Journal of Human Development, 2010. Symposium on Estimation of Poverty and Indentifying the Poor. *Indian Journal of Human Development*, 4(1).

Indian People's Tribunal on Environment and Human Rights, 2003. *Report on Human Rights Violations, Industrial Pollution and the Implications of the Proposed Chemplast Sanmar PVC Factory in SIPCOT, Cuddalore, T.N.* Mumbai: Combat Law Publications, http://www.sipcotcuddalore.com/downloads/Cuddalore_IPT_report.pdf   (accessed 15 December 2016).

IndiaSpend, 2016. 'Half full, half empty: 10 years of NREGA'. 9 February, http://tinyurl.com/mxykrj6 (accessed 8 May 2017).

Institute for Human Development, 2014. *India Labour and Employment Report 2014*. New Delhi: Academic Foundation and Institute for Human Development.

Ismail, F. and A. Shah, 2015. 'Class struggle, the Maoists and the indigenous question in Nepal and India'. *Economic & Political Weekly*, 35(29): 112–123.

Jaoul, N., 2006. 'Learning the use of symbolic means: Dalits, Ambedkar statues and the state in Uttar Pradesh'. *Contributions to Indian Sociology*, 40(2): 176–207.

Jayawardena, C., 1963. *Conflict and Solidarity in a Guianese Plantation*. London: Athlone Press.

Jeffrey, C., P. Jeffery and R. Jeffery, 2008. *Degrees without Freedom: Education, Masculinities, and Unemployment in North India*. Stanford, CA: Stanford University Press.

Jeffery, P., R. Jeffery and C. Jeffrey, 2007. 'Investing in the future: education in the social and cultural reproduction of Muslims in UP'. In *Living with Secularism: The Destiny of India's Muslims*, ed. M. Hasan. New Delhi: Manohar.

Jeffrey, R., 2012. 'Missing from the Indian newsroom'. *The Hindu*, 9 April.

Jodhka, S., 2011. 'What's happening to the rural? Revisiting "marginalities" and "dominance" in northwest India'. Paper presented at the Poverty Conference, Oxford Department for International Development.

Jodhka, S., 2015. 'Cast(e) on the hill: "divine" power, social cohesion and hierarchy in Himachal Pradesh'. *Economic & Political Weekly*, 50(21): 58–68.

Jodkha, S. and K. Newman, 2010. 'In the name of globalisation: meritocracy, productivity, and the hidden language of caste'. In *Blocked by Caste: Economic Discrimination in Modern India*, eds S. Thorat and K.S. Newman. New Delhi: Oxford University Press.

Jolliffe, L., 2007. *Tea and Tourism: Tourists, Traditions and Transformations*. Clevedon: Channel View Publication.

Kalva, S., 2016. 'Tracing Ambedkar in Dalit capitalism'. *Economic & Political Weekly*, 51(47): 79–81.

Kannan, K.P., 1988. *Of Rural Proletarian Struggles: Organization and Mobilization of Rural Workers in South West India*. New Delhi: Oxford University Press.

Kannan, K.P., 2010. 'The long road to social security'. Hivos Knowledge Programme 2010/2, http://tinyurl.com/mnr2kbm (accessed 8 May 2017).

Kannan, K.P., 2011. 'The social face of poverty in a fast-growing India: national and regional dimensions'. Paper presented at the Poverty in South Asia Conference, University of Oxford.

Kannan, K.P., 2012. 'How inclusive is inclusive growth in India?' *Indian Journal of Labour Economics*, 55(1): 33–60.

Kannan, K.P., 2014. *Interrogating Inclusive Growth: Poverty and Inequality in India*. New Delhi: Routledge.

Kannan, K.P., 2016. 'At the bottom of durable inequality: the status of India's Dalits and Adivasis'. Paper presented at the Workshop of the Inequality and Poverty Research Programme, Anthropology Department, London School of Economics, London, 30 June–1 July 2016.

Kannan, K.P. and J. Breman (eds), 2013. *The Long Road to Social Security*. New Delhi: Oxford University Press.

Kapadia, K., 1995. *Siva and her Sisters: Gender, Caste, and Class in Rural South India*. Boulder, CO: Westview Press.

Kapila, K., 2008. 'The measure of a tribe: the cultural politics of constitutional reclassi-fication in North India'. *Journal of the Royal Anthropological Institute*, 14(1): 117–134.

Kapur, D., D.S. Babu and C. Bhan Prasad, 2014. *Defying the Odds: The Rise of Dalit Entre-preneurs*. New Delhi: Random House India.

Karat, B. and V. Rawal, 2014. 'Scheduled tribe households: a note on issues of livelihood'. *Review of Agrarian Studies*, 4(1): 135–158.

Karlsson, B., 2003. 'Anthropology and the "indigenous slot": claims to and debates about indigenous people's status in India'. *Critique of Anthropology*, 23(4): 402–423.

Karlsson, B. and T. Subba (eds), 2006. *Indigeneity in India*. London: Kegan Paul.

Kaushal, M., 2001. 'Divining the landscape – the Gaddi and his land'. *India International Centre Quarterly*, 27/28(4/1): 31–40.

Kijima, Y., 2006. 'Caste and tribe inequality: evidence from India, 1983–1999'. *Economic Development and Cultural Change*, 54(2): 369–404.

Kosambi, D.D., 1956. *An Introduction to the Study of Indian History*. Bombay: Popular Book Depot.

Kulkarni, S.D., 1979. 'Class and caste in a tribal movement'. *Economic & Political Weekly*, 14(7/8): 465–468.

Kumar, A., 1999. *The Black Economy of India*. New Delhi: Penguin.

Kumar, D., 1965. *Land and Caste in South India*. Cambridge: Cambridge University Press.

Kumar, D., 1992. *Land and Caste in South India*. New Delhi: Manohar.

Kumar, X.R.A., L. Giridharan, J. Shyamala, P.M. Velmurugan and M. Jayaprakash, 2013. 'Urbanisation impact of groundwater quality in Cuddalore district, east coast of India'. *Journal of Environmental Chemistry and Ecotoxicology*, 5(3): 63–73.

Lal, B.V., 1993. '"Nonresistance" on Fiji plantations: the Fiji Indian experience, 1879–1920'. In *Plantation Workers: Resistance and Accomodation*, eds E.D. Beechart, D. Munro and B.V. Lal. Honolulu: University of Hawaii Press.

Lerche, J., 1999. 'Politics of the poor: agricultural labourers and political transformations in Uttar Pradesh'. *Journal of Peasant Studies*, 26(2/3): 182–243.

Lerche, J., 2008. 'Transnational advocacy networks and affirmative action for Dalits in India'. *Development and Change*, 39(2): 239–261.

Lerche, J., 2010. 'From "rural labour" to "classes of labour": class fragmentation, caste and class struggle at the bottom of the Indian labour hierarchy'. In *The Comparative Political Economy of Development: Africa and South Asia*, eds B. Harriss-White and J. Heyer. London: Routledge.

Lerche, J., 2011. 'Agrarian crisis and agrarian questions in India'. *Journal of Agrarian Change*, 11(1): 104–118.

Lerche, J., 2012. 'Labour regulations and labour standards in India: decent work?' *Global Labour Journal*, 3(1): 16–39.

Lerche, J., A. Mezzadri, D.-O. Chang, N. Pun, L. Huilin, L. Aiyu and R. Srivastava, 2017. 'The triple absence of labour rights: triangular labour relations and informalisation in the construction and garment sectors in Delhi and Shanghai'. CDPR SOAS, Working Paper 32/17, http://tinyurl.com/zs5jvyh (accessed 6 May 2017).

Leve, L., 2011. 'Identity'. *Current Anthropology*, 52(4): 513–527.

Li, T.M., 2010. 'To make live or let die? Rural dispossession and the protection of surplus populations'. *Antipode*, 41(SI): 66–93.

Lovatt, H., 1972. *Above the Heron's Pool: A Short History of the Peermade/ Vandiperiyar District of Travancore*. Kottayam: CMS Press.

Ludden, D., 1985. *Peasant History of South India*. Princeton, NJ: Princeton University Press.

Macfarlane, A. and I. Macfarlane, 2004. *The Empire of Tea: The Remarkable History of the Plant that Took Over the World*. New York: Overlook Press.

Madheswaran, S., 2017. 'Is affirmative action policy for the private sector necessary?' In *Labour and Development: Essays in Honour of Professor T.S. Papola*, eds K.P. Kannan, R. Mamgain and P. Rustagi. New Delhi: Academic Foundation.

Madheswaran, S. and P. Attewell, 2007. 'Caste discrimination in the Indian urban labour market: evidence from the National Sample Survey'. *Economic & Political Weekly* 42(41): 4146–4153.

Madheswaran, S. and P. Attewell, 2010. 'Wage and job discrimination in the India urban labour market'. In *Blocked by Caste: Economic Discrimination in Modern India*, eds S. Thorat and K.S. Newman. New Delhi: Oxford University Press.

Manohar, D., 2001. *Bagh ke Bacche hain Hum* [We Are the Children of Tigers]. Original in Marathi; Hindi translation Jayashree. Hosaghagabad: Disha Samvad.

Marx, K., 1867. *Capital: A Critique of Political Economy*, vol 1. Moscow: Progress Publishers.

Mayaram, S., 2007. 'Caste, tribe, and the politics of reservation'. *The Hindu*, 2 June, http://tinyurl.com/lzrzhxq (accessed 19 December 2016).

Mayer, A.C., 1961. *Peasants in the Pacific: A Study of Indian Rural Society*. Berkeley: University of California Press.

McNally, D., 2015. 'The dialectics of unity and difference in the constitution of wage-labour: on internal relations and working-class formation'. *Capital and Class*, 39(1): 131–146.

Mehrotra, S. and E. Delamonica, 2007. *Eliminating Human Poverty: Macroeconomic and Social Policies for Equitable Growth*. London: Zed Books.

Mehta, J. and S. Venkatraman, 2000. 'Poverty statistics: bermicide's feast'. *Economic & Political Weekly*, 35(27): 2377–2379 and 2381–2382.

Meillassoux, C., 1981 [1975]. *Maidens, Meal and Money: Capitalism and the Domestic Community*. Cambridge: Cambridge University Press.

Middleton, T., 2016. *The Demands of Recognition: State Anthropology and Ethnopolitics in Darjeeling*. Stanford, CA: Stanford University Press.

Mines, D. and N. Yazgi (eds), 2010. *Village Matters: Relocating Villages in the Contemporary Anthropology of India*. New Delhi: Oxford University Press.

Ministry of Housing and Urban Poverty Alleviation, 2017. *Report of the Working Group on Migration*, http://tinyurl.com/kqjgy58 (accessed 27 April 2017).

Moodie, M., 2015. *We Were Adivasis: Aspirations in an Indian Scheduled Tribe*. Chicago: University of Chicago Press.

Mooij, J., 1999. *Food Policy and the Indian State: The Public Distribution System in South India*. New Delhi: Oxford University Press.

Mooij, J., 2014. 'Redressing poverty and enhancing social development: trends in Indian welfare regime'. In *Persistence of Poverty in India*, eds N. Gooptu and J. Parry. New Delhi: Social Science Press.

Mosse, D., 2010. 'A relational approach to durable poverty, inequality and power'. *Journal of Development Studies*, 46(7): 1156–1178.

Mosse, D., 2012. *The Saint in the Banyan Tree: Popular Christianity and Caste Society in South India*. Berkeley: University of California Press.

Mosse, D., S. Gupta and V. Shah, 2005. 'On the margins in the city: Adivasi seasonal labour migration in western India'. *Economic & Political Weekly*, 40(28): 3025–3038.

Mosse, D., S. Gupta, M. Mehta, V. Shah, J. Rees and KRIBP Project Team, 2002. 'Brokered livelihoods: debt, labour migration and development in tribal western India'. Journal of Development Studies, 38(5): 59–88.

Munshi, I. (ed.), 2012. The Adivasi Question: Issues of Land, Forest and Livelihood. Hyderabad: Orient Black Swan.

Nair, K.R., 2006. The History of Trade Union Movement in Kerala. New Delhi: Manak.

Narula, S., 2007. Hidden Apartheid: Caste Discrimination against India's 'Untouchables'. New York: NYU School of Law.

Nathan, D. and V. Xaxa (eds), 2012. Social Exclusion and Adverse Inclusion: Development and Deprivation of Adivasis in India. New Delhi: Oxford University Press.

Navlakha, G., 2010. 'Days and nights in the heartland of rebellion'. Sanhati, 1 April, http://tinyurl.com/lqllkwz (accessed 7 May 2017).

Nayak, V. and S. Prasad, 1984. 'On levels of living of Scheduled Castes and Scheduled Tribes'. Economic & Political Weekly, 19(30): 1205–1213.

NCEUS (National Commission for Enterprises in the Unorganised Sector), 2007 [2008]. Report on Conditions of Work and Promotion of Livelihoods in the Unorganised Sector. http://dcmsme.gov.in/Condition_of_workers_sep_2007.pdf (accessed 19 June 2017). Hard copy published as 2008, New Delhi: Government of India, Academic Foundation.

NCEUS (National Commission for Enterprises in the Unorganised Sector), 2009. The Challenge of Employment in India: An Informal Economy Perspective, vol 1. New Delhi: Government of India, Academic Foundation, http://nceuis.nic.in/The_Challenge_of_Employment_in_India.pdf (accessed 19 June 2017).

Neff, D., K. Sen and V. Kling, 2012. 'The puzzling decline in rural women's labor force participation in India: a re-examination'. Indian Journal of Labour Economics 55(3).

Neilson, J. and W.E. Pritchard, 2009. Value Chain Struggles: Institutions and Governance in the Plantation Districts of South India. Chichester: Wiley-Blackwell.

Ness, I., 2016. Southern Insurgency: The Coming of the Global Working Class. London: Pluto Press.

Nilsen, A., 2010. Dispossession and Resistance in India: The River and the Rage. London: Routledge.

Noble, C., 1987. Over the High Passes: A Year in the Himalayas with the Migratory Gaddi Shepherds. London: Collins.

Omvedt, G., 1994. Dalits and the Democratic Revolution: Dr Ambedkar and the Dalit Movement in Colonial India. New Delhi: Sage.

OPHDI, 2010. Country Briefing: India. Oxford Poverty and Human Development Initiative, Working Paper 38. Oxford: OPHDI.

Osella, F. and C. Osella, 2000. Social Mobility in Kerala: Modernity and Identity in Conflict. London: Pluto Press.

Oxfam, 2016. An Economy for the 1%. Oxfam Briefing Report. London: Oxfam.

Oxfam, 2017. An Economy for the 99%. Oxfam Briefing Report. London: Oxfam.

Padel, F. and S. Das, 2010. Out of this Earth: East India Adivasis and the Aluminium Cartel. New Delhi. Black Swan.

Pai, S., 2000. 'New social and political movements of Dalits: a study of Meerut district'. Contributions to Indian Sociology 34(2): 189–220.

Pai, S., 2014. 'Dalit entrepreneurs, globalisation and the supplier diversity experiment in Madhya Pradesh'. In Dalits in Neoliberal India: Mobility or Marginalisation? ed. C. Still. London, New York, New Delhi: Routledge.

Palmer-Jones, R.W. and K.K. Sen, 2003. 'What has luck got to do with it? A regional analysis of poverty and agricultural growth in rural India'. *Journal of Development Studies*, 40(1): 1–31.

Panagariya, A. and V. More, 2013. 'Poverty by social, religious and economic group in India and its largest states 1993–94 to 2011–12'. Columbia University, SIPA and ISERP, Working Paper 2013–02. New York: Columbia University.

Pandian, M.S.S., 1990. *The Political Economy of Agrarian Change: Nanchilnadu 1880–1939*. New Delhi: Sage.

Pandian, M.S.S. and A. Kalaiyarasu, 2013. 'Why the Tamil Nadu model trumps Gujarat'. *Hardnews*, 23 December, http://tinyurl.com/lsrvy7c (accessed 15 December 2016).

Paranjape, S., 1981. 'Kulaks and Adivasis: the formation of classes in Maharashtra'. *Bulletin of Concerned Asian Scholars*, 13(1): 2–20.

Parry, J., 1999. 'Lords of labour: working and shirking in Bhillai'. In *The World of Indian Industrial Labour*, eds J. Parry, J. Breman and K. Kapadia. New Delhi: Sage.

Parry, J., 2007. 'A note on the "substantialisation" of caste and its "hegemony"'. In *Political and Social Transformation in North India and Nepal*, eds H. Ishii, D. Gellner and K. Nawa. New Delhi: Manohar.

Parry, J., 2009. '"Sociological Marxism" in central India: Polanyi, Gramsci, and the case of the unions'. In *Market and Society: The Great Transformation Today*, eds C. Hann and K. Hart. Cambridge: Cambridge University Press.

Parry, J., 2013. 'Company and contract labour in a central Indian steel town'. *Economy and Society*, 42(3): 348–374.

Parry, J., 2014. 'Introduction'. In *Persistence of Poverty in India*, eds N. Gooptu and J. Parry. New Delhi: Social Science Press.

Patnaik, P., 2007. 'The state under neo-liberalism'. *Social Scientist*, 35(1/2): 4–15.

Picherit, D., 2009. '"Workers, trust us!" Labour middlemen and the rise of the lower castes in Andhra Pradesh'. In *India's Unfree Workforce: Of Bondage Old and New*, eds J. Breman, I. Guerin and A. Prakash. New Delhi: Oxford University Press.

Piketty, T., 2013. *Capital in the Twenty-first Century*. Cambridge, MA: Harvard University Press.

Pinney, C., 1990. 'Colonial anthropology in the "laboratory of mankind"'. In *The Raj: India and the British, 1600–1947*, ed. C. Bayly. London: National Portrait Gallery.

Planning Commission, n.d. 'Data tables', http://tinyurl.com/mgwn5p4 (accessed 2 December 2016).

Prakash, A., 2015. *Dalit Capital: State, Markets and Civil Society in Urban India*. London, New York and New Delhi: Routledge.

Prakash, G., 1990. *Bonded Histories: Genealogies of Labor Servitude in Colonial India*. Cambridge: Cambridge University Press.

Pratap, S. and J.C. Bose, 2015. 'Development as politics: a study of emerging workers' movements in India'. *Journal of Economic & Social Development*, 11(1): 41–52.

Pun, N. and L. Huilin, 2010. 'Unfinished proletarianization: self, anger, and class action among the second generation of peasant-workers in present-day China'. *Modern China*, 36(5): 493–519.

Quddusi, M.I., 2002. *Khandesh under the Mughals: 1601–1724 A.D.* New Delhi: Islamic Wonders Bureau.

Raj, J., 2014. *Burden of Stigma: Crisis, Identity and Alienation in a South Indian Plantation Belt*, unpublished doctoral thesis, University of Bergen, Norway.

Rajshekar, V.T., 1979. *Apartheid in India*. Bangalore: Dalit Action Committee.

Raman, R.K., 2002. *Bondage in Freedom: Colonial Plantations in Southern India c. 1797–1947*. Centre for Development Studies Thiruvananthapuram, Working Paper 327. Thiruvanathapuran: Centre for Development Studies.

Raman, R.K., 2010. *Global Capital and Peripheral Labour: The History and Political Economy of Plantation Workers in India*. London and New York: Routledge.

Rammohan, K.T., 1998. 'Kerala CPI(M): all that is solid melts into air'. *Economic & Political Weekly*, 33(40): 2579–2582.

Raveendran, G., 2016. 'A review of Rangarajan Committee report on poverty estimation'. *Indian Journal of Human Development*, 10(1).

Rawat, R.S., 2011. *Reconsidering Untouchability. Chamars and Dalit History in North India*. Bloomington and Indianapolis: Indiana University Press.

Rawat, R.S. and K. Satyanarayan, 2016. *Dalit Studies*. Durham, NC: Duke University Press.

Reed, A., 2002. 'Unraveling the relation of race and class in American politics'. *Political Power and Social Theory*, 15: 265–274.

Reed, A. and M. Chowkwanyun, 2012. 'Race, class, crisis: the discourse of racial disparity and its analytical discontents'. *Socialist Register*, 48.

Robb, P., 1993. 'Introduction: meanings of labour in Indian social context'. In *Dalit Movements and the Meanings of Labour in India*, ed. P. Robb. New Delhi: Oxford University Press.

Roberts, N., 2016. *To Be Cared for: The Power of Conversion and Foreignness of Belonging in an Indian Slum*. Berkeley: University of California Press.

Rodgers, G. and J. Rodgers, 2001. 'A leap across time: when semi-feudalism met the market in rural Purnia'. *Economic & Political Weekly*, 36(22): 1976–1983.

Roediger, D., 1991. *The Wages of Whiteness: Race and the Making of the American Working Class*. London: Verso.

Roesch, M., G. Venkatasubramaniam and I. Guerin, 2009. 'Bonded labour in the rice mills: fate or opportunity?' In *India's Unfree Workforce: Of Bondage Old and New*, eds J. Breman, I. Guerin and A. Prakash. New Delhi: Oxford University Press.

Rogaly, B., D. Coppard, A. Safique, K. Rana, A. Sengupta and J. Biswas. 2002. 'Seasonal migration and welfare/illfare in eastern India: a social analysis'. *Journal of Development Studies*, 38(5): 89–114.

Ruud, A., 2014. 'Notions of rights and state benefits in village West Bengal'. In *Persistence of Poverty in India*, eds N. Gooptu and J. Parry. New Delhi: Social Science Press.

Saad Filho, A., 2011. 'Growth, poverty and inequality: policies and debates from the (post-) Washington Consensus to inclusive growth'. *Indian Journal of Human Development*, 5(2): 321–344.

Saberwal, V.K., 1999. *Pastoral Politics – Shepherds, Bureaucrats and Conservation in the Western Himalaya*. New Delhi: Oxford University Press.

Saggar, M. and I. Pan, 1994. 'SCs and STs in eastern India: inequality and poverty estimates'. *Economic & Political Weekly*, 29: 567–574.

Samata, 2000. *Surviving a Minefield. An Adivasi Triumph. A Landmark Supreme Court Judgement Restoring the Rights of Tribals*. Hyderabad: Samata.

Sanan, D., 2004. 'Delivering basic public services in Himachal Pradesh: is the success sustainable?' *Economic & Political Weekly*, 39(9): 975–978.

Sanhati, 2011. '20 suicide attempts a day – Tirupur, Tamil Nadu: textile workers in a globalised workplace'. 18 June, http://tinyurl.com/mla3u36 (accessed 6 December 2016).

Sawant, S., 2002. *Purushottamnama: Ma. P.K. Anna Patil Yanchi Charitra Kahani*. Shahada: Saneguruji Vidya Prasarak Mandal, 338–339 (in Marathi).

Scully, B., 2016. 'Precarity North and South: a southern critique of Guy Standing'. *Global Labour Journal*, 7(2): 160–172.

Sengupta, A., K.P. Kannan and G. Raveendran, 2008. 'India's common people: who are they, how many are they and how do they live?' *Economic & Political Weekly*, 43(11): 49–63.

Setalvad, T., 2004 [2001]. 'Hidden apartheid'. In *Caste, Race and Discrimination: Discourses in International Context*, eds S. Thorat and Umakant. Jaipur: Rawat Publications.

Shah, A., 2006. 'The labour of love: seasonal migration from Jharkhand to the brick kilns of other states in India'. *Contributions to Indian Sociology*, 40(1): 91–118.

Shah, A., 2010. *In the Shadows of the State: Indigenous Politics, Environmentalism and Insurgency in Jharkhand, India*. Durham, NC and London: Duke University Press.

Shah, A., 2011. 'India burning: the Maoist revolution'. In *A Companion to the Anthropology of India*, ed. I. Clark-Deces. Chichester: Wiley-Blackwell.

Shah, A., 2013. 'The agrarian question in a Maoist guerrilla zone: land, labour and capital in the forests and hills of Jharkhand, India'. *Journal of Agrarian Change*, 13(3): 424–450.

Shah, A., 2014. 'Religion and the secular left: subaltern studies, Birsa Munda and Maoists'. *Anthropology of this Century*, 9.

Shah, A., forthcoming. 'Tribe, egalitarian values, social reproduction and the state'. *Contributions to Indian Sociology*.

Shah, A. and B. Harriss-White, 2011. 'Resurrecting scholarship on agrarian transformations'. *Economic & Political Weekly*, 24: 13–18.

Shah, G., H. Mandar, S. Thorat, S. Deshpande and A. Baviskar, 2006. *Untouchability in Rural India*. New Delhi: Sage.

Shanin, T. (ed.), 1983. *Late Marx and the Russian Road: Marx and the 'Peripheries of Capitalism'*. New York: Monthly Review Press.

Shramik Sanghatana, 1973. *Shahada Chalval: Teen Varshanchi Vatchal*. Mumbai: Magova.

Shramik Sanghatana, 1979. *Shramik Sanghatanechya Karyachya Adhava, September 1978–79*. Shahada: Shramik Sanghatana.

Shrinivasan, R., 2016. 'SCs in TN better off than FCs in Jharkhand'. *The Hindu*, 1 April, http://tinyurl.com/lcdsa74 (accessed 15 December 2016).

Sikand, Y., 2005. *Bastions of the Believers: Madrasas and Islamic Education in India*. London: Penguin.

Simhadri, S. and P.L.V. Rao (eds), 1997. *Telangana: Dimensions of Underdevelopment*. Hyderabad: Centre for Telangana Studies.

Simpson, E., A. Tilche, T. Sbriccoli, P. Jeffery and T. Otten, forthcoming. 'A brief history of incivility in rural post-colonial India: caste, religion and anthropology'. *Comparative Studies in Society and History*.

Singer, M.B., 1972. *When a Great Tradition Modernizes: An Anthropological Approach to Indian Civilization*. Chicago: University of Chicago Press.

Singh, K.S. (ed.), 1982. *Tribal Movements in India*, vols 1 and 2. New Delhi: Manohar.

Skaria, A., 1997. 'Shades of wildness: tribe, caste, and gender in western India'. *Journal of Asian Studies*, 56(3): 726–745.

Sorge, A. and J. Padwa, 2015. '"The abandoned village?" Introduction to the special issue'. *Critique of Anthropology*, 35(3): 235–247.

Srinivasulu, K., 2017. 'The caste question in the Naxalite movement'. *Economic & Political Weekly* 52(21): 47–52.

Srivastava, R., 2012. 'Changing employment conditions of the Indian workforce and implications for decent work'. *Global Labour Journal* 3(1): 63–90.

Srivastava, R., 2013. *A Social Protection Floor for India*. New Delhi: International Labour Organization.

Srivastava, R. and A. Jha, 2016. *Capital and Labour Standards in the Organised Construction Industry in India*. CDPR, SOAS, London. http://tinyurl.com/msjg8w2 (accessed 16 December 2016).

Standing, G., 2017. *Basic Income: And How We Can Make it Happen*. London: Penguin.

Stern, N., 2017. 'A village, a country and the discipline: economic development in Palanpur over seven decades'. Eva Colorni Memorial Lecture, London School of Economics, 7 June.

Stiglitz, J., 2002. *Globalization and Its Discontents*. New York: W.W. Norton.

Still, C., 2011. 'Spoiled brides and the fear of education: honour and social mobility among Dalits in South India', *Modern Asian Studies* 45(5): 1119–1146.

Still, C., 2014. *Dalit Women: Honour and Patriarchy in South India*. New Delhi: Social Science Press.

Sundar, K.R.S., 2012. 'Counter-tendencies to labour flexibility regime in India: achieving decent work for non-regular workers'. *Indian Journal of Labour Economics*, 55(4): 551–572.

Sundar, N., 1997. *Subalterns and Sovereigns: An Anthropological History of Bastar, 1854–1996*. New Delhi: Oxford University Press.

Sundar, N., 2016. *The Burning Forest: India's War in Bastar*. New Delhi: Juggernaut.

Swatantra Bharat. 1958. 5 and 30 September 1958, Marathi daily, Dhule town.

Symington, D., 1938. *Report on the Aboriginal and Hill Tribes of the Partially Excluded Areas of the Bombay Presidency*. Bombay: Government of Bombay.

Taylor, C., 1992. *Multiculturalism and 'the Politics of Recognition'*. Princeton, NJ: Princeton University Press.

Teltumbde, A., 2009. 'Reservations within reservations: a solution'. *Economic & Political Weekly*, 41(46): 16–18.

Teltumbde, A., 2010. *The Persistence of Caste: The Khairlanji Murders and India's Hidden Apartheid*. London: Zed Books.

Teltumbde, A., 2011. 'Dalit capitalism and pseudo Dalitism'. *Economic & Political Weekly*, 46(10): 10–11.

Teltumbde, A., 2013. 'Ambedkarites against Ambedkar'. *Economic & Political Weekly*, 48(19): 10–11.

Teltumbde, A., 2016. *Mahad: The Making of the First Dalit Revolt*. New Delhi: Dakar.

Thakur, V., 2014a. 'Logjam: peasantisation-caused deforestation in Narmada Valley'. In *Shifting Ground: People, Animals and Mobility in India's Environmental History*, eds M. Rangarajan and K. Sivaramakrishnan. New Delhi: Oxford University Press.

Thakur, V., 2014b. *Unsettling Modernity: Resistance and Forced Resettlement due to a Dam in Western India*, unpublished doctoral thesis, Yale University.

The Hindu, 1997. 'Revolt by CPI MLA puts Babu in a fix', 7 October.

The Hindu, 2015. 'Gutti Koyas despoiling forest, says KCR', 18 January.

Thompson, E.P., 1963. *The Making of the English Working Class*. London: Penguin.

Thompson, E.P., 1978. 'Eighteenth-century English society: class struggle without class?' *Social History*, 3(2): 133–165.

Thorat, A., 2010. 'Ethnicity, caste and religion: implications for poverty outcomes'. *Economic & Political Weekly*, 45(51): 47–53.

Thorat, S., 2017. 'Caste and labour market discrimination: discussion on forms and remedies'. In *Labour and Development: Essays in Honour of Professor T.S. Papola*, eds K.P. Kannan, R. Mamgain and P. Rustagi. New Delhi: Academic Foundation.

Thorat, S. and K.S. Newman, 2007. 'Caste and economic discrimination: causes, consequences and remedies'. *Economic & Political Weekly*, 42(41): 4121–4124.

Thorat, S. and K.S. Newman, 2010. 'The legacy of social exclusion: a correspondence study of job discrimination in India's urban private sector'. In *Blocked by Caste: Economic Discrimination in Modern India*, eds S. Thorat and K.S. Newman. New Delhi: Oxford University Press.

Thorat, S., M. Mahamallik and N. Sadana, 2010. 'Caste system and pattern of discrimination in rural markets'. In *Blocked by Caste: Economic Discrimination in Modern India*, eds S. Thorat and K.S. Newman. New Delhi: Oxford University Press.

Tilche, A., 2016. 'Migration, bachelorhood and discontent among the Patidars'. *Economic & Political Weekly*, 51(26/27): 17–24.

Times of India, 2015. 'Cash starved Maharashtra bans all new job posts'. 28 May, http://tinyurl.com/pf8sp6j (accessed 25 November 2016).

Times of India, 2016. 'Kerala becomes 1st state in country to achieve 100% primary education'. 12 January, http://tinyurl.com/juz9mcn (accessed 26 November 2016).

Tinker, H., 1974. *A New System of Slavery: The Export of Indian Labour Overseas, 1830–1920*. London: Oxford University Press.

Tsing, A. L., 2009. 'Supply chains and the human condition'. *Rethinking Marxism*, 21(2): 148–176.

Umamaheshwari, R., 2014. *When Godavari Comes: People's History of a River. Journeys in the Zone of the Dispossessed*. New Delhi: Aakar Books.

UNDP, 2010. *Human Development Report 2010: The Real Wealth of Nations: Pathways to Human Development*, http://tinyurl.com/mlnjc7k (accessed 16 December 2016).

UNESCO, 2015. 'National consultation on 'Children and Internal Migration in India', 22–23 September 2015, India Habitat Centre, New Delhi'. Background Note, http://www.unesco.org/fileadmin/MULTIMEDIA/FIELD/New_Delhi/images/background-note_02.pdf (accessed 5 May 2017).

UNHCR, 2016. *Report of the Special Rapporteur on Minority Issues*. United Nations General Assembly A/HRC/31/56, 28 January, http://tinyurl.com/yc3z7rza (accessed 2 May 2017).

Varma, S., 2014. 'Between 2000 and 2012, jobs grew by a mere 2% per year'. *Times of India*, 9 February, http://tinyurl.com/o72pxwz (accessed 16 December 2016).

Varshney, A., L. Iyer and T. Khanna, 2013. 'Caste and entrepreneurship in India'. *Economic & Political Weekly*, 48(6): 52–60.

Vincentnathan, S.G., 1996. 'Caste politics, violence, and the panchayat in a South Indian community'. *Comparative Studies in Society and History*, 38(3): 484–509.

Vishwanath, R., 2014. *The Pariah Problem: Caste, Religion, and the Social in Modern India*. New York: Columbia University Press.

Viswanathan, S. and S. Saqaf, 1999. 'The Tirunelveli massacre'. *Frontline*, 16(31).

Webber, J.R., 2011. *Red October: Left-indigenous Struggles in Modern Bolivia*. Chicago: Haymarket Books.

Whitehead, J., 2010. *Development and Dispossession in the Narmada Valley*. New Delhi: Pearson.

Whitehead. J., 2016. 'Intersectionality and primitive accumulation: caste and gender in India under the sign of monopoly-finance capital'. *Monthly Review*, 68(6): 37–52.

World Bank, 2002. *Globalisation, Growth and Poverty: Building an Inclusive World Economy*. New York: Oxford University Press.

World Bank, 2012. *World Development Report 2013*, http://tinyurl.com/8nhyrpw (accessed 16 December 2016).

Xaxa, V., 2001. 'Protective discrimination: why Scheduled Tribes lag behind Scheduled Castes'. *Economic & Political Weekly*, 37(29): 2765–2772.

YASHADA, 2014. *Maharashtra Human Development Report 2012*. New Delhi: Sage, http://tinyurl.com/lg2tsn8 (accessed 5 May 2016).

Zelliott, E., 1992. *From Untouchable to Dalit: Essays on the Ambedkar Movement*. New Delhi: Manohar.

Acknowledgements

Malasree Neepa Acharya; Rita Astuti; Harry Axelby; Helen Axelby; Moya Axelby; Laura Bear; Lewis Beardmore; Henry Bernstein; Hassan Bhatia; Bhangya Bhukya; Chunnilal Brahmane; Maurice Bloch; Jan Breman; David Castle; Simon Chambers; Uday Chandra; Dee Chanter; Sahil Chowfla; Stuart Corbridge; Noelle Counord; Magnus Course; Santosh Das; Sangeeta Dasgupta; Geert De Neve; Kassim Deen; Smita Deshmukh; Divya Devarajan; Kishore Dhamale; Prakash Dhami; Nitin Dhami; Manu Dhami; Margaret Dickinson; Caitlin Donegan; Fiona Donegan; Henrike Donner; Peggy Froerer; Ricardo Fuente-Nieva; Chris Fuller; C. Gautam; Katy Gardner; David Gellner; David Graeber; Isabelle Guerin; Gulzar; Chris Hann; Ian Harper; John Harriss; Barbara Harriss-White; Greg Hasnip; Carolyn Heitmeyer; Sruthi Herbert; Thomas Herzmark; Judith Heyer; Rob Higham; John Hills; Michael Hoffman; Feyzi Ismail; Chain Singh Jadiyal; Vikas Jadiyal; Deborah James; Muhamed Ali Jan; Nicolas Jaoul; Diya Jayaseelan; Jakson Jebadas; Patricia Jeffery; Steven Johnson; Don Kalb; Karin Kapadia; Bruce Kapferer; K.P. Kannan; George Kunnath; Nicola Lacey; Jessica Lerche; Staffan Lindberg; LSE Department of Anthropology; Asmita Kabra; Nisam Kallupurackal; Kalpana Kannabiran; Ranjana Kanhere; Vikram Kanhere; Praveen Kaushal; Beppe Karlsson; Asif Ali Khan; Nagaraju Koppula family; Arun Kumar; Ajay Kumar; Suneel Kumar; Vivek Kumar; Andrew Lattas; Hussain Lodhi; Janarth NGO team; Lakshman Madakam; Madhu; Mara Malagodi; Dinanath Manohar; Susan MacMillan; Mathew McCartney; Allessandra Mezzadri; Megnaa Mehta; Lucia Michelutti; Uttam Chand Minhas; Ajay Minhas; Gautam Mody; David Mosse; Munno; Neha; Rohit Negi; Alf Nilsen; Itay Noy; Dilip Patil; Jonathan Pattenden; Jonathan Parry; Mathijs Pelkmans; David Picherit; Vikram Pawar; Vijay Pawara; Thakur parents; Paru; People in Peermade and Munnar, Tirupur, Dumka, Melpuram, Pondicherry, Chennai, Nandurbar, Chamba, Bhadrachalam; Jai Prasad; Banu Pratap; Sirisha Pusan; Charles Ramsey; Baburam Rao; Shantakumar Rao; Nate Roberts; Dennis Rodgers; Indrajit Roy; Charlie Rumsby; Orlanda Ruthven; Mira Sadgopal; Mike Savage; Rajesh Seagal; Julius Sen; Hasan Sen; Kunal Sen; Edward Simpson; K. Sivaramakrishnan; Mohinder Slariya; SOAS Department of Development Studies; Ravi Srivastava; Srinivas; Luisa Steur; Clarinda Still; Jayaraj Sunderesan; Anand Teltumbde; Louise Tillin; Bharat Vasave; Chaudhary Vasave; Aswathy Vasudevan; Meena Verma; Judith Whitehead; K. Satyanarayan; Gavin Smith; Virginius Xaxa.

Index

Rao, K. Chandrashekar (KCR), Chief
  Minister of Telangana, 116
rape, 208, 214, *see also* sexual harassment
ration card, 67, 76
Reddy caste in Tamil Nadu, 89
Reddy caste in Telangana and Andhra
  Pradesh, 6, 7, 122
reproductive work, 160
reservations, xiii, 27, 97, 109, 113, 125,
  130, 158, 168, 183, 206–7; reserved
  constituency, 120, 167; reserved seat,
  xiii, 122, 159, *see also* affirmative
  action
Reserve Bank of India, 184
reservoir, *see* dams
resettlement, 9, 138, 177, 178, 184, 195–6,
  199, 200, 202
retirement, 58, 61, 127
Revenue Settlement, *see* land settlement
Revenue Survey, *see* land settlement
rights, x, 16, 30, 169, 215; abuses, 30, 26,
  215, *see also* forest rights, labour rights,
Right to Education Act (2011), 205
road construction, 8, 18, 27, 74, 133, 155,
  163–6, 171, 173, 182, 185,
ryotwari system, 180

Saal Valley, Himachal Pradesh, 8, 147, 148,
  149
saldari system, 181, 193, *see also* bonded
  labour
Salwa Judum, 138
Santhal Parganas Act, 28, 213
Sarapaka village in Telangana, 120, 125,
  129, 133–4, 139–40
Satpura hills, Western India, 8, 176, 177,
  178
Scheduled Area, 115, 119, 120, 124, 129,
  135, 136, 142
Scheduled Caste (SC), xiii, 1, 26, 206, *see
  also* Dalits
Scheduled Tribe (ST), xiii, 1, 26, 206, *see
  also* Adivasis
seasonal migration (SC), *see* migration,
  seasonal
sedentarisation, 117, 144, 151, 152, 154
segregation, 4, 73, 98, 112, 162
'self-racialisation', 212
sexual exploitation, 3, 29, 181, 187, 214,
  see also rape

Shahada taluka, Maharashtra, 178, 188, 191
shifting cultivation, 10, 115, 138, 179
Shramik Sanghatana, 181, 190
Singareni Collieries, Telangana, 115, 120
Singh, Bhagat, 108
SIPCOT (State Industries Promotion
  Corporation of Tamil Nadu), 83–4, 87,
  91, 104, 106
SIPCOT Area Community Environmental
  Monitors, 106
slavery, 3, 19, 52, 54
social / cultural capital, 99, 125, 158, 174
'social cost of production', 22, 23, 59, 75, 142
'social floor', 204
social justice, 85, 116
social mobility, 6, 29, 30–1; in Cuddalore,
  93, 112; among Gujjars in Himachal
  Pradesh, 172–3; in Kerala 50, 65–6; in
  Nandurbar, 191; among Tamil Dalits in
  Kerala 50, 65–6
social relations, xvi, 13, 26, 28, 82, 83, 93,
  112, 144, 200
social exclusion, 45, 144, 161, 174
social inclusion, 204
social reproduction, 2, 12, 28, 30, 84
social security, *see* welfare
solidarity, 78, 80, 108, 132, 133, 189
South Arcot, Tamil Nadu, 86
Special Economic Zones (SEZ), 213
state policy targeting, 206
state sector employment, xiii, 6, 9, 31, 206,
  207; in Himachal Pradesh, 8, 18, 144,
  145, 147, 149, 158, 159, 160, 162, 163,
  168; in Maharashtra, 9, 179, 182, 183,
  189, 191, 192, 198–9, 201, 202; in Tamil
  Nadu, 95, 96–7, 98, 100, 108, 113, 114;
  in Telangana 125, 130
stigma, social, xvii, 2, 3, 15–16, 24, 25, 26,
  28, 29, 30; in Kerala, 25, 70–1, 72; in
  Himachal Pradesh, 159, 162, 171; in
  Tamil Nadu, 25, 112; in Telangana, 25,
  130, 133
strikes, *see* trade unions
'Swami Nagar', Tamil Nadu, x, 26, 65, 104
suicide, x, 26, 65, 104
super-exploitation, 2, 16, 19–24, 27, 30
Suratwanti, Ambarsing, Bhil leader, 181
'surplus populations', 9–12
Syrian Christians, 54, 55, 66, 71, 79
Tamil Nadu, 39, 85–6